The Greek City and its Institutions

The Greek City

and its Institutions

By

G. GLOTZ

NEW YORK

BARNES & NOBLE, INC.

First published 1929

Published in the United States of America 1969
by Barnes & Noble, Inc., New York, N.Y.

Translated by
N. MALLINSON

Printed in Great Britain

CONTENTS

v

FOREWORD

This work which contributes in one of its aspects to the study of the " Greek miracle " fills also an important place—between "From Tribe to Empire" *and* " Roman Political Institutions " *—in the study of political institutions.*

There are—as has already been noted—historians as well as sociologists for whom sociology is quite distinct from history ; sociologists who recognize only necessity in their science and historians who recognize only chance in their discipline find themselves in agreement upon this point of distinction. From our point of view, however, history, the all-embracing study of past events relating to man, necessarily includes sociology. The closely woven web of facts of every kind of which history is composed is interwoven with events demonstrating an inherent necessity in social development—with what we may call mental logic—as well as with innumerable chance happenings. Specialists working in the field of abstractions and generalizations can, undoubtedly, by comparative studies—whether of institutions on the one hand or of religion and intellectual and æsthetic activity on the other—set forth general facts ; but history furnishes the material for these generalizations, and the result of the comparison, when brought to bear on the facts of history, throws human evolution into relief, picks out the path it has followed from the mass of groupings, recurrences and regular stages, and leads one to seek in logic—in the meaning we give to this word —for the fundamental cause of these recurrences.

In " From Tribe to Empire " *the social aspect as such was dealt with.*[1] *We there put forward the problem of the origins of society, of the relations between society and the individual, and, as an hypothesis, distinguished various phases of social organization—phases characterized precisely by the varying nature of these relations. It is our belief that society only exists by virtue of the individuals who compose it, but that in order to consolidate its position and attain to maturity, it has at a certain point to*

[1] *v. Foreword to* " From Tribe to Empire," *p. ix.*

vii

submerge the individual until the day when the latter asserts himself in some way and consciously strives to bring society to perfection by means of the intellectual and spiritual development which it has made possible.

We followed in the East of antiquity the progress of " political organization from the humble germs of individualized power to the formation of strongly centralized kingdoms and vast empires."[1] We showed how the growth of societies in these " cosmocracies " encouraged the division of labour and how, in a general way, the development of the individual followed upon this division of labour no less as a result of technical inventions than of specula- tive and æsthetic activity. But the development was limited by the part which, from a political point of view, privileged indi- vidualism played. As the chief of the clan gathered up the totemic mana, so the king embodied in himself sacred power : since in his person the human and the divine were united, it was he who gave birth to law ; the men who presided over administra- tion and justice were his representatives.[2] Greece as a whole, but Athens in particular, realized a form of political organiza- tion which was totally new and, at the same time, a development of the individual which was wholly unprecedented. In opposi- tion to the Barbarian who was subjected to despotism and deified it, the Greek was a free citizen ; in opposition to the Empire, the stupendous creation of the East, he ingeniously managed the affairs of his microscopic State. The Greek city is just as " miraculous " as Greek art or thought ; it represented an " ex- periment ";[3] it is an example, a model εἰς ἀεί.

This book, which Gustave Glotz was peculiarly well-equipped by all his previous works to write, has a twofold interest : on the one hand it traces, with remarkable erudition, the evolution of Greek institutions, brings out their essential characteristics and, to a certain extent, enters into the details of their construction ; and, on the other hand, it formulates and suggests the general ideas which such a subject admits of, and leads on to considera-

[1] v. Foreword to " The Nile and Egyptian Civilization," p. xix.

[2] We must not forget, however, the Egyptian revolution in which " the individual had given rein to his appetites and kicked over every kind of discipline." v. Moret, " The Nile and Egyptian Civilization," p. 220.

[3] v. Jardé, " The Formation of the Greek People," Foreword, p. xii. Renouvier, in the Introduction to "La Philosophie analytique de l'Histoire" (p. 92), makes a striking contrast between the great empires " which con- demned whole races to moral death " and the peoples who created " un- fettered science and law and organized the first republics."

tions of a sociological bearing. It combines strict realism and explanations of deep insight.

Fustel de Coulanges explained marvellously well ; he explained too well, too simply, too logically. The respect which Glotz feels for his " masterpiece " does not prevent him from criticizing it. Human societies " are not geometrical figures, but living organisms "; " Truth is always complex when it is concerned with men . . . who toil and struggle and are subject to the common needs of humanity." [1]

* * * * * *

This book deals first, therefore, with the genesis of the πόλις. The " fluid " term polis signified the acropolis—the fortified town as opposed to the open village, κώμη—before it was applied to the city.[2] *From a few scattered facts, " guided by precarious conjecture," Glotz reconstructs its small beginnings. He makes discreet and legitimate use of philology, archæology and " the innumerable analogies which a comparative study of human societies affords " (p. 5). He, too, sets out from the clan*[3]*— the γένος, the patriarchal clan, the " first unit of society "—and passes through the associations of families, the phratries—whose characteristics he discusses—and the military groupings of clans, the φυλαί, tribes, to the political organism which grew out of a settled life and synœcism.*[4]

The Homeric poems show us a society in process of evolution. The king of kings, " the most royal," βασιλεύτατος—for the βασιλεύς, originally, is the chief of the γένος, the man who advances ahead of the others[5]*—intermediary between the gods, from whom he is descended (διογενής), and man, has uncontested sacerdotal authority, but only a precarious political authority: in the Homeric monarchy we can see elements of the oligarchy which is to succeed it, and even of the democracy, δήμου κράτος, which eventually will establish the voice of the people, δήμου φῆμις (pp. 59-60).*[6]

[1] *Pp. 3, 4.*
[2] *Cf. Jardé, " The Formation of the Greek People," p. 291.*
[3] *v. Davy, " From Tribe to Empire."*
[4] *Cf. for Rome, Homo, " Primitive Italy." On the names of clans and their origin, v. Ad. Reinach, " Atthis, les origines de l'État athénien " (extract from the R.S.H., 1912), pp. 19-20.*
[5] *Ad. Reinach, p. 30 : βαίνω and λαός—etymology discussed.*
[6] *Δῆμος=part of the territory which belongs to a community, country ; population of a country, mass of the people ; later only people as opposed to the chiefs, or mass of free citizens, democracy.*

When aristocracy destroys the king in his capacity of leader in war and justiciary, he still remains a βασιλεύς, high-priest, just as at Rome after the fall of the kings there remained a rex sacrorum. For centuries a single class, more or less numerous, and very variously recruited, holds power in the cities. Glotz emphasizes the " disconcerting " multiplicity of forms which oligarchic government assumes: as a general rule it is not the government of the " best " (ἄριστοι). Moderate oligarchy, moreover, borders upon moderate democracy, and " it is impossible to say exactly where one ends and the other begins " (p. 79). His keen sense of the complexity of reality prevents Glotz here from making distinctions which would be too absolute and theoretical.

Finally, democratic government is established—the rule of state authority in place of the authority of chiefs, of individual responsibility in place of collective responsibility—a system prepared by the " tyrants," whose guiding principle and transitory function is " to humble the aristocracy and uplift the lower classes " (p. 111): " An inherent contradiction doomed tyranny to death as soon as it had infused life into democracy " (p. 116).

The latter comes to full maturity thanks to the liberation of the individual, who repays to the city in strength what he has gained from it in independence. The " great mistake " which Fustel de Coulanges made was to establish " an absolute antinomy between the omnipotence of the city and individual liberty, whereas, on the contrary, state power and individualism progressed side by side, each supporting the other " (p. 5). Whilst oligarchical survivals persist for a long time in the Peloponnese and northern Greece, Athens leads the maritime cities in the direction of "natural development " (p. 118). It is her vocation to be the school of democracy. The dates 594-3—the constitution of Solon—and 508-7, the constitution of Cleisthenes, are great dates in the political history of the world. This " Hellas of Hellas " was to give the people, to use a phrase of Plato's adopted by Plutarch, " the purest liberty with unstinting hands " (pp. 355, 125).

The demos, we must remember, is the body of members of the city, and not the inhabitants of the town, for slaves and metics are excluded from it ; it is not man as such, but the citizen who is of value[1]—that, at all events, is the principle. The assembled

[1] Phrase used by Cournot in "Traité de l'enchaînement des idées fondamentales," p. 460.

*demos is sovereign ; " its functions were universal and its powers
unlimited " (p.* 181). *The delegates of the demos—in so far as
delegates are necessary for deliberative, judicial and executive
power—are again, in principle, appointed by lot. Glotz attempts,
in the middle section of his book, to define the nature, detail the
organization and examine the working of the Athenian democracy : its Assembly, its Council, its various magistracies. . . .*

*After his illuminating study of the closed, autonomous
society which is the City in general, and Athens in particular,
he shows how practical needs were gradually, in spite of everything, to open up this " microcosm," how common interests of
defence and common preoccupations created leagues and federations : but—as we have seen before—" in some cases the federal
bond was so loose that it allowed the isolation of the cities to
survive, and in others the union, imposed by force, collapsed as
soon as the small States thought that they could escape from the
control of the great State which dominated them."* [1]

Though Athens did much for the unification of Greece (p. 286),
*she was actuated by an imperialist spirit, which encountered
lively opposition. Undoubtedly the sense of Panhellenic solidarity, of the oneness of their civilization, as it became more
conscious tended to be translated into the political sphere :* [2] *the
bestowal of citizenship, not only upon individuals but upon whole
towns, and the multiplication of leagues are proofs of it ; but
the atavistic urge towards autonomy was stronger than cultural
affinities and the need for unity. " It is a law of nature," Plato
says, " that between all cities war shall be continuous and ever-
lasting."* [3]

*We know that a united Greece, a Greek people, was to come
only with the Empire ; and the substitution of the Empire for the
city-system was due far less to an internal need for unity than to
increasing anarchy. Glotz makes this point absolutely clear.
There was not only war between cities, but also war between
citizens. The growth of individualism, unbridled egoism, the
disappearance of the middle class, the glaring inequality of wealth*

[1] *Jardé,* " Formation of the Greek People," *p.* 294.

[2] *v. pp.* 354-356 *and—on the part played by Pericles—Jardé, ibid.,
pp.* 285-289: " *By his comprehension of the interests of Hellenism, by the
breadth of his views, which embraced the entire Greek world, he was worthy
to realize the unity of Greece, had this unity been possible.*"

[3] *Jardé, ibid., p.* 265. *On the question of unity see the whole of Part IV
and the Conclusion of this volume.*

which made the proletariat dangerous, led to a state of affairs in which " the city was composed of two opposing and antagonistic sections, of two enemy cities " (p. 316). Although Athens was less embroiled than other cities in intestine strife, after the archonship of Euclides, 403-2, the sovereignty of the people there became increasingly tyrannical and was increasingly used for the benefit of individual interests at the expense of the exchequer and the state.

We shall see here the process of political, judicial, financial and military disorganization which made Greece an easy prey to the onslaughts of ambition. And, since the lust for power was not the least of these unbridled appetites, " the idea of monarchy was in the air " (p. 385). Thus it was exaggerated individualism—both collective and particular—which, by causing the decline of the city, was to put Greece at the mercy of a master and lead to the restoration of the king-god.[1]

Gustave Glotz is too good an historian to be satisfied with merely outlining and describing the constitutions and institutions of the City in the abstract : he is keenly alive to their actual life, and by his use of contemporary works, which he draws upon wherever it is apposite and profitable, he summons up the political and social activities of the Greeks in striking and picturesque scenes. We seem to see the men who stood at the top of the social scale— nobles, nouveaux riches, tyrants[2]—and the mass of the population, the humble folk, farmers, workmen, merchants, fishermen, sailors.[3] We might almost think that he had been present in the Ecclesia, had taken part in the elections on the Pnyx or sat in the Boule ; that he had seen the blatant luxury of the " magnificent mansions " built in the declining city.[4] By the casual use of a word—habeas corpus, Tammany clubs, the "haussmannisation" of the towns,[5] aptly and without straining, he brings before our very eyes this civilization separated from us by more than two thousand years. In all this we see the hand of the author of the " Ægean Civilization " who, by his learning and his talent, has done more than any other Hellenist to familiarize a large number of readers with a world which, barely thirty years ago, was unknown.

From what has gone before it will, we think, have been

---

[1] *v.* Jouguet, " Macedonian Imperialism."
[2] E.g., *pp.* 66-67, 75, 114. [3] *E.g., pp.* 146, 149.
[4] *Pp.* 153-156, 162, 302, 311. [5] *Pp.* 120, 216, 217.

gathered that Glotz allows their just share in the development of Greek institutions to historical circumstances, to those contingencies of every kind which were the subject of " The Formation of the Greek People " *and which he vividly and brilliantly passes in review.* But we wish to emphasize everything which in this book confirms or supplements what we have said elsewhere on the question of the inherent necessity of institutions and on the part which the logical factor plays in social evolution.

Glotz naturally notes the close connection which existed in the beginning between political organization and religion : " The need for mutual defence of which the acropolis and the ramparts are evidence, was expressed, as was every social function in antiquity, in a religious form.   Every city had its deity, as had every family " (*p* 19).   But, he says, " supernatural notions of this sort are always capable of a natural explanation.   This fear of the gods was, at bottom, fear of a social force which day by day took to itself new strength.   Men feared the demos " (*p.* 9).   *Thus our thesis gains support : society utilizes, annexes, institutionalizes beliefs, but religion has its source in the psychology of the individual and not in a strictly social need.*[1]   *The social need properly so called was embodied in their political institutions and their economic institutions, which were at one and the same time clearly distinguished and closely related.*

The agora, which was the market, was originally also the public meeting place :[2] " *with merchants and customers mingled. gossips and loungers.   At all hours it was the rendezvous where men strolled around, learnt the latest news or talked politics ; and there public opinion was shaped* " (*p.* 22).   *The popular Assembly had its birth in the agora.   We see economic development taking place here, and at the same time we can gauge the intensity of the repercussions of economics on politics (pp.* 23, 69, 101).   *The development of the city was closely bound up with the increase of moveable wealth, with the formation of the class of craftsmen and an aristocracy of* nouveaux *riches, with the progress of shipping and the rule of money, in short with the emergence of* chrematistike, *that is of capitalism.*

This new system created in the aristocratic city a situation

---

[1] *v. General Introduction to* " The Earth before History," *p. ix.   For the theory of the Durkheim school as to the religious origin of institutions cf. our* " Synthèse en Histoire," *p.* 201.

[2] *Cf. Foreword to Toutain,* " Ancient Economic Organization."

in which the demos—*now a proletariat—stood opposed to the nobles and the rich, and became first a dangerous, eventually a victorious party (pp. 101, 311). In the democratic city, and at Athens especially, there was, corresponding to a period of economic prosperity and comparatively fairly distributed wealth, a wise organization in which " a just balance between the legal power of the state and the natural right of the individual " (pp. 124, 143) was more or less preserved. But when an unbridgeable gulf was cleft between rich and poor, when this demos, " which was in name sovereign," was made wretched by inequality of conditions, when class conflict raged and communist theories flourished, democratic institutions became corrupt beyond hope of remedy.[1]*

In the originally undifferentiated field of political organization we see the usual process of differentiation, the progress of the division of labour. The separation of judicial from purely political functions, which hitherto had been combined in the person of the king, can be clearly traced. The latter, together with the " elders," delivered the themistes, those inspired judgements which formed " the sacred and mysterious code of family justice (themis) " (p. 7). The substitution of written law, of νόμος for oracular tradition—in one sense too rigid and in another too flexible—of individual responsibility—involving definite rights and duties in relation to the State—for collective responsibility, marked an epoch in development (p. 106).[2] And the organization of justice advanced side by side with law. Because " the progress of the State at the expense of the genos and the economic development of the whole of Greece increased the number of suits," justice became " a trade " (p. 50). Athens above all was a centre of litigation, simply because law, and consequently chicanery, tended there to take the place of violence (p. 251).

[1] *v. pp.* 311 *ff. On the relations between economics and politics cf.* Jardé, ibid., *p.* 160 *ff.;* Kowaleski, " Annales de l'Inst. int. de Sociologie," *vol. XIV, pp.* 187-238 *;* R. Hubert, " Manuel de Sociologie," *pp.* 212-213.

[2] *Note that between* θέμις *and* νόμος, *there was* δίκη, *which originally was inter-family justice. But the conception of* δίκη *was extended, and ended by being identified with the* νόμοι: δίκαιος *and* νόμιμος *were synonymous. When the idea of equality became associated with the idea of justice, the city looked for* κόσμος, *good order (works of Herodotus and Thucydides). It was from the city that the concept of* κόσμος *passed to the universe, as also that of* νόμος: " *the notion of natural law is explained only by the progress of judicial development." v. on these various points an interesting discussion in the* " Année Sociologique," *vol. XI, pp.* 282-286.

There are some remarkable passages in which Glotz describes the part which Athens played in the development of law—a part which has often been misunderstood. We have had occasion to allude elsewhere to the excellent work in which Henri Ouvré examines " the literary forms of Greek thought." Ouvré grants the Greeks a capacity for creating constitutions, " ambitious compositions, the extempore creations of the wonder-working vote, regulating everything, providing for everything, and preparing for the peoples an eternal happiness, which lasted a few months." He emphasizes and exaggerates the abstract and theoretical character of their public law. " In Athens, for example, the government seems rather like a practical application of the decimal system : ten tribes, ten strategoi, *five hundred councillors, five thousand active heliasts and a thousand in reserve, fifty citizens in the prytany, only ten months to the official year. . . ."*[1] *As for civil law the Greeks were incapable, according to Ouvré, of giving it " the calm attention which it demands." The Romans, on the other hand, " went into details ; being a closely reasoning people, they expounded the minutest questions." In what way should this toll be fixed, this mortgage be made, the water in this channel be directed ? They had the stolid patience of the farmer who counts the ears of his corn, and measures inch by inch the land which has been watered less by rains than by his own toiling efforts. " The Roman was a civil lawyer, the Greek not."*[2] *The whole chapter which Glotz devotes to justice must be read if the Greeks are to be judged fairly. In his eyes the ancestors of the Roman* jurisprudentes *were the dramatists, the philosophers, the* logographoi. *Zealous care for equity and the sentiment of humanity were essential characteristics of Athenian law.*

At Rome practical sense constructed a juridical monument which was in a measure definitive. At Athens an inherent humanitarianism and democratic principle made laws yielding and flexible. Athens " carried philanthropy so far as to sap the national basis of the institution of slavery—an institution without which it seemed that the city must perish."[3] *And, in spite of the principle according to which the foreigner was an enemy, the advances of humanitarianism and pacificism alike had*

[1] *Cf.* Glotz, *p.* 123.
[2] *Ouvré,* " Les formes littéraires de la pensée grecque," *pp.* 209-213.
[3] *v. pp.* 254-262.

tremendous influence upon international law both public and private.[1]

To sum up, in Greece law and ethics were not rigorously differentiated until a late date, with the result that ethics was a vital and constant factor in law. Though sometimes we meet in the works of the ancient philosophers the expression " unwritten law," νόμος ἄγραφος, or " innate law," a careful reading of the texts shows us that the term νόμος is used in the ordinary sense of " custom " or " usage."[2] But thought acted as a kind of leaven upon nomos.

The part played by " logic " also is very clearly brought out in this book. In the first few pages we see " the social impulse," which we have spoken of elsewhere, at work, together with that " nameless collective will " (p. 9) which subordinated the clans, the γένη, to a common interest, to the δῆμος, just as previously it had subordinated individuals to the clan. There are many passages, on the other hand, in which the close connection between institutions and the general level of social morality, represented by customs and ideas, is traced and emphasized : " Legal enactments are of no avail against the force of customs " (p. 356). There were two forces, one proceeding from an inherent yet vague feeling, the other from a comparatively clear recognition of the social bond, of social needs. Society had its basis in the social instinct : individuals are the material of society. But they can also be social agents, or rather, social inventors, that is to say, conscious creators of social " logic." So it was in Greece ; to a greater extent than in any other country of antiquity the individual there exercised a powerful and perceptible influence over political institutions. He even developed his personality to a point at which it became a danger to society.[3]

---

[1] v. pp. 263-272.

[2] Brochard, " La morale ancienne et la morale moderne," in Étude de phil. ancienne et de phil. moderne, p. 492. Cf. Gomperz, " Penseurs de la Grèce," vol. III, p. 341: " The domains of law and custom, of the coercive and the non-coercive spheres, were far from being clearly defined, as we see . . . from the use of a single word to denote them both. Every usage, even the most trifling and unimportant, such, for example, as that of having hair or wearing a beard, was called nomos; while the most important and serious law, even one which involved death, as, for instance, that against murder, was likewise called monos." v. also Declareuil, " Rome the Law-Giver," Foreword, p. xiv and pp. 3-4.

[3] Greek individualism v. Max Wundt, " Griechische Weltanschauung," analyzed in A. Diès, " Autour de Platon," vol. I, pp. 55 ff.

Tyrants, legislators, leaders of the people (p. 109) *and later
(pp.* 335-336) *politicians, first established, then perverted, democratic government. In his interesting chapter on tyranny,
Glotz describes—comparing it in certain respects with the Italian
podesta*[1]*—the part played by the " demagogue," who became the
servant of the people in order to be its master, and whom the
people used until it found him useless and oppressive. But
there were more direct and more deliberate makers of democracy.
At Athens in particular there arose men who gave their name to
constitutional and judicial achievements (pp.* 119-120) *: Draco,
Solon, Cleisthenes, Ephialtes, Pericles.*

*" Athens of the fifth century lived according to the civil laws
of Solon and the political laws of Cleisthenes " (p.* 123). *Draco
had previously amended the ancient patriarchal law, which was
linked up with religion*[2] *by the intervention of the State and the
principles of a lay moral code ; Solon with his wise economic
and social reforms and his introduction of democratic elements
into the constitution completed the downfall of oligarchy. " To
judge him by his reforms Cleisthenes was a great man, a true
Ionian type, with a mind both practical and logical . . . balanced
yet innovating "; bolder than Solon, " he was not content to stay
within the confines of tradition ; he was not content merely to
amend and perfect. Paying no heed to current practices and
customs he received and reinvigorated in its most essential
organs the very life of the Republic. . . . His is the earliest
attempt of which we know to found a constitution based not on
tradition but on reason."*[3] *Finally, Pericles, the pupil of the
philosophers, realized complete democracy.*

*In this evolution of democratic institutions it is scarcely
possible to ignore traces of religious survivals, but they are not
easy to specify. Thus was drawing " by the bean " at bottom an
abandoning of decision to the gods? Can we say that " all the
principles which seem to us to-day emanations of human reason
derive from a desire to discover the will of the gods," that " all
the forms which dominate modern states—the will of the people,
the infallibility of universal suffrage—owe their character to the*

[1] *Cf. Ad. Reinach, op. cit., pp.* 16, 66, 67.
[2] *Glotz examined this ancient law in his important studies* " La Solidarité de la famille en Grèce " *and* " L'ordalie dans la Grèce primitive."
[3] *v. Ad. Reinach, op. cit., pp.* 46, 70, 71-72 *; the last lines are translated
from G. De Sanctis,* 'ΑΤΘΙΣ.

fact that the people has taken the place of the king, who succeeded to the place of a god?"[1] *Whatever the case, Athens effected a swift and radical transformation, a complete rationalization of the religious elements inherent in primitive societies. Glotz quotes Thucydides' wonderful commentary on Athenian democracy, "whose every word is like a medal of pure gold to the image of Athena Polias," and in which "there are maxims which one might say had inspired the Declaration of the Rights of Man"* (pp. 141, 142; cf. p. 175).

It is impossible to insist too strongly on the novelty and importance of this study of society, which henceforth exists side by side with the study of nature. The search for the common good became increasingly a theoretical study: it ended in a pitiless criticism of democratic government, of the excesses to which it was liable, and into which, in actual fact, the professional politicians did drag Athens; to the desire that "philosophers should be the rulers of cities, or that kings and dynasts should be good philosophers," that "political power and philosophy should coincide."[2]

Theorizing gave birth to the most fantastic conceptions, but Athens at the height of her powers has none the less proved to be the "school" of humanity in general and not merely of Greece. She had supreme moments in which she succeeded in achieving an harmonious reconciliation between the needs of the State and the desires of the individual, under the sovereignty of law which "secured the reign of reason, nous, logos" (p. 136)—*i.e., logic.*[3]

When circumstance had made the Empire possible, and even necessary, the Hellenization of the world popularized the form of the polis *and perpetuated many democratic principles, though not "the provisions which best illustrated the spirit of Athenian*

[1] *v. Ad. Reinach*, op. cit., pp. 76-85.
[2] Plato, "Republic," 473*b. v. E. Brehier*, "Hist. de la Philosophie," *I*, Part I, p. 143; cf. p. 250. *On the contrast between Plato, constructer of societies, and Aristotle, observer of societies, cf. P. Janet*, "Histoire de la science politique dans ses rapports avec la morale," 3rd edition, vol. *I*, pp. 229 ff.
[3] "... *The substitution of codes for customs, the establishment of a written law of nations, and finally the Declaration of Rights, ... all this is but the natural development from one and the same fact; the progressive extension of reason, and the government of human concerns by reason ...*" (*P. Janet*, op. cit., *p. lxx*). *On the preambles of laws in antiquity, v. ibid.*, p. 60.

legislation, which caused vigorous individualism and a fine philanthropy to flourish " (p. 391). *In modern times, " the men of the Revolution and the philosophers their masters were inspired more by Athens than by Rome when they laid the foundations of the modern State."*

But, as Glotz so well says, the City was " a very small affair " both in area and in the number of its citizens. This was to be a major problem for modern States, to adapt the most logical elements of Greek institutions to societies completely different in structure. On a copy (editio princeps, Amsterdam, 1762) of the " Contrat Social," *so obviously inspired by Greek democracy,*[1] *I read these words dated 1791: " Though all parts of the system set forth in this social contract* are not applicable to the government of a people inhabitating a large area, *it will always be worthy of praise for its broad outlook on questions of the general welfare."*[2]

The " Cité antique " must always be read because it embodies a large portion of the truth and because it is a remarkable piece of work, clear-cut and finished. But in exaggerating the connection between institutions and beliefs Fustel is led to exaggerate the resemblance between the Greeks and Romans and the difference —which he regards as " fundamental and essential "—between ancient peoples and modern societies.

The " Greek City and its Institutions "—and, further, " Roman Political Institutions," " Rome the Law-Giver " and the " Roman Empire " in this series—must be read if we are to understand social development in Greece, the permanent contribution made by the Athenian Republic in spite of its elements of weakness, the extension of the Roman city into a territorial State and an Empire.

From reading this book which is so rich in erudition, in

---

[1] *v. a note in Rousseau, Book I, Chap. VI, which begins in this way :* " The real meaning of this word has been almost wholly lost in modern times ; most people mistake a town for a city, and a townsman for a citizen. They do not know that houses make a town, but citizens a city." *For the ideas of Rousseau (and of Condorcet) on direct government by the people v. H. Sée, " L'évolution de la pensée politique en France au xviiie siècle," pp. 293-94.*

[2] *Rousseau realized this problem :* " In Greece, all that the people had to do, it did for itself ; it was constantly assembled in the public square. . . . All things considered, I do not see that it is possible henceforth for the Sovereign to preserve among us the exercise of its rights, unless the city is very small " (Book III, Chap. XV). *He suggests federations.*

thought, in apt quotation, in vivid pictures, just as from reading the " Cité antique " a keen æsthetic pleasure is derived—a pleasure which proceeds from more than one source, for in these pages besides the charm of life and colour we find the intellectual satisfaction which vigorous writing gives.

HENRI BERR.

THE GREEK CITY AND ITS INSTITUTIONS

INTRODUCTION
FORMATION OF THE CITY

I

THEORIES

THE most striking feature of ancient Greece, the fundamental cause both of its greatness and its weakness, was its division into innumerable cities, each one of which formed a State. The ideas which a division of this sort implies were an inseparable part of the mental equipment of the Greeks, so much so that in the fourth century the most discerning minds considered the existence of the *polis* as a fact of nature. They could not conceive of any other organization for men worthy of the name. Aristotle himself took the effect for the cause, and defined not the Greek, but man, as a " political animal." There were for him two kinds of human beings: those who were submerged in savage, formless hordes or in the vast tribes of some monstrously large monarchy, and those who were harmoniously associated in cities; the former were born for servitude in order that the latter might enjoy a nobler way of life.

In actual fact the geographical conditions of Greece were a powerful factor in its historical development. Sea and mountains split up the land into narrow valleys imprisoned by hills and having no easy outlet save on the coast, and thus a great number of cantons was formed, each the natural home for a small society. Physical partitioning gave rise to, or at least facilitated, political partitioning—to every division a distinct nationality. Imagine an isolated valley with pasturage bordering on streams, with wooded slopes, fields, vineyards and olive groves sufficient to maintain some tens of thousands of inhabitants, seldom more than a hundred thousand, and, in addition, high ground for refuge in case of attack, and a port for communication with the outside world, and one then has some idea of what an autonomous and sovereign State meant to the Greeks.

One cannot, however, attribute the creation of the city-state solely to inevitable circumstance, to the all-powerful influence of the land on its inhabitants. Proof of this lies in the fact that Aristotle gave no thought to it when he spoke of man as a " political " being. In Asia Minor and in Italy, moreover, geographical conditions were very different from those existing in Greece itself: there the mountains were lower and less wild, the plains more extensive, communication easier; and yet there the Greeks faithfully reproduced the type of constitution which they had devised for the needs of a smaller and more divided country. One must, therefore, admit that in the formation of the city historical circumstances were combined with the influence of physical environment.

Aristotle in ancient times and Fustel de Coulanges in our own day considered only the former.

According to the author of the *Politics*,[1] the Greeks passed through three stages. The first community, which persists in all times simply because it is natural, was based on the association of husband and wife, master and slave; it embraced all who ate at the same table and breathed the smoke from the same altar: the family, the *oikia*. Out of the family grew the village, the *kome*; its inhabitants, children and grandchildren of the family, obeyed a king who exercised in the larger group all the powers which fell to the eldest in the primitive household. Finally, from the association of many villages, the complete State was created, the perfect community, the *polis*. First founded that men might live, it continued that they might live happily, but only so long as it remained self-sufficing could it exist and endure. The city-state, therefore, was a work of nature just as were the earlier associations which found their fulfilment in it. Thus man, who can begin to develop only in the family, can come to full maturity only in the *polis*; he is by nature, therefore, a " political animal."

[1] Arist., *Pol.*, I, 1, 6 *ff.*

By a narrow use of the comparative method the author of the *Cité antique* has, in modern times, arrived at conclusions different from these in certain respects, but similar on the whole. He looks for the explanation of institutions in primitive beliefs, in the worship of the dead and of the sacred fire—in short, in domestic religion. This was the formative principle of the family in its wider sense—of the Greek *genos* as of the Roman *gens*. The obligation to honour the common ancestor brought with it the obligation to assure the continuance of the family; it gave their essential character to the laws which governed marriage, the right of property and the right of succession; it conferred absolute authority on the father of the family, on the eldest of the direct descendants of the divine ancestor; it was the foundation of all morality. Exigencies of an economic and military nature compelled the families successively to group themselves into phratries, the phratries into tribes and, finally, the tribes into a city. Religion had to keep abreast with the development of human society, but the gods outside the home differed from the family gods only in the wider allegiance they commanded. Now there was a public hearth and the city had a religion which permeated all its institutions. The king was first and foremost a high-priest, and the magistracies which succeeded the monarchy were, in essence, priesthoods: political power sprang from a sacred function. What was law but a command from on high ? What was patriotism but municipal piety ? What was exile but excommunication ? Divine power created the omnipotence of the State, and claims for individual liberty could be regarded as nothing less than revolt against the gods. In cities so constituted the heads of the *gene* formed a privileged class; they were in a position to resist the kings, they lorded it over the men of the lower classes who gathered. round them as clients, and, in particular, over the plebeian mob, the descendants of aliens. Such an exclusive power inevitably gave rise to a series of revolutions. The first deprived the kings of political authority, and restricted them to religious ascendancy. But the leaders of the aristocracy were still veritable monarchs, each in his own *genos*, and so there was a second revolution which changed the constitution of the family, suppressed the law of primogeniture and destroyed the client-system. A third brought the plebs within the city, modified the principles of private law and made the common interest the first consideration in government. For a moment, however, it seemed as if privilege of fortune were to step into the place of privilege of birth, and a fourth revolution was called for to establish the laws of democratic government. The city had now exhausted its capacity for development; and in the struggles between rich and poor it was to meet its end. The criticism of the philosophers began to point out that this regime was too circumscribed; the Roman conquest deprived the municipal system of all political character; and finally, with Christianity, came the triumph of a universal conception which transformed for ever the conditions of all government.

The impressiveness of the structure which Fustel de Coulanges has built up, his breadth of thought combined with precision of detail and lucidity of style, impel admiration; but nevertheless, we cannot to-day accept all his conclusions unreservedly. I shall not attempt any criticism of his half-hearted use of the comparative method, partly because no use is made of it in this work, but still more because, when the *Cité antique* was published, no one since the time of Montesquieu had employed it with such masterly skill. It is in other matters that the fascination which his masterpiece exercises is to be guarded against. It is obvious that the author, as he passes from the family to the phratry, the tribe and the city, merely carries over to the larger groups the beliefs and customs observed in the primitive group; they remain identical though in a wider sphere. With imperturbable logic he proceeds by strict comparison to place the family in the centre of a series of concentric circles. But human societies do not evolve in this way: they are not geometrical figures, but living organisms which can only endure and preserve their identity so long as they suffer profound change. In reality, the Greek city, while retaining the institution of the family, grew at its expense. It was compelled to appeal to individual forces which the original group repressed. For a long time the city had to fight against the *genos*, and each of its victories was gained by the suppression of some form of patriarchal servitude. The great mistake which Fustel de Coulanges made is, therefore, clear. Conforming to the theory which dominated the liberal school of the nineteenth century, he established an absolute antinomy between the omnipotence of the city and individual liberty, whereas, on the contrary, state power and individualism progressed side by side, each supporting the other.

We shall not, therefore, see two opposing forces—the family and the city,—but three—the family, the city and the individual, each in its turn predominant. The history of Greek institutions thus falls into three periods: in the first, the city is composed of families which jealously guard their ancient right and subordinate all their members to the common good; in the second, the city subordinates the families to itself by calling to its aid emancipated individuals; in the third, individualism run riot destroys the city and necessitates the formation of larger States.

II

FACTS

We have seen how, from Aristotle to Fustel de Coulanges, the origin of the city-state has been conceived of in a purely logical manner. Unfortunately, the problem is not so simple. History does not follow a rectilinear line. Truth is always complex when it is concerned with men who live, toil and struggle, and are subject to the common needs of humanity. And if the event one is attempting to explain took place in times which have left no direct documents, when migration was mingling races and civilizations throughout all the lands of the Ægean, one must expect to find contamination of ideas and customs, a deceptive irregularity in the curve of evolution, and spasmodic progress followed by startling retrogression.

The first Greeks to arrive in Greece, the Achæans (some of whom later became known as Ionians and Æolians), were semi-nomadic shepherds from the Balkan peninsula. Since they had spent their lives wandering with their flocks over the plains and through the mountain forests, they had never formed a State. The unit of organization was the patriarchal clan, to which the name of *patria,* or more often *genos,* was given, and whose members were all descendants of the same ancestor and worshippers of the same god. The clans combined in greater or smaller numbers to form wider associations, brotherhoods in the broadest sense or *phratries*, warrior bands known as *phratores* or *phrateres*, *etai* or *hetairoi*. When the phratries went out on great expeditions they formed themselves into a small number, always the same, of tribes or *phylai*; each tribe had its own god and its own war cry, each recruited its own fighting force, the *phylopis*, and obeyed its own king, the *phylobasileus*; but all recognized the authority of a supreme king, the *basileus* in chief.

At this time the *genos* alone had a solid and durable organization. A picture of it can be constructed from the data supplied by various sources—from traditions handed down in very ancient songs and in the relatively recent Homeric poems; from the legendary tales repeated from generation to generation until writing gave them a permanent form; from survivals enshrined in religious ceremonies; from archæological details and from the innumerable analogies which a comparative study of human societies affords.

When the *genos* became established on Greek soil all in whose veins ran the blood of the common ancestor continued to gather round the common hearth. They lived under the same roof, they had imbibed the same milk (ὁμογάλακτες), breathed the same altar smoke (ὁμόκαπνοι), shared bread from the same oven (ὁμοσίπνοι). All the clansmen were brothers (κασίγνητοι)—to attempt to define more precisely the bonds of kinship is impossible. For long men remembered the great households embracing many hundreds of kinsmen: Homer tells of the fifty brothers and twelve sisters living under Priam's roof together with their wives and husbands, not to speak of the children.[1]

Thus constituted, the clan enjoyed complete independence, recognizing no limits to its sovereignty. It knew no obligations save those imposed by its own religion, no virtues save those which contributed to its honour and prosperity. Bonds of the closest nature united all the elements of the clan—men, beasts and chattels: a relation expressed by the Greek *philotes*, a word which must be translated, for lack of an exact equivalent, by "friendship," though it represented a tie

[1] *Iliad*, VI, 244 *ff.*; XXIV, 495.

rather juridical than sentimental. *Philotes* alone aroused and determined *aidos*, consciousness of duty. Duty, always a reciprocal obligation, did not exist, therefore, save between kinsmen.[1]

This world in miniature could only preserve the independence which was its pride, the solidarity which was its strength, if it was self-sufficing: in Greek parlance, autonomy was dependent upon *autarkeia*. The clan possessed, therefore, together with the house consecrated by the hearth-stone, all the surrounding land consecrated by the tomb of the ancestor, all the fields, pasturage, vines and olives required to feed so many mouths. The demesne, with its livestock and slaves, belonged in common to the whole group; and, being collective, property was consequently inalienable and indivisible. There were no rules of succession—it passed in an unbroken chain from the dead to the living.[2] And to earn his title to a share, each, whether young or old, man or woman, had to work for all.[3]

The chief of the *genos* was clearly marked out: he was king who, by male succession, traced his origin most directly to the divine ancestor, and in whose veins, therefore, flowed the purest blood. He was the priest of the god whose incarnation he was; he presided over all the ceremonies which gathered the clansmen together round the common hearth, and offered the sacrifices and libations which assured their prosperity. Not only did he possess absolute power over his wife, whom he could expose, sell or kill without having to justify his action, but, in addition, he exercised unrestricted authority over all the members of his group. To secure domestic peace he proclaimed, interpreted and executed the divine will. With the sceptre he received knowledge of the *themistes*, infallible decrees which a super-human wisdom revealed to him through dreams and oracles, or suggested to his inner conscience. Handed down from father to son since the beginning of time, increasing from generation to generation, the *themistes* formed a sacred and mysterious code of family justice (*themis*). Those who had exposed themselves to divine wrath by acting in a manner hostile to the clan were entirely at the mercy of the chief, the dispenser of

---

[1] Cf. **XXXIII**, p. 96 *ff.*, 139 *ff.*   [2] Cf. **XXXIX**, p. 46 *ff.*
[3] Cf. **XXXV**, p. 12 *ff.*; **XXXVI**, vol. I, p. 120 *f.*

justice. He could put them to the ordeal or the judgment of God to expiate their offence or establish their innocence; he could place them under the ban of the *genos* by the terrible punishment of *atimia*. In his hands were the weapons of punishment and intimidation, and to him, therefore, fell the duty of providing for the protection of society.

Yet in spite of their nature, there was regular intercourse between the *gene*. For long neighbouring families were in a state of almost perpetual warfare. Raids on enemy territory took place; the chief gloried in the number of women and beasts he carried off; blood flowed and called for avenging blood, and so interminable reprisals followed. Even when they were united in phratries and tribes the clans did not abandon the vendetta; they were only compelled to subordinate it to those common rules which constituted then a higher law than *themis*, namely, *dike*. The members of the injured *genos* were always entitled to avenge themselves on the members of the attacking *genos*. But it was admitted that the murderer freed his kinsmen from all responsibility by exile: this kind of compounding by flight tranquillized passions and helped to restore order. A way was found of extending to members of different or even hostile clans the sentiments and obligations which up to that time had existed only between members of the same clan. Reconciliation could be achieved by the application to adversaries of *aidos*, by *aidesis*. By means of adoption or marriage the murderer would sometimes take the place of the dead man in the group he had depleted; most often he would make atonement by paying blood - money (*poine*). A treaty of " friendship " (*philotes*) followed, when with solemn ceremonies the families recently enemies offered a sacrifice to their gods, sat at the same table and mingled their blood in a loving-cup.[1] Thus, above family law custom gradually created an inter-family law, whence, by degrees, public law was to spring.

The rule which subordinated the clans to the common interest was not devoid of sanction. To override the decrees of custom was to expose oneself to divine anger ($\ddot{o}\pi\iota\varsigma$ $\theta\epsilon\hat{\omega}\nu$).[2] But supernatural notions of this sort are always capable of a natural explanation. This fear of the gods was, at bottom,

---

[1] Cf. **XXXIII**, p. 94 *ff.*, 103 *ff.*, 135 *ff.*
[2] *Odyssey*, XIV, 82, 88; XX, 215.

fear of a social force which day by day took to itself new strength. Men feared the *demos*. This name was applied to the whole mass of clans assembled under one rule, whether it was conceived in terms of the country or its inhabitants. Public opinion (*demou phatis* or *phemis*) exercised an influence which no clan could escape. It exerted by means of *nemesis* a pressure powerful enough to prevent crime or to compel the criminal to expiate his offence.[1] True it had no official voice; it was represented neither by a person nor by an accredited body; yet one cannot say that it was simply a moral force, for in extreme cases, when passions were at fever-pitch, indignation would burst tempestuously forth and sweep all obstacles before it. In theory the family remained sovereign; in fact it often had to yield to that nameless collective will which was able to place so formidable a weapon in the hands of the king.

The Achæans appear to have reached this stage of civilization when they settled in the midst of the peoples established on the shores of the Ægean. They were only an armed minority which had for the most part to adapt its ideas and institutions to the customs of the majority which it governed. The Pre-Hellenes, who had been a settled people since the earliest times, seem also to have known the system of the gentile clan: the ruins of spacious dwellings unearthed at Vasiliki, Chamaizi and Tiryns, as well as the enormous bee-hive tombs (*tholoi*) in the Messara, afford a retrospective commentary on those passages in the epics where Priam is shown with the sixty-two families over which he ruled, Nestor and Æolus with the households of their six sons and of their daughters, Alcinous with his six children, two of whom were married.[2] But in the most progressive regions of the Ægean world this stage had long been passed; the enormous families had been broken up, and cities and monarchical government established. Crete, in particular, had magnificent palaces whence its lordly rulers governed a vast and wealthy people, and unfortified towns with roads flanked by rows of small houses. In the Cyclades are to be seen fortifications such as those of Chalandriani on Syra and of Haghios Andreas on Siphnos, which could only have been constructed at the

---

[1] *Iliad*, IX, 459 *ff.*; VI, 351.
[2] *Iliad*, VI, 244 *ff.*; *Odyssey*, III, 387 *ff.*, 412 *ff.*; X, 5; VI, 62 *f.*

command of powerful chiefs for the protection of large populations. On the mainland, along the great road which leads from Thessaly to the extremities of the Peloponnese, were scattered agricultural centres. Many of them were prosperous; Orchomenus began to enrich itself by reclaiming land from Lake Copais, a task involving considerable labour, and surrounded itself with a whole escort of new villages. As a general rule hamlets and villages were situated near a hill which served for refuge in time of war, and to which the chief summoned the elders to make decisions concerning the common welfare. These heights were usually fortified; some were surrounded with simple wooden palisades which now have disappeared, others with walls of stone.

The Achæan conquerors took possession of the richest plains and the strongest positions. Within the walls rose the palaces of the kings. When there was sufficient space the houses of the chief officers and dignitaries were attached to them. At Athens, close by the " stronghold " where the Erectheum lay, was a small group of more modest dwellings. At Mycenæ, towards the middle of the fifteenth century, the fortifications were even extended so as completely to encircle the royal headquarters. At the foot of these hills were huddled the huts in which the peasants and serfs lived, along with the artisans and merchants who supplied their needs—sometimes so large a settlement that the villages formed almost a separate town. When he was in a favourable position and controlled access to his territory, the chief levied forced tolls from travellers, and where roads met population increased greatly.

It was the high town which was at first called the *polis* (πόλις or πτολίεθρον), while the lower town was the *asty* (ἄστυ). In many of the Homeric poems the two words still retain their distinct meaning.[1] The *asty* was the inhabited part to which the roads led, and the surface of which was only hired.[2] To the *polis* was appropriated the term " lofty "; it was the *acropolis*, and there were words innumerable to describe its characteristics—its escarpments, its massiveness,

---

[1] *Iliad*, XVII, 144; VI, 257, 327 *ff.*; *Odyssey*, XIV, 472 *f.*

[2] *Iliad*, IX, 589; XV, 680 *f.*; *Odyssey*, X, 103 *f.*; XXIV, 468; *v.* **XVIII**, for the word ἄστυ.

its towers, its great gates;[1] moreover, since it contained the temple of the god of the city and the king's palace, it alone was sacred, rich, magnificent, treasure-filled.[2] When Hecuba wished to bring to the goddess Athene her offering and her supplications, she assembled the Trojans in the *asty* and climbed with them to the *polis*.[3] This distinction continued for long in a great part of Greece: in 426, the Hyeans, a people of western Locris, successfully resisted the Spartans so long as they remained masters of a paltry fortress called the Polis;[4] official documents gave the Acropolis at Athens this name even at the beginning of the fourth century, and the Achæan fortress at Ialysus as late as the third century.[5]

But in the latest books of the *Iliad*, and in practically the whole of the *Odyssey*, no distinction is made between the *polis* and the *asty*. As the lower town became larger through the development of agriculture and commerce, it acquired an importance which counter-balanced that of the upper city. It was Mycenæ of " the spacious ways " which filled the coffers of Mycenæ " abounding in gold," and the lord of the heights was forced to consider with growing interest and solicitude the activities of the plains: it is more than symbolic that the kings of the first dynasty were entombed in graves on the fortified hill, while those of the second wereburied in beehive tombs outside the walls. The people and property of the upper and lower towns were beginning to mingle. When the lords of Tiryns were extending their stronghold by building lower than the *Oberburg* the walls of the *Mittelburg*, then lower still those of the *Niederburg*, gradually they brought within the *polis* the territory of the ancient *asty*. Similarly, in the epics it was no longer the upper town of Ilium which was encircled with towers, but the lower town, the *asty*.[6] It was natural that the two words should become synonymous; in many cases the same identification is seen. Both words were used indiscriminately to denote Ilium, Ithaca, Cnossus, Lacedæmon, Scheria.[7] It seems, however, that the main

[1] *v*. **XVIII**, for the words πτόλις and πτολίεθρον. *Acropolis* appears in the *Odyssey*, VIII, 494, 504.
[2] *Iliad*, VI, 88, 96, 297, 305; VII, 345 *f*.; XI, 46.
[3] *Iliad*, VI, 87 *ff*.; 287 *ff*.   [4] Thuc., III, 101.
[5] *v*. **LIII**, vol. II, ii, p. 717; *IG*, vol. XII, 1, no. 677.
[6] *Iliad*, VIII, 519; XVIII, 274 *f*.; 286 *f*. Scheria was likewise surrounded with walls and with palisades (*Od*. VI, 267).
[7] Cf. **XVIII**, ll. *cc*.

agglomeration, as opposed to the surrounding country, was more particularly called the *asty*, the name which the country people had always given to the place where the market was held.[1] On the other hand, the upper town had not merely absorbed the lower town of " the spacious ways,"[2] for the general name *polis* was extended also to all the rural communities which lived under its protection. It was an easy step to extend it to the whole country which recognized the authority of the same chief.[3] The word which in the beginning had denoted an acropolis ended by denoting a city.

This development did not involve the breaking up of the existing social system. The " polis " became a really " political " institution without destroying the clans, the phratries or the tribes; indeed, it was only possible for it to become so by incorporating these groups. They occupied a relatively large area to which the name of *demos* was given —a name which had naturally been transferred to the body of people inhabiting it.[4] The city gave the *demos* the unity which it lacked; but it dealt with the organized society of clans, not with individuals. The king could only give orders and ensure their execution with the consent and through the mediation of the tribal chiefs, who, in their turn, could do nothing without the family chiefs. At most, one may surmise that public opinion (*demou phatis*) worked by indirect methods to undermine the solidarity of the family for the benefit of a larger unit.

These developments might have led Greece even as early as 1000 B.C. to the conception of the city which, in fact, only triumphed some centuries later. But at this point Greece was inundated with semi-barbarian Greeks who had not felt the influence of the Ægean civilization. At the end of the twelfth century there came in successive waves all the peoples of the north-west, some of whom at a later day were to be known as Dorians. Confusion reigned. The old monarchies crumbled and fell, and the glory of Mycenæ vanished for ever. No doubt certain obscure cantons of Greece proper, for

---

[1] *Od.*, VI, 296; X, 104 *ff.*; XV, 308, 681; XVI, 461 *ff.*; *Iliad* III, 116.
[2] *Iliad*, II, 12; IV, 51 *f.*; *Odyssey*, XV, 384.
[3] Cf. *Odyssey*, VI, 177 *f.*; VIII, 151 *ff.*
[4] *Demos*=territory: *Iliad*, V, 78, 710; XVI, 437, 514; *Odyssey*, XIV, 329; XVII, 536. *Demos* =people: *Iliad*, XX, 166; *Odyssey*, II, 291; IV, 666; VIII. 157; XIII, 186; XVI, 114.

example the part of Attica sheltered by Mount Parnes and Arcadia protected by the sharp rise of its plateaus, escaped the storm and could even offer shelter to fugitive bands; but these were small rural districts, divided into innumerable villages, none of which was sufficiently strong to dominate the others. Elsewhere the invaders seized the land and reduced the vanquished to servitude; and the oldest customs of the race once more held sway. The progress of many centuries was lost. The system of clans and tribes regained the mastery, with strongly-marked military characteristics, and the movement which was gradually bringing it into subordination to the State, to the city, was cut short. Everything had to be started afresh.

The *polis* became once more the fortified place or camp whence the conqueror kept watch over his serfs who toiled upon the land. In Lacedæmon it bore the name of Sparta and was a combination of four villages. In Argos it comprised the two citadels of Larissa and the Aspis, with a lower town where the three Dorian tribes looked suspiciously upon a neighbouring non-Dorian tribe. In Crete it consisted of all the heights which rose above the fertile valleys.

There was, however, a vast region in which the Achæans, later to be distinguished as Æolians and Ionians, could transplant the relatively progressive institutions with which they had become familiar. Since early days they had known Asia Minor; at first they had occupied Pamphylia, Cyprus, Rhodes, Lesbos and the Troad; since then they had settled in certain places, preferably islands, from which they could easily explore the interior, either to pillage or to trade. Now they came in larger and smaller bands with no thought of returning to their native lands. They established themselves all along the coast in the midst of a dense population. Since they had to defend themselves against tribes which in some cases were for all practical purposes States, they were compelled to live together in strong strategic positions, in towns naturally or artificially fortified. On the banks of the Hermos grew up the New Fort, Neon Teichos; the port of Colophon received the name South Fort, Notion Teichos; the land of Teos was studded with fortresses to the number of twenty-seven, which served as places of refuge for the farmers, and which eventually became the centres of adminis-

B

tration (*pyrgoi* or castles). Topography confirms the information furnished by place-names. Erythræ was originally situated on a hill; the old town of Miletus had its origin in a citadel built a hundred yards or so from the sea.[1] " The great men defend the towns," as the Homeric expression is (ἄριστοι . . . πτολίεθρα ῥύονται),[2] and even the peasants had their houses there if they were free and of Greek birth; the flat country was left for the natives, for those whom the people of Miletus and Priene called the Gergithes. They thus constituted an aristocracy of Hellenic city-dwellers, as opposed to an alien rural proletariat; and within this aristocracy there were again very clearly defined class-distinctions. Whence the early demand for institutions more complex than elsewhere.

Another factor, the extraordinary mixture of immigrant bands, made this necessity still more urgent. From Crete to Thessaly every country had furnished its contingent. More than once waves of hybrid invaders had swept over the towns of the East. A place in the social structure had to be made for these heterogeneous elements. The Dorians had indeed brought with them the three-tribe system, just as the companions of the Neleidæ were divided into four Ionian tribes; but what was to be done with groups which did not belong naturally to any of these tribes ?

Let us see exactly what the position was. The tribes always kept their gentile character. The great families, the *patrai*, maintained a strong organization and gave their name to the locality in which their domain lay: beneath the royal families, the Neleidæ, Androclidæ, Penthilidæ, Basilidæ, there were still to be seen at Miletus the Thelidæ, the Skiridæ, the Hecætadæ; at Chios, the Demotionidæ, the Thraikidæ; at Camirus, the Hippotadæ, the Græadæ, the Thoiadæ; at Cos, the villages of the Antimachidæ and the Archiadæ; at Calymna, that of the Scaliodæ; at Rhodes, that of the Boulidæ, etc.[3] Around the most important families others were grouped, in such a way as to form phratries. The phratry often bore the name of the controlling *patra*, so that it is sometimes impossible to distinguish them: it must have been so for long with the Clytidæ at Chios, where they

---

[1] Wiegand, *Abh. BA*, 1908, p. 494 *ff.*; cf. *Sb. BA*, 1925, p. 275.
[2] *Iliad*, IX, 396.   [3] Cf. **VII**, vol. I, p. 249.

built a chapel to enshrine the common objects of worship, preserved until then in their own homes. The god of the phratries might be either a Zeus Patrios as with the Clytidæ, or a Zeus Phratrios as with the Euryanactidæ of Cos.[1] The social importance of these cults is attested by the fact that wherever there were Ionians, at Miletus, Priene and Samos, as well as at Delos and Athens, a great feast of the *patriai* and the phratries, the Apaturia, was celebrated. Their political importance is sufficiently demonstrated by the passages in Homer in which he seems unable to conceive of the formation of an army, and, as a consequence, of a people, without the division into phratries. The whole system of clan organization, dating back to the very origins of the cities, is remarkably illustrated, many centuries later, by a veritable family tree traced on an inscription from Camirus; at the top is written as a general heading the name of the Althaimenidæ, descendants of the heroic founder; underneath are ranged the phratries, each containing a certain number of *patrai*, named as such.[2]

What, then, was the position of those Greeks who inhabited the same territory as the members of the family groups without being of their number ? That they might not remain isolated, individuals or small families formed artificial groups analogous to the *patrai* and the phratries, though very different in origin. They were called *thiasoi*. It is a Pre-Hellenic word preserved among the descendants of the oldest Achæans, and diffused in the Greek world by Attic settlers who lived in scattered groups there before the period of the great migrations. These associations kept faintly alive many very ancient beliefs, many elements of civilization which one day were to burst into full life again: it will never be known what part they played in the diffusion of the Dionysian and Orphic cults, and in the rebirth of industry and art, but their influence must have been great. At all events they succeeded in attaching themselves to the phratries. That this happened in Attica is certain;[3] and the same may be said of Asia Minor. It explains the fact that in the third century a phratry of Chios still contained, besides the *patrai* bearing the family name (Demogenidæ, etc.), small communities

[1] *RIG*, nos. 997, 797.   [2] *IG*, vol. XII, 1, no. 695.
[3] *v.* **XXXVI**, vol. I, p. 414.

called by the name of their chief (people of Telargus, etc.).[1] And, still more striking, side by side with the gentile tribes were secondary tribes in which individuals and families of racial minorities were grouped. At first their rights were doubtless small, but sooner or later they succeeded in attaining an equal footing with the other tribes. In this way two tribes, possibly pre-Ionian, the Boreis, and the Oinopæ, attached themselves to the four Ionian tribes at Miletus. And this same town affords the most striking example we know of a non-gentile association forcing its way into the political organism. There was there a religious fraternity of *molpoi* which dated back in all probability to Mycenæan days. In historic times it had at its head a president (*aisymnetes*) and five assistants (προσέταιροι) representing, that is to say, each of the six tribes. One can see how the necessity of making a hybrid population live peacefully together gave extension to the idea of community in the centuries which followed the great migrations.

It was in Asia Minor, as we have just seen, that this stimulus towards progress was felt the earliest and the most powerfully: in a country which had for a considerable time served as a centre of colonization for the Hellenic race the Greeks, so various in their origin, could free themselves more easily than elsewhere from traditions in many respects obsolete. There also another factor contributed early to the same result. In Asia Minor economic conditions were not the same as in Greece proper. An exclusive system of landed property is essentially fitted for the maintenance of patriarchal customs and institutions. In the Greek settlements of Asia there had existed from the beginning resources other than the exploitation of rich land. All along the coast were excellent ports, well supplied with fresh water, near fine and extensive islands and situated often on isthmuses which made defence easy and favoured commerce, or at the mouths of rivers which penetrated far into the interior of the peninsula.[2] There were thus splendid facilities for communication with all the countries of the old civilization, with those of the Ægean as with those of the East. Shipping and commerce were not slow to take advantage of all these opportunities.

---

[1] *RIG*, no. 1144.
[2] On the importance of the isthmuses *v.* Thuc., I, 17.

The city-system developed; thriving markets gave birth to large towns. At Miletus, for example, the old town crept down from the Acropolis and stretched in the direction of the Lion Gate. Thus fluid capital competed with landed wealth and created a new class side by side with the landed and family aristocracy. Here was another reason for modification of the unduly narrow conceptions of former times.

The change which one can dimly discern taking place on the coast of Asia was effected in a similar fashion in Greece, though more slowly and usually still more obscurely. Everywhere were villages bearing ancestral names: for example, Akaidai and Keondai at Histiaia in Eubœa. Everywhere were phratries grouping a number of families around an illustrious *genos*: for example, at Delphi the Labyadæ formed round a sacerdotal *genos* dedicated formerly to the Cretan cult of the Double Axe. Sometimes even the three Dorian tribes admitted a non-Dorian tribe to their ranks: for instance, the Hyrnatians of Argos. It is of Attica, naturally, that we have the fullest information. Clans of Eupatridæ were numerous. Many of them took their name from a sacred office, as for example the Eumolpidæ, and the Kerykes of Eleusis, the Gephyreans of Aphidna, the Bouzygæ, the Aletridæ, the Heudanemoi, the Phreorykhoi, the Aigeirotomoi. Many of them were sufficiently powerful to be able to dominate a whole *demos* and impose their name upon it, as the Scambonidæ, the Philaidæ, the Paionidæ, the Boutadæ, etc. According to ancient custom the phratries celebrated the Apaturia in honour of Zeus Phratrios and Athena Phratria and the tribes were four in number. But Attica is unique in that one can follow there the progressive fusion of all small communities into one community larger than the majority of Greek cities. In this rural country each group had at first its " prytaneum and its archons."[1] After the struggles of which legend has preserved the memory, religious and political associations of various types were created. The most famous was a group of towns which worshipped Athena—the Athenai who took for chiefs the Erechtheidæ and for nucleus an acropolis destined to be the Acropolis *par excellence*. But there were many others: the Amphictyony of the Epacria and that of the Mesogæa; in one place

[1] Id., II, 15, 2.

a Tricomia, in another a Tetracomia or a Tetrapolis. This last example proves that even places so insignificant as Marathon, Tricorythus, Œnœ and Probalinthus were *poleis*, like the seven villages Homer speaks of on the outskirts of Pylus,[1] or like the hundred small towns which were inhabited by the people whom the Spartans made Perioikoi.[2] It proves also that these " cities " formed a " city " four times as large before being absorbed by synœcism into a " city " which united in one single *demos* the *demoi* of the whole of Attica, and which took for its capital the Acropolis of the Erechtheidæ.

III

ELEMENTS AND CHARACTERISTICS OF THE CITY

Though the origin of the city is shrouded in darkness, through which the historian must grope his way lighted only by the feeble glimmer of stray facts, and guided only by precarious conjecture, at least when once it is in existence he can see a little more clearly its constituent elements.

Self-defence was its first necessity. Even in its earliest days the city had possessed a hill to which the country-folk could fly when threatened by an enemy force or pirate bands. Almost always it had one acropolis or even more. Moreover, the development of the lower town usually made necessary the construction of more extensive walls; in the epics we see the *asty* surrounded with walls flanked with towers and pierced by gates. One realizes what Aristotle meant when he asserted that the defensive system of the acropolis was favourable to monarchy and oligarchy, whilst democracy preferred fortresses in the plains.[3] Undoubtedly there were open cities very early in the historic period. When the Dorians of Laconia descended from the heights where they had first settled, they established a camp on the banks of the Eurotas, and, trusting in their native courage, built no ramparts around the four villages which composed Sparta.[4] Many places in Asia Minor had no walls to protect them against the Lydian armies, and were com-

---

[1] *Iliad*, IX, 149 *ff.*   [2] *DA*, art. " Perioikoi."
[3] Arist., *Pol.*, IV (VII), 10, 4.
[4] Xen., *Hell.*, VII, 5, 10; Pol., IX, 8.

pelled hurriedly to make good the deficiency in the face of
the Persian menace.[1] Camirus was not fortified at the end
of the fifth century, nor Elis at the beginning of the fourth.[2]
When a town had extended itself, however, especially if it
were rich and aspired to political importance, it surrounded
itself with strong walls. Miletus in Ionia, Assus in Æolis
and Cnidus in Doris were fortified towns.[3] The Pisistratidæ
had built round the Acropolis and its Pelargicon with Pelasgic
walls a wall of a circumference considerable for those days.[4]
It was not without cause that Thucydides in his rapid survey
of the remote past of Greece made the age of fortified towns
succeed that of open villages.[5]

The need for mutual defence, of which the acropolis and
the ramparts are evidence, was expressed, as was every social
function in antiquity, in a religious form. Every city had
its deity, as had every family. Just as the kinsmen gathered
before the altar of the family hearth, so the citizens celebrated
the religion of the city before the " common hearth " (κοινὴ
ἑστία). There were offered the sacrifices which were to
call down upon the people the protection of the gods: there
were held the official banquets where the flesh of the victims
was divided among the leading men of the city, high magistrates or members of the council, and citizens or strangers
worthy of such an honour. For a long time the public
hearth had for its home the palace of the king, the high-
priest of the city: the banquets at which Alcinous, surrounded
by the elders, magnificently entertained Ulysses, differed in
no way from those where later ambassadors were received
as public guests (τὰ ξένια).[6]

When monarchy fell the common hearth, deified under
the name of the goddess Hestia,[7] was inseparable from the
building where dwelt the chief or the chiefs of the city, the
prytanis or the committee of *prytaneis*: it became the centre
of the Prytaneum and Hestia was its guardian.[8] According
to the ruins of Olympia one must imagine at the entrance

---

[1] Her., I, 141, 163.
[2] Thuc., VIII, 44; Xen., *Hell.*, III, 2, 27.
[3] Cf. **XXXVI**, vol. I, p. 559. [4] *Ibid.*, p. 451.
[5] Thuc., I, 2, 1; 5, 1; 7; 8, 3.
[6] Cf. **LIII**, vol. II, 11, p. 778-780.
[7] The name of Hestia appears for the first time in the *Theogony* of
Hesiod (v. 454).
[8] Pind., *Nem.*, XI, 1.

a small sanctuary, in the middle of which was placed an altar
with a well filled with glowing embers, and, further within,
banqueting halls and a kitchen supplied with all the necessary
utensils.[1]   There could be no city without a prytaneum:
" the prytaneum is the symbol of the city," *penetrale urbis*,
Livy called it.[2]   At the time when Attica was divided
into a great number of little cities, each had its own;[3] when
it became one city it had a single prytaneum, the dwelling
from which the archon had expelled the king, but to which
the king returned with the tribal kings to deliver judgments
of marked archaic character.[4] Whenever a colony was
founded the emigrants took from the hearth of the mother
city the embers which were to be cherished in the new
prytaneum.[5] The place made holy by the undying fire
might bear another name; for the name was of no account.
At Cnidus where the supreme magistrate, the agent of the
people, was the *damiourgos*, the public banquets were held
in the *damiourgeum*.   Among the Achæans of Phthiotis
the prytaneum was called the " house of the people," *leiton*:
the word recalls the *leitourgiai*, or liturgies, those public
services, originally largely ritual, which burdened the richest
citizens, the most characteristic being the *hestiasis*, the provision and preparation of a sacred feast.[6]

Not far from the prytaneum arose the *Bouleuterion*,
where the Council sat.   Whatever the political system of the
city the Council was an institution with which it could not
dispense.   When the great men, who formerly had surrounded the king as *gerontes* or *boulephoroi*, became heads
of the government, it was not enough that they were represented in the prytaneum by the *prytaneis*, they needed also
a special meeting-place for their deliberations.   And in the
same way, wherever democracy took the place of aristocracy,
the people, who could not be in permanent session, needed
a limited body of men to prepare decrees, to keep in touch
with the magistrates, to receive foreign ambassadors, to send

[1] *Ausgr. von Olympia*, vol. II, p. 58 *ff.*; Weniger, *Klio*, vol. VI
(1906), p. 1 *ff.*; **XXX**, p. 167 *ff.*
[2] Schol. Aristid., *Panath.*, 103, 15; Livy, XLI, 20.
[3] Thuc., II, 15, 2; cf. Plut., *Theseus*, 24.
[4] *v.* **XXXVI**, vol. I, p. 398, 399, 424.
[5] Her., I, 146.
[6] *GDI*, nos. 3501 *f.*; Her., VII, 197.

representatives to the ' Commons.' Whether the Council was called the *Boule*, as was most frequently the case, or as in certain cities, the *Gerousia*, whether its deputies in the prytaneum bore the commonly accepted name of *prytaneis* or the name *aisymnates* peculiar to the Megarians, there is no example of a city which had none. The Bouleuterion, as distinct from the prytaneum, dates far back. That of Olympia, rebuilt many times, followed the apsidal plan which goes back to prehistoric days;[1] perhaps it was towards a building of this type that Alcinous was turning his steps when Nausicaa met him at the threshold of his door as he was departing to the Council of the Phæacians.[2] In Attica every small town had its Boule before the synœcism; the synœcism caused all to disappear, save that of Athens. When Thales suggested to the Ionians that they should unite he supplied them with a scheme: allow every city the right of administering its affairs as a deme, and establish in a federal capital a single Bouleuterion. The scheme failed, but the idea was sound. More than a century later it was put into practice at Rhodes. The three cities of Lindus, Camirus and Ialysus had been founded early at the expense of the demes of the island; when, in 408-7, they decided to form a single state they themselves were reduced to the position of demes, and, though they preserved the right of issuing decrees in what were henceforth municipal assemblies, they had only one common Boule.[3]

According to the constitutional regime of the city the mass of the citizens either exercised no political rights at all, or, on the contrary, possessed them all; but whatever the constitution it was always essential that they should be able to meet together. For that gathering, which was called the *agora*, a public meeting-place was required, and it bore the same name. It was before everything else the market-place. " For of necessity in almost every city," wrote Aristotle, " there must be both buyers and sellers to supply each other's mutual wants; and this is what is most productive of the comforts of life; for the sake of which men

---

[1] *v.* Wernicke, *Jb. AI*, vol. IX (1894), p. 127-135; G. Leroux, *Les orig. de l'édif. hypostyle*, p. 75-77; **XXX**, p. 271-274.

[2] *Odyssey*, VI, 53-55.

[3] Thuc., II, 15, 2-3; Her., I, 170; *RIG*, nos. 432-435; cf. **XXIII**, p. 195 *ff.*

B*

seemed to have joined together in one community."[1] The place set apart for commerce ought, therefore, according to Aristotle, to be " easily accessible for goods coming over the sea or from the interior of the country," and the facilities which it offered for supplies generally attracted the prytaneum into its neighbourhood:[2] the excavations at Priene, for example, confirm this assertion. But the market-place was not only the scene of commercial transactions; for there with merchants and customers mingled gossips and loungers. At all hours it was the *rendez-vous* where men strolled around, learnt the latest news or talked politics; and there public opinion was formed. The *agora*, then, was expressly designed to serve for full assemblies of the people, for those which were convened by the king or the leaders of the aristocracy to discuss decisions made by the government, as well as for those which deliberated as sovereign assemblies. Even in that military city, the camp, an agora was needed: there was one during the Trojan war, where the Achæan chiefs, like the Roman prætors, delivered their proclamations to the warriors and administered justice.[3]

In the hundreds of cities of which Greece was composed there were naturally many variations of this institution, as of all others. The agora in the topographical sense might be duplicated. In the oligarchical cities of Thessaly the market-place was abandoned to buying and selling, was " sullied with trade," while the place of Liberty, situated at the foot of the hill where the prytaneum stood, was reserved for gymnastics for the privileged citizens.[4] In democratic cities, especially in those which had grown much, the ancient agora was often too small and obstructed to accommodate the increasing numbers of the popular assemblies: the Athenians of the fifth century went to deliberate on the hill of the Pnyx which was fitted for the purpose, and no longer assembled in the agora except in extraordinary cases. Nor did the assembly retain the name of agora except in cities of the second rank, for example in Delphi, Naupactus, Gortyna and Cos,[5] and especially in subdivisions of the city, in the tribes and demes,

---

[1] Arist., *Pol.*, VII (VI), 5, 2 (*v.* trans. Ellis, p. 196).
[2] *Ibid.*, IV (VII), 11, 2-3.
[3] *Iliad*, IX, 807.   [4] Arist., *loc. cit.*, 2.
[5] **IV**, p. 45, 59 *f.*; *SIG*³, nos. 47, l. 21; 525, l. 11; 1045, l. 9, 34; 1012, l. 2.

or again in religious associations, the *phratries*, the *thiasoi* and the *orgeones*.[1] *Ecclesia* was the usual term for the assembly of the people, save with the Dorians who employed more often that of the *Halia* (the tribunal of the Heliæa of the Athenians), and with the Spartans who used the name *Apella*.[2] But these differences did not prevent the Greeks from regarding the agora as an essential condition of city life. For Homer the Cyclopes were savages because they had not a " deliberative assembly " (ἀγοραὶ βουληφόροι). For Herodotus the thing which most clearly distinguished the Greeks from the Persians was the fact that the one had the institution of the agora whilst the others had not in their feudal villages even market-places.[3]

The capital, whose pre-eminence was attested by the Acropolis, the Prytaneum, the Bouleuterion and the Agora, possessed surrounding territory, varying in extent according to its requirements. Most often the harbour was to be found there; for the Acropolis, which fixed for all time the site of the city, was generally some distance from the coast, in a position chosen by people who lived in fear of piracy.[4] It was by means of the port that the city, whose territory was usually encircled by mountains, communicated with the outside world and added to its own resources the riches which it lacked. In all cases a larger or smaller number of hamlets, villages, and small towns called *komai*, demes, or sometimes even, as in Laconia, *poleis*, were in dependence on the principal agglomeration, the *asty*. In small cities there were fewer scattered villages, since the free peasantry frequently continued to live in the town, while going out to work in the fields from morning till evening. In the large cities, on the other hand, they were numerous, and some even acquired a certain importance. There were more than a hundred *poleis* inhabited by the *perioikoi* of Laconia, and even more demes in Attica. These constituent elements of the city always enjoyed a large independence in administrative matters; but they had no political powers save as fractions of the greater community. Nowhere, perhaps, was the dependence of the part on the whole more remarkable than in certain cantons

---

[1] Cf. *RIG*, nos. 139, l. 23; 142, l. 5; 961, B, l. 28; 969, l. 2; 979, l. 16.
[2] Cf. *DA*, art. " Ekklesia," p. 512.
[3] *Odyssey*, IX, 112; Her., I, 153.   [4] Thuc., I, 7.

which, retaining a purely rural economy, contained only the *komai*, and not a single town. Elis, for example, had no capital before 471; but for long the supreme magistrate and the petty kings of each locality were subject to the *hellanodikai* and the *demiourgoi* who represented the central power.

But the most striking feature of the Greek city was the division of its citizens into tribes and phratries. I shall not emphasize these groups here, because I have already shown at some length that the formation of the city cannot be explained without them. I shall confine myself to pointing out that the gentile and aristocratic character which they owed to their origin was in some degree modified by the progress of democratic government. The phratries had often to admit within the ranks of the *gene thiasoi* composed for the most part of men of humble birth. The ancient tribes had often to tolerate side by side with them tribes of different nationality, before even the new ideas had made the conception of territorial tribes prevail.

The city thus constituted was a small State. Let us try to get a more detailed conception of it.[1] Sparta and Athens were exceptional on account of the extent of their territory. Sparta, when it had aggrandized Laconia at the expense of Messenia, was the first power in Greece, since it commanded a country of 3,360 square miles, two-fifths of the Peloponnesus[2] (a little more than the department of the Marne, much less than that of the Gironde); one must also note that the land reserved for the citizens, the πολιτικὴ χώρα, comprised only a third of that surface, the rest belonging to a hundred *poleis* of *perioikoi*. Athens, the city which holds so great a place in the history of civilization, at the time of its greatest extent, that is, including the island of Salamis and the district of Oropus, possessed only 1,060 square miles (less than the department of the Rhône). One must pass to the West, to the conquering colonies, to find figures comparable to these: after annexing Gera, Acræ, Casmena and Camarina, the territory of Syracuse covered 1,880 square miles, surpassing that of Acragas, which measured 1,720. Everywhere else the surface of the Greek cities was hardly equivalent to that of

---

[1] *v.* **II, III**, vol. III, 1, p. 263 *ff.*; cf. Cavaignac, " La popul. du Péloponnèse aux Vᵉ et IVᵉ siècles " (*Klio*, vol. XII, 1912, p. 261 *ff*).
[2] Thuc., I, 10, 2.

French *arrondissements* or even cantons; often it happened that they were considerably smaller. In the Peloponnesus Argos, mistress of Cleonæ, ruled in all 560 square miles; Corinth 352; Sicyon 144; Phlius 72. In the fifth century the Bœotian League extended over 1,032 square miles, of which Thebes accounted for about 400 and the rest was divided among a dozen cities, each averaging about 52 square miles. The 656 square miles of Phocis were divided among twenty-two principalities. In Asia Minor, where there was no lack of land, the Ionian cities possessed from 80 to 600 square miles; the Æolian cities only about 40. As for the islands, the smaller and most of the medium-sized ones each formed a single city; such were, for example, Delos (2¼ square miles, 9 with Rhenea), Thera (32½ square miles), Ægina (34), Melos (60), Naxos (176), Samos (188), Chios (331). But Ceos, which had an area of only 70 square miles, was, until the fourth century, divided into four cities, each of which coined its own money. As for the larger islands, those of 400 square miles or more, one alone achieved political unity—Rhodes, whose three cities, covering 584 square miles, disappeared only toward the end of the fifth century. Lesbos, with its 696 square miles, contained five cities even in the time of Herodotus, who states that earlier there were still more.[1] Eubœa, with an area of 1,508 square miles, was at the same epoch divided into eight parts. The 3,440 square miles of Crete were divided in Homeric days among ninety cities; more than fifty of them still existed in historic times.

To imagine that density of population compensated for scantiness of territory would be to allow oneself to be misled by fallacious inferences and false interpretations of the facts. It is true that the steady flow of emigration which scattered Greeks on all the shores of the Mediterranean is a phenomenon which gives rise to reflection. Plato saw the cause in the " niggardliness of the soil " and the impossibility of nourishing an over numerous population;[2] and, just at the time of the great colonizations, the author of the *Cyprian Songs* explained the fatal law which decimates mankind by war in a way which certain theorists of modern times would not have been disposed to quarrel with: " Myriads of men wandered in the

[1] Her., I, 151.
[2] Plato, *Laws*, IV, p. 707e-708b; cf. Isocr., *Paneg.*, 34-36.

vast bosom of the earth; Zeus took pity, and of his great
wisdom resolved to lighten the burden of the suckling earth;
he sent forth among them the harsh strife of war that the
dead might make room for the living."[1] But in reality the
excess of population in Greek cities was relative: it proceeded
from a permanent cause, the large extent of barren land, and
from historic causes, the monopoly of property by the aristocracy and testamentary divisions. Moreover, with this
people which had " poverty for its foster sister "[2] colonization
was not the sole factor which prevented the growth of the
population to large proportions. Always and everywhere
the Greeks dreaded large families. To prevent such misfortune, recourse was had to birth control. Hesiod even in
his day was appealing for the " one-child family " ($\mu o\nu\nu o\gamma\epsilon\nu\grave{\eta}s$
$\pi\acute{a}\iota s$).[3] They indulged in all the practices of an unbridled
Malthusianism—abortions, infanticide, exposure of the newly
born, homosexuality: all were authorized by custom, tolerated
by law and fully approved by the philosophers.[4] For these
reasons the Greek city was as small in the number of its
inhabitants as it was in the extent of its territory.

According to Hippodamus of Miletus, that sociological
architect who built both on the soil and in his dreams cities
of faultless symmetry, the ideal city ought to have ten
thousand inhabitants.[5] Plato wished the number of citizens
to be sufficiently great for the city to be able to defend itself
against its neighbours or to assist them in case of need, but
sufficiently small to enable them to know each other and to
choose their magistrates with knowledge: he fixed this
necessary and sufficient number according to a Pythagorean
method at $1 \times 2 \times 3 \times 4 \times 5 \times 6 \times 7 = 5,040$.[6] Aristotle examined
the question at great length. He saw in the number
of citizens, and the extent of territory, the first materials
which the statesman and the legislator required for their
labours; it was necessary that they should have the essential
qualities, and that they should be of just proportions in order
that the city might fulfil the task assigned to it. Nor ought
one to confuse the great city with the populous city. Slaves
and strangers, whether domiciled or not, were merely worth-

[1] *Cypria*, fr. 1, Kinkel.   [2] Her., VII, 102.
[3] Hes., *Op. et Dies*, 376.   [4] *v. DA*, art. " Expositio."
[5] Arist., *Pol.*, II, 5, 2.   [6] Plato, *Laws*, V, p. 737d-738e.

less refuse; only the citizens counted. Experience proved
that it was difficult, and perhaps impossible, to organize
efficiently an over-populous State; for how could good laws
be applied and order be maintained there ? There was a
determinate size for the city as for all other things. If the
city failed to conform to that standard, either from deficiency
or excess, it could not achieve its proper end. A society of a
hundred thousand members was no more a city than one of
ten members.[1]

The theorists only reduced to a system the facts which
were before them. Very few cities exceeded the number
approved by Hippodamus. One can calculate that the
Athens of Pericles numbered about 40,000 citizens. Three
cities had 20,000 or a little more in the fifth century: Syracuse,
Acragas and Argos. It is true that in the following century
Syracuse reached the figure of 50,000 or 60,000 by the
necessary assimilation of conquered peoples, by the colonization of the interior, but she was then by far the greatest city
in Greece.[2] Cities inhabited by 10,000 citizens, those which
realized the ideal of the great town, the πόλις μυρίανδρος, were
not numerous. One can place in that category in Asia Minor
the Miletus of Hippodamus, smaller at this time than in
the sixth century, Ephesus, and Halicarnassus; in Greece
proper, Thebes, Corinth and its ancient colony Corcyra, and
the towns of recent growth, Rhodes, Megalapolis and Messena;
in Chalcidice, Olynthus; on the Bosphorus, Byzantium after
the incorporation of Chalcedon; in Libya, Cyrene; in greater
Greece, Tarentum and Croton; in Sicily, Gela. The proof
that the population of these towns was in accordance with the
Greek ideal of the fifth century no less than with that of
Hippodamus, lies in the fact that the Athenians, when they
founded Ennea Hodoi, and similarly Hiero, when Catana
was superseded by Ætna, sent out the ideal number of ten
thousand colonists.[3] Investigation shows that of the hundreds
and hundreds of Greek cities, barely twenty attained or
surpassed that ideal figure.

To pass on. The towns where the body of citizens
varied between 10,000 and 5,000 and which were reckoned

---

[1] Arist., Pol., IV (VII), 4, 3-8; Nic. Eth., IX, p. 1170b.
[2] Plut., Timol., 23, 25; Diod., XVI, 52.
[3] Thuc., I, 100, 3; Diod., XI, 49, 1.

of importance[1]—such as Mitylene, Chios and Samos, Eretria and Chalcis, Megara, Sicyon, Phlius and Elis—were not considerable in number. Well-known towns such as Mantinea and Tegea did not touch this level; Ægina, for long so rich and important as a result of its commerce, had only 2,000 to 2,500 citizens to its 44 square miles. In the beginning, according to tradition, the Spartans formed a body of from 9,000 to 10,000 men; there were still 8,000 at the time of the Persian wars; but the defects of an obsolete constitution led rapidly to a dearth of men, ὀλιγανθρωπία; they numbered only 2,000 in 371 at the battle of Leuctra, while in 242 King Agis could muster only 700. Undoubtedly the oligarchical principle, which rigorously restricted the dignity of citizen to a minority, played a large part; nor when calculating the population of democratic cities must one forget the mass of aliens and slaves who were excluded from the agora; nevertheless, from a quantitative point of view the Greek city was a small affair.

But it was superlatively rich in moral qualities, and it was to exercise a decisive influence on the civilization of the future. The Hellenic world was a network of virile, active communities. Aristotle described 158 of them,[2] but there were ten times more. Everywhere, some few miles apart, were hills serving as frontiers. A small tract of land shadowed by a mountain, watered by a stream and indented with bays—such was a State. One had only to climb to the acropolis which was the reduit to survey the whole of it. The town, the fields, the woods, the creeks—that was the fatherland, the country founded by their ancestors, the country which each generation must leave more beautiful and more prosperous. Some eminent men realized that the Greek people as a whole differed from other peoples in its language, its poetry, its art, its worship of sublime deities; but for long even these were content and did not aspire to Hellenic unity, because, in their opinion, the superiority of the Greeks lay simply in their conception of the *polis*. The barbarian world was composed of unwieldy monarchies, lifeless masses; the Greek world alone answered to the definition of man who is, in all the fullness of its meaning, a *political* being.

---

[1] Xen., *Hell.*, V, 3, 16; Diod., XIV, 78, 6.
[2] Diog. Laërt., III, 1, 27.

The autonomous city had, as its essential complement, liberty. Collective liberty, if that expression may be used; for though individual liberty might exist as well it was not indispensable. Concerning this Herodotus gives us a piece of information as strange as it is illuminating: for when he wishes to oppose Hellenic freedom to Persian servitude he makes two Spartans speak, two of those Greeks whose whole existence was bound by the most minute regulations. The scene is enacted at Susa. Sperthias and Boulis come to offer their lives to the king of kings in order to appease his wrath for the two heralds of Darius put to death at Sparta. A satrap asks them why they refuse to be the friends of a king who knows how to honour the brave, and their reply is: " Hydarnes, the counsel you give us is not good; it comes from a man who has tried one kind of life and has experience of no other: you know what servitude is but you have never tasted liberty; you do not know whether it is sweet or not. If you had experienced it you would urge us to fight for it, not from afar with javelins, but with axes at close quarters."[1]

That passion for independence made of the city, however small, a sovereign State. Take two neighbouring cities; everything divides them. The sacred bounds which mark the limits of their territory trace almost insurmountable barriers between religions and laws, calendars, money-systems, weights and measures, interests and affections. What was the *patria* in the great centuries of ancient Greece ? The word speaks for itself. It denoted everything which united men who had a common ancestor, a common father. The *patria* was at first the *genos*, as it always was in Asia Minor; by a gradual extension, as in Elis for example, it became the wider group generally called the *phratry*, and it finished by being everywhere the community in which all smaller societies were absorbed, the city. The patriotism of the Greeks seems to us to-day nothing more than municipal loyalty; but it was a feeling the more intense and profound as it was directed towards a smaller object. When the *ephebos* had taken the public oath his thoughts, his very blood, were consecrated to the city. Not to an abstraction did he dedicate body and soul, but to a reality which he saw day by day before his eyes. What was the sacred earth of the fatherland ?—it was

[1] Her., VII, 135.

the home of the family, the sepulchre of the ancestors, the fields whose every owner was known, the mountain where wood was cut, where the flocks were driven, where honey was gathered, the temples where one took part in the sacrifices, the acropolis to which one walked in procession; it was all that one loved, all that one was proud of, and which each generation wished to leave more glorious than it found it. A town, a single town, and often small, and yet it was for this that Hector courted death, for this that the Spartan considered it the crown of " virtue " to " fall in the first ranks," for this that the heroes of Salamis hurled themselves aboard the enemy ships with triumphal songs, and Socrates drank the hemlock in his reverence for the law.

As soon as he left the limits of the microcosm which was the city the Greek was in a strange country, often in an enemy country. Terrible consequences followed from this conception. The hatreds of *genos* towards *genos*, deme towards deme, had at great effort been allayed under the authority of public power, though traces always remained. In Attica, for instance, members of the family of Pallene were not allowed to marry those of Hagnus, and party strife was for long identified with family vendettas. Topography sometimes sufficed to maintain within a city strange enmities: Aristotle mentions the hostility which existed even in his time between the island of Clazomenæ and the district of Chytron.[1] With still more reason were there rivalries, unending and bloody, between neighbouring cities. The history of ancient Greece is a tissue of sordid and cruel wars, in which all the passions of which patriotism is capable were unloosed for the conquest of a few paltry fields.

Many attempts were made to break down these insuperable barriers, to introduce the cities into wider units. But they demanded the renunciation of a portion of sovereignty and hence they were always confronted with invincible opposition.

The Amphictyonic Councils of Calaureia, Delphi and the Panionium could easily, it seems, have transformed themselves from religious associations into political confederations; they did not succeed, but remained hotbeds of intrigue where the representative cities fought for supremacy. The

---

[1] Arist., *Pol.*, VIII (V), 2, 10.

federal system, however, demanded no sacrifice save a mutual understanding on questions of foreign policy. If ever it arose from urgent necessity it was in Asia Minor in the seventh and sixth centuries when the danger of Lydian or Persian domination threatened all the cities. Far from submitting to it Greeks fought Greeks under the eyes of the barbarians, Chios against Erythræ, Samos against Priene and Miletus; and the armies of Darius were preparing to secure the reign of peace by servitude when a project of union which humoured all susceptibilities nevertheless broke down pathetically before general indifference.[1] It was in vain that the Bœotian Confederacy left to each city its own institutions and the right of coining money; continual conflict raged between Thebes, who intended to be mistress, and the other towns which were unwilling to obey. In Arcadia, where pastoral life scattered the people more than elsewhere,[2] two attempts were made to counteract the centrifugal force, in the seventh century under Aristocrates, king of Orchomenus, and in the fourth century under Lycomedes of Mantinea; both times the attempt failed.

As for the system of hegemony which Athens and Sparta sought to impose, it naturally encountered a vigorous opposition. It could not even depend upon political sympathies, upon the solidarity of parties from town to town. During the Peloponnesian war the democrats and oligarchs of Athens were each in their turn striving to uphold their own system; nothing was effective: when a subject city revolted all the factions worked together. Cleon spoke truth when he said that he knew of only one means to maintain the empire— terror; only one effective government—tyranny;[3] and Alcibiades showed true discernment in thinking that every city, rather than be enslaved under the government it preferred, would choose to be free under any.[4]

This narrow and jealous particularism exposed the whole race to dangers which it could not always avert. The danger of barbarian conquest, which Asiatic Greece could not combat, almost engulfed European Greece. She escaped, but not before safety had been long endangered by the petty conflicts of local egoisms. But when finally the cities, worn out by

[1] Her., I, 170.
[3] Thuc., III, 37 ff.

[2] Arist., Pol., II, 1, 5.
[4] Id., VIII, 48.

indecisive and aimless struggles, felt the need of healing unity, there was not one capable of winning a unanimous vote, and the intervention of Macedon and Rome became necessary.

Autonomy was, at all events, rich in benefits.   Each city had its own character, its own personality, its own life.   By its institutions and its law, by its religion and its festivals, by its monuments and its heroes, by all its methods of interpreting and applying the economic and political, moral and intellectual principles of a common civilization, each city helped to give to that civilization an infinite variety of expression.   A fruitful spirit of emulation gave rise to numerous experiments, encouraged originality in imitation and, in order to realize all the latent forces of communities so small, called upon all the energies of the individual.

PART I
THE CITY UNDER ARISTOCRACY

CHAPTER I
THE HOMERIC CITY

I
ORGANIZATION OF THE CITY

In Homeric times, as we have seen, the small districts of which Greece was composed each constituted a city. The word *demos* denoted either their territory or their population, and only rarely stood for the mass of the people as opposed to the dominant class.[1]

The headquarters of the city—the *polis* or the *asty*—were of paramount importance, and, as both these terms were used to cover the whole country, the citizens were known sometimes as *astoi*,[2] sometimes as *politai*.[3] The Homeric city usually had for centre, therefore, a stronghold where the principal chiefs resided, and which offered refuge to the mass of the population in case of danger.

But the rest of the country contained villages more or less considerable. They too bore the name of *asty* or *polis*. It is surprising to note that in the epics there is no word for village or hamlet, although one knows that in Greece there were always regions with no other form of association, regions, that is to say, where the population was organized in *komai* (κατὰ κώμας).[4] Perhaps the poet hesitated to use a vulgar term, and wished to sing only of heroes who came from far-famed places; perhaps he was well-acquainted only with Asia Minor, where landowners lived together in large groups whilst their land was cultivated by tenants or

[1] *Iliad*, II, 198; XII, 213; *Odyssey*, II, 239; VI, 34.
[2] *Od.*, XIII, 192; cf. *Il.*, XI, 242.
[3] *Il.*, XV, 558; XXII, 429; *Od.*, VII, 131.
[4] Cf. **XXXVI**, vol. I, p. 125.

serfs scattered in the surrounding country. Whatever the explanation of this omission, the fact remains that there was in the city-state, under the protection of the principal town, a confused mass of villages. The name *asty*, which was given to the most celebrated towns, was applied likewise to the innumerable settlements (ἄστεα πολλά) of purely rural areas.[1] Crete was an island with ninety or a hundred towns; but of " well peopled " ones the poet mentions only seven.[2] But of what proportions were even the " well peopled " towns of this epoch ?   Agamemnon promised seven as dowry for his daughter; but they were all " near sandy Pylos," in the midst of pastures and vineyards.[3] Menelaus contemplated depopulating a Laconian town in order to establish Ulysses there with his followers;[4] the place in question cannot have been very big.   In short, the capital, where chiefs of great families dwelt in magnificent splendour, was surrounded with innumerable small towns, villages and hamlets where lesser families lived in relative obscurity.

At the time of its fullest development the Homeric city was divided into three classes: the nobles, the craftsmen (*demiourgoi*) and the hired men (*thetes*).

The nobles belonged to families which were descended from the gods: they were the sons, the nurslings of Zeus. Each of them tenderly preserved the genealogy which was his pride; any occasion was sufficient for him proudly to enumerate the ancestors through whom he traced his origin to the ancestral deity.   But even then riches, as well as purity of blood, counted for much.   When he had run through the number of his forefathers the Homeric hero sought to strike awe into his hearer by enumerating his possessions.   Rich cornfields, vine-clad slopes were his, and pastures where oxen and horses grazed in their thousands and vast fields where cattle swarmed.   Jars of wine and perfumed oils, ingots of bronze and iron, chests filled with embroidered raiment, precious cups and arms of damascene enriched his treasure-house.   He loved to parade his strength, to lead raids and reprisals by land and sea, killing men and carrying off women and cattle; or to hurl his chariot into the front of the battle, and, leaping to the earth, a bronze-clad

---

[1] *Il.*, II, 660.   [2] *Od.*, XIX, 174; *Il.*, II, 646 *ff.*
[3] *Il.*, IX, 149 *ff.*   [4] *Od.*, IV, 174 *ff.*

figure, erect behind staunch shield, sword by side, javelin in hand and defiance on his lips, to await an adversary worthy to challenge him in conflict. In the intervals he delighted in displaying his wealth and enjoying his prestige: he went to the king's palace for sessions of the Council and for banquets; he stood in the agora ready to give advice in disputes between citizens; he was foremost on feast days when sacrifices, libations and banquets were followed by songs, dances and games. Life was good indeed for the great; a life such as the immortals, their forbears, led.

But on the other hand life was hard for those who formed no part of their *gene*. We are not speaking of slaves, for they were merely living chattels with whom the master could do as he wished, and with whom the city did not concern itself; there were, moreover, but few of them at this time. At the moment we are speaking only of free men. Some of them had managed with the sweat of their brow to clear a small patch of ground. The most fortunate were those who by dint of breaking up the soil, manuring and irrigating it, had succeeded in bringing to fruition an orchard like that of old Laertes. Others installed in some mountain nook might even form a family; but since they were reduced to eating roots more often than bread or barley porridge, they hesitated to bring more than one son into the world. There were some who could barely afford to keep the single servant who helped with the work.[1] And what was the fate of those who had no land at all ? Some of them were in a tolerably good position. The *genos* could not always be self-sufficient; hence there existed, especially in large centres, craftsmen who worked for the public, *demiourgoi*. The profession they followed was almost always hereditary, because from one generation to another there was no other means of livelihood and a very rudimentary division of labour left little scope for choice. Some entered what one might call the liberal professions: they became soothsayers, heralds, physicians, bards. Others worked as artisans; they were classified according to the material they used—namely, carpenters who combined stone-work with wood-work, leather workers, smiths and potters. The majority took up their abode in the towns, where manual crafts concentrated round the

[1] *Od.*, XI, 489 *f.*

market-place. Some of the *demiourgoi* won a great reputation; the most proficient were regarded as divinely inspired.
Sometimes they were attracted to foreign lands on some
lucrative commission and were able to amass a considerable
fortune. But always they felt themselves inferior to the
landed proprietors: even the soothsayer Calchas, who con-
sorted with kings, recognized that he was a man of little
consequence.

There remains the mass of people who were landless and
tradeless. These lived as best they could. The idle would
beg from door to door or station themselves outside some
wealthy house where banquets were frequent. The in-
dustrious became *thetes*, hirelings. They hired themselves
out for wages. When they were working on a long contract
they were housed, fed and clothed in some sort of fashion;
when they were engaged for one particular piece of work
they obtained a wage in kind, deducted most often from the
product of their own labour. But although they were free
men they enjoyed no security. The very fact that they
belonged to no *genos* meant that they had no place in the
social structure of the city: to be without hearth (ἀνέστιος)
was to be without phratry (ἀφρήτωρ), deprived of the protection which *themis* (ἀθέμιστος) secured for man, devoid
of all social worth and consequently outside all law (ἀτίμητος).[1]
The hireling was bound by a contract which in no way bound
his employer: having completed his task he might find the
wages agreed upon withheld; he might be thrown out of doors,
beaten unmercifully, threatened with slavery. The man
who had no *genos* behind him could obtain no redress against
injustice.

The Homeric city, indeed, was not the confused assemblage
of all individuals who inhabited the same country; it was a
combination of *gene*, of phratries formed by *gene*, of tribes
formed by phratries. It did not embrace indiscriminately
all those who were domiciled within its territorial limits, but
only those who formed part of the closed societies of which
it was composed. It had nothing to do with isolated individuals. Its framework was that of the societies which
dovetailed one into the other and which had existed before
it. To be accounted a citizen one must first belong to a

[1] *Il.*, IX, 63, 648.

group of " brothers " (κασίγνητοι), that is to say of kinsmen
of some degree, who stood by one another in all circumstances
of life; one must in addition be attached to a group of " companions " (ἔται), united in virtue of a fictitious relationship
by the reciprocal obligations of a wider responsibility.[1] The
great community had no life apart from the small communities
of family origin to which it owed its birth.

In a city of this kind no administration was possible save
through the medium of the tribes, the phratries and, finally,
the *gene*.

For the recruitment of the army every father of a family
was called upon, under pain of a fine unless redemption
had been obtained, to furnish one man chosen as he thought
good: a Myrmidon, for instance, draws lots among his seven
sons to decide which one shall go.[2] The units of this army
were formed by the association of " companions," by classes,
and in these companies the ἔται assumed the name of ἑταίροι.[3]
In battle array the troops were grouped by phratries and by
tribes. It was a rule of which Nestor reminded Agamemnon:
" Dispose your men by tribes and by phratries that phratry
may assist phratry, and tribe assist tribe."[4] And so the
word *phylopis*, which originally meant the war cry uttered
by the tribe, was commonly used for the tumult of battle or
even for the host of combatants.[5]

The same principle held in the recruitment of the navy.
The *Catalogue of Ships* enumerated in the *Iliad* always gives
one the impression that the ships and their crews had some
numerical relation either with the towns placed under the
command of the chiefs or with the subdivisions of the cities.
Rhodes, inhabited by the Dorian τριχάϊκες,[6] was composed
of three large towns, each divided into three tribes: it was
represented by nine vessels.[7] From Pylos there were ninety.
As if to explain this number the poet names nine localities;
but they were of too unequal importance to owe equal contingents. The true explanation is revealed in the passage
in the *Odyssey* in which the Pylians are represented as being

---

[1] **XXXIII**, p. 85-91.
[2] *Il.*, XXIV, 399 *f.* For the fine, *v. Il.*, XIII, 669; for the redemption, XXIII, 297.
[3] **XXXIII**, *loc. cit.*
[4] *Il.*, II, 362 *f.*
[5] *Il.*, IV, 65.
[6] *Od.*, XIX, 177.
[7] *Il.*, II, 654 *f.*, 668.

assembled in nine sections.　Each of the nine sections offered
the same number of victims for the public sacrifices; in the
same way each equipped an equal number of ships for the
navy.[1]　When only a single vessel was required the system
remained unchanged; the duty of the groups consisted then
in furnishing men for the crew.　When Alcinous was preparing the ship which was to bring Ulysses home again he
announced that oarsmen to the number of fifty-two would
be recruited "from the people" (κατὰ δῆμον).　Why that
number ?　Because at Scheria there were thirteen kings,
thirteen chiefs: each of them owed four men.[2]

Other impositions were allotted in similar fashion.　We
have seen how at Pylos the expenses for the feasts fell equally
upon the nine sections of the people.　To obtain the gifts
which he wished to bestow upon Ulysses Alcinous ordered
each king to bring a cloak, a tunic, and a talent of pure gold,
besides a large tripod and a sacrificial basin; but he added
that each should recoup himself from the people as a whole
(it is always κατὰ δῆμον).[3]　Thus all the public services,
whether one considers the army, the navy or what one must
call the exchequer, respected the natural groupings without
which the city could not exist.

All the chiefs, those of the genos, the phratry and the
tribe, as well as the chief of the city, bore the hereditary
title of king (βασιλεύς).　A king, too, was the landowner who,
standing on a swath, sceptre in hand, watched over the
harvesting, and through his heralds made preparations for
the harvest feast.[4]　From the greatest to the least these
kings were sons and foster-children of Zeus (Διογενέες,
Διοτρεφέες);[5] divine birth conferred on them the right to
the sceptre,[6] the sacred badge of priests, heralds and soothsayers.　They were the lords (ἄνακτες), the elders (γέροντες),
the guides and counsellors (ἡγήτορες ἠδὲ μέδοντες).　Since
they represented groups subordinated one to the other, they
naturally formed a hierarchy of suzerains and vassals, a
sort of feudal system.　Royalty, therefore, was capable of

---

[1] Il., II, 591-602; Od., III, 7-8.
[2] Od., VIII, 35 f.; 48, 390 f.; cf. XXXIV, p. 240.
[3] Od., VIII, 392 ff.; XIII, 10 ff.; cf. XIX, 196 f.
[4] Il., XVIII, 556 ff.
[5] v. for the ordinary soldiers, Il., IV, 280; V, 544 ff.
[6] Od., VIII, 41, 47; cf. Il., XVIII, 507.

THE HOMERIC CITY   39

degrees; all were kings, but one more kingly than another
(βασιλεύτερος),¹ and one most kingly of all (βασιλεύτατος).²
At Scheria one can see fairly clearly how such a system was
organized. The king Alcinous appears with his twelve peers
round him. Though he may modestly say: " Twelve great
kings rule the people, and I am the thirteenth,"³ yet in
actual fact he was the first, the only one who issued commands, because it was he who bore the title " Sacred Power "
(ἱερὸν μένος 'Αλκινόοιο) and he whose words were heeded
like those of a god.⁴ But if he associated in his authority
the most powerful chiefs, the kings of the tribes, he was also
compelled, in order to ensure the execution of measures
concerted with them, to summon " gerontes in greater
number," the ordinary chiefs of the gene.⁵

II

THE KING

The king of the city, the king of kings, was, therefore,
he whose divine origin was most incontestably established.
Everyone knew his genealogy. Agamemnon and Menelaus
were descended from Zeus by Tantalus, Pelops and Atreus;
Achilles by Æacus and Peleus; Ulysses by Arcesius and
Laertes; Idomeneus by Minos. Some, as, for instance, Ajax,
had Apollo for ancestor, others, such as Nestor and Alcinous,
Poseidon. A king embodied all the puissance of a god. In
certain States it was admitted that this supernatural power
exhausted itself in time; it had to be renewed: every nine
years in Crete Minos had to enter the cave of Zeus to render
him account of his administration and to be invested for a
new period;⁶ once every nine years in Sparta on a clear
moonless night the ephors kept silent watch, with eyes fixed
on the sky, and if they perceived a shooting star it was a
sign that the kings had committed some sin against the gods
and had, therefore, to be declared deposed.⁷ But usually
the king exercised power for life and transmitted it to his

¹ Il., IX, 160, 392; X, 239; Od., XV, 533.
² Il., IX, 69.   ³ Od., VIII, 390 f.
⁴ Od., VII, 167, 11.   ⁵ Ibid., 189.
⁶ Od., XIX, 179; cf. Plato, Minos, p. 319b; Laws, I, p. 624 a-b, 630d,
632d; Strab., X, 4, 8, p. 476; 19, p. 482.
⁷ Plutarch, Agis, 11.

eldest son.¹ Even at a time when monarchy was in jeopardy the Ithacan suitors did not dispute the hereditary right of Telemachus;² they sought merely to free themselves of him, and the only way they could see to usurp his position was to attach themselves to the extinct dynasty by marrying the wife of the last king. Failing a son the king's daughter perpetuated the line. She was the *epicleros*, one who did not inherit but brought the heir into the world. In order that the line might remain pure she married the nearest male kinsman of her father. Alcinous, for example, became king of Scheria by marrying his niece Arete, the daughter of his brother and predecessor Rhexenor.³ Only in Asiatic countries could the king choose for son-in-law and successor a foreign prince; even then it was essential that by his marvellous exploits he should have proved himself the scion of a god.⁴

All the kings were sceptre-bearers (σκηπτοῦχοι), but the king of the city was so pre-eminently; for his badge of office was the very same which the great god, the ancestor of the dynasty, had borne. The golden studded sceptre which shone in the hands of Agamemnon had a history which rendered it venerable: it had been fabricated by Hephæstus and transmitted by Zeus to Hermes and by Hermes to the Pelopidæ.⁵ This staff of office which subjected the people to the king was the visible will of a god: it showed to all the man whom Zeus in his wisdom had invested with τιμή, with superhuman power and the loftiness of mind which was its necessary complement.⁶

The king of kings had received from Zeus, therefore, the right of representing the city in every circumstance. In truth the city was the king, as one day Æschylus was to say: σύ τοι πόλις, σύ δὲ τὸ δήμιον. He had "sovereignty and power," "freedom of action and of speech."⁷

First and foremost he was the religious chief, the high-

---

¹ On the right of the eldest son, v. *Il.*, II, 106 f.; *Od.*, XIX, 181-184; cf. *Il.*, XV, 204.
² *Od.*, I, 387; XVI, 388, 401.
³ *Od.*, VII, 63 ff.; cf. *Il.*, XX, 180 ff., 231 ff.
⁴ *Il.*, VI, 191; cf. XX, 180 ff.
⁵ *Il.*, II, 101 ff.; cf. 46, 186; IX, 38; VII, 412. The sceptre of Agamemnon was the object of a cult at Cheronæa (Paus., X, 40, 11).
⁶ *Il.*, II, 196; cf. I, 279; VI, 159; IX, 37, 99.
⁷ Æsch., *Suppl.*, 370; *Od.*, VI, 196; XI, 346; cf. 353; VIII, 382.

priest. Who better than he could in the name of all hold communion with the gods, secure their favour and turn aside their wrath ? With his own hand he performed the sacrifices, clipped the hair from the heads of the victims and distributed it among the onlookers or cast it into the fire, and sprinkled the lustral water and the sacred barley; he recited the prayers and presided over the preparations for the sacred feasts.[1] His palace was the prytaneum; his hearth the public hearth round which the leading men of the community assembled to take part in the offerings which preluded their deliberations on public affairs or the reception of illustrious guests.[2] He was the mediator between the gods and man; and more, he was the representative of the gods among men. With the sceptre he received knowledge of the *themistes*, those supernatural principles which enabled all difficulties to be smoothed away, and, above all, made it possible for internal peace to be restored by the words of justice.[3] According as he fulfilled his mission well or badly, according as he knew or did not know what was meet and fitting (τὰ αἴσιμα), the royal wizard determined the happiness or unhappiness of his people.

" When a blameless and god-fearing king maintains impartial justice the brown earth is rich in corn and in barley, and the trees are laden with fruit; the ewes constantly bring forth young, the sea abounds in fishes; nothing that does not prosper when there is good government, and the people is happy."[4]

In time of war, even more than in time of peace, the king was the all-powerful leader. Then especially did he bear the title which had already been assumed, according to a Hittite document, by one of the Atreidæ in the thirteenth century, the title of *koiranos*.[5] Then especially was it true to say: " Division of power (πολυκοιρανίη) is not a good thing: a single *koiranos* is called for, a single king, he whom the son of Cronus has pointed out."[6] If, however, he was too old to take the field, he delegated his powers to his future

---

[1] *Il.*, II, 402 *ff.*; III, 271 *ff.*; VII, 314 *ff.*; IX, 534 *f.*; *Od.*, III, 444 *ff.*; VIII, 59 *ff.*; XIII, 181.
[2] *Od.*, VIII, 40 *ff.*; 56 *ff.*
[3] *Il.*, IX, 98 *f.*; *Od.*, XI, 569; cf. *Il.*, XVI, 542.
[4] *Od.*, XIX, 109 *ff.*
[5] **XXXVI**, vol. I, p. 90; *Il.*, II, 487, 760; VII, 234; XI, 465; *Od.*, XVIII, 106.
[6] *Il.*, II, 204 *f.*

successor.[1] In the army the supreme king might, indeed, summon to his tent, as council of war, the kings who were subordinate to him, just as formerly they were summoned to his palace; but, once they had voiced their opinions, it was the king who made the decision. He decided upon the plan of campaign, assigned to each unit its place, and chose the captains.[2] To give effect to his orders he exercised his *themis* in the agora of the camp; he had power of life and death over all: the soldier who was cowardly or who disobeyed orders was not " certain of escaping the dogs or the vultures."[3] No one save the king could treat with the enemy or with foreigners in general: he received the heralds and ambassadors sent into his camp or town, heard their proposals, informed them of his reply, and, if an agreement were reached, offered the sacrifice and took the oath which hallowed it.[4]

Justice demanded that the chief on whom fell the heavy burden of watching over the welfare of the city should enjoy special privileges. He wore robes of purple; he occupied the place of honour on all ceremonial occasions, and walked at the head of the processions. Brimming cups and the choicest morsels of the victim's flesh were always his, unless he desired to do honour to one of his guests.[5] But he had need of more substantial privileges, for it fell to him to meet the cost of the sacrifices, of the libations offered to the gods, of the feasts to which great men and strangers of distinction were invited. Like a god, he possessed a domain cut off from the communal lands, a *temenos*, half in corn fields, half in vineyards;[6] but he enjoyed only the use of this domain which formed no part of his patrimony.[7] Like a god, he levied gifts and dues called *themistes*, in the shape of domestic animals, in addition to the contribution which he levied through his *gerontes* in case of extraordinary outlay for the reception of a public guest: one sees, for example, a man of Sicyon furnishing Agamemnon with a race horse in order

[1] *Il.*, IX, 252, 438; XI, 783.
[2] *Il.*, II, 65 *f.*; 362 *ff.*, 553 *f.*; IX, 69; XVI, 129, 155, 171 *f.*
[3] *Il.*, XI, 807; II, 391 *ff.*; cf. Arist., *Pol.*, III, 9, 2.
[4] *Il.*, III, 105 *ff.*, 250 *ff.*; VII, 354 *ff.*; *Od.* III, 82; IV, 314.
[5] *Il.*, X, 133; VIII, 162; IV, 262; *Od.*, XIX, 225; VIII, 4, 46, 104, 162.
[6] *Il.*, VI, 194 *f.*; IX, 578 *ff.*; XX, 184 *f.*; *Od.*, VI, 291 *ff.*; XI, 184 *f.*
[7] Cf. *Od.*, I, 397 *ff.*; XI, 174; XXIV, 205 *ff.*

to gain exemption from military service.¹ He even levied customs duties on imported goods: in this sense one ought to interpret the passage in the *Iliad* in which a Lemnian, having arrived with a cargo of wine, offers a hundred measures of it to Agamemnon and Menelaus before exposing the rest for sale.² Finally, in the division of booty, the king acted like any pirate chief: he deducted first the γέρας, his share as chief, which accrued to him even if he had taken no part in the business and which might amount to as much as half; and he received also the μοῖρα, his share as combatant.³ Telemachus, indeed, spoke truly when he declared with charming naïveté: " It is no bad thing to be a king."⁴

This feudal king, however, exercised only a patriarchal sovereignty, similar to that which he had inherited on his own domain. The ideal for him was to act as a " good father."⁵ The stewards of his lands were not great magistrates but servants. Ulysses had for stable-companion, if one may use that expression, an old slave, Eumæus: the " divine swineherd " was a chief (ὄρχαμος ἀνδρῶν), just as was his master Ulysses. He had under his command, to tend a flock of from seven to eight thousand head, a carefully graded hierarchy of neatherds, shepherds, swineherds, goatherds and ordinary menials.⁶ But the king in his palace had not only a large staff of men of free or servile birth; he had besides a numerous " household " recruited from the noble families of the country, the *therapontes*, that is to say servants or squires. They bore official titles and dwelt in the palace itself or in the neighbourhood.⁷ Their duties were of unequal importance. Thus the *therapontes* were subordinated one to the other: behind the personages known by their names and the names of their fathers was a nameless host, employed in inferior tasks. Consider, for instance, in the *Iliad* Achilles' attendants: to Phœnix fell the duty of teaching him the art of war and eloquent speech; Patroclus was his right-hand man, he gave orders to Automedon, the

¹ *Il.*, IX, 154 *f.*; XXIII, 296 *f.*
² *Il.*, VII, 470 *f.*; cf. XXIII, 744 *f.*
³ *Il.*, I, 124, 161 *ff.*, 368 *f.*; II, 226 *ff.*; VIII, 286 *ff.*; IX, 130 *ff.*; XVII, 231; *Od.*, VII, 10; IX, 42; XI, 534.
⁴ *Od.*, I, 392.   ⁵ *Od.*, II, 48, 235.
⁶ *Od.*, XIV, 48, etc., 121, etc., 100 *ff.*
⁷ *Il.*, XI, 322; XV, 431 *ff.*; XVI, 685; XIX, 281; XXIII, 90; XXIV, 396 *f.*; *Od.*, XV, 96.

keeper of the stables, and himself had *therapontes* attached
to his person. Or again, consider in the *Odyssey* the court
of Menelaus, where his first squire, Eteoneus, was at the head
of a whole administration.[1]

In the first rank of the *therapontes* were placed those who
assisted the king in his religious duties and partook of his
sacred character, namely the heralds. Messengers of Zeus
and of men, they were " divine," dear to the gods, honoured
above all others by the most powerful chiefs. The sceptre
which they bore attested to the wisdom which they had received from on high.[2]   Their functions were far-reaching, since
they were the ministers of the king in all the circumstances
of public life. They helped him in the offering of sacrifices
and libations and officiated at the banquets which followed,
sprinkling water on the hands of the guests, giving to each
his rightful share.[3]   In the performance of their mission no
one, whatever his rank, dared disobey them.[4]   They convoked
the Council.[5]   Armed with proclamations to the people[6] they
also convoked the Assembly, maintained order and silence
there, and gave their sceptre into the hands of the speakers
to render them inviolable.[7]   They aided the elders in settling
quarrels in the agora; they calmed men's over-violent passions
and passed their sceptre to the judges as each in turn spoke.[8]
In the army they carried important messages and gave the
signal for battle [9]   Their sacrosanctity was respected even
among foreigners, even among enemies. Whenever Ulysses
sent out spies into an unknown land he sent a herald with
them. During the Trojan war the heralds of the belligerents
went without fear from one camp to the other as ambassadors
or envoys of peace, and their intervention was necessary for
the sanctioning of treaties. In the midst of the battle, if
they but extended their sceptre between two combatants the
duel was brought to an end.[10]   What the heralds were in the

[1] *Il.*, IX, 438 *ff.*; XVI, 148, 279; *Od.*, IV, 22 *ff.*, 35 *ff.*, 216 *f.*; XV,
95 *ff.*
[2] *Il.*, I, 334; VII, 275; VIII, 517; X, 315; XII, 343; XXIV, 412,
575; *Od.*, XVII, 173; XXII, 357 *ff.*
[3] *Il.*, XIX, 196 *ff.*, 247 *ff.*; XVIII, 558 *ff.*
[4] *Il.*, I, 320 *ff.*, 334 *ff.*   [5] *Od.*, VIII, 8.
[6] *Il.*, VIII, 517.
[7] *Il.*, II, 50, 97 *ff*, 279 *ff.*; XXIII, 567 *ff*; *Od.*, II, 6, 37 *f.*
[8] *Il.*, XVIII, 503 *ff.*   [9] *Il.*, II, 442.
[10] *Od.*, IX, 90; X, 59, 102; *Il.*, VII, 372 *ff.*; XXIV, 149 *ff.*, 180 *ff.*;
III, 116 *ff.*, 245 *ff.*

Homeric era they always remained. Why, then, since their moral force remained unimpaired, did their social position decline ? The reason is to be found in the fact that their office remained specially and exclusively religious. When the high-priest, whose acolytes they were, ceased to be the veritable ruler of the State, they were no longer employed save in leading victims to the altar, in mixing the wine and water in the cups, in scouring the banqueting tables, in washing the hands of the guests, in serving them with bread and meat.[1] It was of no avail that they passed into the service of the city and became *demiourgoi*;[2] even when a family of heralds made itself into an hereditary caste, as did, for example, the Talthybiadæ of Sparta and the Kerykes of Eleusis, it was incapable of transforming a quasi-sacerdotal into a political magistracy.

It was not so with the other *therapontes*. Under the regime of patriarchal monarchy their office had undoubtedly a domestic character; one is constantly being brought up against that fact. In the palace the chief *therapon* usually filled the office of cupbearer, carver and master of the horse. Patroclus poured out the wine, prepared the food after the sacrifice, carved the flesh and served the guests, not forgetting to offer the first morsels to the gods.[3] In the field the servants of the king vied in gallantry to do him honour.[4] The humblest assisted their master to don his armour, led away the men whom he had taken captive, stripped those who had fallen beneath his blows, and, if he were wounded, tended and protected him.[5] The sons of great families looked after his horses and his chariot. The most distinguished of all acted as his charioteer: he bore him to the front of the battle and stood aside during the fray, ready to lead him back to the camp.[6] This was the duty which the illustrious Automedon gloried in.[7] But one sees that on occasion the duties of the chief *therapon* were capable of being extended in remarkable fashion. Patroclus, the servitor of Achilles, was none the ess the intimate friend who helped him in the reception of

---

[1] *Od.*, XX, 276; I, 109 *ff.*; VII, 163 *ff.*; VIII, 474 *ff.*; XVIII, 423 *ff.*
[2] *Od.*, XIX, 135. [3] *Il.*, IX, 190, 202 *ff.*, 211 *ff.*
[4] *Il.*, XVI, 271 *f.*
[5] *Il.*, VI, 531; V, 48; XIII, 600; XI, 843; XV, 401.
[6] *Il.*, VIII, 109, 113, 119; XII, 76, 111; XIII, 386.
[7] *Il.*, XVI, 145 *ff.*, 865.

c

his guests, the confidant whom he named as guardian of his son should misfortune arise.[1] When a king, on account of old age or for some other reason, did not wish to place himself at the head of his troops, he gave his armour to one of his *therapontes*, and by that act invested him with supreme command.[2] As in all patriarchal monarchies it was but a short step from domestic functions to public functions.

III

THE COUNCIL

Powerful though the king seems at certain moments, we know that he could do nothing without the chiefs of the groups which constituted the city. They formed the Council, the Boule, which was ever near him. The other kings stood in the relation of " counsellors " (βουληφόροι) to the supreme king. Since they derived their right from the life sovereignty which each exercised in his *genos*, phratry or tribe, the name of "elders " or " elders of the people" (γέροντες or δημογέροντες) was also given to them: a name which signified that they were for the most part, though not necessarily, men advanced in years. The assembly of the Council or *thokos* was also given the more general name of *agora*; for this word, before being applied to the place where the assemblies of the people were held, meant any gathering whatever. Thus the counsellors were essentially " men of the agora," ἀγορηταί.[3]

The Council met together on the initiative and through the exertions of the king. According to the business to be despatched the summons was either addressed to the chiefs of highest rank or to all the chiefs. In closing a session of the smaller Council where only his twelve peers were assembled, Alcinous decided that the deliberations should be resumed the next day with " *gerontes* in greater number."[4] The meetings were usually held in the king's palace or on his ship;[5] there is one instance, however, in the *Iliad*, when an assembly took place near Nestor's ship, and in the *Odyssey* there is an

[1] *Il.*, IX, 190 *ff.*; XIX, 331 *ff.*; cf. XXIII, 78.
[2] *Il.*, VII, 149; XVI, 129 *ff.*, 145, 164 *ff.*, 257 *ff.*
[3] *v.*, for all these words, **XVIII.**
[4] *Il.*, II, 404 *ff.*; X, 300 *f.*; *Od.*, VII, 189.
[5] *Od.*, VI, 156; *Il.*, X, 326.

exceptional case when Alcinous, in place of summoning the Phæacian kings to his palace, was himself summoned by them to an assembly outside it.[1]

Certain proof that the king's palace was originally the building later called the Prytaneum or Bouleuterion lies in the fact that every session of the Boule commenced there with a banquet and the great men could come there " throughout the year " (ἐπηετανόν) to eat and drink.[2] An invitation to dine was equivalent to a convocation of the Council.[3] The councillors bore the semi-official title of " table companions " (ἄνδρες δαιτυμόνες), and " the wine of the elders " (γερούσιος οἶνος) was part of their prerogative (γέρας γερόντων).[4] When they were not in session their cups and their tables were piled in the vestibule of the palace;[5] when they met all these were moved into the great chamber, into the *megaron.* There the hearth was situated, the hearth of the king and the common hearth of the city, before which were offered the libations which preceded the banquet. Along the walls were ranged the thrones where the kings sat to eat and later to deliberate.[6] In the centre, in the place of honour, sat the king. He paid the expenses for these perpetual banquets, for had he not the fruits of his *temenos* and gifts and *themistes* for his use and enjoyment ? He was merely discharging a public duty. To drink the " wine of the elders " was, in reality, to drink at the expense of the people (δήμια πίνειν).[7] One can understand a little why, in the absence of Ulysses, the petty chiefs of Ithaca considered his house as their own.

When they had eaten, the king opened the consultation either by disclosing the reason for the summoning of the assembly or by calling upon some chief who had a report to present.[8] But that formality was superfluous when the business of the day was known in advance. In that case the *gerontes* did not wait to be consulted. Custom demanded that the eldest should speak first: it was the privilege of Nestor in the council of the Achæans, and of Echeneus in that of the

[1] *Il.,* II, 55; *Od.,* VI, 53 *ff.*   [2] *Od.,* VII, 95 *ff.*
[3] *Il.,* IX, 70 *ff.,* 89 *ff.*
[4] *Od.,* XV, 468; *Il.,* IV, 259; IX, 422.   [5] *Od.,* XV, 466 *f.*
[6] *Od.,* VII, 95 *f.*; VIII, 422; cf. XVI, 408; XXII, 23.
[7] *Il.,* XVII, 247; cf. IV, 344; VIII, 161; IX, 70 *ff.*
[8] *Il.,* II, 56 *ff.*; IX, 672 *ff.*

Phæacians; Diomedes excused himself for coming forward, though the youngest present, and thought it advisable to justify his intervention on the score of his birth and his wealth.[1] The speaker, whoever he might be, the president no less than the others, rose to address the assembly.[2]   His listeners would from time to time applaud.[3]   There was no voting. The king decided alone, in the fullness of his sovereignty. Nestor well knew that he could do no more than offer advice; he himself makes this clear:

" Illustrious Agamemnon, king of men, thou art the first and the last object of this discourse; for thou art king of numerous peoples, and Zeus has given thee the sceptre and the *themistes* that thou mayest have them at thy command. More than all others ought thou to listen and consider, in order to give effect to the advice of him who shall be inspired to speak for the common good; it is for thee to decide which counsel shall prevail."[4]

Although the *gerontes* had only an advisory voice in the Council, their competence seems to have extended to all matters of importance.   They accompanied the king to the Assembly,[5] and there sat in places set apart for them.[6]   On their own initiative they could offer a *temenos* to the prince.[7] They had a part to play in everything concerned with external relations.   The king never omitted to summon them for the reception of a distinguished guest and informed them of his intentions when he wished to bestow gifts upon him and send him back to his own country in a state ship; he made them responsible, each in his group, for the execution of the measures agreed upon, the recruitment of the crew, and the recovery of expenses, etc.[8]   He conferred with them on the despatching of embassies to foreign countries.[9]   In the field they naturally formed the council of war and had an effective say in the conduct of operations.[10]   By their oath, the γερούσιος ὅρκος,[11] they helped in the fashioning of treaties.

Besides the powers which they exercised under the hegemony of the king, the *gerontes* possessed one which they

[1] *Il.*, II, 76, 433; *Od.*, VII, 155; *Il.*, XIV, 122 *ff.*
[2] *Il.*, II, 76.
[3] *Il.*, VII, 344; IX, 173, 710; *Od.*, XIII, 16, 47.
[4] *Il.*, IX, 76 *ff.*   [5] *Il.*, II, 86; *Od.*, VIII, 46.
[6] *Od.*, II, 14; VIII, 6.   [7] *Il.*, IX, 578.
[8] *Od.*, VII, 155 *ff.*; VIII, 40 *ff.*, 386 *ff.*; XIII, 7 *ff.*, 47 *ff.*
[9] *Od.*, XXI, 21.
[10] *Il.*, II, 53 *ff.*; VII, 313 *ff.*; XV, 721 *ff.*; XVIII, 249 *ff.*
[11] *Il.*, XXII, 119.

could exercise apart from him. Accustomed as they were to administer sovereign justice within their *genos*, they appeared as the natural arbitrators for disputes which arose among members of different *gene*. They, like the king himself, had received with the sceptre the secret of the *themistes*. Of these *themistes* they, the *boulephoroi*, could make use on all occasions, since the *themistes* were, like the oracles, the *boulai* of Zeus.[1] It was through them that little by little the principles of the family *themis* penetrated into the customs of the inter-family *dike*. Not that they had an obligatory jurisdiction: each remained free to defend his person and his goods with the aid of his kinsmen; no authority could infringe the primordial right of private vengeance and of private transactions, not even to succour the orphan.[2] But the disputing parties might, if both agreed, appeal to the *gerontes*. They were there to soothe angry passions and to restore peace by means of one of those adages which they had learnt from their fathers and which expressed heavenly wisdom in the language of men. Here is a vivid picture of them at their work.[3] In the agora a crowd is collecting: a quarrel has just broken out. Two men are disputing about a murder: the one swears that he has paid the blood money, the other that he has not received it. They decide to refer the matter to an arbitrator. Each has his partisans who urge him on with their cries. Heralds keep them apart. The *gerontes* are seated on benches of polished stone in the sacred circle. One after the other they arise, take in their hand the sceptre which one of the heralds offers and propose a sentence, until one is found which seems "most just." To its author are given the two talents of gold deposited by the disputants as the price of justice.

For a long time arbitrations of this kind were comparatively rare; the king then had time to preside over the tribunal and it was his judgments which brought upon the city the blessings of heaven. But the progress of the State at the expense of the *genos* and the economic development of the whole of Greece increased the number of suits submitted to the *gerontes*. Henceforth it was necessary to be in session

---

[1] Cf. *Od.*, XVI, 402 *f.*; XIX, 297; *Il.*, VII, 45.
[2] *Od.*, XXII, 55 *ff.*; IV, 164 *ff.*
[3] *Il.*, XVIII, 497 *ff.*; cf. **XXXIII**, p. 115 *ff.*, 127 *ff.*

from morning till night.[1] The king, even if he had been willing, was not equal to the task. The *gerontes*, or at least those of them who found it most agreeable, received the name of " judges " (δικασπόλοι). They pocketed the deposits of the disputants and were present at the feasts of reconciliation.[2] Justice became a trade. The kings became those " devourers of gifts " who were to be the despair of Hesiod and suited their sentences to their interests. Thus to the picture of blessings diffused by the equity of the king was opposed the description of calamities unloosed by the injustice of the *gerontes*:

" When the anger of Zeus rages against men who abuse their power in the agora by pronouncing false judgments and who drive out justice without fear of divine vengeance, then all the rivers burst their banks, torrents everywhere ravage the slopes, their onslaught casts mountains into the sea with thunderous noise and destroys the works of men."[3]

IV

THE ASSEMBLY

When the *gerontes* had been consulted the king had to make known his decisions to the people and to inform them of his plans. In addition to the opinion of the Council there was that of the *demos*, of the lesser folk as opposed to the great: θῶκος δήμοιό τε φῆμις.[4] The agora was essentially the plenary assembly where all the λαοί gathered, all the citizens in the town, all the warriors in the camp, in short " the whole mass (πληθύς) of those who had no place in the Council."[5] It completed the number of institutions which seemed necessary to the very existence of the city and without which men were merely savages living like the Cyclopes.[6]

It was the king who convened the Assembly, as he did the Council. Only very exceptional circumstances could justify Achilles in taking the initiative in place of Agamemnon in the army of the Achæans.[7] The rule was strict and unquestioned. It explains the anarchical condition of Ithaca in the *Odyssey*: during the twenty years of Ulysses' absence the island had known " neither *agora* nor *thokos*," and when Telemachus,

[1] *Od.*, XII, 440.
[2] *Il.*, I, 238; *Od.*, XI, 185 *f*.
[3] *Il.*, XVI, 385 *ff*.
[4] *Od.*, XV, 468; cf. II, 26; III, 127.
[5] *Il.*, II, 143; cf. 268.
[6] *Od.*, IX, 112, 215.
[7] *Il.*, I, 54; XIX, 40.

having come of age, assumed his father's prerogative the advocates of strict legality were at a loss as to what to think.[1] Often the king summoned the Assembly and the Council together in order that he might without delay announce to the people all the decisions arrived at with his intimate advisers. In these circumstances the summons to the common people was made in the usual way, through the proclamation of the heralds, while the king reserved to himself the right to summon the " chief men."[2]

The meeting took place in the early morning " in the first light of the rosy-fingered dawn."[3] It was in despite of custom (οὐ κατὰ κόσμον) that Agamemnon and Menelaus once convened an assembly of warriors at sunset, and they were punished by the riotous behaviour of half-drunk, uproarious men.[4] In the field the assembly might be held anywhere, on some sweeping stretch of beach, for example.[5] In the towns the seat of the agora was definitely fixed. At Troy it was on the Acropolis, not far from the palace and the temples of Apollo and Athene; in maritime cities such as Pylos and Scheria it was near the harbour, before a temple of Poseidon.[6] It was fashioned in the form of a circle, as the Skias of Sparta and the Tholos of Athens were to be; at Pylos it was an amphitheatre with nine tiers, each capable of holding five hundred people.[7] In the middle, in the " sacred circle," were the seats of honour, benches of polished stone reserved for the king and the *gerontes*.[8] Thus everybody was seated; it was a custom so firmly established that even in the assemblies of warriors everyone sat on the ground and only in a crisis would they remain standing.[9]

It might seem from the matters brought before the Assembly that it had considerable powers. Before it came everything concerning the people, everything which was δήμιον.[10] Remedies for public evils such as pestilences or dissension among the chiefs were discussed there;[11] rewards

[1] *Od.*, II, 26 *ff.*
[2] *Il.*, II, 50 *ff.*; IX, 9 *ff.*; cf. *Od.*, II, 6-8; VIII, 7 *ff.*
[3] *Il.*, II, 48 *ff.*; VIII, 1 *ff.*; *Od.*, II, 1 *ff.*; VIII, 1 *ff.*
[4] *Od.*, III, 138 *ff.*   [5] *Il.*, II, 92.
[6] *Il.*, II, 788; VIII, 325, 382; *Od.*, III, 5-6; VI, 266; VIII, 5.
[7] *Od.*, III, 7-8; cf. VIII, 16.
[8] *Il.*, XVIII, 504; *Od.*, II, 14; III, 31; VIII, 6.
[9] *Il.*, II, 96, etc.; IX, 13; XIX, 50; *Od.*, III, 149; *Il.*, XVIII, 246.
[10] *Od.*, II, 32.   [11] *Il.*, I, 59 *ff.*; XIX, 55 *ff.*

to be given for services rendered to the State were there considered; immigrants who were to be repatriated were presented before it; news of the battlefield was announced to it; and proposals for the opening of peace negotiations were made there.[1] In the agora of the camp the question of liberating prisoners and captives was discussed, or the arguments for and against prolonging the war were put forward, and proposals submitted by the enemy were examined.[2] Such were the programmes which might easily lead one to believe in the political power of the people; but we shall see that its rôle for the most part was limited to that of a passive and almost silent audience.

On leaving the Council, the king generally went to the agora accompanied by the *gerontes*. He opened the session with an outline of the matter to be discussed, unless he delegated that task to the chief who had been most prominent in seeking a meeting of the assembly.[3] Those who wished to speak rose and were invested by a herald with the sceptre which rendered them sacrosanct.[4]

But one must not think that every Tom, Dick and Harry ventured on this step. Normally the *gerontes* alone took part in the proceedings, and nearly always the same ones who had spoken in the Council then came down to voice their opinions in the agora: βουληφόρος and ἀγορήτης, the two words were complementary.[5] Consequently the oldest of the nobles were the usual speakers in the Assembly. Great store was set by their orations: a reputation for wisdom and eloquence was of no less worth than a reputation for valour;[6] the poet never tires of praising the mellow voice of Nestor and extolling the old men of Troy " like unto grasshoppers."[7] Sometimes for form's sake the orators would address the whole audience, Danaans, Trojans or Ithacans; but in reality the king spoke only for the chiefs,[8] and the chiefs for the king.[9] The discussion was nothing more than a colloquy between two or

---

[1] *Od.*, VII, 150; II, 30; *Il.*, XVII, 345 *ff.*
[2] *Il.*, I, 15 *ff.*; II, 110 *ff.*; VII, 382 *ff.*
[3] Cf. *Il.*, II, 50 *ff.*, 86, 110 *ff.*; IX, 16 *ff.*; XIX, 55 *ff.*
[4] *Il.*, I, 234, 245; II, 100; *Od.*, II, 37.
[5] *Il.*, VII, 126.
[6] *Il.*, I, 490; XII, 325; XV, 283 *f.*; *Od.*, XI, 510 *ff.*
[7] *Il.*, III, 150.
[8] *Il.*, VII, 385; IX, 17; *Od.*, VIII, 26.
[9] *Il.*, I, 59; XIX, 56.

three great personages. The chiefs, it is true, might be free-spoken. Nestor went in for persuasive methods, but Diomedes adopted a truculent tone and did not even hesitate at violence: such was the " right of the agora " ($\dot{\eta}$ θέμις ἐστιν ἀγορῇ).[1] What part did the common man (δήμου ἀνήρ) play ? If one were a man " of the people " (δήμου ἔων), " one did not count."[2] Nevertheless in extraordinary circumstances an old man might take it upon himself to voice popular disquietude and curiosity. But for a Thersites, a man of nothing, whose father was unknown, to dare to rise to his feet and, without arming himself with the protecting sceptre, to burst forth into invective against the kings, that was contrary to all forms (οὐ κατὰ κόσμον). The whole audience jeered at the insolent fellow, then grew angry, and applauded Ulysses when first he rebuffed him and finally beat him with his staff.[3]

But this does not mean that the opinion of the people was negligible. It always found means of expressing itself either by signs of approbation or murmurs of discontent or even by silence. The imprudence of making a decision contrary to the temper of those who will be responsible for its execution is always obvious. The power of the multitude, vague in the *Iliad,* begins to define itself in the *Odyssey.* But in façt it was seldom that men other than members of the Council spoke in the agora, and, in theory, power of decision belonged to the king alone. Let us see what actually happened in the great assemblies described in the epics.

At the very beginning of the *Iliad* a foreign priest named Chryses comes to ask that his daughter who has been taken prisoner shall be released for a ransom. He appeals to " all the Achæans and especially to the two sons of Atreus." All the Achæans are of the opinion that the offer should be accepted, yet nevertheless Agamemnon, with threats on his lips, refuses. Just as Apollo avenges his servant by sending down a pestilence, so Achilles, urged by the goddess Hera, takes it upon himself to summon the people to the agora. There arises an altercation of unparalleled violence. Achilles, overcome with passion, hurls forth bitter insults and even goes so far as to draw his sword from its scabbard.

---

[1] *Il.*, IX, 31 *ff.*   [2] *Il.*, II, 198, 202; XII, 213.
[3] *Od.*, II, 15 *ff.*; *Il.*, II, 211-264.

C*

Agamemnon furiously retorts, only recovering his majesty with the unanswerable speech: " This man wishes to place himself above all others; he wishes to be in command over all, to rule over all, to give orders to all; but I know one man who will not obey him." After this quarrel, which Nestor has in vain attempted to compose, the Assembly dissolves. At no point in the proceedings did the dispute become generalized.

When Agamemnon thinks that the day has come for the decisive battle he resolves to test the morale of his army. He summons it to the Assembly. Escorted by the Council, whom he has informed of his intentions, he proposes that they shall re-embark. Immediately the erstwhile docile mass turns and rushes towards the ships. But Ulysses hurls himself in front of the mob, Agamemnon's sceptre in his hand: to the leaders he explains that they have mis- understood the king's meaning; the common people he thrusts back into the agora with angry words and blows. Once more they sit down. Thersites alone begins to shout that there has been enough of fighting to furnish a king with women and treasure. They laugh at him, they grow angry, and the punishment inflicted on the insolent wretch delights the crowd. When Ulysses asserts that hostilities must be continued he is greeted with shouts of acclamation. When Agamemnon adopts the plan of campaign proposed by Nestor he too is acclaimed. And so they depart before the soldiers can decide otherwise. No formal consultation, no voting: the king has spoken, it is enough.[1]

Once it happened that occurrences during the Assembly caused the king to modify his opinion, but without impairing his authority. Agamemnon proposes to the Assembly of war- riors, seriously this time, that the Troad shall be abandoned and that they shall return to Greece. Icy silence greets this proposal. Diomedes refuses, avails himself of the privilege of the agora, and utters the word cowardice, while the crowd applauds. It is a difficult moment. Then Nestor arises and, to shield the king, asks that the matter be dealt with by the Council. The elders gather together. Nestor is careful to put forward no claims in opposition to the royal prerogative, in which every discussion has its beginning and its end. He

[1] *Il.*, II, 50-378.

merely suggests to the king that he shall be reconciled to Achilles whom he has offended. To this Agamemnon consents: he can acknowledge his mistake without prejudicing his sovereignty; Achilles will receive presents but he will be compelled to submit to one who is "more royal" than himself.[1]

Here, finally, are instances of the way in which the Assembly of the Trojans and that of the Achæans might participate in negotiations. In an agora seething with tumult and terror Antenor proposed to the Trojans that peace should be made. The proposal, amended by Paris, was accepted by king Priam who, of his own initiative, added a demand for an armistice in order that the bodies of the dead might be burned. Furnished with formal instructions the herald Idæus went to the Achæan camp. He was received in the agora but he addressed himself only to the king and the chiefs. His proposals were received in significant silence. In a few words Diomedes demanded that the terms offered should be rejected. "You have heard," said Agamemnon, "the reply of the Achæans; I make it mine, and so it shall be." He granted, however, without consulting anyone, a brief cessation of hostilities and confirmed it with an oath. Idæus could do nothing save return and make known to the agora the eagerly awaited reply.[2]

In the *Odyssey* the Assembly has not changed its character, at least in normal circumstances. The king Alcinous is still the king " to whom the people hearken as to a god," because with him lies " action and speech."[3] After having come to an understanding with the twelve other kings on the question of the repatriation of Ulysses, he convened the Assembly: to it he presented the noble stranger, announced that a ship was to be prepared for him, and then withdrew with his illustrious escort. The people looked and listened, and said nothing.[4] Even in such an extraordinary situation as that of Ithaca during the absence of Ulysses the people acquired no new rights. On the contrary: no king, no Assembly. When finally Telemachus, having reached his majority, convened an Assembly, all that he desired was to excite the

[1] *Il.*, IX, 9-161.   [2] *Il.*, VII, 345-417.
[3] *Od.*, VII, 11; XI, 346; cf. 353; VI, 197; VIII, 382.
[4] *Od.*, VIII, 4-46.

compassion of the people that he might turn it into anger
against the suitors, to achieve by violence the expulsion of
the intruders who were eating up his wealth. Two citizens
supported him; three of the suitors made brutal reply.
What would the Assembly do ? Moved with compassion, it
preserved a mournful silence, and when the last of the orators
commanded that they should disperse, that each should
return to his own business, the people scattered without
having made the slightest effort to make their wishes known.[1]

Yet the times were troubled. How was it possible that
force of numbers should not exert itself ? The acclamation
by which the crowd expressed its preferences could make it
clear to what lengths popular passion could go; it could
announce recourse to arms in case of resistance. Take, for
example, the Assembly in which Diomedes rose against
Agamemnon; passions were roused and Nestor saw clearly
whither they were tending: towards civil war ($\pi\acute{o}\lambda\epsilon\mu\sigma\varsigma$
$\grave{\epsilon}\pi\iota\delta\acute{\eta}\mu\iota\sigma\varsigma$).[2] Telemachus' speech when he tried to rouse the
Ithacans against his private enemies was leading in the same
direction. No other solution is possible when there is no
sovereign will to impose its commands. The vote is the
prophylactic against civil war; where it does not exist there
remains, in default of absolute power, only the alternatives
of civil strife or anarchic inertia. In two instances in the
Odyssey we see a meeting of the Assembly cut short by the
uprising of the commonalty. After the taking of Troy
Agamemnon and Menelaus, being at variance on the question
of returning, assembled the agora; they exchanged bitter
words, and the Achæans rose in frenzied tumult: some remained with Agamemnon, others departed with Menelaus.[3]
In the same way after the murder of the suitors the people
of Ithaca assembled in the agora. The adversaries of Ulysses
demanded vengeance and cried: " Let us depart !" ($\emph{ἴ}o\mu\epsilon\nu$).
His partisans replied: " Let us remain !" ($\mu\grave{\eta}$ $\emph{ἴ}o\mu\epsilon\nu$). Law
could show no way to deaden such antagonism, and so two
camps were formed. There was a rush to arms and blood
flowed freely. To put an end to this internal strife ($\pi\acute{o}\lambda\epsilon\mu\sigma\varsigma$
$\acute{o}\mu\omicron\acute{\iota}\iota\sigma\varsigma$), a general reconciliation with the customary formalities of a covenant was necessary.[4]

---

[1] Od., II, 6-257.
[2] Il., IX, 64.
[3] Od., III, 137-157.
[4] Od., XXIV, 420-548.

The people had no actual rights in judicial affairs, just as they had none in political. How could it be otherwise when even the *gerontes* themselves could only arbitrate on differences which were submitted to them by the mutual consent of the persons involved ? But here again the people could exercise a moral pressure or could resort to violence. *Demou phemis* compelled the murderer, whatever his power and whatever the weakness of the injured family, to take without delay the path of exile.[1] When Telemachus recounted the misdeeds of the suitors before the agora and declared that he was unable to defend himself, he summoned to his aid popular indignation. It is true he did not succeed; but his adversaries trembled in their shoes lest another time he should be more fortunate and a furious mob mshandle them and chase them from the country.[2] In case of any hostile attempt against the city the people did not bother about questions of competence, but resorted to lynching. " Were not the Trojans so cowardly," said Hector to Paris, " they would long ere now have stoned thee."[3] After an act of high treason Eupeithes was hunted down by the Ithacans, who burned with eagerness " to kill him, to tear out his heart and consume his substance."[4] It was this same Eupeithes who, when Ulysses had killed his son, attempted to rouse the multitude against the murderer.[5] To conclude, in an epoch when nothing resembling separation of powers existed, in judicial affairs as in everything else, two courses of action alone were open to the people—ineffectual words or a revolutionary outburst of collective feeling.

V

FORESHADOWINGS OF THE FUTURE

Thus the age-long traditions which are enshrined in the Homeric poems give us a picture of associations which, in spite of appearances, were always developing. The city was made up of all the inter-related groups which had an existence earlier than its own; it was an agglomeration of *gene*. Powerful though the king of the city was, all around him were other

[1] *v.* **XXXIII**, p. 53 *f.*, 233.
[3] *Il.*, III, 17.
[5] *Od.*, XXIV, 421 *ff.*

[2] *Od.*, XVI, 375 *ff.*
[4] *Od.*, XVI, 424 *ff.*

kings who derived their power, as he did, from their *genos*. No one was ever to contest the sacerdotal authority with which he was invested, but his political powers were at the mercy of fortuitous events and new ideas.

One foresees in certain parts of the *Iliad* and still more in the *Odyssey*, how patriarchal monarchy was to decline. Peleus, now an old man, is in a precarious position, while his son, far from him, in agonized suspense wonders whether he has been forced to suffer insults and contempt, whether even he has been stripped of his majesty.[1] Quarrels between brothers, that of Agamemnon and Menelaus after the fall of Troy, for example, were bitter trials for the royal families. Still more dangerous were minorities. Achilles relied upon Patroclus, should he himself die, to place his son in possession of his patrimony; but Ulysses likewise had entrusted his son to the devoted care of the aged Mentor, and one knows what the outcome was. The suitors did not deny dynastic right; but each of them hoped one day to enjoy the position of the queen's husband; and, meanwhile, there was Eurymachus whom the Ithacans began to regard " as a god," and Antinous on whom on occasion was bestowed the title of " Sacred Power."[2] Foreigners were led to wonder whether an oracle had turned the people from their rightful heir.[3] When finally Ulysses returned and massacred the suitors a whole party arose to avenge them, and the king only triumphed over them and became once more "king for ever"[4] by making a bilateral covenant analogous to that which was to bind the kings and the people at Sparta and among the Molossians.

It was to the members of the Council, kings of tribes and chiefs of *gene*, that the powers lost to the monarch were to go. When Alcinous treated as equals the twelve kings who surrounded him, he spoke as a sovereign condescending and courteous; but even then his language expressed something which was to be a reality in the future. Not many incidents such as that in which Diomedes, before the whole Assembly, heaped objurgations on the head of Agamemnon were necessary to show that public authority was no longer inseparable from the royal title. Even the enormous strength which

[1] *Od.*, XI, 495 *ff*.   [2] *Od.*, XV, 520; XVIII, 34.
[3] *Od.*, III, 214-215.   [4] *Od.*, XXIV, 483.

military command gave to the king was threatened: a petty chief of Crete refused to place himself under the command of Idomeneus, fought with a band of followers side by side with the regular army, and assassinated the king's son who attempted to deprive him of his share of the booty.[1] Moreover, of the nobles who had formerly esteemed it an honour to serve their master as *therapontes*, we see already some in exceptional circumstances being designated by the king as guardian and future regent, or as general. Appointments of this sort were to be extorted from the weakness of the king or even made without his participation. The time was to come when, aristocracy having reduced the monarchy to a simple magistracy, the one-time major-domo, now Mayor of the Palace, would control the State as archon or as pole-march.[2] The household of the king was to be transformed into the public administrative body, and the simple " carvers of meat " ($\delta a\iota\tau\rho o\grave{\iota}$ $\kappa\rho\epsilon\acute{\iota}\omega\nu$)[3] were to be raised to the management of the treasury with the title " collectors of the fragments " ($\kappa\omega\lambda a\kappa\rho\acute{\epsilon}\tau a\iota$).[4]

The birth and expansion of the aristocratic regime can be seen clearly in the monarchy of the epics; and there too can be seen, though in a purely embryonic state, an element of democracy. Though the agora was reduced for the most part to playing a passive rôle, there are instances, especially in the later parts of the Homeric poems, of the voice of the people, the $\delta\acute{\eta}\mu o\upsilon$ $\phi\hat{\eta}\mu\iota s$, becoming a by no means contemptible force. On one occasion it was sufficiently threatening to compel a chief to set out for war. " There was no way of resisting," remarked the person in question.[5] But the people could exert only a moral pressure or have recourse to arms; no middle legal course existed. The rule of the subordination of the minority to the majority, the legal procedure of the vote, has not always been known. Even acclamation had, in theory, no obligatory force, such as the *boa* was to have with the Spartans. Civil wars and disasters without number were necessary before the Greeks could be

---

[1] *Od.*, XIII, 262 *ff.*
[2] The " kings " of the Phæacians were called ἀρχοί (*Od.*, VIII, 391), as was the ruler of several peoples, including the Athenians (*Il.*, XV, 337) whose *archos* was, in that case, a *polemarchos.*
[3] *Od.*, I, 141; IV, 57; XVI, 252 *f.*; XVII, 331.
[4] **XXXVI**, vol. I, p. 401.   [5] *Od.*, XIV, 237-239.

induced to define the rights of the agora.   The time was not yet ripe.   When two families quarrelled they had no weapon save the vendetta, and private war could be ended only by a formal treaty of peace: they had not even reached the stage of recognizing that it was better for family quarrels to be settled by calculating the strength of each by means of conjuration and awarding the victory without bloodshed to the one which presented the greater number of combatants. When there was dissension in the agora, if the king was incapable of taking a strong line and if no compromise could be reached, civil war of necessity broke out.   The day had not yet come when, to judge the strength of the opposing sides, each in turn was made to shout its war cry, or else each citizen was called upon to raise his hand and swear upon which side he would fight, if it were necessary to fight. It was only through the vote that the opinion of the people was to prevail, that the *demou phemis* was to become the *demou kratos*.

CHAPTER II

ORIGINS AND FORMS OF OLIGARCHY

I

ORIGINS OF OLIGARCHY

THE king, who embodied in himself the power of the city, had as natural enemies the petty kings of the tribes and the phratries who had at their command all the strength of the *gene*. The outcome of the struggle was never doubtful. Even in the *Odyssey* one sees a very different monarchy from that which had existed in the great times of the *Iliad*. Alcinous, king of the Phæacians, with twelve other kings around him, humbly styles himself the thirteenth; let us say that he was the first, *primus inter pares*, yet even so he could do nothing without consulting the others. Ulysses had only to be away from Ithaca and his son a minor for all the chiefs of the neighbourhood to aspire to take his place by marrying his wife. By the end of the eighth century all was over, the Homeric monarchy was no more.

The only exceptions were the Battiadæ of Cyrene and the Kinyradæ of Cyprus, to whom perhaps can be added the Aleuadæ of Larissa and the Scopads of Crannon. But the former, far overseas, were in the vicinity of Egypt or in touch with the Phœnicians, and the latter did not assume the title of king in spite of their power and the example of the Macedonian dynasty. The Hellenic conception[1] is well illustrated by this fact: at Panticapæum in the Euxine the chiefs chosen from the family of the Archeanactidæ, then from that of the Spartacidæ, were kings of the Scythians and archons of the Greeks.[2]

Although there remained kings whose office was for life and hereditary they were nothing more than magistrates

---

[1] " Hereditary monarchy is unendurable when men are equal," says Aristotle, *Pol.*, VIII (V), 1, 6.

[2] Dem., *C. Lept.*, 29, 31; *IGPE*, vol. II, nos. I *ff.*; *RIG*, nos. 98, 124.

with relatively little power. At Sparta the Agidæ and the
Eurypontidæ, generals and high-priests, were held in check
by the actual masters, the ephors. Nor is this the only
example to be found among the Dorians: the king of Argos
retained his military function till the middle of the fifth
century;[1] at Corinth the dynasty of the Bacchiadæ was
successful until the time of its definite fall (657) in nominating
from its own number a king with an honorific and life title,
as well as the *prytanis*, the annually appointed head of the
government.[2] Even in Ionia the Basilidæ, descendants of
Androclus, continued to furnish Ephesus with its king; but
this king, although always clad in the purple and bearing
the sceptre, was only a sacerdotal dignitary.[3] Others of
the family of the Basilidæ at Chios, Erythræ, Skepsis and
probably Clazomenæ[4] lost the royal dignity but still
remained at the head of the ruling aristocracy. It was
the same with the Neleidæ at Miletus and the Penthilidæ
at Mitylene.[5]

Usually monarchy, when reduced to the position of a
magistracy, ceased to be a life office and was removed from
the family in which it had originally resided; it became an
annual office open to all the families of the ruling class. At
the same time it was restricted to those functions of which
religious sentiment would not suffer it to be deprived—
namely, sacred functions. The most celebrated example is
that of Athens, where the king was only one of the nine
archons, the one who was responsible for dealings with the
gods, and where he had not even the honour of giving his
name to the year. This *rex sacrificulus* appears in a great
number of Ionian islands and towns: at Siphnos, Naxos, Ios,
Chios and at Miletus whence the institution was transported
to the Milesian colony of Olbia.[6] At Megara the king was
likewise an ordinary magistrate with religious duties; but in
the Dorian city he was eponymous as he was in the small

---

[1] Her., VII, 148 *f.*; *BCH*, vol. XXXIV (1910), p. 331; Paus., IV, 35, 2
(cf. II, 19, 2; Diod., VII, fr. 13).
[2] Her., V, 92; Diod., VII, fr. 9.
[3] Strab., XIV, 1, 3, p. 633; cf. Diog. Laert., XX, 6.
[4] Her., VIII, 132; Strab., XIII, 1, 52, p. 607; Arist., *loc. cit.*, 5, 4;
Ath. Const., 41, 3.
[5] *CRAI*, 1906, p. 511 *ff.*; Arist., *Pol., loc. cit.*, 8, 13.
[6] Arist., *op. cit.*, III, 9, 8; Isocr., *Ægin.*, 36; *IG*, vol. XII, v, nos.
54, 1008; *CDI*, nos. 5653c, 5495; *IGPE*, vol. I, no. 53.

towns of his domains and in his colonies.[1] By an unexplained chance the king of Samothrace was not only eponymous but also enjoyed political powers.[2]

This persistence of a meaningless title is one of the traits which best illustrates the reluctance of the ancients to interfere with institutions of the past. Even the smallest local kinglets were maintained as magistrates. In certain places, " kings " similar to those who administered justice in the villages of Bœotia in the time of Hesiod were recognized until the very end. Athens preserved its *phylobasileis*, its " kings of the tribes," and they came to the Prytaneum to associate themselves with the king of the city in protecting the people from divine vengeance by judging accusations of murder brought against inanimate objects and animals.[3] In Elis the *basileis* of the phratries formed a tribunal presided over by the highest magistrate of the locality.[4] But it is in Asia Minor in particular that one sees " kings " of this kind functioning. In conjunction with the *prytanis* they made enactments at Mitylene on questions relating to landed property,[5] at Næsus they heard accusations of insults to magistrates and of desertion.[6] At Kyme they sat under the presidency of the *aisymnetes* and their administration was subject to the control of the Council.[7] At Chios, after a revolution which took place about 600, " the kings " were named in a law in conjunction with a demarch; but in a city which had at one and the same time a king fallen to the rank of *rex sacrorum* and a *prytanis*, one may conclude that the demarch had been substituted on the spur of the moment by the victorious party for one or other of these oligarchical magistrates.[8]

The weakening and the eventual collapse of the primitive monarchy turned to the profit of those who, consciously or not, had worked towards this end from the beginning. The

[1] *IG*, vol. VII, nos. 1 *ff.*, 188 *ff.*, 223 *ff.*; *RIG*, nos. 166, 172, 338, 1227.
[2] *IG*, vol. XII, viii, nos. 164 *ff.*, 186 *ff.*
[3] Arist., *Ath. Const.*, 41, 2; 8, 3; 57, 4. Cf. *REG*, vol. XIII (1900), p. 156.
[4] Cf. **XXXIII**, p. 248.
[5] Theophr. ap. Stob., *Flor.*, XLIV, 22; *RIG*, no. 356, 1. 1, 9, etc.
[6] *IG*, vol. XII, ii, no. 646, *a*, 1. 45; *b*, 1. 14, 37.
[7] Plut., *Qu. gr.*, 2, p. 291 *f.*; Arist. ap. Schol. Eurip., *Medea*, 19.
[8] Wilamowitz, *Nordionische Steine* (*Abh. BA*, 1909, p. 66 *ff.*); *RIG*, no. 33; *GID*, vol. III, no. 5653.

chiefs of powerful families became masters of the city; and
this they remained for many centuries. The archaic period
was entirely subjected to a half patriarchal, half feudal rule
in which the common interest was an unstable compromise
between a few persons each accustomed to command in his
own circle.[1]

They had on their side noble blood; they traced back
their origin to some god. The value that was attached to
birth is attested by the very persistence of the *gene*, which
had long since split up into small families, and by the care
with which the great men preserved their genealogical tree
and the traditional history of their house (their πάτρια).
A man was as proud to be one of the Alcmæonidæ at Athens
or of the Eumolpidæ at Eleusis as he was in Asia Minor to
be connected with the royal lines. Towards the year 500
Hecatæus of Miletus made a proud display of his family tree
and traced it back to the sixteenth generation, that is to say,
reckoning three generations to a century, to the second half
of the eleventh century, to the foundation of the city. A
little later an inscription on the tomb of a noble of Chios
contents itself with enumerating fourteen of his ancestors,
thus taking the origins of his family back to the beginning
of the tenth century. The Philaïdæ of Athens prided themselves on an equally distant origin: one of their number,
Hippocleides, archon in 556-5, claimed to be the twelfth
descendant of the hero Ajax. The Spartan kings did not go
back so far, for the Agid Polydorus and the Eurypontid
Theopompus, who were reigning round about 720, belonged
respectively, so it was said, to the seventh and ninth generation of their dynasty.[2]

No vicissitudes of fortune could wrest from the nobles
their natural prestige and right to respect.[3] As a matter of
fact very few noble houses declined: it was sufficient to belong
to an illustrious *genos* to have a share in the revenues and lands
of a wide domain and to enjoy the riches won at the point
of the sword by numerous generations. In all parts of
Greece a class of gentlemen grew up. They were designated
by general terms, such as " the good " (ἀγαθοί), " the best

    [1] *v.* **XXVIII**, l. IV, chap. IV.
    [2] Her., II, 143; *GDI*, no. 5656; Pherecydes, 20 (*FHG*, vol. I,
p. 73); Paus., III, 2, 1-3; 7, 1-5.
    [3] *Od.*, XXI, 335.

men " (ἄριστοι, βέλτιστοι), " the great and good ' (καλοὶ κἀγαθοί), " men of blood " (εὐγενεῖς, γενναῖοι), " men of quality " (ἐσθλοί, χρηστοί), " men of honour " (γνώριμοι, ἐπιεικεῖς). Sometimes more precise terms were employed: they were " well born men," Eupatridæ; they were " lords of the earth," Geomoroi; they were " knights," Hippeis.

It was to this last title that they clung most tenaciously. The noble, who was both landowner and soldier, devoted himself to rearing the horse which gave him superiority in combat. Whilst the wretched foot-soldier was armed only with the short javelin or sometimes only with a sling, the noble approached the enemy clad in heavy brazen armour, his head enclosed in visored helmet, and the rest of his body protected with a cuirass of metal sheets and with greaves, with buckler in his left hand, a long lance in his right, and a two-bladed sword by his side. He fought on foot; but up to the middle of the seventh century he was driven into the midst of the battle field in his chariot by a charioteer (the παραβάτης with the ἡνίοχος); later he dispensed with the chariot and rode on horseback, followed by a servant similarly mounted (the ἱπποβάτης with the ἱπποστρόφος).[1] The war horse whether yoked or mounted was the distinctive mark of the nobility. Several times Aristotle points out the connection which existed originally between oligarchy and cavalry:

" The first states in Greece which succeeded those where kingly power was established were governed by the military. First of all the horse, for at that time the strength and excellence of the army depended on the horse, for as to the heavy-armed foot, they were useless without proper discipline; but the art of tactics was not known to the ancients, for which reason their strength lay in their horse. . . . This cannot be supported without a large fortune; for which reason in former times those cities whose strength consisted in horse became by that means oligarchies. . . . Where the nature of the country can admit a great number of horse, there a powerful oligarchy may be easily established; for the safety of the inhabitants depends upon a force of that sort, and those who can support the expense of horsemen must be persons of some considerable fortune."[2]

There was, therefore, in a very great number of Greek cities a ruling class of knights. Such were the Hippobotæ, the breeders of horses, at Chalcis, and the Hippeis, the horsemen, at Eretria, in Thessaly, at Colophon, at Magnesia ad

---

[1] Cf. Helbig, Les ἱππεῖς ath. (MAI, vol. XXXVII, 1902, p. 157 ff.).
[2] Arist., Pol., VI (IV), 10, 10; 3, 1-2; VII (VI), 4, 3 (v. Pol. translated William Ellis [Everyman ed.], p. 131-2, 195).

Mæandrum, and in other towns of Asia, and it was the same in Attica before the epoch when the landowners who cultivated more than five hundred measures of land rose above the other Eupatridæ.[1]

But in the seventh century there occurred an economic revolution which had powerful repercussions in the social and political conditions of the whole of Greece. The discovery and colonization of a new world led, by an immense development of commerce and industry, to the substitution of a monetary system for the old natural economy. The great landholders, accustomed to appropriating the lion's share of the booty won in raids and pirating expeditions, were just as favourably placed for making capital out of these new sources. They possessed fields and forests, vineyards and olive plantations, mines and quarries; they built ships and brought home from foreign lands wealth to swell their treasuries. They had not even to move into the towns, for they had lived there always, since the agora was the centre of government as well as of commerce. Thus in innumerable cities aristocracy changed its character. The knights of Chalcis who cultivated the fields of the Lelantine plain were the same who exploited rich copper mines, possessed smelting furnaces, founded colonies in Thrace and in the West, and controlled the flourishing corporation of ship-owners (the *aeinautai*).[2] The breeders, who monopolized the whole of the pasture lands of Megaris, converted the wool which they obtained from their sheep into *exomides* which they sold to the common people, or sought the corn and fish of the Euxine in the warehouses of the Propontis.[3] A Lesbian of high birth, Charaxus, the brother of the poetess Sappho, shipped cargoes of wine to Egypt and squandered the proceeds on the most beautiful courtesan of Naucratis.[4] The Athenian Solon, whose family was related to the royal dynasty of the Medontidæ, by prosperous voyages restored his dwindling patrimony.[5] It was no longer only landed wealth which gave the nobles their power, but money also.

[1] Id., *ibid.*, VI (IV), 3, 2 and 8; VIII (V), 5, 10.   Cf. **XXXVI,** vol. I, 309, 312, 403 *ff.*
[2] **LXXXI,** p. 123; cf. **XXXVI,** vol. I, p. 312 *ff.*
[3] Cf. **XXXVI,** vol. I, p. 326 *ff.*
[4] Her., II, 135; Athen., XIII, 69, p. 596*b*; Strab., XVII, 1, 33, p. 808.
[5] Plut., *Sol.*, 2; Arist., *Ath. Const.*, 11, 1.

The nobles, however, were not the only ones to lay hands
upon the mass of fluid capital, of precious metal, which was
circulating now from one end of the Mediterranean to the
other. In all the cities the *demiourgoi*, both artisans and
traders, were able to take their share and formed an intermediary class above the *thetes*: they possessed neither land
nor horses; but they had the means of arming themselves
as hoplites, and they were sometimes sufficiently strong, with
the advantage afforded by their numbers, to endanger the
position of the knights. Some by their ability, intelligence
and energy managed to rise above the others and brought
themselves before the public eye by flaunting their newly
gained wealth. The old nobility were contemptuous of these
" nouveaux riches," and the poet Theognis was a merciless
critic. Nevertheless many great lords whose resources were
no longer adequate for their position were not unwilling to
have them for fathers-in-law or even for sons-in-law: it was
an alliance of needy pride with wealthy vanity. Thus a
hybrid aristocracy was formed in which race and land retained
their prestige, but in which the scale of social values was
determined by wealth, however gained. " Money makes the
man," " money mingles blood," sighed the extollers of times
past;[1] but their protests were fruitless, nothing could be
done. Ostentatious wealth constituted a claim to political
power. To be entitled to stand for the magistracies a man
must be prepared to offer magnificent sacrifices in the ceremony of installation, to entertain the people with banquets
and feasts, to adorn the city with temples and statues; and
that was why it was wise policy to display in the agora tunics
white as snow and mantles of purple, to deck one's hair with
jewels, and to honour the dead of one's family by sacrificing
upon their graves whole hecatombs and pouring forth libations
from enormous perforated jars.[2] " Ah! 'tis not without
reason that men honour thee, O Plutus," said Theognis;[3]
and in fact aristocracy was being transformed into plutocracy.
The people of the upper class added henceforth to all the
epithets earned for them by nobility of blood the new epithets

---

[1] Alcæus, fr. 49; Theognis, 190; cf. 662 *ff*.
[2] Arist., *Pol.*, VII (VI), 4, 6; Asius ap. Athenæus, XII, 30, p. 525.
and Xenophanes, *ibid.*, 31, p. 526*b*; Thuc. 1, 6; Plut., *Sol.*, 21.
[3] Theognis, 523.

of " rich " (πλούσιοι, εὔποροι, τὰς οὐσίας or τὰ χρήματα ἔχοντες) and " stout " (παχεῖς).[1]

In the innumerable cities where this system prevailed power was always placed in the hands of a few, the *oligoi*. It was for this reason that the Greeks usually called it *oligarchy*, and not *aristocracy*, a name specially reserved for the government of the " best men," that is to say the ancient nobility, or, according to the vocabulary of the future philosophers, those morally and intellectually the finest.[2] But the composition of the ruling class varied infinitely according to its origins.   There were some countries which took no part in the colonial and commercial expansion, who withdrew into themselves and remained faithful to rural civilization; the great landowners continued to prevail there.   Such was the case in Thessaly and Elis.   On the other hand one can mention the case of an island where the paucity and barrenness of the land had long hindered the formation of a landed aristocracy, but which as a result of its excellent position on the sea was exalted suddenly to the first rank: it was Ægina which henceforth only knew an oligarchy of merchants.   For the most part there was a working compromise between landed wealth and movable wealth, and riches, serving as a common measure, then seemed the most striking trait of oligarchy.   We have just seen examples of this regime at Chalcis, at Megara, in Lesbos and at Athens.   The most remarkable example is, perhaps, that offered by Miletus.   On the one hand were the masters of the soil, those who found " the horn of Amaltheia " in their fields and who cultivated them by means of their serfs, the Gergithes;[3] on the other hand were the manufacturers who controlled the mass of manual workers, the *Cheiromacha*, and the *aeinautai* who directed colonization and commerce;[4] together they formed the *Ploutis* which wielded political power and had at its head the dynasty of the Neleidæ.[5]

[1] The last of these expressions frequently occurs in Herodotus: V, 30, 77; VI, 91; VII, 156.   Cf. Aristophanes, *Peace*, 639.
[2] v. Arist., *Pol.*, III, 5, 2.
[3] Phocylides, fr. 7; Her., V, 29 (cf. I, 17, 19, 21); Heracleides Ponticus ap. Athen., XII, 26, p. 523 f.
[4] Plut., *Qu. gr.*, 32, p. 298c.
[5] Id., *ibid.*   Cf. *CRAI*, 1906, p. 511 ff.

II
FORMS OF OLIGARCHY

We know enough of the origins of oligarchic rule not to be surprised when we find it assuming very diverse forms. The essential difference between democracy and oligarchy consisted in this: in the one all native-born were full citizens; in the other full citizens were distinguished from natural citizens. Oligarchy always supposed the division of citizens into two classes, of which one only participated in government. But, according to the city, the superior class might be greater or smaller, and extend either to the majority of the people or be confined to a more or less exclusive minority. The privilege which it enjoyed might comprise a varying number of rights. It might pertain to birth, or to landed property estimated according to revenue, or to wealth whether real or movable, assessed either according to capital or to income; in the two last cases it might be determined either by a property qualification, or by a limited number of participants. From one city to another these elements formed different combinations.

In this confusing diversity Aristotle[1] distinguishes four principal forms. His classification, though purely logical and hence artificial, is none the less convenient. We shall, therefore, keep to it, although making some alterations. Aristotle examines oligarchy after democracy; that is to say he passes from the most moderate form to the most extreme; we shall invert the order adopted by the philosopher and follow, as is most proper for the historian, the natural evolution of institutions. Aristotle as a theorist remains in the realm of abstractions; we must give life to the theory by concrete examples.

Extreme oligarchy (the fourth form of oligarchy according to Aristotle) is that in which the supreme magistrate possesses hereditary power and commands such wealth and rules over so many followers and subjects that sovereignty, in place of pertaining to law, is in the hands of a man. This regime is reminiscent of the patriarchal monarchy of the city organized according to *gene*; it is " dynastic " oligarchy.

---

[1] *Pol.*, VI (IV), 5, 1 and 6-8.

The history of ancient Thessaly is that of a few dynasties.[1] In the most extensive plain of the whole of Greece, the conquering people had divided the land between families grouped in tribes and subdued those of the vanquished who had not taken refuge in the mountains of the frontier. The masters possessed vast *kleroi*. Their arable land was cultivated by gangs of serfs or *penestai*, who owed them a yearly service; they themselves devoted their time to stock breeding. They were intrepid horsemen and loved hunting and bull fighting. When they set out for war they were followed by a troop of mounted vassals and a throng of lightly armed *penestai*. According to a regulation laid down by one of the chiefs each *kleros* had to furnish a contingent of forty horsemen and eighty *peltastai*.[2] Many of these great landowners were able to do even more: in the fourth century one man brought to the Athenians two or three hundred horsemen with their *penestai*, and a tyrant undertook by himself to revictual the whole Athenian army with meat at an absurd price.[3] Political rights were the monopoly of these great proprietors, the " good men."[4] Beneath them, indeed, was formed a class of free peasants and, in certain places, a class of merchants and artisans; but few of them were in comfortable circumstances, for in the army there were only two hoplites to each knight.[5] Moreover, the middle class had no place in the State. Even in great towns the names of the tribes showed that they had for long been composed of breeders and nobles, and records gave lists of families.[6] In these towns the agora was at all times closed to the humble peasants and craftsmen.[7] Thessaly, therefore, was entirely subjected to a landed nobility. But the bulk of these lords obeyed a few great suzerains, and it was among these that the dynasts were found. The Aleuadæ were the masters of Larissa: their merits were sung by Pindar and they hoped to become the satraps of Greece in the name of Xerxes. At Crannon the Scopads were celebrated for their treasures. Pharsalus belonged until the middle of the fifth century to the house of Echecratides and later to that

---

[1] Cf. **XXXVI**, vol. I, p. 309 *ff.*   [2] Schol. Eurip., *Rhes.*, 307.
[3] Dem., *C. Aristocr.*, 199; *Pub. Econ.*, 23; Plut., *Reg. et imper. apophth. Epamin.*, 17, p. 193e.
[4] Pind., *Pyth.*, X, 71.   [5] Xen., *Hell.*, VI, 1, 8.
[6] *IG*, vol. IX, ii, nos. 458 *f.*; 513; 517, l. 20; 524.
[7] Arist., *Pol.*, IV (VII), 11, 2.

of Aparos.[1] All these princes had resplendent courts to
which they attracted poets such as Simonides and Anacreon.
Each of them asked nothing better than to unify Thessaly
in order that he might rule over the whole of it.

Dynastic oligarchy was just as suited to a large town of
traders and ship-owners as to an agricultural and stock-
raising country. Corinth offers proof of this. There meagre
and barren land prevented the formation of a landed nobility;
but an excellent position on two seas enabled energetic and
intelligent ship-owners to take the first place in Mediterranean
commerce and to acquire vast fortunes. This the Bacchiadæ
did. This indeed was a dynasty, which maintained its purity
to the end by permitting no alliance with other families.
In all probability it had formerly been invested with royal
power, and it kept for its chief the royal title, while at the
same time reserving to itself the prerogative of naming one
of its own number for the principal office, that of *prytanis*.[2]
Its policy was essentially mercantile: a harbour was made on
the Saronic Gulf and a second on the Gulf of Corinth, a road
of wood was laid down between the two for the portage of
vessels, trading centres were established all along the north-
west coast of Greece, and the colonies of Corcyra and Syracuse
were founded. In reality the Bacchiadæ transformed their
private affairs into public enterprises and enriched themselves
while enriching their city. So long as they were successful
they were the absolute masters of the city.

When the chiefs of noble families were not subordinated
to one of their number there existed a dynastic oligarchy of
greater, though still small, numbers. The circle of choice
for all offices of State was confined to a few families; and all
the offices were transmissible from father to son. It differed
essentially from the former system, according to Aristotle,
in that since all powers were no longer concentrated in the
same hands, law necessarily intervened to guarantee the
inheritance of privileges. But there is nothing to prove that
it had always been so, at any rate in the beginning. In rural
cities this type of oligarchy seems to have had a purely
traditional character: one finds there traces of the time
when there existed kings " more royal " one than other,
with this difference, that among them now no one could say

---

[1] Cf. **VII**, vol. I, p. 359 *f*.   [2] *v*. **XXXVI**, vol. I, p. 319.

that he was "the most royal" of all. It was only in towns of relatively recent origin, the colonies, and above all in those where commercial wealth had monopolized the government, that one can imagine a constitution of this type fixed by legislative enactment. But one can see how rivalries would spring up in the oligarchy of multiple dynasties. On the one hand "kings" of inferior order would demand a share in the privileges of those who were "more royal"; on the other hand, the richest families, for example those of the ship-owners in the ports, would attempt to monopolize more completely the powers which they shared with others less rich.

Take for example an agricultural country. Elis, whose population was scattered among hamlets and which did not possess a single town until the fifth century, obstinately adhered to its ancient institutions and the customs of "the sacred life": Polybius tells how in his time one met families not a single member of which had been to Elis for two or three generations.[1] There were a great number of phratries there, each of which had its chief and its kings, a local aristocracy composed of *gene* each of which ruled in its hamlet. The central government was in the hands of ninety *gerontes* who no doubt represented the three tribes of Heraclides. These *gerontes*, appointed for life, were always chosen from the same families by a "dynastic" system ($αἵρεσις$ $δυναστευτική$); they chose by rote from these families the *Hellanodikas* and the *demiourgia* who exercised control over the phratries. Aristotle, who tells us of this system, also tells us how it fell. "If the members of an oligarchy agree among themselves, the state is not very easily destroyed without some external force . . . for though the place is small yet the citizens have great power, from the prudent use they make of it. But an oligarchy will be destroyed when they create another oligarchy under it; that is when the management of public affairs is in the hands of a few, and not equally, but when all of them do not partake of the supreme power, as happened once at Elis. . . ."[2] What happened was that an oligarchy of two degrees took the place of an oligarchy in which all the privileged persons had equal rights: their chance of

---

[1] *Pol.*, IV, 73, 8-10.
[2] Arist., *Pol.*, VIII (V), 5, 7-8 (*v.* translation William Ellis [Everyman ed.], p. 155-156).

entering the Gerousia and of being appointed to the dignity of *Hellanodikas* was henceforth reduced by half and dependent upon election by lot.[1] How many then were active members of the oligarchy of Elis ? Since they appointed two supreme magistrates instead of one, one jumps to the conclusion that there were twice as many as the *gerontes* of the old regime; and, indeed, to confirm this hypothesis we find that at Epidaurus the oligarchy was composed of the " Hundred and Eighty," the masters of the " Dusty-feet " (*Konipodes*), who appointed the members of the Council and the magistrates, and whose number was likewise connected with the three Dorian tribes.[2]

Here is a second example, this time of a great commercial port. Massalia was governed in the time of Strabo[3] by a Synedrion of six hundred members appointed for life: they were called the *timouchoi*. From the Six Hundred was drawn the Council of Fifteen responsible for the management of current affairs: three of the Fifteen exercised executive power; one of the Three was the official head of the city. A man could not be a *timouchos* unless he had a legitimate child and unless he belonged to a family which had possessed citizenship for three generations. Exclusive though the government of the Six Hundred was it succeeded an even more exclusive one. The name of the *timouchoi* goes back, indeed, to the very origins of the town, since it is peculiar to Ionia, the country of its founders.[4] Originally, as the etymology of the word and the example of Ionian cities indicate, it could mean only a small number of persons invested with public duties. At that time the body of citizens comprised only a few privileged families and the office of *timouchos* was exclusively confined to their chiefs. That extreme form of oligarchy could not last indefinitely. It became more " political," Aristotle declares ($\pi o\lambda\iota\tau\iota\kappa\omega\tau\epsilon\rho a$). What does this mean ? " For those who had no share in the government ceased not to raise disputes till they were admitted to it: first the elder brothers, and then the younger also."[5] Such a reform made the particular interests of collateral branches

[1] Cf. *REG*, vol. XVI (1903), p. 151 *ff*.
[2] Plut., *Qu. gr.*, 1, p. 291e.   [3] Strab., IV, 1, 5, p. 179.
[4] *v.* M. Clerc, *DA*, article " Timouchoi "; **VII**, vol. I, p. 357, n. 3; *Massalia*, vol. I (1927), p. 424 *ff*.
[5] Arist., *loc. cit.*, 2 (trans. Ellis, p. 154).

prevail over the unity of the *genos*; its result was to give to the richest families a larger representation in the government. Oligarchy became more " political," that is to say more civic, more republican, in the sense that henceforth a greater share was given to wealth than to nobility of blood: the importance of the *genos* diminished in favour of the individual. Since primogeniture was the rule of succession it was necessary to make some arrangement by which the best of those who were excluded, the *élite* of the *plethos*, should pass into the body of active citizens, into the *politeuma*: henceforth a periodical revision of the " Golden Book " was made.[1] But it was decided, either at this time or in a subsequent reform, that the number of the privileged should be limited to six hundred. The title of *timouchos* belonged to all of them; but it changed its significance since it now only conferred on the ordinary members of the Synedrion the virtual right of being promoted to the Council of Fifteen. Many other cities, among which Aristotle numbers Heraclea, Istros and Cnidus, underwent the same vicissitudes as Massalia.[2] One sees then oligarchy extending its bounds, and even perhaps passing from one to the other of the categories distinguished by Aristotle. But these reforms were less profound than they appeared. In the prosperous ports, where population increased rapidly, to increase the number of active citizens was not necessarily to alter the relation of that number to that of passive citizens. Even if the list of privileged persons was lengthened a little, the principle of the constitution did not change, and it was easy enough to render the measure nugatory by forming a new oligarchy within the enlarged oligarchy. When the *timouchoi* of Massalia numbered six hundred the Fifteen took the place of the old *timouchoi*, and Cicero was to see in the condition of the Massaliot people " a striking picture of servitude " similar to that of Athens under the Thirty.[3]

When oligarchy ceased to be " dynastic " and became really " political " it still confined power to a minority of the citizens, but to a comparatively numerous minority. " It supposes," says Aristotle, " men of property less numerous than in the first hypothesis (the last for us), but with more

<hr>

[1] Id., *ibid.*, VII (VI), 4, 5.   [2] Id., *ibid.*, VIII (V), 5, 2-3.
[3] Cic., *Rep.*, I, 27, 43; 28, 44.

considerable fortunes. As ambition increases with strength they arrogate to themselves the right of nominating to all the offices of government; but as they are not powerful enough to govern without law, they make a law for that purpose."[1] This regime was usually instituted by a law which rigidly fixed the number of active citizens.

Thus it happened that a great number of cities were ruled by the Thousand. We know of two in Asia Minor: Kyme, where the Thousand seized power from the knights, which probably means that an aristocracy of wealth replaced an aristocracy of birth;[2] and Colophon, where the Thousand appeared in the agora clad in mantles of purple which were worth their weight in silver, adorned with diadems of gold and scented with perfumes.[3] In eastern Locris the capital, Opus, was governed by the assembly of the Thousand; the majority of these citizens, compelled to keep one war horse, belonged without doubt to the " hundred households," to the families which traced back their noble titles to the time of Ajax. Towards the beginning of the seventh century Opus handed on its institutions to its colony Epizephyrian Locri: there also the Thousand administered the laws, and the principal families claimed descent from the women of the " hundred households " who had followed the first colonists.[4] Two neighbouring towns of Epizephyrian Locri, Croton[5] and Rhegium,[6] possessed in the same way their assembly of the Thousand, which later continued to sit side by side with the popular assembly under the name of *Syncletos* or *Escletos*. It was the same away in the south of Sicily at Acragas.[7]

But no mystic quality was attached to this number of a thousand. In relatively small cities the body of citizens might be much smaller, but the government was not for that reason so much the more oligarchical; in very large cities it might be much greater, without approaching any nearer to

[1] Arist., *Pol.*, VI (IV), 5, 7.
[2] Heracl. Pont., XI, 6 (*FHG*, vol. II, p. 217).
[3] Xenophan. ap. Athen., XII, 31, p. 526*a*; Theop., *ibid.*, *c* (*FHG*, vol. I, p. 299, fr. 129); cf. Arist., *loc. cit.*, 3, 8.
[4] *IJG*, vol. I, no. xi (cf. *IG*, vol. IX, 1, no. 334), B, l. 14 f.; Polyb., XII, 5, 26. *v.* Wilhelm, *Jh. AI*, vol. I (1898), Beiblatt, p. 50, l. 15.
[5] Iamblichus, *v. Pyth.*, 35, p. 260; Val. Max., VIII, 15, 12; cf. Diod., XII, 9, 4.
[6] Heracl. Pont., fr. 25 (*FHG*, vol. II, p. 219); cf. *RIG*, nos. 555, 952.
[7] Timæus, fr. 88 (*FHG*, vol. I, p. 213).

democracy. Thus at Massalia and Heraclea Pontica a comparatively generous measure of reform was necessary to
bring the numbers of the oligarchy up to six hundred, whilst
the Synedrion of six hundred which legislated at Syracuse for
twenty years had a strongly oligarchical character in a town so
populous.[1] The constitutional history of Athens towards the
end of the fifth century is rich in partisan experiments in
which rival parties endlessly disputed as to the ratio to be
established between the number of inhabitants and that of
active citizens.   In 411-10, whilst the extreme oligarchy of
the Four Hundred was making itself hateful to a people of
close on thirty thousand, what were the theorists proposing
in their search for a just mean ?   Theramenes brought in a
law which entrusted the whole government " to the Athenians
most capable of serving the State with their person and their
possessions, to a number of not less than five thousand."
The constitution of the Five Thousand, whose minimum was
in fact a maximum, thus deprived five-sixths of the citizens
of their political rights.   It functioned for some months after
the fall of the Four Hundred in 410.[2]   In 404, the opposition
of Theramenes compelled the Thirty to imitate it and to
draw up a list of three thousand citizens who had the right
to participate in government and were guaranteed against
the arbitrary power of tyrants.[3]   Finally, in 312, Antipatros
decided that to be a citizen it was necessary to possess a
capital of two thousand drachmas—equivalent to an income
of from 200 to 240 drachmas: this property qualification
excluded twelve thousand out of a total population of twenty-
one thousand.[4]

Such constitutions could, however, cloak a much more
strictly oligarchical rule.   The common run of citizens often
had for their sole privilege the right of attending a powerless
Assembly, while all actual power resided in a small Council.
The history of the Athenian oligarchies makes this fact clear:
the paper nomination of the Five Thousand and the Three
Thousand limited in no respect the omnipotence of the Four

[1] Arist., *Pol.*, VIII (V), 5, 2 (cf. 4, 2); Diod., XIX, 5, 6; (cf. 4, 3;
6, 1 and 4).
[2] Arist., *Ath. Const.*, 29, 5; 33, 1-2; Thuc., VIII, 65, 3; 67, 3; 97,
1; Lys., *P. Polystr.*, 13.
[3] Arist., *op. cit.*, 36 *ff.* Cf. **XCII**, p. 3 *ff.*, 7 *ff.*
[4] Diod., XVIII, 18; Plut., *Phoc.*, 28.

Hundred and the Thirty. None the less these were revolutionary tentatives. But elsewhere oligarchies within oligarchies were of normal and frequent occurrence. The most celebrated example is that of Sparta with its oligarchy in the form of a pyramid: above the *Helots*, who were not free, and the *Perioikoi*, who were not citizens, were placed the Spartiates; above the " Inferiors " who were admitted to the great assembly or Apella, the " Equals," provided with a patrimony and paying their quota towards the common meals, formed alone the small assembly where they gathered in ever decreasing numbers; above all was the Council of the thirty *gerontes, itself* controlled by the five ephors, which actually exercised sovereignty. In the same way at the time when Athens had for its masters the Four Hundred, Thasos was in the hands of the Three Hundred and Sixty.[1] After the fashion of Sparta, Croton, according to the constitution of Pythagoras, had its Assembly and its Gerousia, in addition to its Syncletos of the Thousand.[2]

The last form of oligarchy (the first for Aristotle) was characterized by a property qualification sufficiently high to exclude the poorest from the magistracies but sufficiently low to give easy access to the privileged classes and to admit, for example, anyone who was capable of serving as a hoplite. While not having enough money to live without working the citizens had sufficient not to be a burden to the State. At all events, their number was too great for sovereignty to be concentrated in one person, and it necessarily found its expression, therefore, in the law.

Such was the regime in countries where there existed many people of small substance. With peasants such as the Malians the right of full citizenship belonged to the veteran hoplites, that is to those who possessed a complete suit of armour and had completed their term of service.[3] The towns which formed the Bœotian Confederation, in the second half of the fifth century and the first third of the fourth, confined political powers to an assembly of men who had the required minimum wealth—all landed proprietors: at Thebes a fixed number of inalienable estates was maintained by law and access to any magistracy was forbidden to anyone who had

---

[1] *IG*, vol. XII, viii, no. 276. [2] *v. infra*, p. 84.
[3] Arist., *Pol.*, VI (IV), 10, 10.

D

followed a trade during at least the last ten years; at Thespiæ those who had learnt a mechanical trade and even those who tilled their own land were excluded.[1] It is true that the qualification was not very high: at Orchomenus it appears to have been 45 medimni or 23 sacks of corn,[2] which meant in an age of small yields and a biennial rotation of crops about 12 acres of land. From the contingents of hoplites and knights furnished by each city in the confederation one can estimate the number of active citizens at 3,000 for Thebes, more than 1,500 for Orchomenus, 1,500 for Thespiæ and Tanagra, 500 for Eutresis and Thisbe, rather fewer for Platæa, 500 for Haliartus, Lebadea, Coronea, Acræphia, Copæ and Chæronea.[3] In Cretan cities the qualified people consisted of citizens who had been admitted into the *hetaireiai*, where after having completed their service as members of an *agela*, they lived in common and ate together at the expense of the treasury.[4] They formed a considerable body. In a town of secondary importance, at Dreros, a class of *agelaoi* comprised, in the third century, 180 youths,[5] a figure which corresponds to a body of about 7,000 citizens. But the tribes, which embraced them all, accorded a special place to the *startos* composed of privileged families from which were recruited the *kosmoi* who were entrusted with executive power.[6]

It was constitutions of this type which were eulogized in Spartan propaganda at the end of the fifth century. One of its agents, a sophist speaking in the name of a Thessalian party, proposed this model to his fellow-citizens: " People will say to me: ' But the Lacedæmonians have established oligarchy everywhere.' Yes, an oligarchy which we have long invoked in our prayers, . . . if the name of oligarchy can be given to such governments in comparison with those which merit the name in our country (a country of dynastic governments). Is there in their league a city, however small it may be, where a third of the citizens does not participate

---

[1] *P. Oxy.*, XI, 2; cf. Xen., *Hell.*, V, 4, 9; Arist., *Pol.*, II, 9, 7; III, 3, 4; VII (VI), 4, 5; Heracl. Pont., fr. 43 (*FHG*, vol. II, p. 224). *v. BCH*, vol. XXXII (1908), p. 271 *ff.*
[2] Poll., X, 165; Arist., fr. 518 Rose.   [3] *P. Oxy.*, XI, 3-4.
[4] *IJG*, vol. I, p. 410 *ff.*   [5] *RIG*, no. 23, l. 12 *f.*
[6] Arist., *Pol.*, II, 7, 3-8.   Cf. *IJG, loc. cit.*, p. 414 *f.*; **XXXVI**, vol. I., p. 301 *f.*

in the affairs of government ? He who has not the means to procure armour and to take part in politics, not Lacedæmon, but fortune excludes him from public life. He is excluded only until he can show the lawful property-qualification."[1]

Modified oligarchy merges into modified democracy, and it is impossible to say with precision where the one ends and the other begins. The oligarchic constitution which had existed in Athens since the middle of the seventh century needed very little reform at the hands of Solon to yield place to a system which prepared the way for absolute democracy. This *timocratic* constitution divided the people into four classes, among which offices and honours were partitioned in proportion to their income from land.[2] When Cleisthenes had abolished this system and proclaimed almost complete equality for all Athenians, the opponents of democracy never ceased to regret " the constitution of their ancestors." We know this from the examination of a pamphlet in which one of them put his own views into a supposed constitution of Draco. He proposed to concede political rights, including therein access to the Council and minor offices, to the citizens who were in a position to arm themselves as hoplites, but to elect the archons and the treasurers from those who possessed a capital of ten *minæ* (a thousand drachmas), and the *strategoi* and the hipparchs from those who could show a capital of a hundred *minæ* and had lawful children over ten years of age.[3] As a matter of fact each time that the opponents of Athenian democracy succeeded in attaining their ends they instituted a violent oligarchy, such as that of the Four Hundred and that of the Thirty, or at the least gave power to a minority, as did Theramenes and Antipatros. There were, however, politicians who thought it was possible to turn away from democracy without falling into oligarchy. In 403 a man named Phormisios proposed to confine political rights to Athenian landowners, that is to about fifteen thousand citizens out of a total of more than twenty thousand native born Athenians:[4] thus a very mild form of oligarchy would have been instituted, but it would nevertheless have meant the end of democratic principle.

---

[1] Ps. Herodes Atticus, Περὶ πολιτείας. *v.* **XCIV**; cf. **LIX**, p. 207.
[2] *v. infra*, p. 120.   [3] Arist., *Ath. Const.*, 4, 2-3.
[4] Lys., XXXIV. Cf. **XCII**, p. 420 *ff*.

To all these types of oligarchy is added a last—nominal democracy.   Aristotle gives interesting details of the subterfuges by which the people were deprived in practice of the rights which were theirs in theory and of the simple deceptions which were used.   These subterfuges were directed towards five objects: the Assembly, the magistracies, courts of justice, possession of arms and gymnastic exercises.

" With respect to their public assemblies, in having them open to all, but in fining the rich only, or others very little for not attending; with respect to offices, in permitting the poor to swear off, but not granting this indulgence to those who are within the census; with respect to their courts of justice, in fining the rich for non-attendance, but the poor not at all, or those a great deal and these very little, as was done by the laws of Charondas.   In some places every citizen who was enrolled had a right to attend the public assemblies and to try causes; which if they did not do, a very heavy fine was laid upon them; that through fear of the fine they might avoid being enrolled, as they were then obliged to do neither the one nor the other.   The same spirit of legislation prevailed with respect to their bearing arms and their gymnastic exercises; for the poor are excused if they have no arms, but the rich are fined; the same method takes place if they do not attend their gymnastic exercises, there is no penalty on one, but there is on the other: the consequence of which is that the fear of this penalty induces the rich to keep the one and attend the other, while the poor do neither."[1]

---

[1] Arist., *Pol.*, VI (IV), 10, 6-7 (*v*. trans. Ellis, p. 130-131).

CHAPTER III

OLIGARCHICAL INSTITUTIONS

OLIGARCHY had the same institutions as democracy. On a superficial consideration it would seem that the only difference between the two systems was the number of people who benefited by them. In both fully qualified citizens could attend the Assembly, sit in the Council, be chosen as magistrates. But a closer examination shows that the difference of numbers was of such importance that it gave to institutions of identical appearance a totally different character.

I

THE ASSEMBLY AND THE COUNCIL

In principle sovereignty resided in the mass of active citizens. They exercised it in the Assembly called the Ecclesia or the Halia. They excluded from their meetings all the rest of the *demos*, the unprivileged mob, the *plethos*. In Thessalian towns the agora was called " the place of Liberty "; but in what sense must one understand that term ? The magistrates were charged to keep the public square " free from the contamination of merchandise "; it was closed to "the artisan, the peasant and all other such persons."[1]

In oligarchies where the rich were relatively numerous, the very nature of the system demanded that the less rich should abandon the direction of affairs to the richest, that is to say to the Council, to a limited Assembly, or to the magistrates. There were several ways of achieving this end. Sometimes the Assembly was allowed to discuss only motions initiated from above, so that it was given a deliberative voice while being deprived of the power to alter the constitution; sometimes it was given the right of sanctioning but not of rejecting decisions made outside itself; sometimes it was

[1] Id., *ibid.*, IV (VII), 11, 2.

conceded only a consultative voice, while the right of decision resided in the magistrates alone.[1] In the towns of Crete although the citizens of the *hetaireiai* might come in their thousands to the agora they could only give formal ratification, by show of hands or ballot, to the proposals which the Council and the *kosmoi* brought before them;[2] and for the rest they were the passive and silent witnesses of certain official acts such as the choice or the reception of foreign ambassadors.[3]

It was found to be much more convenient not to convoke all the citizens at one time. In the Bœotian cities of the fifth century the people included in the property census were divided into four sections, each of which in turn acted as Council and introduced measures into the plenary assembly for its final and purely formal ratification.[4] By this means, of the approximately 3,000 citizens of Thebes only about 750 at a time had an effective voice in government. This system was copied by the Athenian theorists who formulated the constitution of the Five Thousand. The Five Thousand likewise were to be divided into four sections: in each section those over thirty formed a Council, and each of these Councils was to sit in turn for a year. The Council in office was, therefore, composed of from 800 to 900 members. In grave crises the Council might be doubled: each councillor might. in this case choose for himself a colleague from citizens with the requisite age qualification. Sessions of the Council were held normally every five days. The executive consisted of five *proedroi* chosen by lot, and every day one of them was elected by lot as president or *epistatos*. If a councillor failed to be present at the opening of the session he had to pay a fine of a drachma, unless he had obtained permission to absent himself.[5] This constitution remained a dead letter so long as the leaders of the extreme oligarchy of the Four Hundred wielded revolutionary power: they were authorized to convoke the Five Thousand when they deemed it necessary; not once did they do it.[6] But it existed in reality for

[1] Id., *ibid.*, VI (IV), 11, 9.
[2] Id., *ibid.*, II, 7, 4; cf. *IJG*, vol. I, p. 416.
[3] Law of Gortyna, X, 33-36; XI, 10-14 (*IJG*, vol. I, p. 386); *RIG*, nos. 53 *ff*.
[4] *P. Oxy.*, XI, 38 *ff*. *v. BCH*, vol. XXXII (1908), p. 271.
[5] Arist., *Ath. Const.*, 30, 3-6; Thuc., VIII, 67, 3.
[6] Thuc., *ibid.*, 97.

some months when Theramenes' constitution retarded the re-establishment of democracy: an official writ gives us details of a commission of *proedroi* with its president.[1]

In place of splitting up the Assembly into sections in this manner oligarchy sometimes preferred to interpose between it and the Council a smaller and more reliable Assembly. This is what happened at Sparta.[2] In principle, all Spartiates over thirty who were enrolled in the tribes and *obai*, and had been through the course of public instruction and were admitted to the common meals, had the right of sitting in the *Apella*. Originally we are told they numbered nine thousand. They gathered in a plain near the banks of the Eurotas, between the Babyca bridge and the Knakion, and deliberated in the open air, the kings and the *gerontes* on special seats, the others massed on benches or on the ground. An ordinary assembly was held at least once a month at the time of the full moon; but extraordinary sessions were frequent. Until the middle of the eighth century the Apella exercised wide powers. It possessed the right of amendment, though not the right of initiative, declared war, superintended operations, concluded treaties of alliance and of peace, nominated the elders and the magistrates and settled questions of succession to the throne. It voted by acclamation, and, in case of doubt, by discession. Thus the Apella possessed at that time " sovereignty and power."

But the number of the " Equals " or *Homoioi* diminished rapidly. The obligation to possess a portion of " civic land " and to contribute to the expenses of the common meals precipitated many into the class of the " Inferiors " or *Hypomeiones*. At the same time the increasing wealth of a small number exalted above the " Equals " a controlling aristocracy (the καλοὶ κἀγαθοί). This great nobility placed the monarchy in tutelage and reduced the Assembly to impotence. Henceforward the Apella met in an enclosed building, which more than sufficed to hold the handful of citizens who were present. It continued to elect the magistrates, but according to an absurd system which in practice made the right nugatory. As a deliberative body it was not

---

[1] *IG*, vol. II², no. 12. Cf. Ad. Wilhelm, *loc. cit.*, p. 43; **LVIII**, vol. II, p. 430 *f.* Glotz, *REG*, vol. XXXIV (1921), p. 2.
[2] *v. DA*, art. " Ekklesia," p. 512-515.

consulted save for form; its opinion was asked but there was no necessity to adopt it. " If the people gives an unfavourable vote," said the law, " the *gerontes* and the kings may set it aside." Before embarking upon a war or signing a treaty the chiefs of the city heard the opinion of the majority; but they none the less did as they pleased. When they had reached a decision concerning internal policy, they announced it as a command given to men whose duty it was to obey.

The twenty-eight elders and the five ephors did not, however, constitute the whole of the nobility. In times of grave crisis they associated with themselves in closed committee the principal magistrates and the richest or most respected persons. It was this Council larger than the Gerousia, this Assembly smaller than the Apella, which was given the name of " small Assembly " ($\mu\iota\kappa\rho\grave{\alpha}$ $\dot{\epsilon}\kappa\kappa\lambda\eta\sigma\acute{\iota}\alpha$). It is mentioned only once in the ancient historians. But we know that the oligarchy of Sparta was surrounded with mystery,[1] so that an institution whose very existence we might not have suspected may well have been one of the principal organs of the Spartan government.

The special body which one finds mentioned quite frequently under the name of *Escletos* or *Syncletos*, was most probably a " small Assembly " of the Spartan type, a very carefully picked Assembly. The institution functioned under one of these names at Rhegium and at Acragas, side by side with the Halia and the Bola;[2] at Croton side by side with the Ecclesia and the Gerousia.[3] There were even cities where the Syncletos definitely took the place of the Assembly.[4]

In oligarchies where the citizens were fewer in number the Assembly could more easily preserve the reality of power. The Thousand of Colophon were all very rich; and all went to the agora, were it only to display their wealth. The Thousand of Opus voted laws in full assembly. The Thousand of Croton, as well as the Syncletos, were consulted on questions of war and peace.[5] At Massalia the six hundred *timouchoi*,

---

[1] Thuc., V, 68.   [2] *RIG*, nos. 555, 553.
[3] Diod., XII, 9, 4; Iambl., *op. cit.*, 35; cf. Val. Max., VIII, 15, 12; Dicæarchus, fr. 29 (*FHG*, vol. II, p. 244).
[4] Arist., *Pol.*, III, 1, 7   [5] *v. supra*, p. 77.

who were elected for life and who assembled in the Synedrion, formed the firm basis of a graded pyramid. Moreover in these restricted oligarchies it is extremely difficult to distinguish the Assembly from the Council. At Massalia, for example, the Synedrion might pass for a general Assembly as well as for a Boule, and the Fifteen for a Boule as well as for an executive committee. We are told that at Epidaurus the Hundred and Ninety chose among themselves *bouleutai* called *artynoi*; but the name of these " orderers " attests that they did not differ greatly from the *artynai* who formed in the neighbouring city of Argos a college of supreme magistrates, clearly distinguished from the Boule:[1] the only difference was that in the small town there was no need to extract from the Assembly a Council, whilst in the large town there was certainly in the time of the oligarchy, as later under the democratic regime, a Bola and a Haliaia.[2]

From all that one can learn of the Assembly in oligarchical cities this conclusion emerges: the oligarchical principle, which by refusing rights to the poor led the richer to exalt themselves over the less rich, generally resulted in the concentration of political power in the Council.

Where the Council had a " dynastic " character it commonly bore the name of Gerousia. The name was well justified, for not only was the age limit high, but also members held their seats for life. At Sparta where one could not enter the Apella before thirty years of age, one could not become a *geron* until all military obligations had been discharged, that is until one was sixty, and the title was retained to the end of one's days. In spite of the high age qualification appointments to the office were rare; for the Spartan Gerousia consisted only of twenty-eight members apart from the two kings, or, if one prefers, of thirty members of whom two were hereditary. Plutarch becomes almost ecstatic when he speaks of these elections. " It was indeed," he says, " the most glorious struggle that could take place among men, and the one most worthy of arousing competition. From the good and the wise had to be selected the wisest and the best;

---

[1] Plut., *Qu. gr.*, I, p. 291*e*; Thuc., V, 47; *IG*, vol. IV, no. 554.
[2] Her., VII, 148 *f.*; cf. Thuc., *loc. cit.*; *IG*, *loc. cit.*, no. 557; *BCH*, vol. XXXIV (1910), p. 331, l. 25.

D*

the prize of victory was a prize for virtue bestowed for life, with an almost sovereign authority in the State."[1]   But in reality it was not so glorious.   Candidates were chosen from the narrowest circle of the privileged, as were the judges whose task it was to declare which one was accorded the most enthusiastic acclamations:[2] one can imagine to what collusions an election of this kind lent itself.   The results of the system were described by Aristotle who cannot be suspected of severity towards an institution of aristocratic character.

" There are also great defects in the institution of their senators. If indeed they were fitly trained to the practice of every human virtue, everyone would admit that they would be useful to the government; but still it might be debated whether they should be continued judges for life, to determine points of the greatest moment, since the mind has its old age as well as the body; but as they are so brought up, that even the legislator could not depend on them as good men, their power must be inconsistent with the safety of the State: for it is known that the members of that body have been guilty both of bribery and partiality in many public afiairs; for which reason it would have been much better if they had been made answerable for their conduct, which they are not."[3]

In Elis the ninety *gerontes*, representing the three tribes, were not recruited in the same manner as the twenty-eight of Sparta: it was not possible to have a minimum age limit there since each represented his *genos*, and the son succeeded the father;[4] but since they remained in office until their death they were, on the whole, old men.   From these instances one can guess what was the probable constitution of the Council in other towns where it bore the name of Gerousia, as for example at Ephesus and Croton.[5]

But the Council did not even need a special qualification in order to have an oligarchical character: it might be styled the Boule, as in a democracy, and consist of members appointed for life.   In this case the oligarchical Boule was usually composed of important magistrates who had completed their term of office.   In ancient Athens it was composed of ex-archons.   This aristocratic Council was never destroyed by democracy, it never ceased to sit on the hill of the Areopagus

---

[1] Plut., *Lyc.*, 26; cf. Arist., *Pol.*, II, 6, 15; 8, 2; Polybius, VI, 45, 5.
[2] Plut., *loc. cit.*; Arist., *loc. cit.*, 6, 18-19.
[3] Arist., *loc. cit.*, 17-18 (trans. Ellis, p. 55).
[4] Id., *ibid.*, VIII (V), 5, 8.
[5] *RIG*, no. 488; Dicæarchus, *loc. cit.*

to try cases of murder; but, before it was reduced to this function by the Boule properly so called, it combined with its supreme jurisdiction an absolute power in all matters concerning the observance of law, the maintenance of order,the responsibility of magistrates, and relations with foreign countries. One must probably recognize an analogous body in the Boule at Chios to which a revolution in about 600 added a double in the form of a popular Boule. In Crete it was certainly so: in every town the *kosmoi* entered the Boule after their year of office and remained there until their death, and to these *bouleutai* Aristotle does not hesitate to apply the name of *gerontes*.[1] At Cnidos the Boule was not recruited in the same fashion as at Crete and Athens, since there it was composed of a fixed number of members; but these members, the sixty *amnemones*, in like manner sat for life and dealt with all affairs of importance under the presidency of the *aphester*.[2]

Certain oligarchies discovered that a too large Boule was dangerous; they, therefore, replaced the great Council by a restricted Council, a committee of *probouloi*. Aristotle sees in these " pre-advisers " an institution essentially opposed to the democratic principle. " One such order is necessary," he says, " whose business it shall be to consider beforehand and prepare those bills which shall be brought before the people that they may have leisure to attend to their own affairs; and when these are few in number the State inclines to an oligarchy. The pre-advisers indeed must always be few; for they are peculiar to an oligarchy: and where there are both these offices in the same State, the pre-adviser's is superior to the senator's, the one having only a democratical power, the other an oligarchical."[3]

Aristotle's opinion was based on many examples. The government of merchants which was established at Corinth after the fall of the Cypselidæ rested upon a Gerousia of eighty members, recruited from the eight tribes. Each tribe nominated nine ordinary councillors and a pre-adviser (*proboulos*). The eight *probouloi* formed a superior Council, which submitted questions previously prepared to the

[1] Arist., *Pol.*, II, 7, 5; cf. Diod., XVI, 65, 6-7.
[2] Plut., *Qu. gr.*, 4, p. 292*b*.
[3] Arist., *Pol.*, VI (IV), 12, 8 (trans. Ellis, p. 138); cf. 11, 9; VII (VI), 5, 10 and 13.

Gerousia.[1]   This institution was transmitted to one at least of its colonies; at Corcyra the pre-advisers acted in concert with the executive committee of the Boule, the *prodikoi*, and their president, the *prostatas*, presided over the Assembly of the people.[2]

It can well be understood that in other cities the name of *probouloi* might be attached sometimes to the councillors or a part of them, sometimes, and most often, to a college of chief magistrates directing from outside the work of the Council. At Delphi the thirty *bouleutai* were divided into two half-yearly sections, and the first of each section were named with the archon in official documents;[3] it is not surprising that these *bouleutai* should have been called *probouloi* somewhat late.[4] But elsewhere at Histiæa,[5] the *probouloi* possessed executive power.   At Eretria they appeared, indeed, as heads of the State.   They guarded the seal and the archives, received the oaths of the citizens, proclaimed public rewards, and directed financial affairs and foreign policy.   At the same time they were presidents of the Boule: by virtue of this they drew up memoranda for consideration and the other officials could only propose decrees through them.[6]   In short, as an inscription expresses it, their duties were those of presidents (ἀρχὴ τῶν προκαθημένων).[7]   When in 411, after the disaster of Sicily, the oligarchical party of Athens once more raised its head, it began by copying this institution; it stripped the Boule of its powers, and vested in a committee of ten *probouloi* the task of protecting the State from danger by introducing emergency measures; then it added twenty new officials to the first ten, entrusting them with the duty of proposing all measures which they judged necessary for the safety of the State and with the drawing up of a new constitution.[8]

---

[1] Nic. Dam., fr. 60, 9 (*FHG*, vol. III, p. 394); cf. Suid., *s.v.* πάντα ὀκτώ; Diod., XVI, 65, 6-8.   *v.* H. Lutz, " The Corinthian Constitution " (*Cl. R*, vol. X, 1896, p. 418); Szanto, " Gr. Phylen " (*Sb. WA*, vol. CXLIV, 1901, p. 16).

[2] *IG*, vol. IX, 1, nos. 682 *ff.*; *v. RIG*, nos. 319 *f.*

[3] Cf. **IV**, p. 45 *ff.*

[4] *RIG*, no. 263, A, l. 26.

[5] *Ib.*, no. 402, l. 6, 14, etc.; *IG*, vol. XII, v, no. 594, l. 19.

[6] *v.* Holleaux, *REG*, vol. X (1897), p. 364 *ff.*; **LXXXI**, p. 314, l. 16. 'Eφ., 1911, p. 6, 24.

[7] *RIG*, no. 345, l. 28 *f.*

[8] Thuc., VIII, 1, 3; Arist., *Ath. Const.*, 29, 1-2.

II

THE MAGISTRATES

To understand the position of the magistrates in the oligarchic city one must go back to the past, as it is depicted in the epics. At that time the king exercised his authority through those who assisted him in his Council, the *gerontes* or the *boulephoroi*. When he ceased to be master, executive power naturally fell into the hands of those who continued to make up the Gerousia or the Boule. The Council became the supreme magistrature, the ἀρχή *par excellence*. This it always remained. This primary fact appears even in cities from which oligarchy had long ago been ousted by democracy; so much so that Aristotle, in his description of the Athenian constitution, groups all the other magistracies round the Boule, the first in importance. But it shows itself most clearly in oligarchical governments, which were bound most closely in origin to Homeric institutions. The close and permanent relations of the magistracies with the Council explain many apparent anomalies.

We have just seen that in certain cities the *probouloi* figured as commissioners preparing business for the Boule, while in others they were in charge of the whole administration. The division of political labour is just as vague in the case of the *artynoi* or *artynai* of Epidaurus and Argos. A number of institutions are particularly interesting in this respect: for instance those of the *demiourgoi*, the *timouchoi*, the *aisymnetai* and the *prytaneis*.

The very name of the *demiourgoi* is witness to their great antiquity. They date from an epoch when the organization of the city was beginning to free itself from the family regime; for they, like the artisans, were " men who worked for the community." Moreover the *demiourgos* is one of the most obscure and ill-defined institutions which we find in Greece. It was, however, widely known, especially in the Peloponnese (Arcadia, Elis, Achæa, Argolis) and in the overseas settlements founded by the Dorians and the Achæans (Amorgus, Astypalæa, Nisyrus, Cnidus, Chersonesus in the Euxine, Petilia in Greater Greece). There were some cities in which it quite distinctly appears as a Council of long standing, as for example in Elis,[1] and in this form it sometimes functioned side by side with a Boule of more recent origin, as at Argos for instance.[2] In other cities it was openly converted into a supreme magistrature, which had almost always the privilege of eponymacy.[3] But usually it is impossible to distinguish its functions, and it looks as if this were the fault not so much of insufficient documentary evidence, as of the nature of the institution itself—a vague, hybrid, undeveloped thing.

The *timouchoi* only existed in the towns of Ionia and their colonies. Their name seems to indicate that they were supreme magistrates;[4] such, indeed, they must have been in some distant epoch. At the end of the fifth century other magistrates were associated with them; but they always kept their religious functions, and, since they had complete control of the Prytaneum they, like the *prytaneis*, were in constant communication with the Council. At Teos they uttered in the name of the city the imprecations which sanctioned the laws, presided over religious ceremonies, and, in conjunction with the *strategoi*, proposed decrees. At Priene they proposed motions in the Council and had for meeting-place the common hearth called the *Timoucheion*. At Naucratis they imposed fines on sacrificers who failed to do their duty in the Prytaneum.[5]

The history of the *aisymnetai* is even more curious. Their title stamps them as conservers of convention, of good customs. We must go back to the time when the Ionians were not yet separated from Greece proper and when Patrai in Achæa took for its god one Dionysus Aisymnetes.[6] In Asia Minor these guardians of propriety, the *aisymnetai*, did not act as members of the Council. Already in the Homeric poems they appear as persons of princely lineage selected to organize the dances and games in the festivals.[7] One is,

[1] *RIG*, no. 195 (cf. no. 194); Thuc., V, 47, 6.
[2] *IG*, vol. IV, no 493 (cf. nos. 487, 560).
[3] *Etym. M.*, s.v. δημιουργός. Examples: Aigion in Achæa (*RIG*, no. 288), Samos (*ibid.*, no. 371), Amorgos (*ibid.*, no. 712), Astypalæa (*ibid.*, no. 416), Nisyrus (*ibid.*, no. 43, 1. 9), Cnidus (*ibid.*, no. 1340, 1. 57, 86), Ithaca (*SIG*³, no. 558).
[4] *v.* M. Clerc, *DA*, art. " Timouchoi; Massalia," vol. I (1927), p. 430 *ff.*; **VII**, p. 357.
[5] *RIG*, nos. 1318, B, l. 29; 498, B, l. 60; 499, l. 12; *IPr.*, 4, 6, 10-12; Athen., IV, 32, p. 149 *f.*; Dittenberger, *Or. gr. inscr. sel.*, no. 120.
[6] Paus., VII, 20, 1; 21, 6.
[7] *Il.*, XXIV, 347; *Od.*, VIII, 258 *ff.*

therefore, not surprised to see at Miletus[1] the ancient and noble fraternity of the *molpoi* appointing annually an *aisymnetes* who presided over public ceremonies, crown on head, and who even in the city appeared as an eponymous *stephanephoros*. The office of *aisymnetes*, therefore, easily became the supreme magistrature in Ionian towns: at Naxos two *aisymnetai* were eponymous; at Teos a single *aisymnetes* exercised a right of jurisdiction which extended to the infliction of the death penalty.[2] The title was perhaps borrowed from Ionia by Æolis; for Aristotle mentions it in his work on the constitution of Kyme. The Æolians, however, gave to the term which denoted " master of conventions " a wide meaning: they applied it to persons armed with extraordinary powers for the re-establishment of peace between parties and the promulgation of a code of laws. The *aisymnetes*, therefore, became a sort of dictatorship of the interior, conferred for a term of years or for life, an " elective tyranny," as Aristotle styles it.[3] Hence Pittacus, who was invested with that power at Mitylene, was treated as a tyrant or a king by his adversaries in whose minds lingered memories of Homeric times.[4] Whilst in Asia Minor the title of *aisymnetes* was thus borne by ordinary or extraordinary magistrates, in a canton of Greece proper it remained attached to the institution of the Boule. The Megarians gave the name of *aisimnatas* in their Dorian dialect to the members of the permanent committee of their Boule, and a chapel near their Bouleuterion was called the *Aisimnion*.[5] The colonies of Megara imitated the mother country in this respect. There were *aisimnatai* in Selinus from the sixth century.[6] They existed at Salymbria, at Chalcedon, at Callatis and at Chersonesus,[7] and, in these towns, they had a president who at the same time presided over the Boule, as did the *epistatos* of the *prytaneis* at Athens.

As for the *prytaneis* it is they who show us most clearly how the *gerontes* who surrounded the Homeric king seized power and how they exercised it, whether they assumed it

[1] *Sb. BA*, 1904, p. 619; 1905, p. 543.
[2] *IJG*, vol. I, no. xv, A; *RIG*, no. 1318, B, l. 4-5, 9.
[3] Arist. ap. Schol. Eurip., *Medea*, 19; *Pol.*, III, 9, 5-6; 10, 1; VI (IV), 9, 2.
[4] Id., *ibid.*, III, 9, 6; Strab., XIII, 2, 3, p. 617; Plut., *Sol.*, 14.
[5] *RIG*, no. 169; Paus., I, 43, 3.   [6] *IO*, no. 22a, l. 5.
[7] *GDI*, vol. III, nos. 3068, l. 4, 10; 3052 *ff.*; *RA*, 1925, I, p. 258; *RIG*, no. 338, l. 56.

as a body or whether they entrusted it to one alone. Each city had its Prytaneum where solemn sacrifices were offered on the common altar and where the flesh of the victims was divided among the public guests. Formerly it was the palace: " the king " there convened " the kings " to hear their opinions and caused the wine of honour to be poured forth for them. Now the " first of the land," including the king, were together masters of the sacred edifice which owed to them its name. They formed the Council. Usually the Council was divided into sections each of which in turn exercised the prytany, and the same practice was to hold even in cities where oligarchic institutions were destroyed by democracy. But it also frequently happened that the whole power of the aristocracy was concentrated in the hands of a single *prytanis*, who was not only the president of the Council, but the virtual head of the republic, invested with executive power. The first of these cases was common in Greece proper: the *prytaneis* there formed generally a committee of the Boule, even when that committee had special functions as at Delphi, where it was exclusively concerned with finance.[1] The second case was customary in Asia Minor: Aristotle mentions the *prytanis* as supreme magistrate at Miletus; inscriptions inform us that he was eponymous at Hal'carnassus, Chios, Teos, Gambreion and especially in the towns of Lesbos, Mitylene, Methymna, Eresos and Antissa.[2] Through Corinth which was an exception in Greece proper the West became acquainted with the institution of the single *prytanis*; he was eponymous at Corcyra and Rhegium.[3]

It appears from the example of the *aisymnetes* and the *prytanis*, that originally there had been no need for a great number of magistrates. The aristocracy merely placed its leader on a level with the king, and the king, himself reduced to the position of a magistrate, saw the greater part of his power rapidly pass to his rival. The Eupatridæ of Athens gave to this annual delegate the name of *archon* and by making him responsible for the maintenance of the ancient rights of the *gene* he was made the first man of the State, the one who gave his name to the year and took the place of the king in

[1] Cf. **IV**, p. 47 *ff.*
[2] Arist., *Pol.*, VIII (V), 4, 3; *RIG*, nos. 451, 33, 499, 356, 360, 358.
[3] Diod., VII, fr. 9; *RIG*, nos. 319, 555.

the Prytaneum.[1] Among the Opuntian Locrians the *archon* had sovereign control over all administration (διοίκησις), and in particular presided over judicial assizes.[2] Where there was a single *prytanis*, it was he who enjoyed this exalted position. At Miletus, Aristotle tells us, his power was so great that with the greatest ease it passed into tyranny.[3] At Corinth it was by appropriating the annual office of *prytanis* and conferring on him all the reality of royal power, that the Bacchiadæ ruled as absolute masters for ninety years.[4] The name of the supreme magistrate varied so much from place to place that a law of the Eleans, being unable to enumerate all the titles which he bore in different parts of the country, indicated him in a vague and general term as " the one who performs the highest function."[5]

As the cities grew larger progress in the division of political and administrative labour tended to augment the number of magistrates. Although to a lesser degree than in the democracies this tendency was also seen itself in oligarchical cities. One example will suffice. The Eupatridæ of ancient Athens installed by the side of the king and the archon a polemarch, invested with military functions, and later six *thesmothetai* responsible for the administration of justice.

The organization of justice was the most urgent necessity during the centuries when Greece was under oligarchic rule.

Formerly the kings with their counsellors around them had been consulted on litigious questions when the persons concerned agreed to adopt that course. When this justice by arbitration was converted into an obligatory jurisdiction, the right of giving judgment was naturally divided among the magistrates who inherited it from the kings and the Council constituted as an independent body. In Bœotia Hesiod and his brother brought the question of inheritance upon which they were at variance to be settled by the kings of Thespiæ.[6] At Athens, the King Archon, assisted perhaps by the kings of the tribes, presided over the Council which settled all suits concerning public order and which tried

[1] Arist., *Ath. Const.*, 3, 5; cf. **XXXVI**, vol. I, p. 397 *ff.*
[2] Arist., *Pol.*, III, 11, 1; *IJG*, vol. I, no. xi, B, l. 16 *f.*
[3] Arist., *Pol.*, VIII (V), 4, 3.
[4] Diod., *loc. cit.*; Paus., II, 4, 4. Cf. **XXXVI**, vol. I, p. 319.
[5] *RIG*, no. 195, l. 3.
[6] Hes., *Op. et Dies*, 38, 263.

criminal cases on the Areopagus.[1] At Corinth it was the Gerousia which arrogated to itself penal and political jurisdiction.[2] At Sparta the kings had no longer competence save in religious matters, while the Gerousia reserved to itself cases of criminal law and, in conjunction with the ephors, dealt with all affairs which directly or indirectly concerned the welfare of the State.[3] At Locri civil law suits were judged by the archons; but doubtful cases were submitted to the *kosmopolis*, and, if one or other of the parties did not accept his decision, it was deferred ţo the full Assembly of the Thousand, which condemned the loser to be hanged, whether he were a private individual or a magistrate.[4]

But since the Homeric epoch, the king, who could not sit from morning to night in the agora to await appeals for arbitration, delegated this task to the *dikaspoloi*.[5] Thus in certain cities there were, side by side with the Council or the magistrate invested with supreme jurisdiction, special judges for cases of minor importance. Such were the *dikastai* who sat at Gortyna beneath the *kosmoi*: they exercised only common law jurisdiction, and each of them had his special competence which he exercised with the assistance of a secretary of the archives or *mnemon*. The *dikasteres* who functioned among the Opuntian Locrians under the surveillance of the *archon* must have been the same. And in the same category also should be included the *ephetai* established by Draco: these *ephetai*, to the number of fifty-one, formed a jury which took the place of the Council of the Areopagus in the trial of cases of manslaughter.[6]

But we can spend no more time in enumerating the various magistrates, but must pass to a description of their main characteristics.

In the dynastic oligarchies they were hereditary and for life; consequently they did not involve responsibility to any body, a grave defect which Aristotle's acute mind did not fail to see.[7] Naturally it was the same in States where sovereign power belonged to a single family, as in the principalities of Thessaly, and even in those where it was divided among a few

[1] *IJG*, vol. II, no. xxi, l. 12; cf. p. 13.
[2] Diod., XVI, 65, 6-8.   [3] **XXXVI**, vol. I, p. 363, 364, 366.
[4] Pol., XII, 16.   [5] *Il.*, I, 238; XVI, 386 *ff.*
[6] *IJG*, vol. I, p. 429-431; *ibid.*, no. xi, B, l. 7-8; vol. II, no. xxi, l. 24 *f.*
[7] Arist., *Pol.*, II, 7, 6.

families, as in Massalia, Cnidus, Istros and Heraclea.[1] In the most moderate oligarchies the magistracies were annual. But even there the principle of life-tenure might reappear in the formation of the Council: the archons of Athens and the *kosmoi* of Crete did not return into private life at the end of their term of office, since they alone constituted the Boule. The oligarchical nature of this principle was so apparent that Athenian democracy would not allow it to be applied in the Areopagus without modification by the drawing of lots.[2]

When the privilege of holding office was comparatively widely diffused[3] the conditions of eligibility were even more variable. They were sometimes determined by birth and gave to otherwise moderate oligarchies a dynastic character. In Crete the citizens of the *hetaireiai*, divided into tribes, were allowed to choose the *kosmoi* from certain families (ἐκ τινῶν γενῶν) which formed the *élite* of each tribe, the *startos*.[4] Certain colonies such as Thera and Apollonia selected their magistrates exclusively from the descendants of the first colonists.[5] Usually a property qualification determined eligibility. For Plato as for Aristotle this timocratic form of appointment is a distinctive trait of oligarchy.[6] At the same time Aristotle makes a reservation: according to him if the choice is made from the whole body of those within the property-census the institution is rather aristocratic, in the highest sense he gives to this word, and it is only really oligarchical when the choice is confined to a small circle.[7] He observes even that it has its *raison d'être* in the governments midway between oligarchy and democracy. He who sometimes identified oligarchy with this single characteristic, the timocratic system,[8] nevertheless allows that democracy may subject the right of exercising public functions to a moderate property qualification.[9] In fact, in Athenian history, the monopoly of the principal offices of state, assigned to the richest by the Eupatridæ, was retained with the system of

[1] Id., *ibid.*, VI (IV), 5, 1 and 8.
[2] Id., *ibid.*, VII (VI), 1, 10.   [3] Id., *ibid.*, VI (IV), 5, 7.
[4] Id., *ibid.*, II, 7, 5; cf. *IJG*, vol. I, p. 414.
[5] Arist., *Pol.*, VI (IV), 3, 8.
[6] Plato, *Rep.*, VIII, 6, p. 550c; 7, p. 553a; Arist., *Pol.*, III, 3, 4; VI (IV), 5, 1; 7, 3; 12, 7 and 10; VIII (V), 5, 5 and 11.
[7] Arist., *Pol.*, VI (IV), 5, 1.
[8] Id., *ibid.*, II, 4, 4; VIII (V), 6, 6.
[9] Id., *ibid.*, VI (IV), 4, 3; 5, 3.

census classes by Solon and Cleisthenes,[1] and for this reason the names of the two reformers, commonly considered as the founders of democracy, were nevertheless on occasion claimed by the parties of reaction.[2] In exceptional cases the magistrates were chosen from the leaders of the army. Among the Malians they were required to have exercised command in battle.[3] In every way the appointment of magistrates tended to constitute an oligarchy within an oligarchy.[4]

One of the rules which this regime always observed was the fixing of a minimum age for the exercising of public functions. There is no doubt that democratic cities took a precaution of this kind: the Athenian constitution, for example, which permitted all citizens to enter the Ecclesia as soon as they had attained their majority and completed their military service, did not open the Boule and the Heliæa to them until they were thirty and they were not allowed to give judgment by arbitration until they were sixty. Even Athenian oligarchy went little further than that: in 411-10 it merely perpetuated the age limit of thirty for the Council;[5] and when certain theorists proposed to apply it to all the magistrates[6] their proposal was defeated; it was thought sufficient to require an age limit of forty for deputies responsible for drawing up the new constitution or compiling the list of citizens.[7] But purely oligarchical cities went much further. They were not content with appointing the members of the Council for life. They recruited the Gerousia from the old men, as at Sparta, where the councillors had to be sixty years old, or else indeed they formed the Boule from ex-magistrates. They rigorously excluded the young from access to important offices. In the towns of Sicily the democrats themselves recognized that there was nothing to be done against the laws which stood in the way of premature ambition.[8] At Chalcis one had to be forty years old to aspire to any office, even to an embassy.[9] The gymnasiarch of Coressus had to be not less than thirty years old; the *nomo-*

---

[1] Id., *ibid.*, II, 9, 2; *Ath. Const.*, 2, 2; 22, 1; 28, 2; Isocr., *Areop.*, 16; *Antid.*, 232.
[2] Arist., *Ath. Const.*, 29, 3; Plut., *Cim.*, 15.
[3] Arist., *Pol.*, VI (IV), 10, 10.   [4] Id., *ibid.*, VIII (V), 5, 8.
[5] Id., *Ath. Const.*, 30, 2 f.; 31, 1.   [6] Id., *ibid.*, 4, 3.
[7] Id., *ibid.*, 29, 2, 5.   [8] Thuc., VI, 38, 5.
[9] Heracl. Pont., fr. 31, 2 (*FHG*, vol. II, p. 222).

graphoi of Teos and certain commissioners of Andania,[1] not less than forty. A decree of Corcyra directed the Boule to select office holders for any function whatever from among the richest men between the ages of thirty and seventy.[2] In short, Greek oligarchies, even when they did not give the members of the Council the name of *gerontes*, had a natural inclination towards gerontocracy.

By their origin and their organization the magistratures clearly show the high place they held in oligarchical cities. The confusion of powers which so often prevents one from distinguishing the rôle of the Council and that of the supreme magistrate, turned usually to the profit of the individual, to the detriment of the nameless multitude. Those who by their appointment stood as an " *élite* within an *élite* " were by the extent of their powers the masters of the republic. It is not surprising that the magistrates were, in general, more honoured in oligarchies than in democracies. Their persons and their honour were vigilantly guarded by law.[3] At Sparta, the ideal type of aristocratic city, the wielders of public authority obtained an unquestioning obedience from all. Whilst in other States the citizens, especially the great men, were unwilling to appear afraid of the magistrates and considered such fear unworthy of a free man, the leading men among the Spartans gloried in humbling themselves before those who were the incarnation of law.[4] It was for this reason that the philosophers considered oligarchy a rigid, authoritarian, in a word, " despotic " system, that is a system in which the magistrate exercised a power analogous to that of a master over his slaves.[5]

Such was the regime which all Greece knew and which persisted in places which remained faithful to rural life. As one would expect it is in a *Hymn to Earth, Mother of All* that this idealized description of the aristocratic city occurs:

" Happy is he whom thou cherishest in thy kindly bosom ! Abundance is his. His fertile fields are burdened with crops, and his pastures are rich in cattle; his house is filled with all good things. In the city are beautiful women, and its masters rule in the name of just laws,

---

[1] *RIG*, nos. 402, l. 21; 34, l. 44 *ff.*; 694, l. 120 *ff.*
[2] *CIG*, no. 1845, l. 47.
[3] Dem., *C. Androt.*, 32; *C. Timocr.*, 75.
[4] Xen., *Laced. Rep.*, 8, 1 *ff.*
[5] Arist., *Pol.*, VI (IV), 3, 5; Plato, *Rep.*, V, *v.* p. 463*a*.

and happiness and plenty flow therefrom. Their sons rejoice in the pleasures of youth, and their virgin daughters joyfully dance and sport through the soft meadow flowers in floral revelry. Such is the life of those whom thou cherishest, O holy goddess."[1]

Such a government could exist only where good order reigned.[2] Anarchic despotism has no durable qualities. Aristotle, however, states that oligarchy and tyranny were the least stable forms of government.[3] What happened was that inequality inevitably created discontent, and lasting discontent always ends by suppressing its cause. Oligarchy maintained itself easily where the conditions which had given it birth persisted, namely wealth comprised exclusively of landed property and the concentration of a large *clientela* round some great proprietor. It usually ceased to have its *raison d'être* in places where the development of a commercial and monetary regime created within the *demos* a powerful class of merchants and artisans. The object of the struggle was often the supreme magistracy. When the oligarchy was determined not to yield an inch, it imposed on the members of the Boule, by execrable oaths, the duty of hating the people, and it reserved power to those who had proved the sincerity of their hate by their deeds.[4] At other times oligarchy felt itself compelled to come to an understanding with the *demos*; it decided then upon curious compromises. After the reforms of Solon when the Eupatridæ had to struggle against the class of small peasants (the *georgoi*) and the urban class of the craftsmen (the *demiourgoi*) the archonship was divided: it was stipulated in an ephemeral agreement that five archons should be chosen from the Eupatridæ, three from the *georgoi* and two from the *demiourgoi*.[5] At Tarentum oligarchy maintained domestic peace by the same means: it duplicated all offices, and confided each to two office holders, the one elected that the work might be well done, the other chosen by lot that the people might have its share.[6] More often still, in order to keep the plebs in submission, the oligarchs gave it minor appointments as a bone to gnaw. According to the constitution drawn up by the Four Hundred in 411 magistrates of any importance were to be chosen by the

[1] *Hymn. Hom.*, XXX, 7-16.   [2] Arist., *Pol.*, VII (VI), 4, 3.
[3] Id., *ibid.*, VIII (V), 9, 21.
[4] Id., *ibid.*, 7, 19; VI (IV), 10, 10.
[5] Id., *Ath. Const.*, 13, 2.   [6] Id., *Pol.*, VII (VI), 4, 5.

Council from among its members, while petty officials were to be elected by lot outside the Council.[1]

But it is always the fate of the oligarchic system that it creates more and more inequality, even among the privileged. The monopoly of the magistratures gave to certain families or to a coterie such power that the majority, excluded from affairs, refused to submit when once it realized its own strength. Aristotle insists on the fact that, time and time again, oligarchy succumbed to attacks directed against it, not by the mass of the people, but by an opposing faction.[2] He gives us for example a terrible picture of Crete under oligarchy:

" To remedy the faults of their constitution the Cretans have adopted an absurd means of a violence opposed to all principles of government: for very often either their fellow magistrates or some private persons conspire together and turn out the *kosmoi*. They are also permitted to resign their office before their time has elapsed. . . . But what is worst of all is that general confusion which those who are in power introduce to impede the ordinary course of justice; which sufficiently shows what is the nature of the government, or rather lawless force: for it is usual with the principal persons amongst them to collect together some of the common people and their friends, and then revolt and set up for themselves, and come to blows with each other. And what is the difference, if a state is dissolved at once by such violent means, or if it gradually so alters in process of time as to be no longer the same constitution ?"[3]

And these consequences of the oligarchic system were so general that Herodotus, when attempting to describe it, can speak only of hatreds, violence, disorder and massacres.[4]

---

[1] Id., *Ath. Const.*, 30, 2.   [2] Id., *Pol.*, VIII (V), 2, 6; 5, 8.
[3] Id., *ibid.*, II, 7, 6-8 (*v.* trans. Ellis, p. 59).
[4] Her., III, 82.

CHAPTER IV

THE BIRTH OF DEMOCRACY AND TYRANNY

I

ORIGINS OF DEMOCRACY

WHILST the great *gene* were monopolizing the growing power of the city, what was happening to all those who by their birth were relegated to an inferior position ? The artisans " worked for the public," and the thetes, hardly distinguishable from slaves, could scarcely hope ever to better their lot. As for the peasants they saw their position grow worse from day to day. The patches of land which they cultivated in the sweat of their brow were swallowed up in the midst of great estates. The land of the nobles, protected against all alienation by the kinsman's right of buying back an inheritance, was always being extended as a result of encroachments upon communal pasture grounds, the purchase of new territory, the realization of mortgages. Thus was formed in certain cities, above even the knights, an aristocracy of great landowners such as the class of *pentacosiomedimni* in Attica. On the other hand, although the villeins yielded themselves to the stern law of labour, " assigned to men by the gods,"[1] they could barely live. The wisest desired only one son in order that their land might not be split up and their children left poverty-stricken.[2] These succeeded, if circumstances were favourable, in forming a middle class of cultivators, possessing their yoke of oxen for ploughing and capable in case of war of arming themselves at their own expense. But the majority lived in privation. In bad years they were compelled to borrow from the neighbouring lord the few *medimni* of grain necessary for their subsistence and for their sowing; they had to return them with interest. Once caught in these toils they could not win free. The insolvent debtor fell into the hands of his creditors, himself, his wife and his

[1] Hes., *Op. et Dies*, 379 *ff.*; cf. 299 *ff.*   [2] Id., *ibid.*, 376.

BIRTH OF DEMOCRACY 101

children. And the most hopeless feature in the condition of the lower classes was that every man who did not form part of a privileged *genos* was delivered over without defence to the justice of grasping and irresponsible lords. For the " devourers of gifts " there was no more lucrative source of revenue than iniquity.[1] Hesiod, witness and victim of " crooked " sentences, could only call upon Zeus the protector of *Dike*[2] and recommend to the unhappy wretches who had fallen into the claws of the oppressors the resignation of the nightingale caught in the talons of the hawk.[3]

This state of affairs might have endured indefinitely if the economic regime of Greece had not been completely transformed at the end of the eighth century. Until then the cities had no resources worth speaking of save agriculture and stock breeding; though one might possibly add the profit gained from barter and piracy. But now the Greeks began to swarm over all the coasts of the Mediterranean looking for new lands and new customers; between the colonies and the mother countries agricultural produce, raw materials and manufactured goods flowed unceasingly; commerce and industry showed a hitherto undreamt of activity; near busy ports workshops multiplied and markets were organized. Henceforth the great thing was bargaining—to exchange some paltry trumpery for a few head of cattle or metal utensils. The reign of money had begun. With the shining coins of electrum, of gold and of silver, credit and the taste for speculation spread. Capitalism, growing more and more daring, dominated the Greek world. Down with the shabby life of ancient times ! Room for *chrematistike*.[4]

The economic revolution necessarily had strong repercussions in the social and political system. Certain cantons, it is true, remained outside the movement: the greater part of the Peloponnese, Bœotia and Phocis, Thessaly, Acarnania, Ætolia and Epirus conserved, with their agricultural and pastoral habits, institutions on the whole faithful to family and aristocratic principles. But everywhere else urban civilization developed in a remarkable manner. A large

[1] Id., *ibid.*, 219 *ff.*, 260 *ff.*   [2] Id., *ibid.*, 20, 252 *ff.*
[3] Id., *ibid.*, 203 *ff.*
[4] This is the term which most nearly approaches to our modern " capitalism " (*v.* Plato, *Gorgias*, p. 477*a*; *Euthym.*, p. 307*a*; Arist., *Pol.*, I, 2, 2; 3, 10).

number of cities which gave themselves up to maritime navigation became great towns. In Asia Minor, in place of a single Kyme which was content to be a rural town under archaic laws, there were ports in dozens, with Miletus at their head, which enjoyed an undreamed of prosperity. In Eubœa, on the shores of the Euripus, Eretria and Chalcis played a considerable part in colonization and joined to the products of the Lelantine plain those of the neighbouring mines. On the Saronic Gulf which was connected with the Gulf of Corinth by an isthmus of some few miles, all the important places, Corinth and Megara, Ægina and later Athens, attained political power through industry and commerce.

Who benefited from this ever-increasing movable wealth ? First of all, to a large extent, those who before had been rich in landed property. The nobles exploited the mines and quarries of their vast estates, converted into money their crops and the bullion piled away in their treasuries, gathered the thetes and the slaves in the workshops whose foundations they made, and, renouncing feats of piracy, threw themselves into safer and more fruitful enterprises. But the nobles were not the only ones to make fortunes. In the cities side by side with them there was now a wealthy middle class, some of whom were cadets or bastards of great families, others of plebeian origin. They were able to buy land whenever an opportunity presented itself; they, too, could breed horses if they so wished; and they lavishly displayed their newly acquired wealth. At first the aristocracy of birth disdained the upstart rich, just as formerly the pirate chiefs despised the captain of a merchant vessel. They did not hesitate, however, to ally themselves with them when they realized the possibilities of profitable misalliances: was it not true that " money makes the man " ?[1] Henceforward plutocracy ruled the cities. At Colophon, for instance, the knights formed only one category of the Thousand. Under a government where power was proportionate to wealth, luxury was more than a satisfaction of pleasure or vanity, it was a social mark, a veritable criterion of political values.[2]

The system of industrial, commercial and monetary economy which altered the composition of the dominant class,

---

[1] Alcæus, fr. 49; v. supra, p. 67.
[2] Cf. Arist., Pol., VI (IV), 3, 1 and 8; VII (VI), 4, 6.

often strengthened other classes or created new ones. It was that which henceforth was to oppose the *demos* to the nobles and the rich. In the Homeric epoch the artisans had no link with the husbandmen, but when the resources of each were estimated in money there was a natural *rapprochement* between people who derived from their labour a small competence. They thus formed a lower middle class. It was composed of citizens who were able to procure for themselves a suit of armour in a time when industrial progress facilitated the acquisition of arms. The number of foot-soldiers fighting in close phalanx was greatly augmented.[1] The fighting strength of the cities increased proportionately; but the knights lost their military superiority. In places where power was not abandoned to the wider oligarchy of the hoplites, as was the case at Sparta, they saw rising against their egoism the claims of those who had rendered services sufficient to justify political rights and access to the offices of state. But the middle class—the μέσοι, as Aristotle calls them[2]—was not very large. It was constantly being depleted, from above by marriages with the nobility, from below by the burdens which were imposed on agriculture and manual labour.

Broadly speaking the new economy rapidly swelled the ranks of the lower classes and aggravated their condition. As the rich became more rich, the poor became more poor. Life was hard for the generations of peasants who had to accustom themselves to buying and selling through the medium of money. They had to pay heavily for the manufactured goods which they bought in the towns, whilst only a low price could be obtained for natural commodities as a result of the facilities offered to foreign competition by the extension of maritime navigation. More frequently than in the past they were compelled to contract debts, and now that all transactions were carried through in money their creditors became more exacting and demanded the commercial rate of interest which was very high. Usury ground down the small men. Once insolvent they were liable to be sold with all their family as slaves to foreign countries, and they thought themselves lucky if they were allowed to cultivate their own land as *partiarii*, sharing the produce

---

[1] Id., *ibid.*, VI (IV), 10, 11.   [2] Id., *ibid.*, 9, 3 *ff.*

with the owner on most unfair terms. One can hardly imagine the misery of these *hektemoroi* who had a right to only the sixth of their produce, in an Attica where the *medimnus* of grain (1⅖ bushels) and the *metreta* of wine (36 quarts) were worth not more than a drachma of silver (9¼d.).[1] If in the most prosperous times the Greek peasant absorbed by his work and isolated on his land held aloof from politics,[2] still less in the archaic epoch when he was haunted and degraded by poverty was he able to frequent the agora of the town and busy himself with public affairs. And yet there were in the lower classes elements capable of taking an interest in politics: namely the plebeians of the town, small artisans and shop-keepers, workmen and labourers, fishermen and sailors, the humblest of the craftsmen whom the epic calls *demiourgoi* and the whole mass of the hired men whom it classes under the name of thetes. This proletariat lived from hand to mouth on wages which the increasing use of that human chattel, the slave, was ever forcing down. Native born there mingled with foreigners of every country; but the very fact that they were herded together in the same suburbs, in the same port, meant that ultimately they must become conscious of a feeling of solidarity and find a means of uniting themselves.

The army for the revolt was ready; it lacked only leaders. The bourgeoisie fitted by its courage, its habits of work, and its intelligence to exercise the political rights which were denied to it, placed itself at the head of the force which it found ready to its hand. From that time the city was split into two camps. The time was past when the discontented were content to groan and invoke the gods: mystics gave place to men of violence. The conflict of classes had begun.

It was long and bitter. From the seventh century to the time of the Roman conquest Greek history is full of revolutions and counter-revolutions, of massacres, banishments and con-fiscations. Party hatred was never expressed with more ferocity than in the small cities where intestine struggles assumed the form of veritable vendettas. In the midst of tempests where always " the oncoming wave towered high above the waves which passed,"[3] one hears blood-curdling cries of joy or savage fury. It is Alcæus the poet of Mitylene

---

[1] Plut., *Sol.*, 23.   [2] Arist., *Pol.*, VII (VI), 2, 1.
[3] Alcæus, fr. 19.

exulting in the news that the leader of the popular party has just been assassinated,[1] or Theognis of Megara raging against the wretches who " but now were strangers to all right and all law, wearing on their flanks goat skins and pasturing outside the walls like deer," venting his spleen on " the merchant-rulers," thinking only of " tearing with his claws a brainless populace," and finally bursting forth with the savage exclamation: " Ah ! could I but drink their blood !"[2] To understand to what paroxysms of hatred human passions can attain one must read Thucydides' description of civil wars aggravated by foreign war.[3] There is perhaps something even more hideous: the vow of hatred and ferocity which, in cold blood before the altar, the oligarchs of certain cities swore before entering the Council.[4]

The first claim which democracy was to make when it was organized in a party had for object the publication of the laws. All the opponents of aristocracy were united in interest on this point. Men had had enough of the " crooked " sentences which the Eupatridæ gave as the expression of the divine will and which were only too often the cynical exploitation of an odious and obsolete monopoly. Many generations had waited vainly for the judge, delivering sentence under solemn oath, to remember Orcus the avenger of perjury, and for the lamentations carried by Dike before the throne of Zeus to have their effect on earth.[5] Now men wished to know what the laws were. The practice of writing, which had almost disappeared for many centuries, once more began to spread, and men began to demand written laws.

This progressive step was first made in the colonies of greater Greece and Sicily. In these new countries the work of codification was more urgent and more simple than in ancient Greece; for customs there were too few in number to afford solutions for all law suits nor had they the sanction of immemorial antiquity. Zaleucos gave a code to Locri about 663-2; thirty years later Charondas gave one to Catana. The work of these legislators met with great success, that of Charondas in particular: it was copied in other Chalcidian towns of the West and doubtless inspired Androdamas of

[1] Id., fr. 20.   [2] Theognis, 53 ff., 677 ff., 847 ff., 349.
[3] Thuc., III, 82-83.   [4] v. infra, p. 319.
[5] Hes., Op. et Dies, 219 ff., 252 ff.

Rhegium when he legislated for Thracian Chalcidice;[1] then it passed into the island of Cos and thence into Asia Minor, to Teos, to Lebedos and as far as Cappadocia.[2] It is not improbable that the influence of the Sicilian colonies was exerted in Corinth and in Thebes when the first of these cities received a code from Pheidon and the second from the Bacchiad Philolaus.[3] But old Greece was not slow to furnish itself with written laws or codes according to its own methods. Crete seems to have made since the seventh century vigorous efforts to put an end in this way to private wars; to this epoch can be ascribed a number of the laws contained in the famous code of Gortyna and a law concerning aggravated assault enacted by the obscure city of Eltynia.[4] The Eleans for their part consecrated in the temple of Olympia a tablet of bronze on which was engraved a juridical document of the first importance, a *rhetra* which inflicted a decisive blow on the principle of collective responsibility.[5] One can see how the best known codes of all, those bestowed on Athens by Draco in 621-0 and by Solon in 594-3, fitted into the general scheme.

The publication of the laws had important consequences. Doubtless a great number of them, wrested from an oligarchy desirous of clinging to as many of its privileges as possible, had still a strongly aristocratic tinge. The inalienability of family patrimony and the establishing of a fixed number of estates; solemn formalities in cases of sale of landed property; the forbidding of transactions by intermediaries, of written contracts and credit transactions: such were the limitations set by the oldest legislators upon the mercantile class and the circulation of wealth. But the very fact that the laws were revealed to the knowledge of all and sanctioned by the city marked an epoch in the history of justice. The chiefs of the great *gene* lost for ever the privilege of making and interpreting at their pleasure the formulas which regulated social and political life. No longer were there *themistes* emerging from a shadowy tradition and distorted by treacherous memories or venal consciences; but in their place was the *nomos*, publicly

---

[1] Arist., *Pol.*, II, 9, 5 and 9.
[2] Herondas, *Mimiambes*, II, 41 *ff.*; *RIG*, no. 34, l. 60 *ff.*, 120 *ff.*; Strab., XII, 2, 9, p. 539.
[3] Arist., *Pol.*, II, 3, 7; 9, 6-7.
[4] *IJG*, vol. I, no. xviii; 'Εφ., 1920, p. 76.
[5] **XXXIII**, p. 244 *ff.*

promulgated, specifying exactly the division of rights and duties and, though it too was regarded as sacred, variable according to the exigencies of common welfare. At one blow the family system was shattered, undermined at its very foundations. The State was placed in direct contact with individuals. The solidarity of the family, in its active rather than passive form, had no longer a *raison d'être*. In all cases where the State itself did not recognize, at least implicitly, the right of private vengeance and private transactions, it imposed its jurisdiction on the injured party and, to enforce it, suppressed all violence with a severity which could not, however, ever go beyond the law of retaliation. When it accorded to the plaintiff pecuniary satisfaction it deducted its share to cover the expenses of justice, thus making the fine come out of the composition. But, by the prohibition of the vendetta, the *genos*, despoiled of a collective right, was freed from a collective responsibility: the jurisdiction of the State could only impute to the individual the acts for which he himself was responsible. It is the proclamation of individual responsibility in the words, " Peace and safety to the kinsmen of the accused," which gives to the Elean *rhetra* of the seventh century such moral grandeur and historic importance.

II

TYRANNY

The legislator had practically always to perform his task in the midst of raging passions and civil wars. For him there was no retiring to his study, quietly to meditate upon his work; his business was to put an end to bloodshed by effecting a reconciliation. It was for him to suggest a compromise and intervene as arbiter between surging factions. Invested with extraordinary powers he became for the necessary time the supreme head of the city. It is not certain what title he bore in general; we only know that in Asia Minor the name of *aisymnetes*, which was often assigned to the chief magistrate, passed naturally to him who had, as the name suggests, to be versed in wise customs and to settle the law. Although Solon of Athens was called *thesmothetes* or simply archon, he was nevertheless an *aisymnetes* in its widest sense, as his contem-

porary Pittacus of Mitylene was in its narrowest. A mission
of this sort was temporary: sometimes it was given for an
indeterminate time until the task assigned was completed,
sometimes for a fixed period, a year, five years or even ten.
In all cases it placed public power in the hands of a single
man: for Aristotle it was an " elective tyranny "; for Dionysius of Halicarnassus, who had in mind the history of Rome,
it was a " dictatorship," a domestic dictatorship, be it understood.[1] When the State had been saved by a peaceful
revolution its preserver returned once more into private life.

It was often difficult to find in a city convulsed by party
strife a man capable of inspiring confidence and of satisfying
everybody: for ten years Pittacus had to struggle against
the hostility of the oligarchic faction; Solon was exposed to
the attacks of rich and poor alike. Frequently resort was
had to foreign arbiters, to a sort of podesta, to put an end
to discords and bring about legislative reform. Towards the
middle of the sixth century the Athenian Aristarchus and the
Mantinean Demonax, called in as conciliators by Ephesus
and Cyrene respectively, formulated democratic constitutions
for these towns.[2] A little later Miletus, exhausted by the
struggles which the Ploutis and the Cheiromacha had indulged
in for two centuries, resolved to refer the matter to the
Parians who, after holding an enquiry, placed the government
in the hands of the landowners who had kept their estates
in a good state of cultivation during the disturbances, that is
in the hands of the middle class who had taken no part in the
civil war.[3]

But the oligarchy of the nobles and the rich had not always
the wisdom to submit to compromise. Then, in order to
overcome all resistance, and to obtain, cost what it might,
some material amelioration of its lot and at least the semblance
of political rights, the people had recourse to an extreme
method: it gave itself up to a tyrant.

What was the nature of tyrannical rule ? Everything
connected with it was extraordinary, abnormal. As a matter
of fact the name of tyrant was almost fading away when it
was introduced into the Greek world. It came probably from

---

[1] Arist., *Pol.;* III, 9 (14), 5; Dion. Hal., V, 73.
[2] Suid., *s.v.* 'Αρίσταρχος ; Her., IV, 161.
[3] Her., V, 28-29.

Lydia in the time of Gyges, and it had at first the signification of master or king, and, like its equivalent *basileus*, was applied to certain gods. On account of its origin, however, because it designated the despots of the East, it was applied in a depreciatory sense by its irreconcilable adversaries to those who held absolute power, not by right of lawful agreement between parties, but as the result of insurrection. They themselves never adopted the title of tyrant. They might have assumed the title of king, which had left behind no unpleasant memories and which would have given them a sort of sanction, had there not existed in most cities a king who was only a religious magistrate of secondary importance. There was, therefore, no official or general title to describe them, and for that reason since antiquity they have necessarily been known by the name with which their enemies stigmatized them. All the libels and·all the calumnies with which the oligarchs assailed them were credited by democracy when it no longer stood in need of them and when it perceived that arbitrary government was not in accord with its principles. From that moment all Greeks vied with each other in attacking the abominable regime—that distortion of monarchy, that usurpation by craft and violence, that elevation of a man above all laws, was the worst of all governments. Since he was placed outside all law the tyrant could not enter within it again, and the life of this omnipotent master, himself proscribed, was at the mercy of anyone who cared to take it.[1]

Before becoming in this way a sinister figure of legend the tyrant had played an historic rôle. He had been the " demagogue " leading the poor against the rich, or the plebeians against the nobles, the leader whom the multitude blindly followed and in whose hands it left all powers provided that he worked for its welfare. But tyranny did not establish itself in all parts of Greece. Apart from Sicily, where tyranny put an end to intestine strife in order to organize national defence, it had arisen only in towns where an industrial and commercial regime tended to prevail over rural economy, but where an iron hand was needed to mobilize the masses and to launch them in assault on the privileged class. With his usual perspicacity Thucydides selected the increase of wealth as the determining cause of tyranny.[2] Nothing could be

[1] Cf. **XXXVI**, vol. I, p. 242-244.   [2] Thuc., I, 13.

E

more true. Class conflict might often be aggravated by race hatreds, as for example at Miletus, where the Gergithes brought ancient bitternesses to the party of the Cheiromacha,[1] and in particular at Sicyon where the Orthagoridæ urged the pre-Dorian populace on to vengeance; but nevertheless it is in proportion as cities grow prosperous that one infallibly sees tyranny propagating itself.[2] From the coasts of Asia Minor bordering on wealthy Lydia to the banks of the Euripus, the Saronic Gulf and the Gulf of Corinth, the list of tyrants coincides as it were with a map of the great ports. If Ægina was an exception it was because the merchants in this barren island had never to face a landed aristocracy. If Athens escaped the *coup d'état* attempted by Cylon in 631 and did not fall to tyranny until 560, it was because in the interval the legislation of Solon had forced a city, until then purely agricultural, into an entirely new path. It may seem paradoxical to affect a greater precision than Thucydides and to establish a connection between tyranny and the exportation of pottery; but the connection is obvious—ceramics, the clue to international commerce, shows us Miletus as mistress of the markets in the time of Thrasybulus, then Corinth under Cypselus and Periander, and finally Athens under the Pisistratidæ.

Just as in former times the first blows were struck at the regime of the *genos* by the cadets or bastards of great families, so the tyrants who made themselves the champions of the lower classes were generally fugitives from the opposite camp. They usually succeeded in seizing power through the exercise of a high office of state or a military command, and by employing at a favourable moment a band of armed partisans, Thrasybulus was a *prytanis*; Cypselus, *basileus*; Orthagoras, *polemarch*; the majority of the Sicilian tyrants, *strategoi*. Sometimes they relied upon the support of foreign countries: Cylon attempted a *coup d'état* with the aid of the Megarians; Pisistratus returned from exile with a band of mercenaries recruited from all sides, including the men whom Lygdamis brought to him; Lygdamis, in his turn, demanded help from Pisistratus in order to return as conqueror to Naxos; under Persian domination the tyrants of Asia Minor were appointed

---

[1] Heracl. Pont. ap. Athen., XII, 26, p. 524*a*.
[2] *v.* **LXXVI.**

by the king of kings, who was their master in all things. In all cases the tyrant established himself on the acropolis surrounded by a strong bodyguard, then proceeded to a general disarmament, banished the most dangerous of the oligarchs and, to control the others, received hostages from them.

It was utterly useless after that to change the constitution, the more so as it might have been extremely perplexing to translate into legal forms the *de facto* situation. Hence the tyrants rarely suspended the political laws and never abolished the civil laws: they were content to accommodate the administration of them to their own interests and to supplement them, if occasion offered, by concessions favourable to the lower classes. They held the office which best fitted in with their plans and took care to reduce their colleagues to servile silence. Often they disdained for themselves public offices, and were content each year to invest their friends and especially their relatives, beginning with their sons, with them. Tyranny thus became a family government, a dynastic regime, and, from being an office of life tenure, tended to become hereditary. Useless for tyranny to consider appearances and respect constitutional forms, to leave the hearing of private suits to the ordinary tribunals, to have recourse from time to time to the Assembly and to take its vote, under the surveillance of club bearers, on proposals in other respects popular; all these devices, even when the master was benevolent and earned a place among the seven sages of Greece, did not disguise the revolutionary origins nor the despotic character of the government.

To humble the aristocracy and uplift the lower classes: such was the general principle which guided the tyrants. One knows the advice given by Thrasybulus to Periander, " to cut down all the ears of corn which tower above the others ":[1] it was an extolling of executions, sentences of exile, confiscations, espionage. Recourse might be had to means more gentle and more permanent in effect. To demolish the framework of nobility one needed only to replace the gentile tribes by territorial tribes in which all the citizens had an equal place: Cleisthenes, the tyrant of Sicyon, invented the notion and furnished an example which was studiously copied

[1] Her., V, 92, 6.

by his grandson and namesake, the democratic reformer of Athens.[1]

It was essential also to diminish the prestige which accrued to the nobility from the possession of hereditary priesthoods and the celebration of traditional rites of worship. The tyrants had a religious policy. " They ought always moreover," says Aristotle, " to seem particularly attentive to the worship of the gods; for from persons of such a character men entertain less fears of suffering anything illegal while they suppose that he who governs them is religious and reverences the gods; and they will be less inclined to raise insinuations against such a one as being peculiarly under their protection."[2] They sought from divine right the legitimacy which human right refused them: it was their power, even their life, which the Cypselidæ, the Orthagoridæ and the tyrants of Sicily were defending when they heaped their offerings in the temples of Delphi and Olympia, when they consulted the oracles before embarking on any enterprise, when they built temples, immolated hecatombs, instituted feasts and led the processions. But they made a choice between religions. Their devotion went first to the pan-Hellenic and civic deities. They carefully avoided, however, giving a national aspect to those which had in the *gene*, the tribes and even the cities assumed an aristocratic character. On the other hand popular gods and rustic heroes received special honours, particularly when they were connected with the locality from which the family of the tyrant had issued and which thus had a dynastic at the same time as a democratic aspect. Cleisthenes ignominiously expelled from Sicyon the Adrastus dear to the Dorian nobility; Pisistratus installed Artemis Brauronia on the Acropolis and loved to dilate on the legend of the Diacrian Theseus. In general the great vogue of Dionysus, god of the vine and of delight, dates from the time of the tyrants.

But the essential duty of the " demagogues " was to ameliorate the material condition of the lower classes. This was a constant preoccupation of the tyrants. The agrarian problem demanded a rapid solution, and for this use was doubtless made of the property of the banished. Whether that were so or not the fact remains that the peasants of Attica

[1] Id., *ibid.*, 68.
[2] Arist., *Pol.*, VIII (V), 9, 15 (*v.* trans. Ellis, p. 178).

who had demanded in vain from Solon a redistribution of property, demanded it no longer after the rule of Pisistratus. In Megara Theagenes had gained power by attacking the flocks of the wealthy breeders at the head of a starving mob;[1] he could not do otherwise than diminish the right of common pasture in order to distribute the lands among his partisans. Thanks to the tyrants there resulted a great work of reclamation which gave new extension to vineyards and olive groves. When once their demands were satisfied the new proprietors had to remain attached to the soil; there was no need for them to swell the urban plebs, nor even to fall into the habit of frequenting the agora.[2] To keep them in their own domains Pisistratus used to send out itinerant justices, Ortyges rendered justice at the gates of Erythræ and allowed no inhabitant of the demes to penetrate within, while Periander established local councils at the extremities of Corinthian territory.[3]

The most complicated problem of all remained to be solved: how were the labouring classes of the towns to be protected and kept in a state of peace ? In this matter also the tyrants were clear-sighted. In an industrial centre such as Corinth slavery was a heavy burden upon wages; Periander prohibited the introduction of new slaves.[4] After assuring to labour a just remuneration and public respect,[5] he thought himself justified, as did his contemporary Solon, in renewing the ancient prescriptions of the *gene* against the parasites who lived on the common stock without taking their share in the common labour: he passed a law against idleness.[6]

The tyrants, at least those who are recorded in history, did even more, for they were great builders. This was one of their principles. Aristotle gives a fantastic explanation of the fact: according to him they wished to impoverish their subjects in order that they should be engrossed in their daily labour and so have no time for conspiracies.[7] But this was

---

[1] Id., *ibid.*, 4, 5; *Rhet.*, I, 2, 7.
[2] Poll., VII, 68; Dion. Hal., VII, 9.
[3] Arist., *Ath. Const.*, 16, 5; Hippias of Erythræ (*FHG*, vol. IV, p. 431); Heracl. Pont., V, 2 (*FHG*, vol. II, p. 213).
[4] Heracl. Pont., *loc. cit.*; Nicolaus Damascenus, fr. 59 (*ibid.*, vol. III, p. 393); cf. Timæus, fr. 48 (*ibid.*, vol. I, p. 202).
[5] Her., II, 167.
[6] Nic. Dam., *loc. cit.*; cf. **XXXVI**, vol. I, p. 321, 434.
[7] Arist., *Pol.*, VIII (V), 9, 4.

not so; if they desired to keep the workpeople occupied, the reason was, on the contrary, that they might grow rich and that they might thereby be deprived not of the time, but of the desire to rebel. They had other reasons too: by works of public utility (aqueducts and breakwaters) they made easier the existence of the townsmen and encouraged maritime commerce; by works of adornment they won over the gods to their cause and inspired in their people a civic pride which made them forget their lost liberty. The name of Periander will be associated for ever with the spring of Pirene. Nothing contributed more to the popularity of Pisistratus than the fountain of the Nine Spouts (the Enneacrounos) and the temple of the hundred feet (the Hecatompedon). The works of Polycrates became proverbial in Greece: Herodotus who knew them *de visu* speaks of them with admiration.[1] Thus in wishing to protect in every way industry, commerce and navigation the tyrants were thinking of the *haussmannisation* of their capital.

To add to its splendour and to augment their personal prestige these sovereigns resolved to live no longer in formidable isolation on their acropolis, in the midst of guards. They led a court life. Around them thronged a numerous household; they had their doctor, their goldsmith, sometimes their favourites. To the people they gave magnificent festivals which did not consist merely of sacrifices, eating and drinking, but whose splendour was enhanced by contests in verse and theatrical representations. Their liberality attracted from all quarters architects, sculptors and poets. Like the princes of the Italian Renaissance the Greek tyrants competed with one another in enticing men of genius to their courts and in raising monuments which should surpass all others in beauty.

These rivalries, however, did not pass beyond the bounds of courtesy. As a general rule, with the exception of the Sicilian *strategoi* who had to justify their omnipotence by victories over the Siculi and the Carthaginians, the tyrants were peace lovers: they knew well that war-fever is an irresistible force and that the smallest defeat would cost them their power and their life. They felt between themselves a common bond: for had they not to cope with a common

[1] Id., *ibid.*; Her., III, 60.

danger, the hostility of the aristocracy ? Periander took counsel with Thrasybulus and offered his good offices to Pittacus; Lygdamis aided Pisistratus, on condition of assistance in his turn, and, at peace in his island, made himself the gaoler of the hostages which his one-time protégé, now his protector, entrusted to his care. To the bond of common interest the tyrants added the bond of marriage; they extended from town to town the family policy which each practised in his own city. Procles of Epidaurus gave his daughter in marriage to Periander, Theagenes took for son-in-law Cylon, while in Sicily alliances of this sort were innumerable. If the regime of tyranny could have endured who knows but that it might not have broken through the narrow autonomy of the cities and led Greece, if not to unity, at least to a type of federalism. Already Pisistratus had attempted, not without success, to force the primacy of Athens on the Ionians of the islands, and Polycrates undoubtedly thought himself adequate to represent the Hellenic race before the Persian empire.

But tyranny nowhere endured. After it had performed the services which the popular classes expected of it, after it had powerfully contributed to material prosperity and to the development of democracy, it disappeared with an astonishing rapidity. Not even genius could save it. The only example of a dynasty which maintained itself in power for a century is that of the Orthagoridæ at Sicyon. Elsewhere the son of the founder managed to retain power, but inheritance went no further than that. When consulted by Cypselus, so it was said, the oracle of Delphi assured him of good fortune " for himself and his children, but not for his children's children ":[1] whether it was prophetic or merely prophecy after the event the oracle was of general application.

Why was so powerful a regime so ephemeral ? The personal character of the tyrants, some cruel, some weak, and the difficulty of assuring the transmission of a usurped power in a family rent by jealousy, these are only contingencies which do not explain a universal fact. Must one, therefore, join in alleging the vices of the regime, such as are depicted by the historians of antiquity, and assign as cause an inevitable reaction against abominable excesses ? Some tyrants, indeed,

[1] Her., V, 92, 5.

found it in accordance with their interests to depress the
public spirit, to excite distrust among the people, to crush
out individual initiative, free thought and talent, and to
admit around them only baseness and mediocrity, espionage
and flattery. It is none the less true that the system directed
against aristocracy persisted everywhere so long as it had
the support of the people. But that support could only be
provisional. The people regarded tyranny only as an expedient. They used it as a battering ram with which to demolish
the citadel of the oligarchs, and when their end had been
achieved they hastily abandoned the weapon which wounded
their hands. " There is no free man, " says Aristotle, " who
would willingly endure such a power."[1] Men bore with it of
necessity, or shook it off with joy. The tyrant, set up on a
pinnacle by the mob and ready to work for it, was followed
by a successor divided from them by his upbringing, usually
more harsh and less capable. In proportion as it became
useless tyranny became oppressive. An inherent contradiction doomed it to death as soon as it had infused life into
democracy.

[1] Arist., *Pol.*, VI (IV), 8, 5.

PART II
THE CITY UNDER DEMOCRACY

CHAPTER I
ATHENIAN DEMOCRACY

I
History of Athenian Democracy

The political evolution of Greece is clearly defined up to the close of the sixth century. The city had grown strong by freeing the individual from patriarchal forms of servitude; the individual had become free through the protection of the city. But after these results had been achieved in some towns political power was seized by great families who succeeded in maintaining their hereditary prerogatives, whilst in others it passed to the whole body of emancipated individuals. Over against oligarchic and aristocratic cities arose cities where the voice of the people was capable of enforcing the sovereignty of the people. In which direction was the future of Greece to lie ?

If it were only a question of material prosperity the answer would not be doubtful. Sparta had at her command enormous forces, since she was the head of the Peloponnesian League—forces so enormous that she was unanimously proclaimed the commander of the Greek army and navy in the struggle against the Medes. But it was a question of much more than military organization. Could the Hellenic genius have free play within such institutions as those of Sparta ? Would it have been able to bring forth all its fruits if everywhere, as on the banks of the Eurotas, the sole preoccupation of the State had been the moulding, physically and morally, of superb hoplites and the maintenance of a constitution which would ensure that result ? No. Sparta, turned in upon itself, looking back to a past which it aimed at perpetuating,

was about the year 550 a perfect example of the ideal aristocratic city; but in the fifth century it was nothing more than
an exceptional case which one can ignore when attempting
to picture the general transformation of the city.[1] For Greece
to fulfil her destiny it was essential that she should march
forward unfalteringly along the path of her natural development, that the energies of the individual should be allowed
to expand freely for the benefit of the common weal. It was
essential that among the cities which had entered most reso-
lutely upon the new paths of democracy, there should be one
ready to march ahead of the others and capable of drawing
the others after it.   Given that condition it would fulfil a
glorious mission, it would be the school of democracy.   This
was the vocation of Athens.

All her past history had prepared her for the democratic
work she was to accomplish.

The Athenians prided themselves on being autochthonous,
that is to say on having neither a dominant race nor a subject
race within their midst: on having nothing comparable to
the helots who laboured for the Spartiates. This homogeneous and free people became a State by a synœcism which
made the men of Attica Athenians and Athens the capital of a
unified people: it was in no way analogous to the Bœotian
Confederation, in which Thebes aspired to hegemony. Thus
from the remotest times ethnical and territorial unity has been
the moral and material condition of political equality.[2] In
this city, as in the others, monarchy declined for the benefit
of aristocracy.[3] The *gene*, at least, were equal among themselves: there was nothing comparable to the Agidæ and the
Eurypontidæ who upheld at Sparta the royal prerogative.
Even within the *gene* equality prevailed, since their decisions
had to be unanimous.[4] Beneath the nobles the multitude
composed of husbandmen, shepherds, artisans, fishermen and
sailors, considered that each should be rewarded according
to his labours, and they were accustomed in the *thiasoi*
and the *orgeones* to deliberate on matters of common
interest.

---

[1] For details of Spartan institutions *v.* **XXXV**, p. 107 *ff.*; **XXXVI**,
vol. I, p. 335 *ff.*, and references to Sparta in the index of the present
work.
[2] **XXXVI**, vol. I, p. 381 *ff.*   [3] *Ibid.*, p. 395 *ff.*
[4] *Ibid.*, p. 390 *ff.*

There as everywhere the popular classes embarked upon a struggle with an oppressive oligarchy. Peasants doomed to slavery on account of their debts, merchants indignant because even wealth did not permit them to hope for political rights, all concerted in a demand for the publication of the laws whose secrets the Eupatridæ jealously guarded; they obtained the appointment of *thesmothetai* deputed for the task.[1] But the projected work came to nothing. Hatred grew more bitter, and conflict submerged the country in blood. A young noble, Cylon, attempted to install himself as tyrant on the Acropolis; he only succeeded in rousing passions to such a pitch that his adversaries did not even hesitate at sacrilege in order to massacre his partisans.[2]

Then Draco arose. One man accomplished in a few months the work which for long years the whole magistracy had striven in vain to do. He left behind a name sinister and feared, because he had armed the State with judicial power; he passed for a bloodthirsty legislator, because he endeavoured to put an end to bloodshed. Civil wars were a succession of private wars in which the *gene* hurled themselves against each other with all their strength. In order to compel the injured party to appeal to the courts Draco laid down the conditions for recourse to vengeance or to composition. In order to break up the family groups he distinguished in each of them circles of kinsmen of varying degrees of proximity, and even, in certain cases, required unanimity to be a condition of decisions taken by kinsmen; he appealed to individualism in the *genos*.[3]

This was a great step forward, but it was, nevertheless, insufficient. The landed aristocracy retained all its privileges; it extended its territories at the expense of the peasants; it enslaved the mass of insolvent debtors and sold them to foreign countries or bound them to the soil, leaving them only a sixth part of their produce (*hektemoroi*).[4] The situation was not without dramatic force. Two parties were at grips, each pushing its claims to the extreme, the one taking its stand upon traditional legality, the other evoking a revolutionary equity. Was Attica to become a country of great proprietors and serfs, like Laconia or Thessaly, or was it, heedless of

---

[1] *Ibid.*, 416 *ff.*
[3] *Ibid.*, p. 420 *ff.*
[2] *Ibid.*, p. 418.
[4] *Ibid.*, p. 411 *ff.*, 425.

established rights, to cancel debts and proceed to a new partitioning of the land ?

Once again Athens found the man who could resolve the problem which tormented her. Solon, rising between the adversaries " like a land-mark," unmoved by the attacks which came from both sides, effected what one might call a peaceful revolution. With one blow he brought down the barriers which divided the Eupatridæ from the other classes and which sheltered the traditional prerogatives of the *gene*. To set free the land he took a general and immediate measure, the " shaking off of burdens " from the *hektemoroi* (*seisach-theia*), while at the same time he suppressed all remaining collective property and liberated the soil by a series of laws on the constitution of the dowry, the right of succession and the freedom of bequest. To emancipate the individual he placed restrictions upon paternal authority, but above all he prohibited any form of enslaving, including therein penal servitude, for debt, and thus proclaimed the *habeas corpus* of the Athenian citizen. He realized clearly that agriculture alone could not maintain a large population in a country naturally poor, and he therefore attempted to give impetus to commerce and industry by attracting craftsmen from foreign countries, by protecting the *metics*, by effecting a monetary reform which opened new paths to the merchant service.

Together with this economic and social revolution there was a corresponding political reform. In the eyes of the State there now existed only free citizens. There was no distinction of birth, but fortune was to be taken into account. In accordance with a system which had for some time been tending to establish itself the citizens were divided into four classes according to the assessment of their property, that is to say into timocratic divisions: first the *pentacosiomedimni*, whose land yielded a harvest of at least five hundred *medimni* of solid (590 bushels) or five hundred *metretai* of liquid (4,290 gallons); secondly the knights who had a yield of at least three hundred (355 bushels or 2,575 gallons); thirdly the *zeugitai* who had a yield of at least two hundred (235 bushels or 1,715 gallons); fourthly the thetes who either possessed no land or whose crops did not reach the minimum of two hundred measures. The obligations and the rights of these classes were fixed in proportion to their assessment. The thetes, from the sole fact that they were citizens, could sit in the Assembly and in the courts; but they owed no military service save as rowers and they were not eligible for the magistracies. The *zeugitai* might serve as hoplites and were eligible for minor offices. The citizens of the first two classes had to enter the army as horsemen and were liable to impositions called liturgies, but they had the right to hold the principal offices. To the *pentacosiomedimni* were reserved the heaviest impositions and the highest offices, the archonship and the treasury. The author of this constitution described it well when he said: " I have given to the people sufficient power to satisfy it, without diminishing or augmenting its dignity." The reform of Solon, prudent and provisional on the political side, but bold and definitive on the social side, marks the advent of democracy (594-3).[1]

Athens, however, did not remain peaceful for long. It became necessary to allow the artisans and the merchants to enter the three first classes: the equivalence of the *medimnus* or of the *metretes* and the drachma was recognized (probably in 581), that is to say the equivalence of landed revenues and movable revenues.[2] But this concession was insufficient. Family organization had disappeared only in theory, and in fact the power of the *gene* still continued to make itself felt. On the other hand the extreme parties had not disarmed, since neither had obtained complete satisfaction, and the third party which adhered to the constitution of Solon had difficulty in defending it. There were three factions in conflict, each representing a social class, each recruited from a particular part of the country, and each having at its head a great family: the Eupatridæ of the plain were led by the Philaidæ; the merchants and the fishermen of the coast by the Alcmæonidæ; the small peasants of the mountain by the Pisistratidæ. Pisistratus won the day (560).

He seized the tyranny which the lower classes had offered in vain to Solon. He settled for ever the agrarian question by dividing out the waste land and the estates confiscated from the nobles, and thus formed a vigorous race of small holders who took deep root in the soil and played a part in

---

[1] *Ibid.*, p. 426 *ff.* [2] *Ibid.*, p. 443.

communal affairs. He encouraged maritime commerce by a far-seeing foreign policy which sent merchants to the Cyclades, to Thrace whence came gold, and to the Hellespont whence came corn. At the same time he fostered the ideal of this rural and urban democracy by festivals which he caused to be celebrated in honour of Dionysus, by theatrical representations and by the construction of magnificent buildings. Finally, since he allowed the constitution to remain in force, he supplied the people with its political education in the sessions of the Assembly and in the courts.[1]

When tyranny had rendered the services which the people expected of it, it disappeared: that was its usual fate in Greek towns. For an instant the oligarchs thought that the fall of the Pisistratidæ would turn to their advantage, but Cleisthenes, the Alcmæonid, disillusioned them.

With an admirable clarity of vision he completed the work outlined by Solon and gave its definitive form to the democratic constitution of Athens (508-7). He wished to prevent the return of tyranny, to destroy the strong organization which the nobles had given themselves in the phratries and the four Ionian tribes, to prevent social classes from grouping themselves by districts. After the proscription of the last tyrant and his children, the other members of the family who remained in Attica went into retirement, for they felt that over their heads was suspended the menace of expulsion by ostracism. The framework of the clan had no longer a place in the State. Districts were created in which the citizens were classified according to their domicile. The whole country was divided into demes,—small parishes which had their own assemblies, magistrates and administration. Each citizen was enrolled on the register of one of these demes, and the deme-name which he bore was proof of his status as citizen. All the demes, which numbered well over a hundred, were grouped into tribes (*phylai*), which no longer, therefore, were family, but topographical groups. Hence it was impossible for the ancient tribes to recognize themselves within the new tribes; but there was the potential danger of regional rivalries being perpetuated by the alliance of neighbouring tribes. To meet this danger Cleisthenes conceived an extremely ingenious device. He realized the

[1] *Ibid.*, p. 441 *ff.*

expediency of establishing intermediate divisions between the demes and the tribes, and so divided each of the three parts of the country, the town or the Asty, the coast or the Paralia, and the interior or the Mesogæa, into ten sections and assigned by lot to each tribe one group in each of the three sections. In this way each tribe was composed of three series of demes, of three *tritteis*. Although topographical then, the tribes were not unbroken territories; they were not representative of interests which might bring them into collision with one another. The decimal system of the tribes was applied to the whole political and administrative organization of the city. The Boule was composed of five hundred members, in the proportion of fifty from each tribe, chosen from the demes in proportion to their population, and each tribe in the Boule in its turn constituted the permanent committee for a tenth òf the year. Since there were only nine archons a secretary was added to them, in order that each of the ten tribes might be represented in the college of magistrates. The army consisted of ten regiments called *phylai*, each one commanded by a *phylarch*. In all circumstances the people thus appeared in ten groups. The decimal system, simple, purely logical and by that very fact contrary to all traditions, became an integral part of the democratic regime, not only at Athens, but often subsequently in Greek cities which were freeing themselves from oligarchic rule.[1]

This constitution, this imposing structure in which political theory assumed a geometrical form, agreed so well with a public spirit moulded by centuries of experimenting, that it was never contested by any party. The democrats were to amend it in certain respects, but they made no essential change. The oligarchs were to bring about revolutions; they were to aspire to re-establish in its entirety " the constitution of their ancestors," meaning by that the constitution which had destroyed the oligarchic regime for ever. Athens of the fifth century lived according to the civil laws of Solon and the political laws of Cleisthenes.

Less than twenty years after the great reform Athenian democracy was put to the searching test of the Medic wars. She came out of it strengthened. Patriotic concord and, at one moment, emigration *en masse*, had mingled classes. The

[1] *Ibid.*, p. 467 *ff.*

oarsmen of Salamis, of Mycale and of Eurymedon, as much as the hoplites of Marathon and of Platæa, were the authors of victory. The city owed its salvation as much to the thetes as to the *zeugitai* and the great landowners. Democratic sentiment naturally became intensified. The maritime cities at once placed Athens at the head of a great confederation, and for long it was the fleet which gave her her strength. The construction of a harbour and a town at the Piræus, the prosperity of industry and commerce, the development of moving capital, the abundance of money: in short, everything which constituted the economic and political splendour of Athens, now the capital of the Mediterranean world, had for result the diminishing of the real value of the property-census and the easy promotion of citizens from one class to another. There was a continual extension of democracy, and a progressive shifting of the centre of gravity towards the mass of producers and seamen.

By the year 500 the constitution of Cleisthenes had undergone important modifications: the Council of the Five Hundred had received its final organization, and the creation of ten elected *strategoi* had struck a serious blow at the college of archons.[1] Thus the way was prepared for the radical alterations in this body of 487-6: it was decided to elect the archons by lot, one from each tribe, from five hundred candidates nominated by the electors of the demes and selected not only from the class of the *pentacosiomedimni* but also from that of the knights.[2] The composition of the Areopagus, recruited from archons retiring from office, was also modified: without changing the aristocratic character of the old Council its importance was diminished. Year by year it grew less equal to the task which tradition had assigned it, so that it was soon to seem an institution of another age. This it was not only because of the permanency of its members drawn from the ranks of the rich and the nobility, but also because of the powers which it had inherited. Its functions, of an order at once judicial and political, were badly defined; but, since they included the surveillance of the laws, they might on occasion become excessive. Moreover, as a result of the services which it had rendered in the most critical moments of the Persian invasion it had magnified its authority and set

---

[1] Arist., *Ath. Const.*, 22, 2.　　　　[2] *Ibid.*, 5; cf. 26, 2.

itself up as arbiter of public life.[1] The people was to launch a fatal attack upon this stronghold of aristocracy.

In 462 the democratic party had for leader Ephialtes. It was from him that the Areopagus, first purged by judicial proceedings, received its death blow. It was deprived of the " superadded " and vague functions which made it the watch dog of the constitution and which enabled it to exercise a control over the government: it lost its jurisdiction over crimes which concerned the city, offences committed against public order by individuals or officials. It retained only functions of a religious character, which were, nevertheless, very extensive, since they included, together with the supervision of the sacred domains, jurisdiction over premeditated murder.[2] The powers withdrawn from the Areopagus passed to the Assembly of the people, the Boule and the tribunals of the Heliæa. This reform was severely criticized by Plutarch: he applies to Ephialtes the saying of Plato concerning men " who give the people unrestrained liberty." He did not see that separation of the powers accumulated by the Areopagus was necessitated by the progress of political institutions in a great city and that, when accomplished by democracy, it could not help but be to its advantage.

Ephialtes paid with his life for his devotion to the people. But he had near him a lieutenant capable of completing his work. Pericles, the great-nephew of Cleisthenes, combined with the intellect of genius and eloquence, an influence, a skill in the handling of men which enabled him to serve the people while dominating it.

Ephialtes' reform created a grave danger. Up to that time the fundamental laws had been assured of strong protection; the Areopagus was, with the Boule, one of the anchors by which the ship of state was moored.[3] If precautions were not taken the laws would be deprived of stability and find themselves incapable of resisting the variable winds of public opinion. Pericles was fully aware of this danger and devised a means of averting it. The criminal action against unconstitutional measures, the *graphe paranomon*, raised law above popular caprice and civil strife, by authorizing every

---

[1] *Ibid.*, 23, 1-2.
[2] *Ibid.*, 25, 1-2; Philoch., fr. 141*b* (*FHG*, vol. I, p. 407); Plut., *Pericl.*, 7, 9; *Cim.*, 10, 15.
[3] Plut., *Sol.*, 19, 2.

citizen to come to its aid as accuser and by making capital punishment the guarantee of its supremacy.[1]

It was also necessary, if democracy were not to be an empty word, to enable the common people, engaged in earning their livelihood, to dedicate their time to the service of the republic. Five hundred citizens were to sit in the Boule for a whole year. The heliasts, whose functions were originally confined to hearing appeals against awards made by the magistrates, were now to judge in first instance and without appeal the increasingly numerous cases in which citizens of Athens and the confederate towns were involved: they formed a body of six thousand members of which half on an average were in session every working day. There were ten thousand officials within the country (ἔνδημοι) or outside (ὑπερόριοι), five hundred wardens of arsenals, etc. Thus public affairs did not merely demand the intermittent presence of all the citizens in the Assembly; they required besides the constant exertions of more than a third of them. But half the citizens, twenty thousand in number, did not possess an income of two hundred drachmas, without which one ranked as a simple *thes*, and which was barely sufficient for subsistence. One could not compel them to forgo a year's income nor even the earnings of several days. On the other hand if the people who possessed nothing were excluded from the Council, the courts and offices of State there was nothing to prevent the government, whatever it might be called, from being in fact an oligarchy. There again Pericles was ready with an appropriate measure. He arranged for the State to make payment (*misthoi*) to the citizens who renounced the exercise of their profession in order to serve the State. *Misthophoria* became an essential element of democracy. But in the fifth century the fact that compensation was allowed only for permanent or exceptional services meant that citizens were not yet paid for the ordinary exercise of their civic right, for attendance at sessions of the Assembly; payment was only made to members of the Council, to the heliasts and to the majority of the officials, especially to those elected by lot.

The archons were among this number. Since 487-6 knights had figured with the *pentacosiomedimni* in the list of the five hundred candidates nominated by the demes for

---

[1] *DA*, art. "Paranomôn graphè." Cf. pp. 134, 178-180.

election by lot. Twenty years later, six years after the reform of Ephialtes, a further step was taken. The hoplites of Athens had just emerged from severe trials in Bœotia, and by way of reward the city granted to the class of the *zeugitai* access to the archonship.[1] But it was for the most part merely an honorary reward; for the reform of Ephialtes had diminished the importance of the archonship, since the body formed by the ex-archons had no longer political functions and the powers which the Boule had won had proportionately reduced the administrative independence of the magistrates. Nevertheless the prestige of the ancient college remained very great. But as soon as the archonship was furnished with a salary and was filled by lot there was no longer any valid reason for confining it to the three highest classes. In their turn the thetes were admitted to it. In order that this concession might not be worthless it was necessary to suppress the preliminary election in the demes, which left a clear field for jobbery on the part of the landowners: hence there was a preliminary drawing of lots to select candidates from the ten tribes, before the final process in which the office-holders were selected. But what need was there for so long a panel of nominees, a complication conducive to intrigue in the demes ? It was decided, therefore, that the panel should include not more than a hundred names, ten from each tribe. Thus the classic system of election by lot " by the bean " was arrived at.[2]

In order to consecrate the rights gained by the people in the fifth century it seemed expedient to protect them against encroachments, which were a constant menace; for it must not be forgotten that democracy, even extreme democracy—if we judge it from our modern point of view and consider not principles, but the people who benefited by it—was never in Greek cities anything but a kind of aristocracy. The citizens in Attica were a minority. Side by side with them lived at least an equal number of slaves and hardly less than half their number of metics. The metics were born of families which had long since been assimilated by the country, and they took advantage of every opportunity, and particularly of the facility of mixed marriages, to thrust themselves into the class

[1] Arist., *op. cit.*, 26, 2.
[2] *v. DA*, art. " Sortitio," p. 1406 *f*.

of citizens. Too many material advantages were attached
to the right of citizenship for the people to be willing to allow
the number of its participants to increase in this manner.
In 451-0 Pericles himself caused a law to be passed according
to the terms of which no one was an Athenian who had not
been born of Athenian parents. This law became a permanent
part of the constitution.

II

PRINCIPLES OF ATHENIAN DEMOCRACY

By the middle of the fifth century the democratic system
of Athens had assumed its definitive form, the form it was to
maintain until Greek independence was destroyed. The value
of a constitution, however, depends upon the spirit which
animates it. In the age of Pericles Athenian political life
showed a perfect equilibrium between the rights of the individual and the power of the State.

Individual liberty was complete. Since the time when
Solon had forbidden debtors to vouch for their debts with
their person this principle had been given universal application. No citizen could, under any pretext, be reduced to
servitude, or subjected to any form of slavery, even though
it might be conditional and temporary. Arrest for debt,
whether on account of indebtedness to the State or to individuals, existed no longer. The principle of individual
responsibility developed in a similar way. The interdiction
decreed by Solon profited a fortiori the family of the debtor
and, consequently, that of the condemned man. It is true
that at the beginning of the fifth century certain outstanding
crimes, such as treason, might still entail collective punishment; but the State progressively abandoned that sinister
prerogative and, before the end of the century, neither the
penalty of death nor proscription involved the children of the
guilty man. Thus Attica became the classic home of liberty.
There one saw no slaves among the citizens.[1] There even
foreigners breathed a quickening air: it attracted the exiles
of the whole of Greece, from Herodotus of Halicarnassus to

[1] Æsch., *Pers.*, 241 *f.*; Eurip., *Suppl.*, 404 *ff.*; cf. **CXXVI**, p. 129 *ff.*

Gorgias of Leontini; and Democritus of Abdera, who established himself there, said that it was better to be poor under democracy than to enjoy the semblance of happiness in the court of a king.

The Athenians, proud as they were of being free citizens, were perhaps still prouder of being equal citizens. Equality was for them the condition of liberty; it was, indeed, because they were all brothers, born of a common mother, that they could be neither the slaves nor the masters of one another. The only words which serve in their language to distinguish the republican regime from all others were *isonomia*, equality before the law,[1] and *isegoria*, equal right of speech.[2] So far from titles of nobility existing, even family names were ignored, and every Athenian without distinction coupled with his own name the name of his deme. At the most people of high birth might indulge in the luxury of perpetuating the name of their father; but they never record that of their *genos*, and the most illustrious of the Alcmæonidæ went under the name of Pericles, son of Xanthippus, of the deme of Cholargus. Though it is true, as one sees from this example, that great houses still preserved sufficient prestige to furnish a leader even to the democratic party, the State did not recognize families but only individuals who were all of equal worth. All had the same rights. They could enter the Assembly to speak, if they wished, and to vote; for the representative system did not exist and would have seemed an oligarchical restriction of *isegoria*. They could sit in the Heliæa as judges when they had qualified in age. They could present themselves as candidates for the Council and other offices, according to the constitutional forms: they were by turns compelled to obey and permitted to command. They took part in public festivals, processions, games, theatrical representations without discrimination save for the precedence (*proedria*) accorded to magistrates. It was equality which the Athenians rated above everything in their constitution. " Advancement in public life," they said, " falls to reputation for capacity, class considerations not being allowed to interfere with merit; nor again does poverty bar the way,

---

[1] Her., III, 80; V, 37; Plat., *Rep.*, VIII, p. 563*b*; Ps. Plat., *Menex.*, p. 239*a*. Cf. CXXVI, *loc. cit.*
[2] Her., V, 78; Dem., *C. Mid.*, 124.

if a man is able to serve the state he is not hindered by the obscurity of his condition."[1]

One might think that by maintaining Solon's system of timocratic classes the Athenians involved themselves in contradiction. But this was not so. Solon had made rights and obligations proportionate to wealth; when rights became equal only inequality of obligations remained and these continued to be in direct proportion to the property-census. The thetes served in the navy as oarsmen and, in case of need, in the army as light-armed foot-soldiers; they owed nothing to the treasury since they did not possess the minimum taxable income. The *zeugitai* served as hoplites and paid the extraordinary war tax, the *eisphora*. The knights served in the cavalry and discharged in turn the ordinary " liturgies." The *pentacosiomedimni* also served in the cavalry, but they were in addition burdened by the onerous imposition of the trierarchy, that is to say the commanding of a ship which they had to equip at their own expense.

Liberty and equality, these rights of the citizens, could not be exercised without imposing certain obligations on the city. The State was called upon to use its power in the service of the individuals who composed it. It was in order to guarantee more fully individual liberty that it destroyed, one by one, the last traces of collective responsibility. It was in order to ensure the reign of equality, to enable the humblest citizens to take their legitimate share in political life, that it granted an indemnity to those who placed their services at its disposal. But the obligations which it imposed were much more far-reaching. Though birth and fortune no longer conferred privileges in public life, there were always rich and poor and it was necessary that protective measures should be taken in order that the poor might avail themselves of their civic rights. Political equality would disappear if social inequality were too glaring; liberty without a minimum of property or easy means of access to it would be nothing more than an abstract principle. It was the duty of the State, therefore, since it was possessed of the power, to remedy an evil dangerous to the whole community and fatal to democracy. It had to safeguard the rights and interests, of

[1] Thuc., II, 37 (Eng. trans. Crawley [Everyman], p. 122); cf. Ps. Plat., *loc. cit.*; Eurip., *loc. cit.*

one group without at the same time disregarding and over-
riding the rights and interests of another group. With
Pericles for leader Athens succeeded in achieving a remarkable work of social service and preservation. There was no
redistribution of lands, no cancelling of debts. In a country
where landed property formed only a part of public wealth,
where movable capital was swelling as a result of commercial
development and the exploitation of a great empire, measures
partial but comprehensive would suffice to relieve the most
urgent needs.[1]

Misthophoria was one. There were many others. The
system of *cleruchies* allowed thousands of thetes to settle
abroad, all provided with land sufficient to bring in a revenue
equal to that of the *zeugitai*. In order to supply work for
artisans who remained in the capital the State turned employer: it required a fleet, arsenals, a corn-market and fortifications to connect the town with the port: and, in addition,
monuments which would make the Acropolis the most beautiful in the world. For those who were unable to work there
was well organized public assistance. War orphans were
brought up at the expense of the exchequer as children of the
nation and received, when they attained their majority, the
full armour of the hoplite. Pensions were granted to those
wounded in war and, later, help was given to disabled workmen. In normal times the city took measures to assure a
supply of cheap bread for all.[2] Several colleges of magistrates
and a series of special laws provided for this. The *sito-
phylakes* saw that grain was sold at a just price, that millers
sold flour and bakers bread at a rate proportionate to this,
and that bread had a standard weight.[3] In order to prevent
forestalling corn merchants were forbidden to purchase more
than fifty " loads " at a time;[4] in order to facilitate provisioning and to obtain regularity in trade every importer was
ordered to send to Athens two-third of the grain brought
into the Piræus,[5] and no bottomry loan could be made unless
it was secured on commodities of first necessity, particularly
corn;[6] all shipowners living in Attica were forbidden to trans-

---

[1] **XXXV**, p. 177 *ff.*; **LXXVII**, p. 13 *ff.*
[2] **XCIX**, p. 344 *ff.*, 364 *ff.*; **XXXV**, p. 354 *ff.*
[3] Arist., *op. cit.*, 51, 3.
[4] Lys., *Against Corn Merch.*, 5; cf. **XCIX**, p. 342 *ff.*
[5] Arist., *op. cit.*, 51, 4.   [6] Ps. Dem., *C. Lacr.*, 51.

port corn elsewhere than to the Piræus.[1]   Add to these the windfalls by which the whole people benefited.   When a foreign prince sent as a gift a vessel filled with grain or when a victorious expedition enabled them to carry off the enemy's harvest, there was a share for all citizens who presented themselves.[2]   Periodically the great sacrifices offered to the gods gave to each one present a goodly portion of flesh.   In years of war, at least from 410-406, there was a daily allowance of two obols, the *diobelia*, to assist the indigent.[3]

As well as providing for the material needs of the multitude the State also procured for it intellectual and moral pleasures. The numerous *choregiai* which it imposed on the rich were devoted to the preparation of lyrical and dramatic contests to which thronged a people delighting in the beautiful, and it was not one of the worst means of rendering oneself popular to show one's generosity by presenting a lavish and well trained chorus.   A time was to come when levies on individuals were to prove inadequate, when the budgetary surplus was to provide the poor with money to enter the theatre and even to feast themselves on holidays.[4]

If the city recognized in this way that it had obligations towards individuals, it was because after all it was nothing more than the whole body of citizens.   The direct government of the people necessarily turned to the advantage of the majority.   But, so long as Pericles was alive, the Athenians did not confuse the mass of individual interests with the common interest.   The obligations of the city towards its citizens were surpassed by those of the citizens towards the city.   And thus they were undertaken readily.

It was not a tacit and vague contract which bound the Athenian.   When he attained his majority, before being enrolled on the register which gave him citizenship he solemnly took the civic oath.[5]   Everywhere in Greece, according to Xenophon, the law exacted a similar oath.[6]   The young Athenians swore it in the temple of Agraulos.[7]   Of the formula

---

[1] Id., *C. Phorm.*, 37; *C. Lacr.*, 50; Lyc., *C. Leocr.*, 27.
[2] Plut., *Pericl.*, 37; Aristoph., *Wasps*, 716 et Schol.
[3] *RIG*, no. 569, A, l. 10, 12, 14, 23; B, l. 5, 6, 9, etc.; Arist., *op. cit.*, 28, 3.   Cf. **CXXIV**, vol. II, p. 212.
[4] Harp., *s.v.* θεωρικά.   [5] Arist., *op. cit.*, 42, 1.
[6] Xen., *Mem.*, IV, 4, 16.   Cf. *DA*, art. " Jusjurandum," p. 753 *ff.*
[7] Plut., *Alc.*, 15; Dem., *Emb.*, 303 et Schol.

in use in the fifth century we know only a single example, that " of recognizing no bounds to Attica save beyond the corn and barley fields, the vineyards and the olive groves."[1] But we have fuller knowledge of the fourth century which must on the whole have conformed to tradition. The scene was not lacking in grandeur.[2] The *epheboi* received their armour in the presence of the Five Hundred and, with hands outstretched above the altar, uttered these words:

" I will not dishonour these sacred arms; I will not abandon my comrade in battle; I will fight for my gods and my hearth single-handed or with my companions. I will not leave my country smaller, but I will leave it greater and stronger than I received it. I will obey the commands which the magistrates in their wisdom shall give me. I will submit to the existing laws and to those that the people shall unanimously make: if anyone shall attempt to overthrow these laws or disobey them, I will not suffer it, but I will fight for them, whether single-handed or with my fellows. I will respect the worship of my fathers."[3]

Such were the obligations which the citizens had to recognize before being invested with rights; such were the vows which renewed year by year before the gods the omnipotence of the city.

This omnipotence was wielded by the whole body of citizens in a democracy. The constitutional theory of Athenian democracy was very simple; it can be expressed in a single phrase: the people is sovereign (κύριος). Whether it sat in the Assembly or in the courts it was absolute sovereign in all that concerned the city (κυριότατος τῶν ἐν πόλει ἁπάντων).[4] A political principle, however, in all times and places, lends itself to various interpretations and gains precise meaning only in practice. The contemporaries of Herodotus employed the same formula as did those of Aristotle and Demosthenes, but they neither understood it nor applied it in the same fashion. In the fourth century the principle: " the people has the right to do what pleases it " (ἐξὸν αὐτῷ ποιεῖν ὅ τι ἂν βούληται),[5] was pushed to its furthest limits; it was even sovereign over the laws (κύριος καὶ τῶν νόμων).[6] In the fifth century it

---

[1] Plut., *loc. cit.*
[2] *v.* P. Girard, art. " Ephebi," *DA*, vol. II, p. 624-625 and illustration 2677.
[3] Poll., VIII, 105; Stob., *Floril.*, XLIII, 48. Cf. P. Girard, *loc. cit.*
[4] Ps. Dem., *C. Neaira*, 88; cf. Her., III, 80; Arist., *Pol.*, II, 9, 3.
[5] Ps. Dem., *loc. cit.*   [6] Arist., *Pol.*, VIII (V), 4, 6.

was king,[1] but it was not yet tyrant.[2]   It admitted that there were limits to the arbitrary power of the majority.   Of the Athenians of this time, as of the Spartans, one can say both of their public and private life: " They are free but they have not an absolute freedom: for above them is a master, the law."[3]

The *graphe paranomon* curbed the enthusiasms of the Ecclesia, as well as the excesses of the demagogues.   Even after the death of Pericles it remained efficacious.   One day, in tragic circumstances, the people refused to heed it; but they were not slow to perceive their error.   In happened in 406 during the terrible trial of the generals who had returned victors from Arginusæ.   In the midst of heated passions, one courageous citizen attempted to suspend the proceedings, sanctioned by a decree of the Council and the people, by raising the plea of illegality.   The crowd protested that it was " monstrous to deprive the people of its power of doing what it pleased " ($\delta\epsilon\hat{\iota}\nu o\nu$ $\epsilon\hat{\iota}\nu a\iota$ $\epsilon\hat{\iota}$ $\mu\acute{\eta}$ $\tau\iota\varsigma$ $\dot{\epsilon}\acute{a}\sigma\epsilon\iota$ $\tau\grave{o}\nu$ $\delta\hat{\eta}\mu o\nu$ $\pi\rho\acute{a}\tau\tau\epsilon\iota\nu$ $\grave{o}$ $\mathring{a}\nu$ $\beta o\acute{\nu}\lambda\eta\tau a\iota$).[4]   It was in vain that certain members of the bench, Socrates among them, protested against putting the matter to the vote; they yielded to threats, Socrates alone excepted;[5] the resolution was adopted, the accused were condemned to death and led out to execution.   But a little later the Athenians repented: they arraigned by a decree of impeachment (*probole*) those who had deceived the people, and the principal culprit was to die of starvation, detested of all.[6]   This exception is excellent proof of the power of the rule: in the fifth century popular sovereignty was something other than arbitrary power, than tyranny.   Democracy must have for foundation respect for the law.

What then did law mean to the Greeks in general, and particularly to the Athenians of the fifth century ?

Opposed though the political ideas of democracy and oligarchy were, they conceived of law in a practically identical fashion.   When, however, one attempts to define what that

1 Aristoph., *Wasps*, 549.
2 Arist., *loc. cit.*; II, 9, 3; cf. VI (IV), 4, 4-5.
3 Her., VII, 104.   4 Xen., *Hell.*, I, 7, 12.
5 Id., *ibid.*, 14; *Mem.*, I, 8; Plat., *Apol.*, p. 32*b*; Ps. Plat., *Axioch.*, p. 368*d*.
6 Xen., *loc. cit.*, 35.

idea was in the classical era, one is surprised to find in it a singular contradiction. Law appears in a two-fold aspect: it is a sacred and immutable thing; and it is a human contrivance—" laic " one might say—and consequently subject to change. One can, by analysis, distinguish these two conceptions,[1] and then they seem irreconcilable; actually they harmonized tolerably well in daily practice.

On the one hand the ancient *themis* of the *genos* was introduced into the *dike* of the city by transforming the most venerable *themistes* into what were called *thesmoi*. Such was the word which signified in the oldest days the fundamental rules of public law. These rules were of an essentially religious nature. They did not distinguish as yet between the temporal and the spiritual. Ritual prescriptions as much as legislative enactments, they differed in no respect when they treated of property, marriage, succession, crimes and delinquencies, political relationships, and when they determined sacrificial rites, honours due to the dead, forms of prayers or oaths. What was their origin ? No one knew, or at least no one knew its date, but they did not doubt that they had been *established* ($\theta\acute{\epsilon}\sigma\mu\sigma\varsigma=\tau\acute{\iota}\theta\eta\mu\iota$) for eternity by the gods. The gods worshipped in the families and the city, but above all the great deity of the city, had in the dim past revealed them to men; and the most venerable of them, those which sprang from the soil at the same moment as the first ear of corn, had for author Demeter Thesmophoros. They were repeated from generation to generation by oral tradition, bequeathed from father to son in the *gene*, communicated by the *gene* to the priests or the magistrates of the city, and transmitted in the city itself from age to age by the archivists, the *mnemones*, the *hieromnemones*, the *aisymnetai*. They were very brief texts, rhythmical that they might be remembered the more easily, and were chanted in monotone.[2] Of preamble they had no need for they were commands from above; they offered no reasons, since they were imposed by virtue of a transcendental authority. When time had obscured them or when they were inadequate, recourse was had to *exegetai*, whose function was sacerdotal, to interpret them. At the most it might be

[1] *v.* **XXVIII,** l. III, chap. XI; l. IV, chap. IX.
[2] Arist., *Probl.,* XIX, 28; Hermippos, fr. 7 (*FHG,* vol. III, p. 37); Strab., XII, 2, 9, p. 239.

necessary ultimately to codify them, a work entrusted to the *thesmothetai*. But their sacred character prohibited any alteration of them. This was to remain an absolute principle: even when the laws were emancipated from divine tutelage, and new ones were made, the ancient ones remained un-abrogated. Hence it happened that litigants adduced in their suits irreconcilable texts. These old beliefs in the supernatural power of the *thesmoi* remained particularly attached to the penalties of criminal law. There were formulas laden with imprecations, the ἀραί. The penalties which they fulminated, especially that of outlawry, *atimia*, had such potency that they fell of themselves on whomsoever had provoked them: there was no need even for judgment to be delivered in order to fall within the orbit of their witchery.[1]

On the other hand there existed a law which owed nothing to revelation, the *nomos*. Here everything was man made. Its essential characteristic was that it was written. It was not the private property of a few privileged persons who had inherited it from the gods; it was stripped of all mystery; it was known to all, it belonged to all. The law bore the name of its author: everyone knew that it was Solon's law, or Cleisthenes', or simply the law of some common citizen. And it could not have been incorporated in the body of legislation unless the people had voted for it; it could not have received the assent of the majority had it not been conceived in the common interest. It had, therefore, to allot to each his share of rights and obligations. The *nomos* was the organization of distributive justice (*nemesis*), and it was for that reason that Aristotle declared that there was no order outside the law (ἡ γὰρ τάξις νόμος).[2] The *nomos* was the mean, the common measure which procured the greatest sum of equity, the impartial rule which restrained individual or collective passions, the master who opposed excesses of liberty.[3] The sovereign law was that which secured the reign of reason, *nous, logos*.[4] Thus, even when idealized, the laws could only take from man the best that was in him. But, in actual fact, they were good or bad according to the constitution, according to the city,[5] and they inevitably remained incomplete, always

---

[1] Cf. **XXXIII**, p. 569 *ff.*; **XXXIV**, p. 53 *ff.*
[2] Arist., *Pol.*, III, 11, 3.
[3] Id., *ibid.*, 10, 4; 11, 6; Her., VII, 104.
[4] Arist., *loc. cit.*, 11, 4.   [5] Id., *ibid.*, 6, 13.

imperfect in some respect.[1] They had no absolute value. When Solon was asked whether he thought that he had given the most perfect laws to the Athenians he is said to have replied: "No, but those which best suited them." Since they were not infallible, human laws were not eternal; they endured only so long as they were accepted by the conscience of the people: if customary law was silently transformed by the insensible evolution of civilization, written law lent itself to change each time that the need was manifested. Law was, after all, a relative and conventional thing: it was not amiss that the word *nomos* was also used to signify a musical mode and all money in circulation.

When the Greeks spoke of laws they did not, as we do to-day, place constitutional laws in a class apart. There was not a single city which had its constitution drawn up in writing; its place was taken by a body of customs and regulations inserted in various laws, through which was manifested "the soul of the city."[2] It is true that Aristotle is constantly speaking of constitutions; but one must understand by that the government of a city, which resulted from the organization of the magistracies in general and of the sovereign magistracy in particular, the partitioning of powers, the attribution of sovereignty, the determination of the goal which the political community set before itself.[3] That suffices, however, to enable one to discriminate, after the example of the philosopher, between the constitution and the laws properly so called, at the same time admitting, as he did, that the one is the reflection of the fundamental character of the other.

But the laws, however, did not with the Greeks form a systematic whole, a code in the modern sense. They had been fashioned from day to day, at least since the epoch when the first legislator, a Zaleucus, a Charondas, a Draco or a Pittacus, had been commissioned to formulate existing customs or new ordinances. But it was imperative that these texts should be classified in some way. This necessary classification was always made, even by great legislators, not in accordance with a logical conception but with a view to practical utility. The aim was to furnish each magistracy with the documents which it required. If there is anything

---

[1] Id., *ibid.*, 11, 8. [2] Isocr., *Areop.*, 14; cf. 78.
[3] Arist., *loc. cit.*, 4, 1; VI (IV), 1, 5.

which remotely, very remotely, resembles our codes, it is the kind of guide or list of instructions with which the officials of the State were provided. Aristotle expresses it with all the lucidity one can wish for: " The laws are something different from what regulates and expresses the form of the constitution; it is their office to direct the conduct of the magistrate in the execution of his office and the punishment of offenders."[1]   Examples are not lacking. The Athenians, named, indeed, a certain number of isolated laws according to their content: law concerning trierarchy (τριηραρχικὸς νόμος),[2] law of eisangelia (εἰσαγγελτικὸς νόμος),[3] laws concerning mines (μεταλλικὸς νόμος),[4] fiscal laws (τελωνικοὶ νόμοι),[5] commercial laws (ἐμπορικοὶ νόμοι).[6]   But as a general rule, when the laws were classified they bore by way of official label the name of the magistrates or the courts whose duty it was to apply them.[7]   In the annual session when the people were consulted as to whether the laws in force should be maintained or amended, they voted in succession on the laws pertaining to the Council (βουλευτικοὶ ν.), on the laws common to the different magistracies (κοινοὶ ν.), on the laws which affected the nine archons, and finally on those which dealt with the other magistracies.[8]   There was a law of the Areopagus,[9] a law concerning the public arbitrators or diaitetai,[10] a law concerning the king,[11] a law of the treasurers;[12] there was a law concerning the archonship, which contained provisions as disparate as the functions of this magistracy.[13] The same practice was followed elsewhere, from Corcyra[14] which had a law of the agonothetes, to Magnesia which had a law of the polemarch,[15] and Miletus which had a law of the agoranomoi and the paidonomoi.[16]   It was the same in the kingdom of Pergamum, where a law concerning the astynomoi has been discovered, which must have been inspired by the

1 Id., ibid., VI (IV), 1, 5 (Eng. trans. Ellis, p. 108).
2 Dem., De Coron., 312.   3 Hyper., P. Euxen., 3, 4, 10.
4 Dem., C. Pantain., 35.   5 Id., C. Timocr., 190.
6 Id., C. Lacr., 3.
7 v. R. Schoell, Sb. MA, 1886, p. 92 f.; cf. VII, vol. I, p. 303 f.
8 Dem., C. Timocr., 20.
9 Id., C. Aristocr., 22; Lys., Murder of Eratosth., 30; C. Andoc., 15.
10 IG, II², no. 179.
11 Athen., VI, 26, p. 234 f.; 27, p. 235c-d.
12 Arist., Ath. Const., 8, 1; 47, 1.   13 Plut., Sol., 24.
14 IG, vol. IX, ii, no. 694.   15 IMa, no. 14.
16 LXXXII, p. 6, l. 54; p. 8, l. 80; cf. p. 17.

ordinances concerning the ædiles of the Roman empire,[1]
and in the Egypt of the Antonines, where we have learnt from
a papyrus of the existence of the *gnomon* of the *ideologos*.[2]

It was, however, to these laws of diverse origin, to these
prescriptions scattered among purely practical regulations,
that the Greeks applied the idea of moral grandeur, of super-
human dignity which the *themistes* of past centuries had
bequeathed to them. They regulated the whole life of the
community and of individuals; they were the moral nexus,
the vital principle of a people. The result was that this
confused assemblage inspired a religious respect. Heraclitus,
the first physician of Ionia to employ his dialectic to the study
of moral questions, attributes to law a divine origin before
making this declaration of more than Ionian civic patriotism:
" The people ought to fight for the law as for the walls of its
city."[3]   All that the Greeks ever thought of the law, from the
most ancient beliefs to the most recent conceptions, even to
the distinction between nature and the laws established by
the sophists and here turned against them, finds itself embodied, not without contradiction, but with lofty grandeur,
in a passage which may be attributed to Demosthenes:

" The whole life of men, whether they inhabit a great city or a
small, is ordered by nature and the laws. Whilst nature is lawless
and varies with individuals, the laws are a common possession, controlled,
identical for all. . . . They desire the just, the beautiful, the useful.
It is that which they seek; once discovered, it is that which is erected
into a principle equal for all and unvarying; it is that which is called
law. To it all owe obedience, for this reason among others, that all
law is an invention and gift of the gods, at the same time as it is an
ordinance of wise men, the common covenant of the city according to
which all in the city ought to mould their life."[4]

But the noblest idea which a Greek expressed of human
laws, quasi-divine as they were considered, is to be found expounded by Socrates in the famous prosopopœia of the *Crito*.
Though deprived of the sublime beauty which a dramatic
form would give it, the fragment still remains of very great
interest, since it shows us of what kind of respect a great
mind believed the laws to be worthy, even though he thought

[1] Dittenberger, *Or. Gr. inscr. sel.*, no. 483.
[2] Cf. Th. Reinach, *NRHD*, 1920, p. 583 *ff.*; 1921, p. 5 *ff.*
[3] Heraclit., fr. 114, 44 (Diels, *Fragm. der Vorsokr.*, 4th ed., vol. I,
p. 100, 86).
[4] Ps. Dem., *C. Aristocr.*, I, 15-16.   Cf. **LXXVII**, p. 18 *ff.*

them bad laws. He who violates the law destroys the city as far as it is in his power to do so. The State cannot subsist when its decrees are rendered nugatory, when individuals are able to destroy their purpose. One must accept them, even though they are unjust. For it is by virtue of an inviolable contract that the citizen owes obedience to the laws. He is beholden to the laws and to the State for his birth and his education. Brought into the world, nourished, reared by the laws, he is their slave; he has not the same rights over them as they have over him. As to his parents and his master, so to the laws and his country, he must not return injury for injury, nor blow for blow. Country is more than a mother: for her sake all things must be endured. It is one's duty to execute her orders, unless by legitimate means she may be induced to alter her decision. Each one is free, after he has been invested with civic rights, to renounce them and leave the country with all his possessions; but he who remains enters wittingly upon a contract to obey the laws.[1]

To sum up, Athenian democracy of the fifth century appears as the exercise of sovereignty by free and equal citizens under the ægis of the law. The law, which protects the citizens one against the other, defends also the rights of the individual against the power of the State and the interests of the State against the excesses of individualism. Before the last years of the fifth century there is no sign that liberty has degenerated into anarchy or licence, nor is the principle of equality carried so far as to entail the denial of the existence of mental inequalities. We are in a city where Anaxagoras, the friend of Pericles, develops the idea that the mind (the νοῦς) " infinite and self-ruled . . . began to revolve first from a small beginning; but the revolution now extends over a larger space, and will extend over a larger still."[2] This theory acquired a political meaning: in order that Greece might govern the barbarians, as she ought to do, one city in Greece must be at the head of all the others and in that city one man must be at the head of the people. To fulfil its destiny Athenian democracy submitted to the moral dictatorship of genius.

[1] Plat., *Crit.*, p. 50a-51a.
[2] Anaxag., fr. 12, 13 (Diels, *loc. cit.*, p. 404 *ff.*).

CHAPTER II

IDEAS ON DEMOCRACY

THE Athenians were perfectly aware that the establishment of a democracy in a town as populous as theirs was a striking innovation. They were proud of their constitution. Of the three systems of government which the Greeks distinguished one only appeared commensurate with human dignity: the one which opposed the principle of equality to the oligarchic principle and maintained against tyranny the right to liberty. Liberty and equality, this was properly the motto of the Athenians; to it they added fraternity under the name of *philanthropy*. It was not without a feeling of pride that they compared their city with all the others, especially with that Sparta towards which all the adversaries of the ideas which they cherished turned with longing. Doubtless the statesmen and poets of Athens indulged in exaggerated praises when they spoke of their constitution; but even these high-flown sentiments have a historic value, for such out-pourings reveal to us the soul of a people; it is enthusiasms which reveal an ideal.

No one has expounded the ideal of Athens with more magnificent and powerful eloquence than Thucydides. The historian carefully avoids the insincerity of speaking in his own name, since he had no particular affection for the policy of his own country. It is to the friend of Anaxagoras, to the animating spirit of Athenian democracy, to the " Olympian " who for thirty years dominated with all the greatness of his soul the petty doings of the agora, to Pericles, that he attributes the splendid commentary whose every word is like a medal of pure gold to the image of Athena Polias.

When called upon to deliver the funeral oration (the *epitaphios*) for the warriors who had died for their country, the orator declared that, without delaying to eulogize those who in the past or the present had contributed to the greatness of Athens, he would examine the institutions and the national

F   141

habits which were the essential cause of its strength and prosperity.[1]

" Our constitution does not," he first of all asserts, " copy the law of neighbouring states; we are rather a pattern to others than imitators ourselves. Its administration favours the many instead of the few; this is why it is called a democracy." Equality is its fundamental principle. In private life the law makes no distinctions between citizens. In public life consideration is accorded neither to birth nor to wealth but solely to merit, and not social distinctions but capacity and talent prepare the way for advancement. Equality thus understood, equality which gives free play to individual merit, in no way prejudices liberty. Each is free to act as he will, without fear of jealous curiosity or injurious looks. But the liberty of individuals is limited by the laws of the State, the obligations of civic discipline. Public order demands submission to the established authorities, obedience to the laws, especially to the laws of brotherhood which ensure the protection of the weak and to the unwritten laws which emanate from the universal conscience.

Such a constitution sheds upon all innumerable benefits. At Athens life holds more delights than anywhere else: frequent festivals there refresh the spirit, and overseas trade brings there in abundance the fruits of the whole world. But this does not preclude apprenticeship in war. Everything however is done in broad daylight, without mystery and without constraint. There is no law which closes the city to foreigners; no painful discipline which would make manliness a product of education. The natural courage of the Athenians is sufficient to enable them in hours of danger to show themselves equal to the enemy whose existence is one long labour. And they have other titles to glory. They cultivate the beautiful without extravagance and knowledge without effeminacy. For them wealth is not a thing to boast about but an instrument to employ, and poverty is only a disgrace if no attempt is made to struggle against it. How could such men be incapable of fostering their own interests and at the same time those of the city ? At Athens the craftsmen are judges of politics, and he who takes no part in public affairs is regarded as useless. The citizens, assembled

[1] Thuc., II, 36-41.

in one body, can judge wisely of decisions to be taken, for they do not think that words are a stumbling block in the way of action, but on the contrary they wish enlightenment to shine forth from discussion. Whilst usually boldness is the fruit of ignorance and reflection a cause of hesitation, Athens proceeds from deliberation to daring. A last trait which distinguishes her from other nations is her generosity. She confers benefits without calculation, without ulterior motives, and it is by her persistence in rendering services that she forestalls the weakening of gratitude. " In short," Pericles concludes, " I say that as a city we are the school of Hellas " (τῆς Ἑλλαδος παίδευσιν).

These ideas are too finely conceived and too consistent to give a faithful and complete picture of reality, but they only throw a flattering light upon it without distorting it. The most striking point in these passages of Thucydides is not the reflections upon democratic equality; they are customary and recall the commonplaces on *isonomia* which already Herodotus and Euripides had delighted in.[1] What merits attention is the exposition of the relations between the State and the individual. In it there are maxims which one might say had inspired the Declaration of the Rights of Man. Political liberty is only the consequence of the liberty which all citizens enjoy in their private life. What then of that oppression to which, according to a widespread prejudice, the omnipotence of the city subjected them ? They were accustomed to order their own lives freely, and they could, if they wished, take part as a matter of course in discussions of affairs of common concern. Thus Euripides understood it when he makes Theseus, the hero of democracy, say: " Liberty is epitomized in these words: ' Let each man who would give good advice to the city come forward and speak.' Each one can according to his will either bring himself into prominence by speech or keep silence. Is there a finer equality than this for citizens ?"[2] In short, by all these principles, Athenian democracy of the fifth century tended to maintain a just balance between the legal power of the State and the natural right of the individual.

But to this brilliant picture is opposed one of appalling blackness. Even the authors who are ready with their

---

[1] Her., III, 80; Eurip., *Suppl.*, 406 *ff.*, 429 *ff.*
[2] Eurip., *loc. cit.*, 438 *ff.*

praises offer also searching criticism. In Herodotus, when Otanes has spoken in favour of democracy, Megabyzus makes answer in bitter terms: " The mob has no common sense; there is nothing more unintelligent, more unbalanced. . . . The tyrant at least knows what he is doing; but the people does not know. And how should it, when it has neither knowledge nor natural perception of the good and the beautiful ? It rushes headlong into undertakings and presses forward in them without reflection, like a winter torrent."[1] In the tragedy of Euripides, the stranger to whom Theseus replies withers with scorn " the orators who excite the multitude and impel it in every direction for their own interests, full of charm to-day and making its delight, to-morrow noxious, and dissimulating their faults by means of calumnies that they may escape punishment." Even when free from demagogy democracy appeared to him unjustifiable; for " how can the people, incapable of right reasoning, direct the city into the right path ?"[2] As for Thucydides he gives as counterpart to the portrait of Pericles that of Cleon and puts these words in the mouth of Alcibiades: " As for democracy the men of sense among us knew what it was . . .; but there is nothing new to be said of an obvious absurdity."[3]

It was not, however, historians and poets resolved to investigate the arguments for and against who inflicted the most telling blows on Athenian democracy, but a politician, an avowed antagonist, the anonymous author of the *Republic of the Athenians* which was for long included in the works of Xenophon. This pamphlet, written probably in 424, is the work of a haughty aristocrat, of a doctrinaire speaking with cool calculation in a *hetaireia*. He pursues his argument with imperturbable logic, sufficiently calm to make a penetrating analysis of the constitution he abhors without allowing his judgment to be warped by hate, but at the same time so full of hatred and so fanatical that he does not censure the democrats, enemies not to be reasoned with, but seeks only to dispel the illusions of the moderate oligarchs. What folly to imagine that democracy is capable of improvement ! It is detestable because it is true to its own nature, because it conforms to its own principle, because it cannot be otherwise.

[1] Her., III, 81. [2] Eurip., *loc. cit.*, 412 *ff.*
[3] Thuc., VI, 89, 6.

Democratic equality, the tyranny of numbers, has for inevitable consequence the impotence of the good and the domination of the bad. No reform can prevent the mob from being ignorant, undisciplined, dishonest, "because poverty impels men to base acts from the lack of education and knowledge which want of money entails."[1] Democratic government causes the worst elements in the city to prevail: such is the fundamental and inevitable fact:

" The objection may be raised that it was a mistake to allow the universal right of speech and a seat in council. These should have been reserved for the cleverest, the flower of the community. But here again it will be found that they are acting with wise deliberation in granting to even the baser sort the right of speech, for supposing only the better people might speak, or sit in council, blessings would fall to the lot of those like themselves, but to the commonalty the reverse of blessings. Whereas now, anyone who likes, any base fellow, may get up and discover something to the advantage of himself and his equals. It may be retorted: ' And what sort of advantage either for himself or for the people can such a fellow be expected to hit upon ?' The answer to which is, that in their judgment the ignorance and baseness of this fellow, together with his goodwill, are worth a great deal more to them than your superior person's virtue and wisdom, coupled with animosity. What it comes to, therefore, is that a state founded upon such institutions will not be the best state: but, given a democracy, these are the right means to secure its preservation. The people, it must be borne in mind, does not demand that the city should be well governed and itself a slave. It desires to be free and to be master. As to bad legislation it does not concern itself about that."[2]

The tirade is cynical. When the pamphleteer maintains that the multitude does not do ill from impulse or error, but from inevitable obedience to the law of the regime and simply because evil is its good, he does not seek to raise a smile by his cutting irony, he hopes to convince by an acute observation. He believes himself to be impartial. And impartial he is, indeed, whenever there is no fear of truth's being prejudicial to his argument. Although he condemns the encroachments of Athenian justice, he recognizes that the great number of judges attached to each court is an obstacle to intrigues and venality, he admits that with any other system sentences would be less equitable. He regrets nevertheless— and what greater praise could there be than such a regret ?— that Athenian democracy commits so few injustices and so does not add to the number of malcontents.[3]

[1] Ps. Xen., *Rep. of the Athen.*, 1, 5.
[2] *Ibid.*, 6-8 (Xen., *Works*, vol. II, p. 277, Eng. trans. Dakyns, [Macmillan]).
[3] *Ibid.*, III, 7, 12.

A theory systematic to this degree was by its essential characteristics admirably suited for the philosophers who recognized no legitimate supremacy save that of intelligence.

The rationalism of Socrates found ample matter for criticism in the democracy of his day. He had not an atom of respect for an assembly " composed of fullers, cobblers, masons, metal-workers, labourers, pedlars, hawkers, dealers in old goods."[1] Not that he despised manual labour, he the son of an artisan, who loved nothing so much as to chat with the people in the workshops and the market-place; but he was convinced that merit and virtue lay only in knowledge and feared to see the city governed by ignorance. The election of magistrates by lot seemed to him purely and simply an aberration.[2]

One can readily understand, therefore, why Socrates was accused by such a man as Anytos of despising the established laws. But he denied that he had ever contemplated the overthrowing of national institutions by force. And in fact whatever he may have thought of it he showed a certain weakness for Athenian democracy; he confessed with disarming frankness that he was in no way tempted to leave his country in order to bring his practice into accordance with his precepts. Though unceasingly he eulogized the constitutions of Lacedæmon and Crete he showed not the slightest desire to see them at close quarters. Consistent with himself, he recognized that to continue to form part of a community which one is free to leave is to take a tacit oath to respect its laws; and yet " how could a city be pleasing to one who did not love its laws ?"[3] Nor did he aspire to play the part of an exile in his own country. Not only did he admire in Pericles the ideal of the orator,[4] but he wished each citizen to contribute his share towards maintaining the high reputation of Athens abroad.[5] He believed it his duty to take part in political life: he was nominated as *bouleutes* and gave, as *prytanis*, a fine example of civic courage in opposing the majesty of the laws as against an assembly delirious with passion.[6] The true Socrates appears indeed to have been the

[1] Xen., *Mem.*, III, 7, 5-6.   [2] Id., *ibid.*, I, 2, 9; *v. infra*, p. 212.
[3] Plat., *Crit.*, p. 52e-53e.   [4] Id., *Phædr.*, p. 269e-270a.
[5] Id., *Apol.*, p. 35a-b.   [6] Id., *ibid.*, p. 32b-c.

one whom Xenophon portrays in the *Memorabilia*:[1] to Char-
mides, a man well versed in public affairs, he denies the right
of abstaining from serving his country; he censures the
cowardice of the citizen who is only too willing to offer advice
on occasion to the magistrates and has a fine flow of talk in
aristocratic clubs, but who is terror-stricken when he stands
before the people. Not he but a disciple inaccurately record-
ing his ideas declared that the case of Athens was hopeless,
that any attempt to intervene would merely doom to death
whoever should attempt it, that the place for a man resolved
to combat injustice without uselessly sacrificing himself was
in private life, not in public life.[2]

Plato indeed condemns democracy in general without
qualification.[3] He takes a stand diametrically opposed to
the theory formulated by the Pericles of Thucydides. Liberty
a boon ? Rather it is the cause of all evil. The Athenian
constitution a model ? It is rather the governments of
Sparta and Crete which more nearly approach the ideal to be
pursued. As in men's hearts so in the city must order be
made to rule; individual diversities must be suppressed, the
personal must be renounced, all men must think alike on all
things. Only thus will the day arrive when a caste of philosophers, upheld by the warriors and freed from all egoism by
community of goods, of women and of children, will dominate
the ignorant throng of workers. Democracy is the exact
opposite of that ideal. It is the rule of individualism, in which
each man does as he pleases. It is, therefore, the prey to
a disconcerting diversity, to a perpetual instability. The
liberty which it institutes and which makes life appear so
good and glorious is nothing other than the negation of order,
a chaos in which even the glimmerings of talent and genius
are only phantasmagoria and impotence. The equality upon
which it prides itself, the placing of unequal men upon an
equal footing, is a flagrant inequality. By allowing to all
desires the same legitimacy, to all aspirations the same rights,
it creates lawlessness and immorality, makes moderation
seem weakness and scrupulousness childishness. When a
city is in that position its constitution is nothing but a many-
coloured cloak. It is even inaccurate to speak of *a* constitu-

---

[1] Xen., *loc. cit.*   [2] Plat., *loc. cit.*, p. 31*e*-32*a*.
[3] Id., *Repub.*, VIII, p. 557, 560 *f.*; cf. p. 563*d*.

tion, for it is eternally changing at the bidding of passions, and there are as many as are demanded in the market-place. In brief, democracy inevitably passes into *ochlocracy*, and the domination of that monstrous beast the multitude (θρέμμα μέγα καὶ ἰσχυρόν) is nothing less than a re-awakening of Titanic nature (παλαιὰ γιγαντικὴ φύσις).[1]

By a penetrating analysis Aristotle reaches a conclusion almost as severe.[2] He starts with the fact that the three pure forms of government, monarchy, aristocracy and republicanism or *politeia*, are equally susceptible to corruption. Whilst monarchy degenerates into tyranny, and aristocracy into oligarchy, republicanism degenerates into demagogy.[3] Let us follow this process.

And first how can democracy be identified ? It is a common error to base it exclusively on the sovereign right of the majority; but in oligarchy also the majority is sovereign. Democracy exists where sovereignty belongs to all free men without distinction of fortune. Consequently there is no democracy when a minority of free men dominates a majority of men deprived of freedom; nor does it exist when sovereignty belongs to the rich, even though they be in a majority. In short " democracy is a state where the freemen and the poor, being the majority, are invested with the power of the state."[4]

Democracy thus defined presents a multiplicity of forms. There are many reasons for this, the most obvious being the great variety of human elements of which the city is composed. All combinations of classes meet in democracies: husbandmen, artisans, merchants, sailors, workmen—all are citizens.[5] On the other hand, though the democratic principle demands that supreme power shall belong to the people, there are various ways of organizing the attendance of the citizens at the Assembly. Similarly, though sovereignty implies the right of deciding on questions of war and peace, on the making and the breaking off of alliances, on legislation, on supreme justice, and the rendering of accounts, there are many ways of distributing these functions between the people and its delegates, the magistrates.[6] As in natural history so here

---

[1] Id., *ibid.*, VI, p. 493a; *Laws*, III, p. 701b.
[2] v. **XXVI**, p. 221 *ff.*; **VII**, vol. I, p. 440-442.
[3] Arist., *Pol.*, VI (IV), 2, 1.
[4] Id., *ibid.*, 3, 6-8.   [5] Id., *ibid.*, 3, 9-15; 4, 1.
[6] Id., *ibid.*, 4, 2; 5, 3; VII (VI), 2, 1-2.

the typical organs of each variety must be determined in order that the different types may be classified.

The first type of democracy, the oldest and the best, is characterized by equality founded on law: rich and poor possess the same degree of sovereignty. It is democracy *par excellence* because it gives to all an equal share in the power of the city. It is found in agricultural and pastoral countries where fortunes are small and where everyone has to work for his living. There, lack of leisure prevents the citizens from gathering in the Assembly save on absolutely necessary occasions, to elect the magistrates or simply to select the electors, and to hear the accounts; for the rest the business of government is left to those few citizens who are sufficiently wealthy to be able to engage in politics.[1] Aristotle sees in this form of government an excellent type of the constitution which he preferred above all others, a constitution which favoured the middle class.

Two other kinds of democracy recognize the sovereignty of law, but differ in the qualifications for eligibility to offices of state and in the rôle which the Assembly plays. The second type, which is fairly common, makes access to offices dependent upon a small property qualification, or else participation in the Assembly is governed by severe conditions. Since this system permits wise choices to be made without awakening jealousies it usually leaves great latitude to the magistrates, so much so that the people is satisfied with electing them and demanding a rendering of accounts. Aristotle approves also of this combination since it gives power to a select few and, by making them responsible to another class, compels them to govern with equity.[2] In the third type all citizens without distinction have access to the magistracies; but the composition and the powers of the Assembly vary considerably. In one place the citizens may sit in the Assembly in alternating sections; in another they may enter by turn in sections into the colleges of magistrates, colleges which meet in limited assembly to deliberate on current affairs, and in that case they are only summoned to the plenary assembly to sanction the laws, to determine constitutional questions and to hear the reports of magistrates.

[1] Id., *ibid.*, VI (IV), 11, 1-3.
[2] Id., *ibid.*, 4, 3; 5, 4; VII (VI), 2, 3-4.

F*

Elsewhere they may assemble for elections, legislation, the rendering of accounts, peace and war, other matters being reserved to the appropriate magistrates.[1]

Finally—last in order of merit as in chronology—comes the democracy in which the multitude no longer recognizes the sovereignty of law, but appropriates it entirely to itself and exercises it by means of decrees.[2] Such a government can exist only in large towns, for it gives predominance to a class which is of no weight in pastoral and agricultural States, the class of manual workers and merchants. This mass, whose existence is degraded, whose labour has nothing in common with virtue, swarms unceasingly in the markets and the streets; it is ever ready to rush to the Assembly, whereas the peasants scattered in the countryside have not the same need to meet together.[3] It is the rule of a monarch with a thousand heads, who refuses to submit to the law and erects himself into a despot. This democracy is, therefore, of its kind what tyranny is to monarchy. In place of giving precedence to the best citizens it oppresses them and honours flatterers. A brood, which never appears where law is sovereign, inevitably arises where it is not, namely the demagogues. They have two methods of action: on the one hand they concoct corrupt decrees which place everything in the hands of the people, for they can only aggrandize themselves by extending the sovereignty of the people whose masters they are; on the other hand they work against the magistrates by bringing in accusations against them before the people's courts.[4] The most extreme form of democracy is that in which the people is consulted directly on all matters and in which no magistrate can make any decision without reference to the Assembly.[5]

When democracy has reached the point when it rules by decrees, there is no longer a *politeia*, no longer a genuine constitutional regime. For an essential condition of such a regime is that the law should be supreme, that it should lay down rules of a general order, while the magistrates determine particular matters according to the principles it has estab-

---

[1] Id., *ibid.*, VI (IV), 11, 3-4.   [2] Id., *ibid.*, 4, 3-4; 5, 3-4.
[3] Id., *ibid.*, VII (VI), 2, 7.
[4] Id., *ibid.*, VI (IV), 4, 3-6; 5, 4-5.
[5] Id., *ibid.*, 11, 5.

lished. Fundamentally the State where everything is ordered by means of decrees is not a true democracy.[1]

Aristotle, however, offers one consolation to the cities which he criticizes with such severity. As the worst constitution is a corruption of the best, democracy which, in its ideal form, is not the equal of aristocracy nor still less that of monarchy, holds nevertheless the highest place among the ranks of degraded forms of government: it is the most endurable of the corrupt regimes. Thus one might say that it is the worst form of good government, the best form of bad government.[2]

It would be childish to show surprise at the varied opinions which were current concerning Athenian democracy. In an epoch when democratic and oligarchical cities existed side by side every party in power found itself faced with a violent opposition, inspired by principles the exact contrary of its own. Thucydides shows us the ideal for which the Athenians engaged in the Peloponnesian war; the Pseudo-Xenophon expounds the ideas which obsessed the people of the *hetaireiai* before bringing about the revolution of the Four Hundred. Moreover both were of an age in which individualism, emancipated by the power of the State, dared attempt nothing against it, and when civil strife had a political rather than an economic or social complexion. But there were to appear generations of Athenians who would hear nothing of oligarchy, who were to force the democratic principle to its extreme limits and who were dominated by selfish and purely material interests; one can understand what philosophers then would think of democracy. In retirement from public life they saw only its blackest sides, and they were the more ready to exaggerate the evil since political philosophy was bound by all its traditions to the banquets of the aristocratic *hetaireiai*.

We can descry, though far away, the city which Plato and Aristotle saw. But first we will turn our attention to the one which Pericles surveyed with justifiable pride.

[1] Id., *ibid.*, 4, 7.   [2] Id., *ibid.*, 2, 2-3.

CHAPTER III

THE ASSEMBLY OF THE PEOPLE

I

COMPOSITION AND WORKING OF THE ASSEMBLY

ENTRY to the Ecclesia was limited by two conditions:

1. One must be an Athenian, that is to say a citizen. Until the middle of the fifth century this title belonged to anyone born of an Athenian father. But in 451-0 Pericles ordained that to be regarded as an Athenian a man must have both an Athenian mother and an Athenian father:[1] children born of a foreign mother (μητρόξενοι) were henceforth in public law " bastards " (νόθοι). The privilege of citizenship might be won, and likewise lost, in exceptional cases: it was granted by decree of the people for outstanding services; it could be withdrawn by *atimia* or civic degradation, either provisionally or permanently.

2. One must have attained one's majority. Majority was attained at eighteen years of age, by enrolment on the registers of the deme; but, since usually two years of military service had first to be done, it was seldom that a man appeared in the Assembly before he was twenty. ·

Control was easily exercised by referring to the πίναξ ἐκκλησιαστικός, which was the copy of the registers posted in the demes. But the registers themselves were not always trustworthy. Metics contrived to get themselves enrolled and so slipped into the Assembly. It was in vain that the terrible action against aliens was brought against them (γραφὴ ξενίας) which entailed condemnation to slavery; the " illegally registered " (οἱ παρέγγραπτοι) were so numerous as to necessitate from time to time a general revision of the lists (διαψηφισμός). Very rarely was the Assembly composed,

---

[1] Arist., *Ath. Const.*, 26, 3; 42, 1; Plut., *Pericles*, 37; cf. Arist., *Pol.*, III, 1, 9; 3, 5. *v. supra*, p. 128. There was the same law at Oreos (Dem., *C. Aristocr.*, 213), at Byzantium (Ps. Arist., *Econ.*, II, 4, p. 1346*b*) and at Rhodes (*IG*, vol. XII, 1, no. 766).

to use Aristophanes' words, of "pure grain" without inter-
mixture of "bran."

On the other hand, never more than a fraction of the
people attended.[1] One can reckon the number of citizens in
431 at about 42,000. The Pnyx could not have accommo-
dated such a multitude, and yet it proved fully adequate. In
time of war the majority of adults were far from Athens
serving as hoplites, knights or rowers. In time of peace the
country people, accustomed to live in scattered communities
and interested only in their land and their cattle,[2] were loth
to undertake a journey often long and costly; the woodcutters
of Acharnæ remained behind in the forests of Parnes, and
the small traders of remote villages did not desert their shops
save on very important occasions; the people of the coast
would not willingly sacrifice one or two days of fishing. As
for the rich they hated to inconvenience themselves. The
knights were reluctant to leave their villa in Colonus to
mingle with the mob. Even those who dwelt in the town
were not always disposed to suffer the tediousness of a long
session: the Athenian when he had nothing to do lingered
happily in the shade of the plane trees planted by Cimon in
the agora, or loitered in the market-place, among the booths,
or in the courts. Sometimes the Scythian archers were
compelled to beat up the people, to hurry them along. In
short, rarely were more than two or three thousand citizens
seen on the Pnyx, and the majority of these were townsmen.
Certain resolutions were supposed to be taken by the "entire
people" (ὁ δῆμος πληθύων); actually, in these cases, 6,000
votes constituted a quorum.

In spite of this abstention in the fifth century was not yet
a great evil. Even the adversaries of Pericles did not quickly
abandon the struggle, and we see them forming strong groups
on the Pnyx in support of their leader, Thucydides son of
Melesias. And even the peasants, when the business on the
agenda made it worth while, put on their holiday garments
and their Laconian shoes, and set out in the night in little
bands, with staff in hand and cloak hanging round their
shoulders or folded over their arm, and tramped down into

---

[1] Thuc., VIII, 72.
[2] Cf. Arist., *Pol.*, VII (IV), 2, 7; cf. *ibid.*, 1; VI (IV), 5, 3; Eurip.,
Suppl., 420 *ff.*; *Or.*, 918; Aristoph., *Birds*, 111.

Athens, singing old refrains as they went.[1]   But the main
body of the Ecclesia was recruited from the suburbs of Melite,
Ceramicus and the Piræus.   Aristotle affirmed that artisans,
shopkeepers and hirelings were almost its sole constituent
elements, and says in explanation of the fact: " As all these
sorts of men frequent the exchange and the citadel, they can
readily attend the public assembly."[2]   Socrates, even in his
day, could find only craftsmen on the Pnyx.[3]   Nevertheless
before the fourth century it was not found necessary to induce
the Athenians to participate in public affairs by instituting
payment for attendance at the Ecclesia ($\mu\iota\sigma\theta\grave{o}\varsigma$ $\dot{\epsilon}\kappa\kappa\lambda\eta\sigma\iota\alpha\sigma\tau\iota\kappa\acute{o}\varsigma$).[4]
Each went of his own accord to the Assembly " carrying in
a little flask something to drink, and a crust of bread, two
onions and three olives."[5]

At first the Ecclesia met only once each prytany, that is
to say ten times a year.   But the progress of democratic
government brought with it an increase in the number of
questions submitted to the people.   Eventually there were
as many as three additional regular sessions each prytany.[6]
The adjective " principal " was applied to the original single
meeting ($\kappa\upsilon\rho\acute{\iota}\alpha$ $\dot{\epsilon}\kappa\kappa\lambda\eta\sigma\acute{\iota}\alpha$).   The three supplementary meetings
became in their turn " lawful " ($\nu\acute{o}\mu\iota\mu\upsilon\iota$ $\dot{\epsilon}\kappa\kappa\lambda\eta\sigma\acute{\iota}\alpha\iota$).   The
order in which sessions succeeded each other and the days
which were assigned to them varied from one prytany to
another,[7] since considerable difficulty was often experienced
in finding places for them in the intervals of holidays and
" inauspicious " days.[8]   In the whole year there were only
two meetings with fixed dates: the first was held on the 11th
of Hecatombaeon in order to afford the recently appointed
Council opportunity of acquainting itself with events; and the
other after the Great Dionysia, on the 21st of Elaphebolion.

  [1] Aristoph., *Ass. of Women*, 268 *ff.*
  [2] Arist., *Pol.*, VII (VI), 2, 7.
  [3] *v.* p. 146; cf. **LXXXV**, p. 7 *ff.*; **XCIII**, p. 9.
  [4] Had the *misthos* existed in 425 Aristophanes would certainly not
have missed the opportunity of satirizing it in the parody of the Ecclesia
with which the *Acharnians* opens.
  [5] Aristoph., *loc. cit.*, 306-307.
  [6] Arist., *Ath. Const.*, 43, 3; Æschin., *Emb.*, 72.
  [7] *v.* **CXV**; cf. *DA*, art. " Ekklesia," p. 519.
  [8] The *Politeia* of the Pseudo-Xenophon asserts that there were more
" inauspicious " days at Athens than in any other city in Greece, and
that great difficulty was experienced in finding the necessary days for the
sessions of the Assembly (III, 2).   Plutarch, *Alcib.*, 24, tells us that it
was forbidden to hold an assembly on an unlucky day.

Although the ordinary sessions did not take place on fixed dates each had its order of the day, its " programme " allotted to it.[1] Since the principal Assembly of the prytany had for long been the only one, it had an all-embracing programme: it proceeded to the *epicheirotonia* or vote of confidence in the administration of the magistrates, deliberated on the question of the provisioning and defence of the country, received the *eisangeliai* or accusations of high treason, heard the reports on confiscated property and on actions entered upon with regard to disputed successions; furthermore, in the sixth prytany, it determined whether there was occasion to apply the law of ostracism and to offer moral support to accusations brought against sycophancy or infidelity in the performance of promises made to the people.[2] The three other ordinary sessions had a less comprehensive programme. One was reserved for the petitions brought by citizens who, after having placed an olive branch upon the altar, appealed for a sort of bill of indemnity in respect of a proposal contrary to an existing law or to a judgment given, a motion leading to reinstatement in forfeited rights or to the remission of punishment.[3] The two last were devoted to remaining affairs: in each of them three matters of religious nature were dealt with, three of international import presented by heralds or ambassadors, and three of lay concern, that is chiefly of an administrative nature.[4] Strict confinement to programme, however, was not obligatory, and the order which they laid down was not rigidly adhered to.[5] Provided that a question had been included in the agenda within the legal term it could be discussed. The term was four days, and the posting of the programme took the place of a summons.[6]

But the Assembly always controlled the order of the day.

[1] Arist., *Ath. Const.*, 43, 4-6; cf. **CXV**, p. 71 *ff.*; **CXXIV**, vol. II, p. 252; **LXXXI**, p. 179 *ff.*

[2] Cf. Swoboda, art. " Κυρία ἐκκλησία," *RE*, vol. XXIII (1924), p. 171-173.

[3] Cf. Andoc., *De Myst.*, 110-116. For the fourth century, *v.* Dem., *De Coron.*, 107; *C. Timocr.*, 12. There was the same procedure at Samos in the second century (*RIG*, no. 371).

[4] Cf. *IG.*, vol. I², nos. 59, 108; Æschin., *C. Tim.*, 22; *RIG*, nos. 89, 92.

[5] *v.* **CXV**, p. 71 *ff.*, 78 *ff.*

[6] Arist., *op. cit.*, 43, 4; 44, 2; Æschin., *Emb.*, 60; Ps. Dem., *C. Aristocr.*; Phot., *s.v.* πρόπεμπτα; *Anecd. gr.*, vol. I, p. 296, 8; *RIG*, no. 129, l. 67 *ff.*

An unforeseen event might demand an immediate measure or
a discussion might not be concluded in one session. In such
cases there was no need to wait for the next regular assembly,
but an extraordinary (σύγκλητος) meeting could be convoked
without publishing the agenda or observing the legal interval;
they might even sit in permanence with instructions not to
stray beyond the limits of the question in hand.[1] Finally,
under the stress of public disaster, when there was urgent
necessity, the *prytaneis* convened an " assembly of panic and
tumult," summoning the citizens of the town by trumpet
blasts and those of the country side by means of a bonfire
kindled on the agora.[2] Thanks to a procedure which had
been gradually evolved and which allowed of modification,
the Assembly of the people enjoyed the advantages of a
systematic organization of work without the inconveniences
of rigid confinement.

The meeting began early in the morning, at daybreak.[3]
The signal was given by a flag flying on the Pnyx. Immediately the police barred the streets which led to the agora, the
rendezvous of loafers, and drove the citizens in the right
direction.

As in all Greek cities the seat of the Ecclesia had originally
been the agora, the public square where the " sacred circle "
was situated in the Homeric era and which retained in certain
towns the name of " sacred agora."[4] But in the fifth century,
the great market-place was used only for the infrequent
meetings at which the " entire people " was supposed to
assemble. The hill of the Pnyx was more convenient for
ordinary assemblies. It was reached by a steep ascent. A
little distance from the summit there was a terrace from which
a magnificent view over the sea, the agora, the Areopagus
and the Propylæa of the Acropolis was gained. A wide
semicircle was drawn out there with a depth of 260 feet by
440 feet in diameter and sloping gently from the periphery,
formed by a strong breast-wall, towards the centre. With

---

[1] *RIG*, no. 74, l. 40.   [2] Dem., *Emb.*, 62; *De Coron.*, 69.
[3] Aristoph., *Acharn.*, 19; *Thesmoph.*, 357; *Ass. of Women*, 20, 100,
238, 291; Plato, *Laws*, XII, p. 961b; Plut., *Phoc.*, 15. This was already
the case with Homeric assemblies (*Od.*, III, 138). The assemblies of
Iasos took place " with the rising sun " (*JHS*, vol. VIII, 1887, p. 103).
[4] Examples: in the fifth century, Halicarnassus (*RIG*, no. 451) and
later Demetrias (*IG*, vol. IX, I, no. 1106).

its surface of 7,180 square yards it could easily give standing accommodation to twenty-five thousand people and, on the benches which had been placed there,[1] there was room for an additional eighteen thousand. The tribune was a platform cut out of the rock and surrounded by a balustrade; it measured 33 feet in front, and three steps gave it a height of nearly 4 feet. In the middle of the tribune arose a square mass of rock 11 feet in height; it was the altar of Zeus Agoraios. Behind and above it was the official daïs, which was reached by means of steps placed to right and left of the tribune. On the front of the daïs on the face of the wall was a sundial, the work of the astronomer Meton, which had been there since the year 433. What was said and done in that enclosure open to the sky could be neither seen nor heard from without; for the breast-wall was continued along the straight part by a partitioning wall, which had the double advantage of rebuffing indiscreet curiosity and of projecting sound towards the auditorium.[2]

The president of the Ecclesia in the fifth century was the *epistatos* of the *prytaneis* appointed each day by lot. The electoral assemblies and the plenary assemblies of the agora formed the only exceptions, for they were presided over by the nine archons. The president was assisted by a herald who, in his name, made communications to the Assembly, and by a secretary, the " secretary of the city " (γραμματεὺς τῆς πόλεως), who read out official documents. At the foot of the tribune, in the first tier of benches, sat the *prytaneis*, responsible for the maintenance of order, and who, for this purpose, had at their disposal archers commanded by six *lexiarchs*.

Before discussion began a religious ceremony was performed.[3] The purifiers, the περιστίαρχοι, sacrificed pigs on the altar, and, with their blood, traced the sacred circle round the assembly. Then the secretary read and the herald

---

[1] In the Homeric assembly the chiefs had benches, while others sat on the ground (*Il.*, XVIII, 503; *Od.*, II, 14; III, 6 *ff.*; VI, 267; VIII, 6). One sat in the Spartan Apella (Thuc., I, 87, 2), as in the Athenian Ecclesia (Dem., *De Coron.*, 169-170). Cf. *Sb. BA*, 1904, p. 918 (Samos); *IG*, vol. XII, vii, no. 50 (Amorgus).

[2] Warning must be given that many objections can be raised against the classic description of the Pnyx since the excavations carried out in 1910 and 1911 (*v. Πρ.*, 1910, p. 127-136; 1911, p. 106 *ff.*).

[3] **XXVIII**, bk. IV, ch. XI.

proclaimed the curse against anyone who should seek to deceive the people. Throughout the Assembly remained beneath the eyes of God: the session was by law suspended in case of storm, earthquake, eclipse, since the *exegetai* recognized in these phenomena a sign of Zeus (διοσημία).[1]

When these formalities had been observed the president ordered the herald to read the report of the Boule on the motion before the Assembly, the *probouleuma*. The president was forbidden by law to initiate (εἰσφερέιν), and to open discussion (χρηματίζειν) on any proposal which had not been referred to the Boule (ἀπροβούλευτον).[2] The Assembly, consequently, was compelled to refer to the Council all privately initiated motions and was not allowed to vote on the first reading. But the Council had not the right of veto: the *probouleuma* never explicitly rejected a motion, since it had already been considered by the people; it was à report either with a favourable decision or without conclusion, and the unfavourable opinion of the Council was implied in the formula " whatever shall please the people is best " (ὅ τι ἂν αὐτῷ δοκεῖ ἄριστον εἶναι).

After the reading of the *probouleuma*, in the normal course of events when the report was favourable, the president went on to the *procheirotonia*, that is voting by show of hands on the alternative which was before them: simple acceptance of the *probouleuma* or the throwing open of the matter to debate.[3] Since this preliminary vote was taken on each article of the report separately the discussion, if it was resolved upon, might be either general or specific.

The herald opened the debate with the words " Who wishes to speak ?"[4] Formerly it had been the custom, it seems, to ask: " Who among the Athenians over fifty wishes to speak ?" and then the question was put progressively to the younger ones. This privilege accorded to age had disappeared. Nevertheless a young man was not allowed to speak first. Moreover, there were in the Ecclesia citizens whose presence was tolerated but who were not permitted to

---

[1] Aristoph., *Ach.*, 171; *Clouds*, 581-586 and Schol.; Thuc., V, 45.
[2] This law is attributed to Solon (Plut., *Sol.*, 19). The *probouleuma* is recalled in decrees in the formula ἔδοξε τῆι βουλῆι καὶ τῶι δήμωι.
[3] Æschin., *C. Tim.*, 23; Dem., *C. Timocr.*, 11-12.
[4] Aristoph., *Acharn.*, 45; *Thesmoph.*, 37; *Ass. of Women*, 136; Dem., *De Coron.*, 170; Æschin., *C. Ctes.*, 4.

speak: namely those who were involved in a suit which might end in the infliction of the dishonourable penalty of *atimia*; for even before judgment was pronounced they were automatically affected by the magic power of the *ara*, the curse attached to the law, and they had to be absolved by the courts before they could resume an active part in public life. If one of them dared to violate the interdict, any citizen could demand that the president should silence him, on condition that he undertook to bring against him a subsidiary action, a demand for a *dokimasia* (δοκιμασίας ἐπαγγελία): by this procedure the accused ran the risk of full and definitive *atimia*, but the accuser was exposed to the penalty inflicted as *pœna temere litigandi*, with the result that it kept the unworthy out of the discussion and at the same time protected liberty of speech against sycophants. In short, apart from this quite exceptional case, every Athenian was permitted to maintain his opinion before the Ecclesia: equal liberty of speech (ἰσηγορία) seemed to be the essential condition of democratic government.[1] But as one might suspect a very small number availed themselves of this privilege. As a general rule it was the party leaders and their lieutenants who bore the weight of the discussion.

The citizen summoned to the tribune placed on his head a crown of myrtle. By that act he became inviolable and sacrosanct. What rights did he possess ?

Every Athenian had the right of initiative. This act of initiating, which entailed a certain responsibility, was recorded in the formula of the decree by the name of the one who had proposed it (such and such a person has said, εἶπεν). Whether the author of a motion was a magistrate acting within the limits of his powers or a citizen intervening by virtue of private right, he could state his case at the first reading and so ensure that the terms of reference to the Boule should dictate to a large extent the *probouleuma*; consequently this often led to the adoption of the definitive decree by *procheirotonia* without discussion. If there was discussion the author of the motion was almost compelled to speak. Every Athenian had likewise the right of amendment. Voting on the *probouleuma* was not necessarily by yes or no. In the

[1] Her., V, 78; cf. III, 80; Ps. Xen., *Rep. of the Athen.*, I, 12; Eurip., *Suppl.*, 436; Dem., *C. Mid.*, 124.

wording of the decree a careful distinction was always drawn between the part borrowed from the *probouleuma* or the original motion and that due to the author of the amendment, who was mentioned by name.[1] In place of a simple addition to the *probouleuma* a counter-project might be proposed in opposition to the original project; this usually happened when the *probouleuma* reached no conclusion, that is when it was unfavourable to the project.

The liberty of speakers was, therefore, absolute; for in that lay the sovereignty of the Ecclesia. It was complete before the intervention of the Boule and remained complete afterwards. But precautions had to be taken that an essential right of the citizen should not degenerate and become prejudicial to the city. The rules of the Assembly provided against this contingency. Every motion, and every amendment or counter-project had to be formulated in writing. The text was handed in to the secretary, who checked its wording and assisted, if there was need, in modifications of form necessary before delivering it to the president. Abuses of the right of initiative were rigorously repressed; all unlawful proposals were rejected by the body of *prytaneis* and might lead to a summons before the courts; without affecting the other very severe penalties, a third condemnation on this count entailed a special degradation, the incapacity to bring forward any motion in the future. Moreover the president was equipped with power to prevent any obstruction or digressions from the matter under discussion: he could bring the speaker back to the question, and there is no evidence of his authority being disputed.

When the discussion was ended the *prytaneis* put the question to the vote (ἐπιψηφίζειν). In doing this their responsibility was involved, for it was their duty to refuse to proceed to the vote, no less than to discussion, upon an illegal motion. But the opposition of one did not prevail against the opinion of his colleagues, and if he persisted in it he was liable to be proceeded against by the summary process of *endeixis* and to be sentenced at least to the payment of a fine: one realizes that no small amount of civic courage was needed for Socrates in such a situation to make a stand against raging passions. Vote was taken by show of hands

---

[1] Ὁ δεῖνα εἶπεν τὰ μὲν ἄλλα καθάπερ τῆι βουλῆι or καθάπερ ὁ δεῖνα.

(χειροτονία). If there was any doubt the herald once more counted the ayes and the noes until the presiding body declared the result clear and indisputable. Secret ballot was reserved for those assemblies in which serious measures were to be taken against individuals, to plenary assemblies where the vote upon ostracism or the removal of legal interdictions (ἄδεια) was taken, and to the ordinary assemblies which judged cases of high treason. The president announced the result of the vote. If the business of the day were finished he declared the session closed; if the discussion was not at an end he pronounced the adjournment to a subsequent session.

Even after the vote had been taken, the *prytaneis* in exceptional cases if they judged, from substantial evidence, that there had been a surprise vote, might submit a question to a second discussion: in those circumstances they either convened a new assembly or agreed to reintroduce the principal question in conjunction with some matter related to it. Thucydides gives us two dramatic incidents of this kind. In 428 the Assembly came to the decision that the Mitylenians who had revolted should without exception be put to death; but during the same night the Athenians became fearful of their bloodthirsty decision, and on the next day a second debate culminated in a less cruel sentence.[1] In 415 the Sicilian expedition had been voted for; but five days later, during a session when the business of preparations was under discussion, Nicias reopened the question; he turned towards the tribune and spoke thus: " And you, Prytanis, if you think it your duty to care for the commonwealth, and if you wish to show yourself a good citizen, put the question to the vote, and take a second time the opinion of the Athenians. If you are afraid to move the question again, consider that a violation of the law cannot carry any prejudice with so many abettors." And he won his cause: the matter was debated again.[2]

---

[1] Thuc., III, 36 *ff*. (Eng. transl. Crawley, p. 412).
[2] Id., VI, 20 *ff*.

II

Powers of the Assembly

1. *The Ordinary Assembly*

Having seen the composition and the working of the Ecclesia it remains to examine its powers more closely. In principle they are easy to define: in an absolute democracy the sovereign people is all powerful. But, however, one must ask what in theory the Athenians understood by sovereignty and whether in practice they admitted that it suffered certain limitations.

According to the definition which Aristotle gives in the fourth century, but which is equally applicable to the preceding century, sovereignty, κυρία, embraces the right of peace and war together with the right of concluding and breaking off alliances, the right of legislation, the right of inflicting the penalites of death, exile and confiscation and the right of hearing accounts.[1] To the Ecclesia, therefore, belonged: (1) foreign policy; (2) legislative power; (3) the most important and particularly the political part of judicial power, it being understood that the cases which it did not reserve to itself passed on to the courts directly drawn from the people; (4) the control of executive power, that is to say the appointment and surveillance of all officers of state.

In the sphere of foreign policy the powers of the Assembly were extensive. Not only did it decide on questions of peace and war as well as of alliances, but it also attended to the minutest details. It appointed the ambassadors, gave them their instructions and received their reports. It received the heralds and ambassadors sent by other cities: in normal times it gave audience to them in two sessions in each prytany, and the understandings reached with them in the Boule were only of the nature of *probouleumata* which it converted into decrees, with or without modifications. Having ratified treaties it designated in addition persons to confirm them by oath or to receive the oath of the other signatory.

The right of controlling foreign policy would have been illusory if it had not carried with it the right of controlling the

---

[1] Arist., *Pol.*, VI (IV), 11, 1.

means; hence all military and naval matters pertained to the Ecclesia. In time of peace, as we have seen, in the principal session of each prytany it heard the report on everything concerning defence, including the state of the fleet; and we know that an old ship could not be put out of action without a decree of the people. In time of war it determined the number of contingents to be mobilized, the proportion of citizens and metics who were to serve as hoplites, and the proportion of citizens, metics, slaves and mercenaries who were to serve as rowers. It appointed the *strategoi* for the expeditions which it ordered, received their reports, directed their operations and ordered retreats by means of decrees. The authority which it exercised over the military leaders was further reinforced by enormous powers which conferred on it judicial sovereignty: one sees it condemning to exile or to death defeated generals and once even victorious generals.

That the most delicate negotiations, that the direction of the armies and the fleets should have depended in this way on forty thousand individuals all enjoying equal rights would appear monstrous and absurd, could one not discern beneath appearances the actual facts. One fact is indisputable: in the fifth century Athens pursued a foreign policy which was certainly not lacking in greatness; it created the most splendid maritime empire which antiquity had known. How can one explain this fact? One must undoubtedly recognize that the forty thousand individuals who made up the Athenian people were capable of subordinating their particular interests and their personal passions to the common interest and the nobler passion of patriotism. They were ready to submit to necessary control. In actual fact the Boule was the controlling force in foreign policy and national defence: an Assembly which, left to its own devices, would have inevitably been fickle and changeable, was thus supplied with an element of stability. Five hundred Athenians spent a whole year in studying the affairs which ought to be submitted to the rest of the people: it was they who first received the ambassadors and negotiated with them, who then presented them to the Assembly and received its confirmation of decisions formulated in advance; it was they who were responsible for the general management of military administration. One must not forget that in spite of all his gifts of mob oratory Cleon did not capture the imagination of the people until he had entered the Boule. And it was undoubtedly through that indispensable medium that Pericles was enabled to impose on the people for more than thirty years the ascendancy of genius.

In order to determine with precision the legislative power of the Ecclesia one must be clear of the exact meaning of the words *nomos* (law) and *psephisma* (decree).[1] It is not for an age such as ours, when the most learned jurists of all countries experience a singular difficulty in defining these two terms—and when French democracy has even introduced into political phraseology the hybrid term of " law-decree " —to criticize Athenian democracy for having left vague the difference which exists between these two fundamental ideas.[2]

At all events the public law of Athens proclaimed in principle that no decree, whether of the Council or of the people, overruled the law[3] (ψήφισμα μηδὲν, μήτε · βουλῆς μήτε δήμου, νόμου κυριώτερον εἶναι). But, on the other hand, Aristotle declares that " the sovereignty of the people extends even to the laws " (κύριος ὁ δῆμος καὶ τῶν νόμων ἔστι), and in his view it had been so since the fifth century since " the Athenians governed then without according to the laws the same respect which they had done hitherto."[4] The contradiction is one of form. It admits of only one explanation. In principle, from religious scruple, the Ecclesia did not take to itself the right of formally abolishing existing laws and of making new ones, but it evaded this principle and invented the necessary forms for legislating by decree. To the Athenians of the fifth century the " laws " implied all the laws and especially the constitutional laws of Draco, Solon and Cleisthenes: none of them was abolished, but that fact did not prevent them from twice reforming the archonship, from depriving the Areopagus of the greater part of its functions, or from placing restrictions upon the power of the city. For Aristotle, who saw the reality lurking beneath

---

[1] Cf. Francotte, " Loi et décret dans le droit publ. des Grecs," (**XXVI**), p. 8 *ff.*; **LXXXI**, p. 265; **LXXI**, p. 122 *f.*; **LXXX**, p. 58; **VII**, vol. I, p. 457 *ff.*

[2] v. the definitions outlined by Xenophon, *Mem.*, I, 2, 43 (cf. IV, 4, 13); Plat., *Laws*, IV, p. 714c (cf. I, p. 644d).

[3] Andoc., *De Myst.*, 87; Dem., *C. Aristocr.*, 87; *C. Timocr.*, 30.

[4] Arist., *Pol.*, VI (IV), 11, 8; *Ath. Const.*, 26, 2; cf. 41, 2.

the convention, this was a regrettable excess; for the historian, who may rely on Aristotle for questions of fact, but who is familiar with the ever changing needs and developments of human society, it is a natural phenomenon which cannot be judged without knowledge of the cause which inspired it. And unquestionably the philosopher declares that " the sovereignty of the law is the essential condition of constitutional government " and that " the State where everything is done by means of decrees is not properly speaking a democracy, since a decree does not admit of general application."[1] It remains to be seen whether the Athenian people, when it made laws under the form of decrees did so in a different manner and with greater precautions than when it passed occasional measures by means of ordinary decrees.

There is no doubt upon this point. We have knowledge of a whole series of decrees which, in their general character, are genuine ordinances of legislative or even constitutional importance, and which were not proposed in the Ecclesia by the normal procedure of the *probouleuma*: decrees such as those in which the status of a federated town was determined, a constitution given to a colony, or the grave question of the first-fruits due to the goddesses of Eleusis settled.[2] In all these cases recourse was had to special and solemn formalities, to those same ones which were employed in renewing by an authorized transcription the principal laws of Draco.[3] A commission of *syngrapheis* was appointed, analogous to the council of *nomothetai*, the legislative committee, which played a prominent part after the fall of the Four Hundred and of the Thirty, and which figured largely again under a regular form during much of the fourth century.[4] The scheme elaborated by the *syngrapheis* was presented by the Boule, together with its observations upon it, to the Assembly for its definitive acceptance. Another precaution was taken: if in the slightest degree the " existing laws " had been interfered with by the new " decree," the author of this sacrilegious

[1] Id., *Pol.*, *loc. cit.*, 7; cf. 4, 3 and 5-6; *Nic. Eth.*, V, 14, p. 1137*b*, 14*ff.* It is to be noted that Demosthenes, *C. Lept.*, 92, saw no difference between decrees and laws, although the distinction existed, for example, in the oath of the *heliasts*.

[2] *IG*, vol. 1², no. 22; *RIG*, nos. 71, 72; cf. nos. 671, 1465, 1495; *v.* **VII**, vol. I, p. 440 *ff.*

[3] *IJG*, vol. II, no. xxi; cf. *RIG*, no. 71.

[4] *v. infra.*, pp. 178, 331, 332.

166   THE CITY UNDER DEMOCRACY

and revolutionary proposal must avert from himself the malediction and the penalty which it involved, and come as a suppliant to beg in advance for pardon, and the immunity which he sought could only be accorded to him in a plenary assembly, by secret ballot, by a vote at least of six thousand. There is not, in fact, any justification for saying that the Athenian Assembly employed its legislative power thoughtlessly.

The people was also sovereign justiciary.   But it delegated judicial power to those sections of the citizens which sat in the courts; the whole body, assembled in the Ecclesia, only reserved to itself the power to intervene in cases where the interest of the State was at stake, in order to furnish the tribunals by unfavourable votes with indications which it thought useful.

Since there existed in Athens no official ministry to represent popular sovereignty, an ordinary citizen, before bringing an action against the author of a delinquency or an offence which was prejudicial to the city, asked the people to grant him moral support in default of a formal mandate. Such was the intent of the preliminary charge or *probole*. This procedure was used to initiate actions against anyone who had violated the sanctity of certain feast-days, against sycophants,[1] and in general against anyone who had deceived the people.[2]   In the fifth century it had been employed by the friends of the victorious generals of Arginusæ against their accusers; in the fourth by Demosthenes against Midias. Although the Ecclesia was not empowered to pronounce condemnation in this case, it was not excluded from taking an active share in the business: it called upon the two parties to state their case, and voted by yes in favour of the accusation (*katacheirotonia*) or by no in favour of the defence (*apocheirotonia*).   But, however, if the accuser won the day he was not obliged to pursue the affair, but might content himself with this moral satisfaction.   In the contrary event, the *thesmothetai* introduced the *probole* and the *katacheirotonia* before the tribunal.[3]

The *eisangelia* was much more serious.   It was levelled

---

[1] Isocr., *Antid.*, 314; Æschin., *Emb.*, 145.
[2] Dem., *C. Lept.*, 100, 135.   One remembers the actions brought under this head against Miltiades.
[3] Arist., *Ath. Const.*, 43, 5; 59, 2; cf. *DA*, art. " Probole."

against the author of a flagrant act against the safety of the State, and it delivered him, bound hand and foot, to the arbitrary decision of the judges. In the fifth century there was no text defining the acts which fell within the range of such an accusation. At the beginning of the fourth century it is true that a law (the νόμος εἰσαγγελτικός) established this prosecution in cases of " grave harm done to the people " (ἀδικία πρὸς τὸν δῆμον); but it determined the applications of the eisangelia in the past (treason, high treason, conspiracy, etc.) without limiting them in the future, so much so that it came by extension to be employed in cases of breaches of public morality, for example in cases of adultery. When an accusation of this kind was made in one of the principal sessions, the Ecclesia voted on the preliminary question of acceptance or rejection. In the case of an affirmative decision, the Council was called upon to say by probouleuma whether the affair should be judged by the Ecclesia or by a tribunal of heliasts, under the presidency of the thesmothetai. If the people as a body retained the right of judgment, its powers were unrestricted in the determination of penalties; if it deputed the task, it specified in the decree introducing the suit the law whose sanctions were to be applied in case of condemnation. As one sees it eisangelia was a formidable weapon. But it must be noted that the Ecclesia seldom judged cases other than those of a frankly political nature, and that, in practice, the indeterminate character of the crime was counterbalanced at any rate by the indeterminate character of the punishment.

The sovereignty of the people in so far as executive power was concerned could be exercised, naturally, only through the magistrates. Their place in the State must be examined more closely, but for the moment it will be sufficient to indicate their relationship to the Ecclesia. The magistrates who were not drawn by lot from the people were appointed by election. The electoral committees were only special assemblies (ἀρχαιρεσίαι) which sat, as the others did, on the Pnyx, and which were likewise called into action by a decree of the Council. When once they had entered upon their duties the magistrates were subjected to vigilant supervision. In each prytany, nine times every year, they had to renew their powers by a vote of confidence, the epicheirotonia, and if they failed to obtain it they were sent before the tribunals. The most stringent control was exercised over the military and political leaders, the *strategoi*; but the precaution was extended to all orders of officials and particularly to those who had the handling of money. The whole of financial administration was dependent on the people: it voted the necessary sums for war, for embassies, etc., even to the ten drachmas required for the writing of the decree which they had just passed; not a single prytany was allowed to pass without its being presented with an account of the state of confiscated property. Finally, at the end of their term of office, the magistrates had to render account of their financial and executive administration before two commissions.

2. *The Plenary Assembly*

As a general rule the decrees of the Assembly were valid without a fixed quorum, whatever might be the number present or the size of the majority: the citizens of the Ecclesia acted in the name of all citizens. But, as we have already seen, there were certain cases in which, in principle, the decision had to be unanimous; in fact this meant that it had to be taken by a proportion of the people sufficiently considerable to represent fairly the whole people. There were two conceptions each of which had its own tradition. The system of unanimous consent, of the *liberum veto*, derived from *themis*, from the ancient family custom which allowed, in important deliberations of the *genos*, the opposition of a single member to override the opinion of all the others (πάντας ἢ τὸν κωλύοντα κρατεῖν).[1] The majority system came from *dike*, from interfamily law based on the reconciliation of opposing forces, and was connected with it through judicial combat and the custom of according victory to the most numerous party (νικὲν δ'ὅτερα κ'οἱ πλέες ὁμόσοντι).[2] At

---

[1] Law of Draco. Cf. **XXXIII**, p. 41-45, 122-123, 296, 313, 324. Example of a unanimous vote demanded from a court at Tegea (*RIG*, no. 585, l. 29).
[2] Law of Gortyna. Cf. **XXXIII**, p. 271 *ff.*, 388 *ff.*. At Sparta, the *boa* (Plut., *Lyc.*, 26; Arist., *Pol.*, II, 6, 16 and 18) is a survival of the war cry, and the practice of the *pedibus ire in sententiam*, which was substituted for the *boa* in doubtful cases (Thuc., I, 87), recalls the formation of enemy bands which, on the point of coming to blows, preferred to settle the issue by counting their numbers.

Athens it was the plenary Assembly (the δῆμος πληθύων), convened in the agora and divided into tribes, which was considered representative of the unanimous opinion of the city; and what one might call the minimum of unanimity was a vote registered by six thousand people.[1]

In the fifth century the plenary Assembly of Athens was convened in two cases: (1) to declare which Athenians should be expelled under the law of *ostracism*; (2) to bestow *adeia*, impunity or pardon, either to the future author of an " unlawful " but necessary proposition, or to persons sentenced to *atimia*. These two cases at first glance seem to have no connection one with another. The connection was, however, there, and it becomes clear when one sees the plenary Assembly in the fourth century functioning in a third case, in the bestowal of citizenship. By *ostracism* as by *adeia* the community violated, in the name of a higher interest, the rules of common law which guaranteed civic rights to individuals. In theory the Athenians did not admit individual law, νόμος ἐπ᾽ ἀνδρί; like the Romans they thought: *Ne privilegia sunto*. But when the interests of the State demanded it they recognized the individual decree, ψήφισμα ἐπ᾽ ἀνδρί. It was decrees of this kind, promulgated under particularly solemn conditions, which were resorted to in order to banish from Attica an individual who had not fallen within the range of the penal code, or in order to grant a bill of indemnity, a pardon or an amnesty.[2]

We must here, therefore, examine one of the most famous of Athenian institutions, ostracism.[3]

All the historians of antiquity agreed in attributing its origin to the founder of Athenian democracy, to Cleisthenes. But not until twenty years after this, in 488-7, does Aristotle note the first instance of the law of ostracism; and then, he tells us, it was applied three years in succession.[4] Hence attempts have been made to deny that Cleisthenes was its

---

[1] It is to be noted that in the assemblies of the demes, as in the Ecclesia, a quorum was demanded for important decisions (cf. *IG*, vol. II, no. 328).

[2] Historical examples: amnesty for citizens condemned to ostracism (481-0), the decree of Batroclides (405-4).

[3] v. A. Martin, " Notes sur l'ostrac. dans Ath." (*MAI*, vol. XII, ii, 1907, p. 384 *ff*.; *DA*, art. " Ostrakismos "; **XXXIII**, p. 483-484; **XXXVI**, vol. I, p. 478-479; **LXXXIX**.

[4] Arist., *Ath. Const.*, 22, 3-6.

creator. It is not impossible, indeed, that Aristotle knew only the oldest instances of ostracism from the decree of amnesty which recalled the victims in 481-0, and since banishment by ostracism terminated of right at the end of ten years, the decree of amnesty named only the citizens ostracized after 491-0. It is none the less very rash, and rather futile, to reject the unanimous testimony of the ancients. The long slumber of the law of Cleisthenes can be easily explained. Ostracism was not originally what it ultimately became. When Cleisthenes established it, Athens was emerging from a period in which civil wars had constantly been calling into play the collective responsibility of the *gene*: many times in the course of a single century the Alcmæonidæ had been banished *en masse*, and the leader of the oligarchs, Isagoras, in 508 expelled seven hundred families. No one better than the Alcmæonid Cleisthenes could realize the invidiousness of such a system, and the Athenians only wished to enjoy, as Aristotle says, " habitual indulgence towards the *demos*." In order to protect the government against the Pisistratidæ it was thought sufficient to proscribe the tyrants and their sons; as for the members of the family " who had not been compromised in the troubles," they were allowed to dwell in the country, with the warning that if they moved they would be exiled for ten years. But during the first Persian war they were suspected of maintaining intercourse with Hippias, a traitor to his ancient country, and even the Alcmæonidæ, or at least some of them, gave rise to suspicions. After the victory of Marathon it was resolved that the friends of the tyrants should be punished and the weapon suspended over their heads fell with crushing blows. In 487, ostracism was decreed against one of the kinsmen of the Pisistratidæ, Hipparchus son of Charmus, who had become the head of the family; in 486, the year when the *pentacosiomedimni* began to share the archonship with the knights, it was decreed against the Alcmæonid Megacles, son of Hippocrates; in 485, in all probability, against Alcibiades the Elder.

But the very fact that it no longer affected only the family aimed at in the first instance enabled it to render the city the service of suppressing intestine struggles. In grave situations, especially in the face of the Persian menace, it would have been fatal to have had continual dissension on the question of national defence. What was to be done when two parties of almost equal strength impeded the administration of the State ? The ancient law of Solon, which inflicted the penalty of *atimia* on citizens guilty of political abstention in times of crisis, was notoriously inadequate and, moreover, it had fallen into desuetude. The superior interest of the republic ordained, therefore, that the work of the majority should be safeguarded against inopportune attacks by banishing from the land the leader of the minority. Thus in the years preceding the second Persian war, according as Themistocles succeeded in enforcing his ideas as to the necessity of a great fleet, his adversaries took the road of exile: Xanthippus was ostracized in 484, and Aristides in 483. If one takes foreign policy into consideration, there is perhaps less contradiction than might appear between these decrees of ostracism launched in successive blows and the amnesty which annulled them in 481 in order to bring all citizens together in sacred union.

The final disappearance of the tyrants and the defeat of the Persians left only the field of internal politics for the exercise of ostracism. In a new epoch it was used in turn by opposing factions to annihilate each other. Themistocles was expelled in 472 by the partisans of Cimon, and Cimon in 461 by the partisans of Ephialtes. Pericles saw his friend Damon sentenced to ostracism before, in 443, striking with this weapon his chief opponent Thucydides, son of Melesias. Thereafter the weapon forged by Cleisthenes and abused in its employment became blunted. At one moment, to which we cannot give a date, the people resolved to proceed to a vote of ostracism; but the voters melted away to such an extent that a quorum was not attained; this abortive attempt would have remained for ever in oblivion had there not been discovered in 1910 among a heap of rubbish which had been thrown aside fragments marked with names.[1] In 417, however, an attempt was made to decide between Nicias and Alcibiades by a vote of ostracism; but at the last moment the partisans of both took fright and united to vote against a wretched politician detested by all, namely Hyperbolus. This was the end of ostracism.

It was in the principal assembly of the sixth prytany,

[1] Brückner, *Πρ.*, 1910, p. 101-111; cf. *AM*, vol. LI (1926), p. 128 *ff.*

immediately after the middle of the year, that the *prytaneis*, in accordance with the order of the day, but without *probouleuma*, submitted to the people the question of whether they wished to proceed to ostracism or not. The vote was taken forthwith without discussion.[1] If the decision was in the affirmative a day was fixed when the action of the *ostrakophoria* itself should take place. Haste was essential, because it only was valid before the elections, and the elections took place every year from the seventh to the ninth prytany.

For the decisive session the agora was divided into ten sections, with an urn for each tribe. The official body was constituted by the nine archons supported by the full Boule. The vote was made by means of potsherds on which each one inscribed the name of the man whom he considered to be the enemy of the public: an ancient custom which had served before Cleisthenes' day for proscription.[2] The quorum was six thousand. But had there to be six thousand votes cast, as Plutarch says, or six thousand directed against one man, as Philochorus would have it ? Consider the spirit of the institution, the principle of unanimous consent; it is improbable that the Athenians would have thought it legitimate to deprive a citizen of his rights without assembling against him as many votes as were necessary in the fourth century to bestow citizenship on a stranger. In the forty-three *ostraka*, which have revealed to us an *ostrakophoria* unknown to history, are five different names without counting five illegible ones. On the day when this vote took place, if it had been enough for six thousand citizens to be present, a citizen might have been ostracized by 1201 or perhaps even by 601 votes. This is inconceivable. The result of the voting was proclaimed on the Pnyx. The victim of ostracism had to leave the country within ten days for ten years. He retained all his civil rights. Originally he could settle wherever he wished outside Attic territory; but in 480, he was forbidden to settle on this side Cape Geræstos (the south point of Eubœa) and Cape Skyllaion (the east point of Argolis).

---

[1] Hence in the *Atthis* of Philochorus (*FHG*, vol. I, p. 396, fr. 79b) this vote is abusively called *procheirotonia*, a term properly applicable to the vote without discussion on a *probouleuma*. The proper name is *epicheirotonia* (Arist., *Ath. Const.*, 43, 5).

[2] Two sherds earlier than Solon's day bearing the word δημώλης (under the ban of the *demos*) have been exhumed.

He was reinstated in all his political rights on the expiration of the fixed term, if an amnesty had not shortened this period, as was the case with the five men ostracized from 487-483, with Cimon and perhaps Thucydides.

The necessity for a plenary Assembly for the granting of *adeia* is explained by religious beliefs. According to the Greek conception the sanction of laws and judgments consisted in the curse which descended spontaneously on anyone who changed them, a curse which doomed him to *atimia*.[1] But, however, it might be necessary for the State to secure the testimony of an unqualified person, an alien or a slave, to persuade a criminal to denounce his accomplices. A very severe law inflicted the penalty of *atimia* on the public debtor and forbade the citizens to propose, and the *prytaneis* to put to the vote, any motion which had as its object the remission of his debt, the granting of time for payment beyond the extreme limit of the ninth prytany or his rehabilitation, before he had discharged his debt.[2] What was to be done if it was to the public interest to suspend the interdict ? The treasures of the temples were protected by laws against impiety; how were they to be evaded in cases of absolute necessity ? It was particularly in financial matters that cases of conscience arose, but the Athenians, scrupulous though they still were in the fifth century, managed to resolve them. Here is an historic example of such a case. In 431 it had been decreed that the treasure of Athena should be utilized for the needs of the war, save for a sum of a thousand talents which was to remain in reserve on the Acropolis: death was to be the punishment for anyone who should make or submit to the Assembly a proposal to broach that reserve, unless the city should be threatened with extinction by an enemy fleet. In 413, after the Sicilian disaster and defection of Ionia, the people, obsessed by fear and at the end of their resources, removed the prescribed penalties.[3] The man sufficiently bold and sufficiently patriotic to contemplate a proposal which might lead to his destruction, had first of all to be freed from legal prohibitions. He required a safe-conduct, an *adeia*, which he could only obtain by an individual decree

---

[1] Cf. *RIG*, nos. 72, 75, l. 46; 563, l. 14, 29, 54.

[2] *v.*, in the fourth century, the speech of Demosthenes, *C. Timocr.*, especially 45 *ff*.

[3] Thuc., II, 24; VIII, 15.

G

issued in a plenary assembly. This extraordinary procedure, trammelled by imposing and complicated formalities, was in constant use in the fifth century in the administration of finance, for the simple reason that there was no public treasure as distinct from sacred treasures.[1]

III

The Historical Rôle of the Assembly

After having followed the people to the exceptional sessions in the agora, we must return with it to the Pnyx, if we wish to gain a general idea of the part played by the Ecclesia.

Much adverse criticism of it is possible, and men were no more sparing of this in antiquity than in our day. Undoubtedly eloquence had in the Athenian Assembly, as in many parliaments of our own time, an influence quite apart from rationality of thought. In the scale of values eloquence ranked far above wisdom. A contemporary declared that the Ecclesia was more like an assembly of sophists than a gathering of citizens deliberating on the interests of the State.[2] Sometimes, it is true, these dupes were mistrustful; but in what cases ? When it was an Antiphon, a partisan of oligarchy, who showed himself in the tribune. By the baits of men such as he they would not be caught.[3] And what type of man was it who, according to Thucydides, put the people on their guard against these orators ? Cleon, the most redoubtable, the most violent of all, and his excellent advice was only an additional cleverness, the ruse of the demagogue who has good reason to believe that States are better governed by mediocrities than by the finest brains and who dissimulates his plans by speaking against smooth-tongued orators.[4] For this people who revelled in any contest whether intellectual or physical, the Pnyx likewise was a stage or a theatre. Whilst sessions concerned with humdrum affairs went on in solitude, the crowd flocked to the oratorical

---

[1] v. the decree of Callias (SIG³, no. 91, l. 45 ff.) and the accounts of the sacred treasurers for the years 418-415 (RIG, no. 563, l. 14, 27, 29, 54).

[2] Thuc., III, 37, 4; cf. Aristoph., Knights, 1262.

[3] Thuc., VIII, 68, 1.   [4] Id., III, 37, 3-4.

contests which took place in great times of political strife. It was of no avail that they were placed in surroundings conducive to reflection, seated on benches in the open air and not in the overcharged atmosphere of a room; friends grouped themselves together, one excited another, and orators speedily inflamed their passions. After a day of tense emotions, when nerves were on edge, came twilight to warn them that the session must come to an end. At such moments hasty votes were taken, by show of hands, for measures which would be repented of at the end of a few months or regarded with horror a few hours later: Pericles was abandoned to the mercy of his adversaries, only to be recalled to power very soon afterwards; the victorious generals were condemned to death and, as soon as they had been executed, their accusers were attacked; it was resolved that the rebellious Mitylenians should be exterminated and the next day a new session was called for in order that they might be pardoned. And then by limiting the political horizon to the semicircle of the Pnyx, men came " to see an oration as they would to see a sight;"[1] they lost sight of the outside world; they imagined that the voting of a decree had an automatic effect; they mistook a resolution for an act; they relied on armies which existed only on paper (ἐπιστολιμαῖοι).[2] Finally, this people which knew itself or believed itself to be omnipotent, was possessed of a royal vanity. Full of admiration for itself it was amazed, indignant, when its whims were not complied with, and it accused of disobedience, suspected of treason those whom it had made responsible for their execution.

One must admit that the Athenian Assembly had many defects. But serious as were the disadvantages of the institution they were compensated by the inestimable advantages which were inherent in the regime and which were as precious as they were little obvious. In spite of everything it was in the Ecclesia that the people received its education. In these ancient democracies, which did not know the representative system, politics was not for the mass of citizens the simple duty of depositing a voting paper in a box at long intervals; it was for them a regular preoccupation, a constant duty. They exercised a general function, undefined and therefore unlimited, which Aristotle calls with precision

<hr />

[1] Id., *ibid.*, 3. [2] Dem., *Phil.*, I, 19.

176   THE CITY UNDER DEMOCRACY

ἀόριστος ἀρχή.[1] Each learnt his business as a citizen by
practical experience. Sometimes by listening to the speeches
of others men acquired the gift of speech; many talents were
quickened in this way, if one is to give credence to an assertion
of Aristophanes and the example of a Demades.[2] By following
the debates of the Pnyx a man could learn the drift of affairs,
great or small, and weigh divergent opinions; and the facts are
there to prove that the Athenians were sufficiently discerning
not to allow themselves always to be swayed by the prestige
of eloquence alone. The general tone of the orations which
have come down to us reveals an audience with very high
standards of taste and accustomed to noble flights of thought.
Whatever charges one may bring against the Athenian
multitude, liable as it was to be carried away by the seductive
enticements of orators, it was nevertheless for that same
multitude that were evolved those maxims on country, on
law, on liberty, equality and philanthropy which have lost
nothing of their grandeur and their beauty although they
have become commonplaces of the moral heritage of mankind.
If it is true, as Aristotle would have it, that the perfect city
is that in which all the members scrupulously fulfil their duty
as citizens, although obviously all could not be good men,[3]
Athens at least approached to that perfection in the time of
Pericles, before free play was given to the caprices of the
individual and public morality allowed to sink to the level
of private morality.

To appreciate properly the rôle of the Assembly one must,
therefore, clearly distinguish between the fifth and the fourth
centuries. That distinction is strikingly revealed by a
scrutiny of the list of leaders of the Athenian people in the
two eras. The amorphous mass had its guiding spirit.
There was an almost unbroken chain of party leaders who,
by the majority which they commanded, were enabled to
exercise a kind of special magistracy not to be found in the
constitution, a hegemony based on persuasion. Though
without official title this person filled the position of first
minister of the democracy; he was the " *prostates* " of the
demos.[4] Surrounded by his supporters, he defended his

---

[1] Arist., *Pol.*, III, 1, 5.
[2] Aristoph., *Ass. of Women*, 244; Stob., *Flor.*, XXIX, 91.
[3] Arist., *Pol.*, III, 2.   [4] Id., *Ath. Const.*, 28, 1-4.

programme against the leader of the opposing party and remained master of the government so long as he succeeded in gaining the assent of the Ecclesia for his proposals. In periods when the people was excited by great questions of general, of national, interest it selected its proxy for preference from the *strategoi* responsible for the supervision of foreign policy; it chose him usually from illustrious families, from those which could boast of numerous ancestors and possessed large estates. Cimon the son of Miltiades and the Alcmæonid Pericles, both great proprietors, are remarkable examples of those *strategoi* who, as *prostatai*, directed the government of the fifth century. Their successors were merchants and traders, not the sausage-seller whom Aristophanes ridicules, but Lysicles the sheep dealer, Cleon the tanner, Cleophon the maker of musical instruments, Hyperbolus the lamp maker: these men represented during the Peloponnesian war a class whose private interests did at least coincide with those of the republic, since in endeavouring to maintain the economic supremacy of their city they sought to protect its maritime empire.[1] In short, the popular Assembly of Athens chose its leaders no more ill-advisedly than do so many of our modern assemblies which emanate from the people by election.

It knew how to protect itself against its own impulses. We have already noticed, when seeing it at work, some of the precautionary formalities with which it hedged in its debates. It forbade the adoption of any proposal which had not first been submitted to the deliberations of the Council, and it voted on decrees only at the second reading. Any individual measure which was contrary to the principles of common law, whether it was favourable or detrimental to a person, was only valid if a large quorum were present. But our attention must be directed in particular to the institutions whose object it was to protect the laws against the abuse of decrees.

In the fifth century the need for regular and permanent means for effecting the modification of existing laws or the adoption of new laws was not yet felt. In certain exceptional cases, for example for the fixing of the status of the confederate cities, for the determining of the weighty question of the first

[1] On the *prostatai* of the *demos* after Pericles, *v.* West, *Classical Philology*, vol. XIX (1925), p. 124 *ff.*, 201 *ff.*

fruits due to the goddesses of Eleusis or for putting in force the laws of Draco, there was appointed a committee of *syngrapheis*, experts whose conclusions were converted by the Council into *probouleumata* and by the Ecclesia into decrees.[1] Each time that democracy was restored after an oligarchical revolution it appointed a committee of *nomothetai* to select from the laws, conjointly with the Boule, those which ought to be abrogated and those which ought to be retained; it was in this way that the *nomothetai* functioned after the fall of the Four Hundred, from 410 to 404,[2] and then after the fall of the Thirty from 403 to 399.[3]   But the *nomothetai* of the fifth century, as well as the *syngrapheis*, differed greatly from the *nomothetai* who, during a large part of the fourth century, were to act as a brake upon the legislative power of the Assembly. At this time they were never more than auxiliaries charged by the people itself with a temporary and special task.

It was to another institution, a judicial institution, that the wisdom of an earlier generation looked for confining in practice the omnipotence of the Ecclesia within just limits. Such was the service which the public action against illegal proposals, the *graphe paranomon*, rendered.[4]   In fact this process was, by its origins, its procedure and its sanctions, one of the most formidable weapons at the disposal of the criminal law of Athens.

In early times the laws bestowed by the gods were protected by the sacred power of the curse.   When written laws came into being they had for guardian the most august tribunal of all, the one which was invested with essentially religious functions, namely the Areopagus.[5]   Then came the reform of Ephialtes which divested the Areopagus of all the functions which made it the guardian of the constitution.[6] It was then that democracy, no longer finding an external check, imposed one upon itself.   The first use which it made

---

[1] *IG*, vol. 1², no. 22; *RIG*, nos. 72, 71; *IJG*, vol. 11, no. XXI; *v.* F. D. Smith, *Athenian Political Commissions*, Chicago, 1920.
[2] Thuc., VIII, 97, 2.
[3] Andoc., *De Myst.*, 83-84; Lys., *C. Nicom.*, 27-28.   *Nomethetai* similar to those of the fifth century were still functioning after the fall of Demetrius Phalereus, from 307 to 303 (*RIG*, no. 1476; Alexis ap. Athen., XIII, 92, p. 610e; Poll., IX, 42; Diog. Laert., V, 38. Cf. Ferguson, *Hellenistic Ath.*, p. 103 *ff.*).
[4] *v. DA*, art. " Paranomôn graphè."
[5] Arist., *op. cit.*, 3, 6; 4, 4; 8, 4.   [6] Id., *ibid.*, 25, 2.

of its sovereignty was to confine it within insuperable barriers.

Every citizen might become the protector of the laws by bringing an action against the author of an unlawful motion and even against the president who had not refused to put it to the vote. The accuser had to bring forward his complaint in writing, and to indicate the law which he considered had been violated.[1] He might announce his intention upon oath (ὑπωμοσία) in the Assembly of the people, before or after the vote upon the provisions which he judged illegal.[2] This official declaration had the effect of suspending the validity of the decree until after judgment had been given.[3] The tribunal, composed of a thousand jurors at least and sometimes of six thousand,[4] sat under the presidency of the thesmothetai.[5] Any motion might be attacked on the ground of error in form: it was sufficient that the severe rules of procedure had not been meticulously observed. A decree was illegal if it had been submitted to the Assembly without having been previously examined and reported upon by the Council or without having been included in the order of the day by the prytaneis.[6] A law was illegal if it was not proposed as the result of a vote expressed in the first assembly of the year, and if it had not been displayed in due time and place. Still more serious, as one might expect, was the illegality which arose not from form but from substance. If it was a decree which was in question the accuser was not debarred from urging the evil which would result from it, in order to prejudice the people against the accused;[7] but he was obliged to establish beyond doubt that the decree was in contradiction of existing laws.[8] If a law was concerned, anyone was allowed to demand reparation for the harm done to the republic, by having recourse to a special action (μὴ ἐπιτήδειον νόμον θεῖναι);[9] but, with the graphe paranomon, the accusation could only be

---

[1] Dem., C. Timocr., 18, 71. [2] Poll., VIII, 44, 56.
[3] Dem., C. Lept., 20, 134 ff.
[4] Dem., C. Timocr., 9; Andoc., loc. cit., 17.
[5] Arist., op. cit., 59, 2; Hyper., P. Euxen., 6; Dem., C. Lept., 98 ff.
[6] Arist., loc. cit.; Dem., loc. cit., 33; C. Lept., 93.
[7] Dem., C. Timocr., 61, 66-108; C. Aristocr., 100-214; C. Androt., 35-78.
[8] Id., C. Timocr., 30; C. Aristocr., 87, 218; C. Androt., 34 ff.; Andoc., loc. cit., 87.
[9] Arist., loc. cit.; Dem., C. Timocr., 33, 61, 138.

made in connection with a new law which was in contradiction to a law which had not been abolished.[1]   Thus all those
whose names were inscribed on a decree issued by the Ecclesia
or on a law adopted by the *nomothetai* were under a grave
responsibility.   The punishment for illegality depended upon
the tribunal:[2] it was usually a comparatively heavy fine;[3]
but sometimes it was the penalty of death.[4]   After three condemnations on the score of illegality the right of making any
proposal in the Assembly was forfeited.[5]   For the author of
an illegal motion prescription was acquired at the end of a
year; but for the motion itself there was no prescription, it
might always be annulled by a sentence of the tribunal.[6]

Thus, as we see, Athens knew how to prevent its citizens
from abusing their right of initiative and, as a consequence,
restrained in practice the legislative power of democracy.
Before introducing a measure an orator had to realize that
for a whole year he must be prepared to answer for it with his
head.   By that device the Assembly prevented its passions
and caprices from prevailing over the traditions and permanent interests of the city.[7]   The sovereign people of its own
will placed itself under the sovereignty of law, and by imposing
upon itself this discipline it gained inestimable advantages.
It had an imprescriptible means for making good its mis-
takes and it permitted the defeated statesmen to appeal from
the *demos* to a better informed *demos*.   It made, so far as was
possible, contradictions and obscurities disappear from the
laws, so successfully that the progressive simplification of the
texts enabled lawyers to be dispensed with.   Finally, by
subjecting itself to the *graphe paranomon* Athenian democracy
was to reap its greatest reward: it made fruitless any attempt
to destroy the constitution by constitutional measures and
left the oligarchic party no alternative save revolution.[8]
Neither the Four Hundred nor the Thirty could adapt themselves to such an institution; but the triumph of democracy
gave it supreme sanction.

[1] Dem., *ibid.*, 18, 32 *ff.*; *C. Lept.*, 93, 96.
[2] Id., *C. Timocr.*, 138; Æschin., *C. Ctes.*, 197 *ff.*, 210.
[3] Hyper., *loc. cit.*, 18; Dem., *C. Mid.*, 182; *C. Theocr.*, 1, 31, 43;
Æschin., *Emb.*, 14.
[4] Dem., *C. Timocr.*, 138; Deinarch., *C. Aristog.*, 2.
[5] Athen., X, 73, p. 451a; Diod., XVIII, 18, 2; Dem., *De Coron.*, 12.
[6] Dem., *C. Lept.*, 144.   [7] Cf. Xen., *Hell.*, I, 7, 12.
[8] Cf. Thuc., III, 67; Dem., *C. Timocr.*, 154; Æsch., *loc. cit.*, 191.

CHAPTER IV

THE COUNCIL

I

THE COUNCILLORS

THE *demos* was sovereign, its functions were universal and its powers unlimited. But, according to the maxim of Lincoln which a penetrating scholar of antiquity has very aptly applied to Athenian democracy, one can secure that a part of the people shall govern all the time, or that all the people shall govern part of the time, but one will never succeed in enabling all the people to govern all the time.[1] To enable the *demos* to make its decisions, it was necessary for its work to be prepared, for decrees to be given a regular form before being submitted to it, in order that it might vote upon precisely worded and carefully considered texts. Moreover it could not be in permanent session to ensure the detailed execution of its will, and to supervise public administration, nor could it as a body conduct negotiations with representatives of foreign powers. It was compelled, therefore, to delegate a part of its sovereignty to a body invested with deliberative power (βουλεύειν) and placed at the head of the executive (ἄρχειν). It was this body to which the Athenians gave the name of Council, Boule, and which they regarded as the first magistracy, the first ἀρχή, of the republic. If, therefore, one seeks in the Athenian constitution anything approximating to the representative system of modern Parliaments, it is not in the Ecclesia that one must look, but in the Boule.

When Cleisthenes replaced the old Council of the Four Hundred by that of the Five Hundred (ἡ βουλὴ οἱ πεντακόσιοι), he gave it an organization which, slightly modified in 501, endured for centuries.[2] It had become so thoroughly assimilated into the regime by 465 that in that year Athens

---

[1] Quoted **CXXVI**, p. 161.
[2] Arist., *Ath. Const.*, 22, 2; cf. 21, 3; 43, 2.

imposed it upon the Erythreans, and the decree issued on this occasion[1] is the oldest document from which we derive detailed knowledge of it. The five hundred seats of the councillors were divided among the demes according to their importance and in the proportion of fifty to each tribe:[2] in the official lists the *bouleutai* are always classified by tribes and demes. It may be truly said, therefore, that the Boule was the great Council of the communes, and it is for this reason that the demes, even when they were deprived of the right of intervening in the election by lot of the magistrates, nevertheless did not lose their right of sending representatives to the Council. The councillors were elected by lot " by the bean " (οἱ ἀπὸ τοῦ κυάμου βουλευταί)[3] from the *demotai* above thirty years of age[4] who presented themselves as candidates. To each of them was attached by the same drawing of lots a substitute (ἐπιλαχών) in case the seat for any reason should fall vacant.[5] It would be wrong to think that there was a scramble for the position of councillor, for it entailed the devotion of a whole year to affairs of state. Certainly they were paid, but the remuneration cannot have been high in the fifth century, and in Aristotle's day it only amounted to five obols a day for the ordinary *bouleutai* and a drachma for the *prytaneis*[6] (half the day's earnings of a workman). Moreover, ambitious men whose lives were not irreproachable dared not put themselves forward as candidates, because they feared the interrogation of the *dokimasia* conducted by the Council in office and the action which might ensue.[7] Thus one is not surprised to find that people of humble family and small fortune were far from forming a majority in the Boule.[8] Even the leisured classes and the rich would hardly regret that they were prohibited by law from being a councillor more than twice,[9] and this deviation from the ordinary rule which prohibited the repeated performance of civil functions seems to indicate that some difficulty was experienced in finding five hundred new *bouleutai* every year. When one

---

[1] *IG*, vol. I², no 10.   [2] Arist., *op. cit.*, 62, 1.
[3] Thuc., 69, 4; 66, 1; Arist., *op. cit.*, 32, 1; *IG, loc. cit.*, l. 7 *ff.*, 11.
[4] *IG, loc. cit.*, l. 10; Xen., *Mem.*, I, 2, 35; Arg. Dem., *C. Androt.*
[5] Plat. Comic., fr., 166 *ff.*   Kock (vol. I, p. 643); Æschin., *C. Ctes.*, 62.
[6] Thuc., *loc. cit.*, 69; Arist., *op. cit.*, 24, 3; 62, 2.
[7] Id., *ibid.*, 45, 3; *IG, loc. cit.*, l. 8 *ff.*
[8] **CXXI**, p. 2 *ff.*   [9] Arist., *op. cit.*, 62, 3.

thinks how many were required in thirty or forty years, one realizes that every reputable Athenian of moderate means could, if he desired, form part of the Council for at least one year of his life.

Before entering upon their office the *bouleutai* had to take an oath. In 501-0 the formula of the oath still in force in the time of Aristotle was fixed.[1] From the fragments which have survived it appears that it alluded to each function and to each duty of the office. The future councillor swore to exercise his function in conformity with the laws and in the best interests of the community, to maintain secrecy on affairs of the State, to respect the liberty of the individual by permitting citizens to escape physical constraint by allowing bail, except in certain cases specifically determined, and to proceed to the *dokimasia* of the *bouleutai* and the archons for the following year. To this formula were added, when circumstances demanded and for a long or short period, certain special promises. The decree of Demophantus, which, after the fall of the Four Hundred, placed outside the pale of the law the author of any attempt against democracy, imposed an oath binding on all citizens, and in a special degree on the *bouleutai*. At the same time the *bouleutai* swore to observe a new regulation: to occupy in the Bouleuterion the place assigned to each by lot. After the restoration of 403 they swore to observe the amnesty by receiving no denunciation or warrant of arrest save in respect of infringement of outlawry.[2]

Entry into office took place, for one century, at the beginning of the official year: this was the year of 360 days, the one which Cleisthenes had brought into conformity with his decimal system and which, in spite of intercalary years, did not coincide with the civil year.[3] For this reason in 411-0 the Council entered upon its duties on the 14th of the last month.[4] But in 408-7 this anomaly was brought to an end by the suppression of the special calendar. On their first day of office the councillors offered an inaugural sacrifice (εἰσιτήρια) and put on the wreath of myrtle which was the sign of their inviolability.[5] From that moment they were

---

[1] Id., *ibid.*, 22, 2. [2] *v. DA*, art. " Jusjurandum," p. 756.
[3] **XXXVI**, vol. I, p. 475 *f.*, 482. [4] Arist., *op. cit.*, 32, 1.
[5] Thuc., VIII, 70; Dem., *Emb.*, 190; C. *Mid.*, 114.

entitled to receive payment, but since they were not always constant in attendance[1] they received only presence-tokens (σύμβολα) which had to be changed later into money.[2] Besides these emoluments they had certain prerogatives: they were exempt from military service during the year of office and they occupied places of honour in the theatre.[3]

These privileges were compensation for special obligations and responsibilities. The body exercised over its members a disciplinary power. If one of them committed a punishable act he might be excluded on the score of unworthiness. For this kind of vote olive leaves were employed; hence the name for this summary exclusion was *ekphyllophoria*. The member thus ejected might appeal from the Boule to an informed Boule: then a formal law suit began. In case of condemnation the Boule might inflict a fine within the limits of its competence. If it considered that the penalties which it was empowered to inflict were inadequate it might send the accused before the popular tribunals.[4] At the end of its period of office the whole Council had to render account to the people, and, although it was regarded as an ordinary magistracy, its rendering of account followed a special procedure. Each year the Assembly gave to the retiring Council an official token of its pleasure or displeasure: it either bestowed on it a crown of gold to dedicate to some sanctuary, or it withheld the gift. Until 343-2 the matter was inserted in the order of the day by the persons concerned; after that date it was done by their successors. In the discussion which took place concerning the crown the whole administration of the Council was surveyed. There was one case in which the law formally forbade the honouring of the retiring councillors, namely when they had not constructed the prescribed number of war ships. The refusal of the reward only involved a moral stigma; but all the personal responsibilities which were brought to light in the discussion were submitted to the examination of a tribunal.[5]

The Council was convened by the *prytaneis* who posted the " agenda " and the place of meeting. In cases of emer-

---

[1] Dem., *C. Androt.*, 36.   [2] *v. DA*, vol. I, p. 741, fig. 841.
[3] Lys., *C. Leocr.*, 37; Aristoph., *Birds*, 794 and Schol.
[4] Æschin., *C. Tim.*, 111 *ff.*; **CVI**, vol. II, p. 277 *ff.*
[5] Dem., *loc. cit.*, 8, 11 *f.*, 16, 20, 35; Arist., *op. cit.*, 46, 1; *RIG*, no. 100, B, l. 5 *ff.*

gency the summons was made by proclamation of the herald or by trumpet blasts. When the State was in danger the Council sat in permanent session: there were occasions when it passed the whole night on the Acropolis, save for the *prytaneis* who remained in the Tholos. In normal times it sat every day, except on holidays and inauspicious days. The ordinary sessions were held in the Bouleuterion, situated to the south of the agora. But there were extraordinary meetings held in the Eleusinion of the city after the celebration of the mysteries, in the arsenal of the Piræus for deliberations on naval constructions and armaments, on the great sea-wall for the departure of the fleet, or again on the Acropolis.[1]

As a general rule the sessions were open to the public. The listeners were only separated from the councillors by a barrier. When secret sessions[2] were held the *prytaneis* sent out archers with orders to thrust back the barrier and keep the crowd at a distance. Private individuals were not admitted to the Council unless they were introduced by *prytaneis* for reasons of public interest or contrived to get in, so malicious tongues said, by means of bribes.[3] There was an exceptional case in 403-2 when a general revision of the laws was being embarked upon; then all citizens were authorized by decree of the people to go there and state their opinions.[4] For the magistrates the rule was the same; but it goes without saying that there were great facilities for them to introduce themselves into the Council and, in any case, to present to it their reports. The *strategoi* in particular were in constant communication with it; they were summoned to the Bouleuterion, and had free admission of right.[5]

In the interior of the Bouleuterion was a sacred place where, around the altar dedicated to Hestia Boulaia, stood statues of Zeus Boulaios, Hera Boulaia and Athena Boulaia. It was there that the councillors performed the preliminary formality of conciliating all the deities " of wise counsel " by an offering and a prayer and by the proclamation through a herald

---

[1] Arist., *op. cit.*, 43, 3; Andoc., *De Myst.*, 36, 45, 111; *IG*, vol. I², no. 114; vol. II², no. 330; *RIG*, nos. 74, l. 53; 604, B, l. 15 *ff.*; Xen., *Hell.*, VI, 4, 20.

[2] *v.* P. Cloché, " L'import. des pouv. de la Boulé ath." (*REG*, vol. XXXIV, 1921, p. 248 *ff.*).

[3] Aristoph., *Peace*, 905 *ff.* and Schol.; *RIG*, no. 72, B, l. 4 *ff.*

[4] Andoc., *loc. cit.*, 84.

[5] Id., *ibid.*, 45; Plut., *Nic.*, 5; Xen., *Hell.*, I, 7, 3.

of a curse against proposers of misleading motions.[1] Then
they seated themselves on benches facing the tribune. Since
the experience of the oligarchic *coup d'état* of 411 had taught
the Athenians that grouping by parties was unfavourable to
liberty of speech, places were assigned to the *bouleutai* by
tribes, and each one swore to occupy no other seat than
his own.[2] The *prytaneis* constituted the committee of the
Council, and their *epistates* was the president of the session.
On the order of the day, in addition to the questions which
were to be brought forward at the next meeting of the
Assembly, were included those connected with the previous
resolutions of the Council or with the decrees of the people.
For the rest the Council always retained control over its
agenda. The presiding body had at its command very
stringent standing orders. Any word or act contrary to these
was liable to be punished, when the session had risen, by a fine
of fifty drachmas. If it were an offence meriting a severer
penalty, the *prytaneis* passed a resolution to this effect and
referred the matter to the next session, when a decision was
taken by means of the secret ballot.[3] We must remember
that permanent exclusion might be pronounced against the
delinquent.

II

THE *PRYTANEIS*

We have reached the point when the directing committee
of the Boule, the *prytaneis* whom we have seen at work in
many different circumstances, must be examined in greater
detail. No more than the Ecclesia could the Boule of the
Five Hundred sit uninterruptedly throughout a whole year.
It required for the expediting of current affairs and the
preparation of its work a committee which might make
for stability, a directing committee. But the democratic
principle could not allow the Council, the epitome of the
Ecclesia, to have the same leaders for a whole year. Hence
it was composed of ten sections each of which corresponded
to a tribe. What could be more simple, more in harmony

---

[1] Dem., *Emb.*, 70; *C. Aristocr.*, 97.
[2] Philoch., fr. 119 (*FHG*, vol. I, p. 403).
[3] Cf. **VII**, vol. II, p. 1027.

with the constitutional ideas of Cleisthenes than to allow each tribe in turn to exercise the *prytaneia* ? To each one a tenth of the year. The order in which the tribes were to be thus honoured was determined by lot: but we do not know whether it was fixed for the whole year at the moment when the Council entered into office or successively at the beginning of the nine first prytanies.[1] In the official calendar the year could be exactly divided into ten prytanies: the 360 days of the ordinary years and the 390 days of the intercalary years gave exactly 36 or 39 days for each tribe. But when in 408-7 the civil year of 354 or 384 days was adopted for public affairs equal partition became impossible. According to Aristotle it was decided that the four first prytanies should be of 36 (or 39) days and the six last of 35 (or 38); but that rule is only followed in some of the documents that we have,[2] whilst the others present a great variety in the allotment of the surplus days.[3]

The *prytaneis* were housed in a special building near the Bouleuterion, the Skias, which was also called, because of its circular form, the Tholos. They took their meals there, and as this meant extra expense for them they received an obol a day more than the other *bouleutai* (a drachma in all), and the *epistates* a further ten obols.[4] On the altar erected in the Skias they offered up sacrifices for the safety of the people.[5] But a connection must not be established between the title of the *prytaneis* and the name of the Prytaneum, the building where the " common hearth " was and to which the city invited those whom it wished to honour, nor must it be imagined that residence in the Skias was rigorously demanded of the fifty *prytaneis*: the tribe was comprised of three *trittyes*, and it was by thirds in rotation that the *prytaneis* mounted guard.[6]

The *epistates* of the *prytaneis* was elected by lot every day. He exercised his high office from sunset to sunset and could only be called to it once. Of the fifty *prytaneis*, therefore, thirty-five at least and sometimes thirty-nine attained to the

---

[1] *v.* **LXXXVII**, p. 23 *ff.*
[2] Arist., *op. cit.*, 43, 2; cf. *IG²*, vol. II², nos. 242, 349, 359.
[3] *v.* **VII**, vol. II, p. 1028, n. 2.
[4] Arist., *loc. cit.*, 3; 62, 2, with the restoration of P. Foucart, *RPh.*, vol. XLII, 1918, p. 55 *ff.*
[5] Dem., *Emb.*, 190. [6] Arist., *op. cit.*, 44, 1.

presidency. That is to say that the average Athenian, since
he had full opportunity to enter the Council if he wished, had
almost as great a chance of being the president of the Republic
for one day in his life—for the position was nothing less than
that. The *epistates* of the *prytaneis*, president of the Boule
and the Ecclesia, had in his possession for a day and a night
the keys of the temples where the treasure and the archives
were kept, as well as the seal of the State. He retained these
privileges even when, in 378-7, he yielded the presidency of
the deliberative assemblies to the *epistates* of the nine *proedroi*
drawn by lot from the *bouleutai* of the non-prytanic tribes.

It will soon be seen, from the powers of the Boule, what
those of the permanent committee were. It was through the
medium of the *prytaneis* that the Boule was brought into
touch with the Ecclesia, the magistrates and the ordinary
citizens, with foreign ambassadors and heralds. They
summoned in case of emergency the Council, the Assembly
and the *strategoi*;[1] they introduced into the Council persons
whose presence the people or they themselves thought
desirable; before them, as a general rule, were presented all
who brought letters or communications which were of public
import;[2] while the policing forces which they had at their
disposal were not only for the maintenance of good order in
the Council and the Assembly but also for the making of
arrests necessitated by flagrant offences prejudicial to the
well-being of the city.[3] On the injunction of the Assembly
they were commissioned, as proxies of the Boule, to denounce
the *strategoi* to the tribunals and to ensure the restitution of
money borrowed by the State.[4]

On account of these various functions the tribe which
exercised the prytanship was not only involved in the common
responsibility of the Boule; it was also responsible for its own
acts, and each *prytanis* for his personal actions. Hence, at
the close of the fourth century, the Boule and the people
adopted the practice of conferring on the prytanic tribes an
additional recompense, not to all indiscriminately, as was
done later, but to the one which had " carried off the victory "

---

[1] Dem., *De Coron.*, 169.
[2] *RIG*, no. 70, l. 12 *ff.*; Aristoph., *loc. cit.*; Arist., *op. cit.*, 43, 6; cf.
VII, vol. II, p. 1016.
[3] Aristoph., *Knights*, 300; *Thesm.*, 654, 754, 923, 929 *ff.*
[4] *SIG*³, nos. 104, l. 11 *ff.*; 91, l. 9 *ff.*

by deserving the best of the city.[1]   But, on the other hand, the direction of the debates of the Assembly exposed the committee to grave criticisms and even to formal accusations.[2] Decrees always mentioned the name of the *epistates* in order that he might be identified even after the vote had been taken. But the *prytaneis* were not bound by indissoluble bonds. Socrates proved in terrible circumstances that each of them might dissociate himself from actions which he considered unworthy of himself, and Demosthenes tells us that the fact of offering libations and sacrifices in common did not prevent the good from distinguishing themselves from the bad.[3]

In order to execute its manifold powers the Boule nominated by show of hands or by drawing of lots special commissions, some for the duration of the year, others for the period necessary for the accomplishment of their mission. Of this number were the " assemblers " or *syllogeis* of the people. They were elected for a year and were thirty in number, three from each tribe, one from each *trittys*. Under the presidency of the prytanic tribe they co-operated with the six lexiarchs to control entries into the Assembly. Their function was extended in the fourth century, when they were made responsible for distributing to the citizens who arrived in time the attendance tokens which enabled them to receive the three obols. In addition they represented the Boule, though for what reason we can hardly tell, at the Olympic festival at Athens and at certain sacrifices in honour of Athena. At all events they contrived to earn titles of honour by their " spirit of justice."[4]   For the supervision of marine administration, one of its principal functions, the Boule nominated from its number two commissions: the one (that of the ten τριηροποιοί) controlled, with the assistance of " architects " or engineers chosen by the people, the constructions in progress and saw that the contractors were paid from a special fund by its treasurer;[5] the other (the ἐπιμελόμενοι τοῦ νεωρίου) was in communication with the directors of the maritime arsenals,

[1] *IG*, vol. II, nos. 864, 866, 871, 872, 1183.
[2] Thuc., VI, 14; Xen., *Hell.*, I, 7, 14 *ff.*; Dem., *C. Timocr.*, 22.
[3] Xen., *loc. cit.*, 15; *Mem.*, I, 1, 18; Plat., *Apol.*, p. 32*b*; Dem., *Emb.*, 190.
[4] Poll., VIII, 104; *RIG*, nos. 648, B, l. 2 *ff.*; 824, I, l. 18 *ff.*; II, l. 12 *ff.*; 1029.
[5] Arist., *op. cit.*, 46, 1.

the νεωροί, who were in charge of ships in service and who had under their command five hundred wardens.[1] Ten commissioners of accounts, the *logistai*, were elected by lot during each prytany to audit the accounts of all the officials who were responsible for monetary transactions. This partial and provisional auditing was a preliminary to the total and final rendering of accounts which took place at the end of their period of office before special magistrates, but in which ten commissioners, the "correctors" or *euthynoi*, participated, each assisted by two assessors, the whole thirty being elected by lot by the Boule.[2] In the inscriptions of the fifth and especially of the fourth century appear also numerous commissions of *hieropoioi* whose duty it was to preside at various ceremonies: at the feasts of Hephæstus, at the sacrifices offered at Eleusis for the consecration of the first fruits or the celebration of the mysteries, at a festival of Dionysus where victims were immolated for the safety of the Council and the people. This kind of commission was usually taken from the whole of the Boule, but once however from the section exercising the prytanship.[3]

The *prytaneis* and the commissioners required, as did the councillors in general, a secretary of the archives who was acquainted with the diplomatic forms necessary for the drawing up of decrees and in whom one might have confidence for the publication, the classification and the guarding of official documents. Until about the year 367 this functionary was "the secretary of the Boule" (ὁ γραμματεὺς τῆς βουλῆς). He was elected by the Boule from the councillors who had not yet exercised the prytanship and, consequently, for one prytany. The popular vote conferred this duty on persons of the greatest nobility and integrity.[4] But though the name of the secretary figured in the preamble and the title of decrees, along with the names of the prytanic tribe and the *epistates*, it was not out of respect for this dignitary, but for the purpose of dating and authenticating acts, and for convenience of reference. In the same

---

[1] Ps. Xen., *Rep. of Ath.*, III, 2; *IG*, vol. I², nos. 73, l. 19; 74, ii, l. 1 *ff*.; Arist., *op. cit.*, 24, 3.

[2] Arist., *op. cit.*, 48, 3-4; cf. *IG*, *loc. cit.*, nos. 46, l. 19 *ff*.; 127, l. 18 *ff*.

[3] *IG*, vol. I², no. 84; *SIG²*, no. 587, l. 28, 296, 301; *RIG*, nos. 1459, l. 25; 648, B, l. 6 *ff*.; 680.

[4] *v.* **LXXXVII**, p. 17 *f*., 25 *f*., 22, 7 *f*.; Schultess, *RE*, vol. VII, p. 1710 *ff*.

way the name of a Boule was indicated by the name of the secretary during the first prytany.[1] In the temple of the Mother of the Gods, the Metroon, were stored tablets and papyri in the midst of which the secretary of the Boule was enthroned. There were accumulated the originals of decrees and laws, a mass of accounts and judicial dossiers and even, since the time of Lycurgus' administration, official copies of great tragedies.[2] The secretary, however, did not keep the key of the Metroon, which passed from day to day into the hands of the *epistates,* and he was of necessity compelled, since he had not time to acquire the necessary experience, to rely upon the actual master within, the public slave attached to the archives.

Between 368-7 and 363-2 the secretaryship was completely reformed. It became a veritable magistracy, annual and filled by lot from the citizens. By a strange paradox the new secretary received the title which properly belonged to the old one, he was called " secretary of the prytany " ($\gamma\rho\alpha\mu\mu\alpha\tau\epsilon\grave{\upsilon}\varsigma$ $\kappa\alpha\tau\grave{\alpha}$ $\pi\rho\upsilon\tau\alpha\nu\epsilon\acute{\iota}\alpha\nu$).[3] Although the period of his office was extended he had not the same prestige as he had had in the days when he was chosen from the *bouleutai.* In order to avoid competition between tribes he was selected in turn from each one, at first following an order determined by lot, and, at the close of the year 356-5, following the official order.[4] As keeper of public documents and commissioned to take care of decrees enacted and to make copies of all other documents, the secretary of the prytany necessarily attended the sessions of the Council, although he formed no part of it. He had as auxiliary and subordinate the " secretary of the decrees " or " of the laws " ($\gamma\rho\alpha\mu\mu\alpha\tau\epsilon\grave{\upsilon}\varsigma$ $\epsilon\pi\grave{\iota}$ $\tau\grave{\alpha}$ $\psi\eta\phi\acute{\iota}\sigma\mu\alpha\tau\alpha$, $\epsilon\pi\grave{\iota}$ $\tauο\grave{\upsilon}\varsigma$ $\nu\acute{ο}\mu\upsilon\varsigma$), who was likewise elected by lot and had entry to the Council, since it was his duty to make copies of decrees and laws.[5]

In addition to these secretaries of the archives there was a secretary of the records, " the secretary of the people " or " of the city " ($\gamma\rho\alpha\mu\mu\alpha\tau\epsilon\grave{\upsilon}\varsigma$ $\tauο\hat{\upsilon}$ $\delta\acute{\eta}\mu\upsilon$, $\tau\hat{\eta}\varsigma$ $\pi\acute{ο}\lambda\epsilon\omega\varsigma$), whose sole function was to read documents to the Assembly and the Council. As it was essential that he should have a good voice

[1] v. **LIII,** vol. II, ii, p. 644 *ff.*; **LXXXVII,** p. 11 *ff.*
[2] Ps. Plut., *Lives of Ten Orat., Lyc.,* 11, p. 841.
[3] v. **LXXXVII,** p. 27 *ff.*
[4] This is what epigraphists call *Ferguson's law (ibid.,* p. 53 *ff.*).
[5] *Ibid.,* p. 97 *ff.*; cf. **VII,** vol. II, p. 1040 *ff.*

he was an elected official.[1]   For proclamations to be made in the Assembly the *prytaneis* had also at their command a herald appointed by the Council (κῆρυξ τῆς βουλῆς) and who remained in office indefinitely.[2]

III

THE POWERS OF THE COUNCIL

At once a preparatory commission, an executive commission and a supreme magistracy the Boule had three channels for the exercise of its various powers: it sent to the Assembly *probouleumata* which served as the basis for the decrees of the people; it issued itself independent decrees in order to secure the detailed execution of decisions made; it collaborated more or less directly, in counsel or action, with the other magistracies.

We have seen that the Assembly of the people imposed upon itself the absolute obligation not to deliberate upon any project save those sent down by the Council, with or without definite conclusions.[3]   A decree of the people always supposed a *probouleuma* of the Boule.   Sometimes it happened that the *probouleuma* was mentioned explicitly in the decree;[4] but most often it was simply alluded to in the formula " it has pleased the Boule and the people " (ἔδοξεν τῆι βουλῆι καὶ τῶι δήμωι).   Even the discussion of a project elaborated by a special commission of *syngrapheis*, even the nomination of *nomothetai* charged with the revision of a law, even the annual meetings for elections commenced with the reading of a *probouleuma*.   Each Boule was responsible for all the propositions which it had made to the Assembly and only for those; as a consequence any *probouleuma* which the Boule had not had time to introduce before the people lapsed with it.

Current affairs called for immediate decisions in a great number of cases which it was not worth while to submit to the Assembly.[5]   The Boule, therefore, drew up executive

[1] Arist., 54, 3-5; Thuc., VII, 10.
[2] Aristoph., *Acharn.*, 45, 123, 172; *Thesm.*, 271; Dem., *Emb.*, 70.
[3] *v. supra*, pp. 158, 177.
[4] *RIG*, nos. 10, l. 5; 80, B; l. 52; 105, l. 9; 110, l. 48.
[5] Ps. Xen., III, 2.

" decrees " (ψηφίσματα) without any other formality.¹ There was implicit authorization for this in its responsibility for ensuring the application of the decrees and the laws of the people. In extraordinary circumstances it was invested with full powers (κυρία, αὐτοκράτωρ) to complete the provisions of a particular decree.² Nevertheless it had to remain within the limits of its powers and to be careful not to transgress the laws and decrees whose application was entrusted to it; if it failed to do this it was liable to prosecution under the law of illegality.³

Finally, the Boule held from the people a general power of attorney which gave it authority over the magistrates. It is in connection with the Boule, as being its subordinates, that Aristotle enumerates a long list of officials; from the greatest to the smallest it supervised them all, administered in conjunction with them, received their reports, gave them their instructions. In short nothing which concerned the city escaped its notice.⁴

In its capacity of intermediary between Athens and foreign States the Boule gave audience to ambassadors before introducing them to the Assembly, and negotiated with them before submitting to the people the result of these conversations in the form of *probouleumata*.⁵ It also gave necessary instructions to Athenian embassies, and sometimes, by order of the Assembly, it appointed them;⁶ in addition it received their correspondence. It apprised States which were affected of decrees of the people and pledged in the name of the city treaties of peace or alliance.⁷ It was expressly charged to receive with all due honour guests of the people, not only ambassadors but also *proxenoi* and *euergetai*. One can imagine, therefore, that the Boule would have a particularly active part to play when Athens was at the head of a confederation. In the fifth century it intervened in the fixing of tributes and prepared, on the motion of the *syngrapheis*, projects which concerned the towns, the districts, indeed the

¹ v. LIII, vol. II, ii, p. 690.
² v. P. Cloché, *loc. cit.*, p. 254-258.
³ Dem., *C. Aristocr.*, 87; Ps. Dem., *C. Euerg.*, 34.
⁴ Arist., *op. cit.*, 47, 1; 49, 5; cf. Ps. Xen., *loc. cit.*
⁵ v. P. Cloché, *loc. cit.*, p. 258 *ff.*
⁶ Cf. *RIG*, no. 71, l. 30; *IG*, vol. II², no. 16.
⁷ Thuc., V, 47, 9; v. LIII, *loc. cit.*, p. 727 *ff.*

whole of the federal domain.[1]   In the fourth century it was
the link which connected the Athenian Ecclesia and the
federal Synedrion.   One fact is sufficient for the realization
of the importance of the power exercised by the Boule in
foreign policy: it was almost always for the discussion of
questions of this order that it sat in secret session.

The Boule was in continual communication with the
strategoi upon questions of foreign policy and still more so
because of its military functions.   It exercised ceaseless
vigilance over the defence of the city.   It had certainly in
the fifth century the right of supervising the list of hoplites,
seeing that in the fourth century it superintended the working
of the ephebic institution, controlled the list of *epheboi* and
received the report of the *kosmetor*.[2]   It concerned itself
especially with the cavalry.   Every year the list of knights
was completed either by the hipparchs, or, in the time of
Aristotle, by special recruiters or *katalogeis*, who passed it on
to the hipparchs; the work of both was submitted for the
approval of the councillors.   They voted upon each name
and struck out those who declared upon oath that they were
not physically or pecuniarily in a position to serve on horse.
The Boule undertook likewise the inspection of the horses;
if it considered that any one was under-nourished it deprived
its owner of the allowance for feeding; it sold off vicious horses,
having them marked with a wheel on the jaw.[3]

But, in a city which set much greater store upon its fleet
than upon its army, the Boule had as one of its principal
functions the supervision of marine administration.[4]   It
attended to matters both of equipment and personnel.   Since
it was responsible for naval constructions and reparations it
had its representatives in the building yards of the Piræus in
the form of the commission of *trieropoioi* and it was empowered
to lay down administrative regulations.   It was especially
for the competent discharging of this duty that the people
awarded it an honorific decree, and that reward could not be
given if it had not constructed the regulation number of ships.
The making and the keeping in repair of hulls and tackle were

[1] Ps. Xen., *loc. cit.*, *IG*, vol. I², nos. 63-66, 218; *RIG*, nos. 70, 72.
[2] Arist., *op. cit.*, 42, 2; *RIG*, no. 610.
[3] Xen., *Hipparch.*, I, 8, 13; Arist., *op. cit.*, 49, 1-2; cf. CIX, p. 328 *ff*.
[4] *v. IG*, vol. II, nos. 802 *ff*.; Arist., *op. cit.*, 46, 1; cf. VII, vol. II,
p. 1032, 1049.

equally the objects of its care, and only on its authorization could rejected parts be sold. For the recruitment of equipment the *bouleutai* of each tribe acted in concert with the demarchs. The directors of building yards and arsenals and the trierarchs fell within the jurisdiction of the Boule: it might punish them within the limits of its competence or hand them over to justice, and it was empowered to double the penalties of trierarchs, condemned by the tribunals to replace a ship or tackle, if they did not fulfil the conditions within the appointed time. Whenever a squadron was got under weigh the *bouleutai* were there on the mole with the *strategoi* and, later, with the *apostoleis* elected for the purpose. The Ecclesia authorized them in that circumstance to apply the rigour of the law to defaulting trierarchs, or it might even go so far as to order the *prytaneis* to bring a capital action against *strategoi* who failed in their duty.[1]

To consider only administrative organization the Boule possessed still more extensive functions in the matter of finance. Of that department one can assert that until the time of Lycurgus it would have been in a state of unmitigated chaos, with a multitude of magistrates in charge of receipts, expenses and the treasury, had there not been the Boule to establish a little order and a semblance of unity.

The Boule again it was which saw to it that the necessary resources for the budget were procured, especially in time of war.[2] In its presence were made, by the *poletai*, all State contracts which were called " sales " and, likewise, real sales. Such was the case for the farming of taxes, the dossiers of which were remitted to the Boule carefully classified; for tenders for mining concessions which were definitively allotted by vote by show of hands; for the sale of property accruing to the State in virtue of judicial condemnations or claimed and recognized by judgment of the courts as public property; for the letting of sacred lands, the registers of which, written on tablets, were brought to it, not by the *poletai*, but by the king, the high-priest of the city. All these accounts, arranged in the order in which they fell due, were entrusted to a public slave. On the days of expiration the *apodektai* or general receivers had them brought before them again and, in the

[1] Ps. Dem., *C. Euerg.*, 42; Xen., *Hell.*, VI, 2, 12 and 14.
[2] Ps. Xen., *loc. cit.*; Lys., *C. Nicom.*, 22.

hall of the Bouleuterion itself, they cancelled the amounts paid or noted the default of the debtor and doubled the arrears. The law in this case gave the Boule the right of securing payment or of putting the defaulters in prison.[1] The *bouleutai*, who were thus responsible for the collection of dues, received even voluntary gifts and supervised the payment and sale of the cereals due as first-fruits of the Eleusinian goddesses.[2] At the time of the first maritime confederation in concert with the *taktai* they fixed the tribute to be paid by the allied towns, and it was in their presence that it was received by the *apodektai* at the festival of Dionysus and transmitted to the *hellenotamiai*.

Throughout the year the Boule closely scrutinized the use made of public funds. By law it was required to investigate the claims of the indigent who applied for the daily allowance of two obols; it was enjoined by a special decree to reduce the costs of a building to the minimum.[3] One of its main concerns was to see that the budgetary law was strictly observed. On their entry into office the *apodektai* received the whole of the cash balance and apportioned it among the different magistrates; the next day they brought into the council-chamber the appropriations inscribed on a tablet; they then read them article by article and asked the Council whether anyone had knowledge of any magistrate or individual having been guilty of any irregularity in the assessment; in this case they demanded an immediate vote on the question of culpability.[4] In the course of the financial year the Boule forbade the transfer and extension of credit; in the fourth century it settled with the *nomothetai* questions of expenses not foreseen in the budget.[5] It is not, therefore, surprising that each prytany it appointed a commission to examine the books of all accountable magistrates and that the inventory of the sacred treasures and their transmission were under its control.[6]

We have just seen that the Boule included within its

1 Arist., *op. cit.*, 47, 5-48, 1; cf. Andoc., *De Myst.*, 79, 93, 134; Dem., *C. Timocr.*, 11, 144.
2 Dem., *C. Mid.*, 161; *RIG*, no. 71, l. 40 *ff.*
3 Arist., *op. cit.*, 49, 4; *IG*, vol. I², no. 54, l. 10 *ff.*
4 Arist., *op. cit.*, 48, 2.
5 *IG*, vol. II², no. 330, l. 18 *ff.*; *RIG*, no. 108.
6 *RIG*, no. 75, l. 20; Arist., *op. cit.*, 47, 1; *IG*, *loc. cit.*, no. 840.

financial competence the expenses of public works. But in such matters its powers were much more extensive. It was concerned with everything connected with the construction and maintenance of public buildings. If the construction of a large building was contemplated, decrees of the Council and the people were first necessary for the drawing up of the estimates by an architect and for the laying down of the specifications; for works of lesser importance, for the conducting of water, for the erection of an altar or a statue, the people referred the matter to the Council.[1] All the contracts were made by the *poletai* in the presence of the Council,[2] and the latter supervised all the works in course of execution through the agency of special *epistatai*. In case of any breach of contract on the part of the architect or the contractor it addressed a statement to the Ecclesia and, if it resulted in a conviction, the matter was referred to a tribunal.[3] Certain accounts of public works make the activity of the Council stand out in bold relief. Those of the Parthenon are dated by the numbers of the Councils which had succeeded each other since the opening of the stone-yard: we have, for example, the accounts of the " fourteenth Boule." A decree issued in the ordinary form settles whether the temple of Athena Nike shall have a door of bronze, of gold or ivory; another, proposed by the Boule in agreement with the *epistatai* and the architect, fixes the salary of the artist.[4]

Finally, the Boule watched over the administration of religion. It took care of the temples as of other buildings, and helped in the annual transmission of the silver, the statues, the ornaments and all the sacred material to the treasurers of Athena and the other gods. The great festivals gave it much to do. For the Panathenæa it had for long to choose the design of the tapestry which was to adorn the robe of the goddess; but it was accused of partiality in its judgments and was, therefore, deprived of this duty which was assigned to a tribunal appointed by lot. Nevertheless it continued to superintend the fabrication of the golden Victories offered to the goddess and to concern itself with the prizes awarded

---

[1] Cf. *IG*, vol. I², nos. 111, 54, 84.
[2] *Ibid.*, nos. 24; 115, l. 8.　　　　[3] Arist., *op. cit.*, 46, 2.
[4] *IG*, vol. I², no. 88; cf. 24-25; *v.* Pogorelski and Hiller von Gaertringen, *Sb. BA*, 1922, p. 187 *ff.*; Pogorelski, *AJA*, 1923, p. 314-317; Dinsmoor, *ibid.*, p. 318-325.

in the Panathenæic contests.[1] It maintained order at the Dionysian games;[2] it chose from its own number *theoroi* as delegates to the Pythian games and various commissions of *hieropoioi*.[3] An inscription of the fifth century shows it appointing heralds to send to the confederate towns and other towns of Greece to demand that the first-fruits of corn should be sent to Eleusis, receiving a statement on the first-fruits of oil and punishing, by request of the king, the crimes committed on the sacred territory of the Pelargicon. Another inscription of the fourth century shows us the Boule busy with the fixing of boundaries and with the supervision of the Eleusinian Orgas and delegating one of its members to consult the oracle of Delphi about this interdicted land.[4]

In virtue of the general delegation which it held from the sovereign people and which made it a supreme magistracy, the Boule had powers of police and justice.

We have already noted that in certain circumstances it exercised the right of censure, of *dokimasia*. Let us assemble here the cases in which it exercised it. The enrolment of adult Athenians on the civic registers was not definitive until it had received the approval of the Boule and, if it was ascertained that any name had been illegally inscribed, it ordered it to be erased and condemned the *demotai* responsible for the fraud to pay a fine. It controlled also the annual enrolments on the lists of knights and cavalry scouts, and passed to the examination of the beasts as well as the men. The same control was exercised over the list of disabled appealing for public assistance. The Boule examined, moreover, at the end of its period of office the *bouleutai* and the archons designated for the succeeding year. It possessed at first a definitive right of exclusion; but later the excluded were allowed to appeal to the tribunal.[5]

When the Boule received from Cleisthenes and then from Ephialtes the political functions exercised hitherto by the Areopagus, it inherited at the same time as the right of control over the execution of the laws, the jurisdiction pertaining to it.

1 Arist., *op. cit.*, 49, 3; cf. 47, 1; 60, 1.
2 *RIG*, no. 100.
3 Dem., *Emb.*, 128; Dein., *C. Dem.*, 82. *v. supra*, p. 189.
4 *RIG*, nos. 71, l. 22 *ff.*, 30 *ff.*, 58 *ff.*; 674, l. 6 *ff.*, 20, 41 *ff.*, 80.
5 Arist., *op. cit.*, 42, 2; 49, 1-2; 45, 3; 55, 2 (cf. Lys., *Dokim. of Evandr.*, 21; *Theomn.*, 31; Xen., *Econ.*, IX, 15; Lys., *Inval.*, 26).

Since it supervised the administration of officials, especially of financial officials, it was qualified to summon them to appear before it and to try them, if they were guilty of neglecting the duties of their office or of infringement of the law.

The penal jurisdiction of the Boule was originally furnished with unlimited sanctions; it included then the sovereign right of inflicting fines, imprisonment and even death, but it had been reduced to a petty fine, the *epibole*. Henceforth the Boule could not condemn without appeal to a fine of more than five hundred drachmas; beyond that sum all sentences pronounced by it were taken by the *thesmothetai* before the popular tribunal, whose decision alone was sovereign.[1] A time came when appeal might even be made against fines inflicted by the Boule within the limits of its competence.[2] Aristotle recounts the circumstances in which the first and the chief of these changes was made. One day, he says, a certain man Lysimachus, delivered by the Boule to the executioner, was already at the place of execution, when he was snatched from death by Eumelides of Alopeke, who declared that no citizen might be put to death without a judgment of the people; he was led before the Heliæa and absolved. Unfortunately we do not know the date of this dramatic incident. It seems probable, however, that the supreme jurisdiction with which the Boule had been invested by Cleisthenes was taken away from it before the Persian wars, perhaps in the year 501-0 which witnessed the institution of the oath of the *bouleutai*: the Boule, therefore, would thus lose at the same time judicial sovereignty, which went back to the Heliæa, and diplomatic sovereignty, which was seized by the Ecclesia. At all events the beginning of the fifth century saw the proclamation of the principle: " No penalty of death without the decision of the people gathered together in assembly," (ἄνευ τοῦ δήμου πληθύοντος μὴ εἶναι θάνατον).[3] Though violated by the oligarchs of 411 and 404, and even by the democracy restored in 403, this principle was again in force before 368,[4] and this time for ever.

---

[1] Id., *ibid.*, 45, 1-2 (cf. 41, 2; 46, 2); *IG*, vol. I², no. 114, l. 32; *RIG*, nos. 71, l. 58; 604, B, l. 10 *ff.*; Ps. Dem., *C. Euerg.*, 43.

[2] *v.* **CVI**, vol. I, p. 45 *f.*

[3] *IG*, vol. I², no. 114, l. 37. *v.* P. Cloché, " Le Conseil ath. des Cinq Cents et la peine de mort " (*REG*, vol. XXXIII, 1920, p. 1 *ff.*).

[4] Arist., *op. cit.*, 40, 2; Lys., *Agst. the Corn-merchants*, 2.

The Boule, however, made frequent use of its right of coercion within the limits imposed by law. It punished, on the request of the king, anyone who violated the sanctity of the Pelargicon; and it punished, on its own initiative, trierarchs who were not at their post, architects who made faults in the repairing of walls, buyers and sellers who employed illicit weights and measures or *metronomoi* who neglected their duties.[1] Although deprived of the right of delivering capital sentences, the Boule was for long able to issue in its own right writs of arrest in serious cases of neglect of duty or of high treason; it did this for example in 406 against the generals who had failed in their duty and, in the following year, against the demagogue Cleophon. But by employing this procedure it exposed itself to virulent criticism and to dangerous attacks. In this sphere also its powers were reduced. In 403 the oath of the *bouleutai* still implied the right of proceeding to arrest; half a century later the same oath guaranteed the liberty of citizens, with the exception of traitors, of conspirators and of tax farmers guilty of malversation, on condition of furnishing three middle class guarantors.[2]

In place of acting in concert with a magistrate or of bringing an action itself, the Boule might be set in motion by a private individual. It heard complaints against magistrates who violated the laws.[3] Sometimes the summary actions of *apagoge* and *endeixis* were used before it: these were prosecutions undertaken without a formal citation, by means of an arrest made by the accuser or a bailiff, against those who were caught in some flagrant breach of the law or were notoriously guilty of certain offences against public order, for example against anyone who entered a public place or participated in a public contract in violation of *atimia*.[4] On other occasions recourse might be had to the jurisdiction of the Five Hundred by means of a written denunciation, a *phasis*: it was the means ordinarily adopted to safeguard the interests of the treasury and of property and to suppress infringements of the customs and commercial laws.[5] Finally, the Boule played a prominent

---

[1] *RIG, ll. cc.*; *IG*, vol. II, no. 167, l. 25.
[2] Dem., *C. Timocr.*, 96, 144.
[3] Arist., *op. cit.*, 45, 2; Antiph., *Chor.*, 12, 35; Ps. Dem., *C. Euerg.*, 41.
[4] Andoc., *De Myst.*, 91, 111; Aristoph., *Thesm.*, 654, 764, 1084.
[5] Aristoph., *Knights*, 300; Isocr., *Trapez.*, 42; *C. Callim.*, 6.

part in the summary procedure adopted in cases of crimes against the State, the *eisangelia*.

Formerly the Areopagus had judged by *eisangelia* attempts against the constitution; a law of Solon assigned to it this right.[1] But as early as the time of the Persian wars the Assembly of the people had taken to itself jurisdiction over actions involving the safety of the city, such as treason or the crime of deceiving the people.[2] After the reform of Ephialtes all crimes falling within the range of *eisangelia*, crimes against the safety of the State or extraordinary crimes not provided for by law, might be deferred either to the Council or to the Assembly. When the Council dealt with *eisangelia* it began by determining the question of guilt.[3] If the question were settled in the affirmative a fresh discussion was embarked upon to decide whether the penalty at the disposal of the Council was adequate (and what was the highest within the legal limits of the *epibole*) or whether the affair ought to be transferred by the *thesmothetai* to the Assembly or the popular tribunal for a severer penalty. When the *eisangelia* was carried directly to the Assembly the latter, likewise, did not enter upon the prosecution until a vote had been taken upon the question of acceptance or rejection. In the case of acceptance it charged the Council to draw up a bill for a decree upon the question of whether it should judge the case itself or send it before a tribunal.

After Cleisthenes had made the deme the constitutional unit of the political body the Council which represented the demes became the central organ of Athenian democracy. Ephialtes increased its authority by making it fill the place occupied by the Areopagus in the " ancestral constitution." It was after this decisive reform that, in the preamble of decrees, the words " it has pleased the people " were replaced by the formula " it has pleased the Boule and the people." Aristotle recognizes, therefore, that the Boule had at first held a prominent place in democracy, but he adds that power had fallen away from it since the people had begun to be paid for their attendance at the Assembly; " for," he says, " the people on whom one lavishes

[1] Arist., *op. cit.*, 8, 4.
[2] Lyc., *C. Leocr.*, 117; Her., VI, 136.
[3] *RIG*, no. 71, l. 58; Xen., *Hell.*, I, 7, 3; Lys., *C. Nicom.*, 22.

misthos attracts all power to itself."[1] Thus there seem to have been two quite distinct periods in the history of the Council. The historians of our day have often protested against such a distinction.[2] In actual fact the Athenians of the fourth century still said that their city was founded on three essential institutions, the Assembly and the Heliæa, in which the people acted directly, and the Boule to which it sent its representatives.[3] In all times politicians found in the Boule an excellent position from which to control government and administration. There were always there, as in the Assembly, a mass of silent listeners (the ἰδιῶται) and a few orators (the λέγοντες);[4] if a party leader obtained a majority in the Council of the Five Hundred he could be almost certain of winning over the people and imposing his ideas on all the magistrates. It was as a *bouleutes* that Cleon began, in 428-7, his astonishing career as demagogue and Demosthenes hoped to play a more prominent part in the negotiations of 346.[5]

But does it necessarily follow that Aristotle was misled by his prejudices and that there was, in truth, no serious difference between the Boule of the fifth century and that of the fourth ? A closer examination of the facts does not lead one to that conclusion. Certainly the Council elected by lot and furnished with the *misthos* remained, until the revolutions which marked the close of the Peloponnesian wars, the mainspring of Athenian government. When Thucydides wishes to indicate democracy as opposed to oligarchy he uses this expression: " the *demos* and the Boule elected by the bean."[6] In fact it was the first care of the oligarchs, when they triumphed in 411, to dismiss the Boule of Five Hundred in order to replace it by a Boule of Four Hundred very carefully selected and unpaid. Though the Council of Five Hundred was re-established by the party of Theramenes, democracy was not considered victorious until the day when it was once more appointed by the drawing of the bean.[7] In the fourth

---

[1] Arist., *Pol.*, VII (VI), 1, 9; cf. VI (IV), 12, 8-9.
[2] Cf. **CXXIV**, vol. II, p. 198; P. Cloché, *REG*, vol. XXXIV (1921), p. 233 *ff.*
[3] Dem., *C. Timocr.*, 9, 99; *C. Aristocr.*, 97; *C. Lept.*, 100; Ps. Dem., *C. Aristog.*, I, 20.
[4] Dem., *C. Androt.*, 36 *ff.*; cf. *RIG*, no. 100.
[5] Cf. **VI**, vol. III, ii, p. 998; P. Cloché, *loc. cit.*, p. 260 *f.*
[6] Thuc., VIII, 66; cf. 69.
[7] Andoc., *loc. cit.*, 96.

century we do not see the Boule playing so important a part in internal affairs. Doubtless the people was forced to refer to it upon questions of foreign policy, and on this count one must admit that the historians are right who adduce the secret sessions of the Boule in refutation of the assertion that its powers had declined from the time of Pericles to that of Demosthenes. But in all other matters one henceforth sees it closely subordinated to the Assembly of the people, and for this reason Aristotle, who considers only the internal life of the cities, was equally not mistaken when he declared that to pay the Assembly is to weaken the Boule.

CHAPTER V

THE MAGISTRATES

I

DEMOCRACY AND ITS MAGISTRATES

EVEN with the aid of its permanent Council the people could only secure the execution of its orders by delegating a portion of its sovereignty to certain magistrates. It was thus led to distinguish among the public offices magistracies properly so called, of a governmental or political nature (ἀρχαί), and purely administrative functions (ἐπιμελείαι), without counting the minor offices (ὑπηρεσίαι) which might be given to metics and slaves as well as to citizens.

By virtue of this delegation of sovereignty the great magistrates possessed, within their several spheres, the following powers:[1] (1) The right of acting on their own initiative in accordance with the laws which qualified them, or of consulting the Assembly or the Council with regard to new decisions (βουλεύσασθαι); (2) the fundamental right of giving orders and of passing obligatory measures (ἐπιτάξαι), which implied the right of punishing the delinquent (ἐπιβολὰς ἐπιβάλλειν) by the imposition of a fine whose maximum varied, according to the magistrature, from fifty to five hundred drachmas, or else of sending him before the courts for severer punishment;[2] (3) judical competence in specified cases (κρῖναι), a competence which no longer carried the right of decision, but only that of receiving pleas, of making investigation and of presiding over the tribunal (ἡγεμονία).

Since the power of the magistrates emanated from popular sovereignty, democratic principle demanded that every citizen should be able to exercise it. But one must not apply

---

[1] Arist., Pol., VI (IV), 12, 2-3; v. Caillemer, DA, art. " Archai," p. 368 f.

[2] Cf. Æschin., C. Ctes., 27; Plat., Laws, p. 764a-c. Examples: Lys., C. Nicom., 3 (the archons); Arist., Ath. Const., 56, 7 (the archon); Ps. Lys., IX, 6; XV, 5 (the strategoi).

to this precept the hackneyed interpretation which there is a temptation to give to it to-day. It did not merely signify that everyone had the right to attain to the exercise of the highest public functions; it proclaimed that everyone ought to attain to it as far as possible. " The first characteristic of liberty," says Aristotle, " is that all should command each and each in his turn all " (τὸ ἐν μέρει ἄρχεσθαι καὶ ἄρχειν).[1] It is also, according to the author of the *Menexenus*, the first condition of equality; for " among brothers born of a common mother, there are neither slaves nor masters."[2] The result is that in a democracy, " no one is compelled to obey unless he may in his turn command: thus liberty and equality are combined."[3] No citizen, therefore, was excluded from honours, whatever his birth or fortune; such was actual fact. The only superiority which might be recognized was that of merit and ability, with the result that the republic would be governed by an aristocracy with the assent of the people: such was the ideal.[4]

In order to accelerate the alternating movement which was to bring citizens to offices of State and then send them back into the ordinary ranks, magistracies were of short duration. Most of them were annual. As a general rule citizens were forbidden to exercise the same function in several successive years or to hold more than one in the same year.[5] These two rules were, however, capable of exceptions. A man might sit for two years in the Council, while with military offices, especially with that of the *strategos*, power might be renewed from year to year indefinitely.[6] But that such repeated tenure had to be justified by exceptional reasons is shown by the fact that in practice hardly ever could even two different magistracies be held in two succeeding years: for before putting oneself forward as a candidate for the second account must have been given of the first; a thing which could only be done by seeking for the second office one of the rare ones which were entered upon, not at the beginning of the civil year, the 1st of Hecatombaion,

---

[1] Arist., *Pol.*, VII (VI), 1, 6.
[2] Ps. Plat., *Menex.*, p. 236 *ff.*   [3] Arist., *loc. cit.*, 8.
[4] Thuc., II, 37; Ps. Plat., *loc. cit.*, p. 238c.
[5] Arist., *Ath. Const.*, 62, 3; cf. Lys., *C. Nicom.*, 29; Dem., *C. Lept.*, 152.
[6] Arist., *loc. cit.*; cf. Plut., *Pericles*, 16; *Phoc.*, 8, 19; Dem., *Prooem.*, LV, 2.

H

but at the Panathenæa, on the 20th of the same month. On the other hand an extraordinary function might be attached to an ordinary magistracy, and ex-archons, although they sat in the Areopagus, might obtain an additional office. Thus Pericles, fifteen times in succession a *strategos*, was at intervals chosen as *epistates* of public works, and Aristides and Themistocles were elected *strategoi* after having been archons.

The same motive which subjected the magistracies to the constitutional rule of yearly office made them also collegiate. The colleges were all independent of one another, and when co-operation was necessary it was effected through the Council. The only exception was in the case of colleges with military functions, where it was essential to have a hierarchy. The *strategoi*, generals in chief, gave orders to the *taxiarchs*, commanders of the infantry, and, through the medium of the *hipparchs*, to the *phylarchs*, commanders of the cavalry.[1] As to the civil magistracies they were all equal in public law. But in practice there was a general and clearly marked distinction between the great offices (αἱ μέγισται ἀρχαί)[2] and the minor ones (ἀρχίδια).[3] And with good reason. The magistracies which involved heavy responsibilities, those whose holders directed the principal affairs of State and exercised command over the army, were not paid. The citizens of the lower classes did not aspire to them, but, on the contrary, found it wholly to their advantage to maintain the property qualification which made effective the pecuniary responsibility of these magistrates. The offices which they aspired to were those which were profitable.[4]

The salaries were, however, very small. For the fifth century we have only rare indications; but they are significant. According to the accounts of the Erectheum (409-8), the working day for labourers and artisans was worth a drachma. The architect responsible for the direction of works and the sub-recorder who kept the accounts were only better off in one respect—they were paid by the year or rather by the prytany, without deduction for non-working days; but the architect likewise received only a drachma per day, and the sub-

---

[1] Ps. Lys., *C. Alc.*, 5.   [2] Arist., *Pol.*, III, 6, 11.
[3] Aristoph., *Birds*, 1111; Dem., *De Coron.*, 261.
[4] Ps. Xen., *Rep. of Ath.*, 1, 3; cf. Arist., *Pol.*, VII (VI), 2, 1; Isæus, *Succ. of Apollod.*, 39.

recorder only five obols.[1] Eighty years later when the pay for skilled work was doubled, one learns from the accounts of Eleusis that the architect was paid two drachmas per day; but the keeper of the accounts now received only a single obol.[2] At the same period whilst the presence-token of the Assembly was equivalent to a drachma or a drachma and a half, the archons each received four obols per day as allowance for keep, as did the *epheboi*, but out of that they had to feed their herald and their flute player; one of the nine, isolated at Salamis, received a drachma, as did the *sophronistai* of the *epheboi*.[3] The *athlothetai* were paid in kind, they took their meals at the Prytaneum, but only during the sixteen days when all their time was occupied with preparations for the Panathenæic games. The amphictyons sent to Delos received a drachma per day from the Delian treasury; the magistrates sent out to the *cleruchies* of Samos, of Skyros, of Lemnos or of Imbros received in money or by a bare allowance for food.[4] Though there were exceptions to the law forbidding the exercise of two offices in the same year, there was none in connection with paid offices (μὴ διχόθεν μισθοφορεῖν).[5]

According to the Athenian conception the principle of equality was to be applied not only to individuals, but also to territorial divisions. It was for that reason that, since the time of Cleisthenes, the number of magistrates had been in almost all colleges in relation to the decimal system of the tribes. Whether elected or drawn by lot they were usually ten in number. If not, some way was contrived to complete the mystic number. The disappointment of the tribe unrepresented in the college of archons was tempered by giving it a secretary. Were the *epistatai* of Eleusis only seven in number ? Then a secretary and two treasurers of the goddesses were added to them.[6] When more than ten were needed the number was not infrequently raised to thirty, in order that the three divisions of each tribe might be represented: thus there had been thirty tribal judges[7] before the

[1] *RIG*, no. 572, l. 56 *ff.*
[2] *SIG²*, no. 587, l. 10 *ff.*, 43 *f.*, 48, 143.
[3] Arist., *Ath. Const.*, 62, 2; cf. 42, 3.
[4] Id., *ibid.*, 62, 2.   [5] Dem., *C. Timocr.*, 123.
[6] *RIG*, no. 817; *SIG²*, *loc. cit.*, l. 3, 36 *ff.*, 114 *ff.*, 137 *ff.*
[7] *IG*, vol. I, nos. 32, l. 8; 226, l. 2; 228, l. 1; Arist., *op. cit.*, 26, 3 (cf. CXXVI, vol. II, p. 168).

Thirty Tyrants had rendered this number odious. When a great number of candidates were needed for the drawing of lots, the total allotted to each tribe was divided among the demes which composed it. For quite a long time this system was applied to the nomination of archons; but, since it readily lent itself to abuse in the small demes, it had to be abandoned except for the appointment by lot of the five hundred councillors and the five hundred keepers of the arsenals.[1] When, on the other hand, ten magistrates was too large a number sometimes only five were appointed, in the proportion of one to two tribes, as for example in the case of road surveyors (ὁδοποιοί) and introducers of cases to be judged within the month (ἐισαγωγεῖς).[2] For the selection of extraordinary magistrates the Cleisthenian rule could not always be followed: for instance the ambassadors sent to foreign countries were chosen in varying numbers from the whole body of citizens (ἐξ ’Αθηναίων ἁπάντων); but whenever it was possible the Athenian democrats adhered to the general custom. It is worthy of notice that the revolutionary oligarchs of 413-11 and of 404 observed it themselves, when they caused the constitution of the Four Hundred to be prepared by ten, then by thirty *probouloi* and when they organized the tyranny of the Thirty. Finally, certain magistracies were taken from the ten tribes in a body: thus the secretary of the Council was supplied from year to year by each tribe in turn.[3]

II

APPOINTMENT OF MAGISTRATES

Magistrates were appointed either by lot or by election.

At the close of the fifth century drawing of lots became the democratic procedure *par excellence*, and by its means were chosen all magistrates whom it was not absolutely necessary to select according to their political ideas or their abilities. One must not think, however, that the drawing of lots was a device invented by the democrats and that it had always possessed the egalitarian character which it

---

[1] Arist., *op. cit.*, 62, 1; 22, 5; 26, 2.
[2] Id., *ibid.*, 54, 1; 52, 2.   [3] *v.* p. 123.

in fact acquired. In order to investigate this subject thoroughly it is profitable to examine the method of appointment employed in the case of the archons throughout the centuries.

The majority of authors have tended to regard the drawing of lots as a relatively late practice and have attributed the idea either to Cleisthenes or Aristides, or even to Ephialtes and Pericles. But Fustel de Coulanges, faithful to his general conception and always tracing back institutions to religious origins, maintained that the drawing of lots, a veritable judgment of God, was used for the appointment of the archons from the beginning.[1] His view was correct. Aristotle says, indeed, in the *Politics* that Solon preserved as he found it the method of appointing magistrates and that this method was essentially aristocratic;[2] while in the *Athenian Constitution* he says that Solon decided that the drawing of lots for the magistrates should be made from lists of candidates previously chosen by the tribes (πρόκριτοι), then four in number, and that for the nine archons, each tribe should put forward ten candidates selected from the wealthiest, the *pentacosiomedimni*.[3] Aristotle does not contradict himself; he merely tells us that while conserving the old method of appointment Solon adapted it to the new constitution: the forty candidates whose names were to be placed in the urn were no longer chosen only by the chiefs of great families and according to birth, but by all the citizens and according to fortune.

The reformer no doubt congratulated himself on having made the drawing of lots a reality; for the Council of ex-archons, the Areopagus, to which was entrusted the recruiting of magistrates,[4] had found it too easy to manipulate the drawing of lots and to turn it for all practical purposes into co-optation. But in that Solon was deceived. Intrigues and frauds continued. During the whole of the sixth century the office of chief archon was the goal of the ambitious. From time to time great men such as Dropides, the friend of Solon, and the leader of the nobility, the Philaïd Hippocleides, might hold it; sometimes sedition and usurpation

210   THE CITY UNDER DEMOCRACY

might prevent it from being regularly filled, whence the years of " anarchy."[1]   Later Pisistratus and his sons, just as if it were a question of ordinary appointment, agreed to fill it with intimate friends such as Pisistratus the Younger, Miltiades and Hebron, and after the expulsion of the tyrants it was given to the leader of the oligarchic party, Isagoras. Then came the reform of Cleisthenes.   It changed the old system in two particulars.   In order not to depart from the decimal system which was applied to political organization, the secretary of the *thesmothetai* was added in subordination to the nine archons, and the ten members of the college were drawn by lot, one from each tribe in turn.[2]   Ten candidates from each of the ten new tribes were to be put forward in place of the ten candidates required from each of the four old tribes.   But as in the past it was always eminent citizens, politicians, who were nominated, Alcmæon, Hipparchus, Themistocles, Aristides.   How was it possible for a magistracy filled by lot to provoke so many conflicts, and to fall regularly to the strongest or the ablest ?   Aristotle supplies the explanation of this fact: " There is also a danger in electing the magistrates out of a body who are themselves elected; for if but a small number choose to combine, the elections will always go as they desire."[3]   It was quite possible, for example, that a tribe might use its right of presentation in putting forward only one candidate and thus render the drawing of lots meaningless.   After the first Persian war the drawing of lots for the archons was equivalent for the most part to an election, but—it must not be forgotten—an election which was a privilege of the Athenians of the first class.

In 487-6 a great reform was achieved in the appointment of the archons.   It was the time when the people was issuing writ after writ of ostracism against persons suspected of having dealings with the exiled tyrants and the Persians. It was essential that their partisans should be prevented from continuing the electoral manipulations which had so often won for them the archonship, and that the lot should be made a reality.   Such a reform was not dangerous since the reins of government were in the hands of elected *strategoi*.

---

[1] Id., *ibid.*, 13, 1.   [2] Id., *ibid.*, 55, 1; cf. 59, 7; 63, 1.
        [3] Id., *Pol.*, II, 3, 13.

The choice of candidates for the archonship might, therefore, be extended over a wider range. From the tribe the right of presentation passed to the demes. In order that all the demes should have their candidates and in a number proportionate to their population, they were allowed for the archonship, as for the Boule, fifty candidates for each tribe: making a total of five hundred. But the first class which could easily put forward forty, could not present twelve and a half times that number; moreover a reward was conferred on at least one of the other classes which had fought at Marathon: the privilege of participating in the drawing of lots for the archonship was extended to the knights.[1] It is possible that after the double invasion of the Persians which had impoverished the landowners and after the victories of Salamis and Platæa won by the patriotic alliance of all classes, a decree proposed by Aristides in 478 allowed the five hundred candidates to be taken from the people as a whole, without distinction of income; but this was in any case an exceptional measure; the law was ignored but not changed.[2] Even the reform of Ephialtes allowed it to remain as it was.

It was only in 457-6 that a further reduction in the property qualification took place. Athens, at war with the Bœotians and the Spartans, had been compelled to make exacting demands on the zeugitai, not only in the infantry, according to the established rule, but also in the cavalry. By way of compensation it gave them access to the archonship.[3] Henceforth one class only, that of the thetes, was excluded, and that distinction could not be maintained much longer. Not even a law was needed to abolish it. Men agreed to close their eyes to the declarations of income made during the dokimasia. Aristotle mentions it not without irony: " When the candidates who presented themselves for the drawing of lots for an office were asked what was their class, no one bethought himself to reply: that of the thetes."[4]

As soon as every citizen became eligible for the archonship it seemed in harmony with strict democratic principle to suppress the method of election for the nomination of candidates proposed by the demes and to replace it by a preliminary

---

[1] Id., *Ath. Const.*, 22, 5.
[2] Plut., *Arist.*, 22; Arist., *op. cit.*, 26, 2.
[3] Arist., *loc. cit.* [4] Id., *ibid.*, 7, 4.

drawing of lots in the demes.[1]   It was this double drawing
of lots, already employed in the recruiting of the Council,
which was, *par excellence*, appointment " by the bean." It
was certainly used as early as the fifth century and probably
shortly after the reform which deprived the two first classes
of their exclusive privilege.[2]   The principal motive which
actuated this reform was the desire to put an end to electoral
jobbery which voting by ballot encouraged in the small
areas of the demes.   But the urns continued to be tampered
with as much in the case of the lot as in election.   What
was to be done ?   It was decided towards the end of the
fifth century, perhaps in 403, to take the drawing of lots
for candidates no longer by demes but by the tribe as a whole.[3]
When this was done there was no longer any reason for retaining the enormous number of five hundred candidates.
Since the tribe had not to provide for all its demes it was
enough for it to put forward ten.   The principle remained
intact, for no limits were set to the number of citizens who
might present themselves for the lot, and the two operations
were much simplified.   Thus was finally fixed a method of
appointment which fraud and the necessity of counteracting
it had caused to vary so much for two centuries.

The drawing of lots for magistrates seems to us to-day
so patent an absurdity that we can hardly conceive that an
intelligent people should have devised and maintained such
a system.   In that we are at one with the oligarchs and
philosophers of antiquity.   " It is foolish," as Xenophon
makes Socrates say, " that the magistrates of the city should
be chosen by the bean, when no one would dream of drawing
lots for a pilot, a mason, a flute-player, or any craftsman at
all, whose faults are far less harmful than those which are
committed in the government."[4]

But it is better to attempt to understand than to criticize.
The drawing of lots had been invented in far distant times
when men knew no better method of appointing their leaders
than by the judgment of their gods.   It was retained by
later generations to whom the judgment of God offered the

---

[1] Id., *ibid.*, 8, 1; 62, 1.
[2] Id., *Pol.*, VII (VI), 1, 10; Xen., *Mem.*, 1, 2, 9; Isocr., *Areop.*, 22.
Cf. art. " Sortitio," (*DA*, p. 1407).
[3] Arist., *Ath. Const.*, 62, 1.   Cf. *DA*, *loc. cit.*
[4] Xen., *loc. cit.*

advantage of appeasing the bloody rivalries of great families. And now it did not fail, even in oligarchic cities, to allay the dissensions of parties, by preventing a victorious faction from making the tyranny of a majority prevail in the whole government, in all the administrative departments, and thus exasperating the opposition; it suppressed the disgrace of electoral jobbery, and Aristotle cites the example of Heraia in Arcadia where election was abolished because it favoured intrigue.[1] Democracy was certainly not going to renounce it because in addition it gave to all citizens an equal right of access to the magistracies. It must be remembered, more-over, that the disadvantages of the lot were much diminished in practice. The incapable were withheld from participating from fear of ridicule and people of doubtful honesty by the prospect of the *dokimasia*; the collegial character of the magistracies ensured an average mean of intelligence, and the nomination of a president introduced the selective prin-ciple into the lot itself; the collaboration of the assessors and especially the presence of an experienced personnel in government departments counteracted the inexperience of the leaders; and finally, in spite of the progress of the system of the lot, the system of election retained an important position.

All the magistrates who were required to have professional knowledge or pecuniary guarantees were appointed by a vote by show of hands. These were, since the fifth century, military officials: the ten *strategoi*, the ten *taxiarchs*, the two *hipparchs*, the ten *phylarchs* and the ten recruiting officers or *katalogeis*;[2] and, in addition, the heads of technical depart-ments: in the fifth century, probably the *Hellenotamiai* or treasurers of the federal exchequer; in the fourth, the ad-ministrators of the theoric fund and the *epimeletes* of waters and fountains.[3] Aristotle also mentions in that category the treasurers of the two State triremes, the *Paralus* and the *Ammonis*; he tells us that the Ecclesia elected the archi-tects in charge of the construction of ships of the fleet and the naval engineers, and that the Council chose from its own number the ten commissioners whose duty it was to super-

---

[1] Arist., *Pol.*, VIII (V), 2, 9.
[2] Id., *Ath. Const.*, 43, 1; 44, 4; 49, 2; 61; Æschin., *C. Ctes.*, 13; Xen., *Mem.*, III, 4; Dem., *C. Mid.*, 171.
[3] Arist., *op. cit.*, 43, 1; cf. Æschin., *loc. cit.*, 24; *RIG*, no. 105.

H*

intend the *trieropoioi*; finally he gives us many details of the method in which the directors and masters of the *epheboi* were appointed.[1] But there were many other elective magistracies. In the first rank, in the second half of the fourth century, was the high office which the orator Lycurgus rendered illustrious, an office which was almost a ministry of public finance, whose holder, called "the keeper of the *dioikesis*" (ὁ ἐπὶ διοικήσει), was elected for four years.[2] Then came extraordinary functions. When the people ordered the execution of public works it elected the architect by show of hands and attached to him by the same method of appointment a commission of *epistatai* provided with a secretary and sometimes with a treasurer.[3] Often it divided the works of naval construction or of fortification between the ten tribes; in this case the tribes each named one or more commissioners (the τειχοποιοί, the ταφροποιοί, the τριηροποιοί), but they were none the less public officials.[4] Finally, the majority of magistrates whose duty it was to preside over great festivals were elected from the citizens who were in a position to enhance their splendour by drawing upon their own incomes. Such were the four *epimeletai* of the mysteries, two of whom were chosen from the whole body of the Athenians, and two from the sacerdotal families of the Eumolpidæ and the Kerykes.[5] It was the same with the ten *epimeletai* of the Dionysia until 451, when it became possible to select them by lot since henceforth a considerable sum was put aside for their expenses.[6] Though the majority of the priesthoods were filled by lot, the oldest were hereditary in certain families, and there were some exceptional ones filled by election.[7] In other religious offices election was more prominent.[8]

The election day (ἀρχαιρεσίαι) was fixed by soothsayers

[1] Arist., *op. cit.*, 61, 7; 46, 1 (cf. Dem., *loc. cit.*); 42, 2-3 (cf. *RIG*, no. 603, l. 29, 55).

[2] Ps. Plut., *Lyc.*, 3, p. 841c; Poll., VIII, 113.

[3] *RIG*, no. 1465, l. 28; *SIG*², *loc. cit.*; l. 12, 43, 118, 143; *IG*, vol. II², no. 463, l. 7.

[4] Æschin., *loc. cit.*, 13 *ff.*, 27 *ff.*, 114.

[5] Arist., *op. cit.*, 57, 1; Dem., *loc. cit.*; *RIG*, nos. 132, l. 10; 683.

[6] Arist., *op. cit.*, 56, 4; Dem., *loc. cit.*, 15; cf. *DA*, art. "Epimeletai," p. 682 *ff.*

[7] Cf. *RIG*, no. 671; *v. DA*, art. "Sortitio," p. 1409.

[8] Dem., *loc. cit.*, 115, 171; *v.* G. Colin, *Le culte d'Apoll. Pyth. à Ath.*, p. 19 *ff.*; A. W. Persson, *Die Exegeten und Delphi* (1918), p. 10 *ff.*

(κατά τὴν μαντείαν): it took place in the first prytany, after the sixth, when the auspices were favourable.[1] Even when the electoral session had opened it was suspended if the gods manifested their disapproval. Thus on the 21st of March, 424, at eight o'clock in the morning preparations were being made for the taking of the vote when, to the great joy of the opponents of Cleon, an eclipse of the sun caused the matter to be postponed to a later meeting.[2] The elections then, unless the gods prohibited it, might be entered upon after the opening of the seventh prytany (the middle of February), but, on the other hand, they might not be delayed beyond the ninth, because sufficient time had to be left for accomplishing the formalities of the *dokimasia* and for settling the suits which sometimes ensued. For the same reason the drawing of lots was held at about the same time as the elections.[3] It was just at the beginning of spring in 440, if one is to trust a piquant anecdote, that the elections which brought Sophocles to the office of *strategos* took place: it was a mark of favour for the success of his *Antigone*,[4] and, therefore, after the Dionysia which were celebrated from the tenth to the fifteenth of Elaphebolion (the end of March), that is to say at a meeting of the eighth prytany. If the anecdote is not authentic, on the question of date, at any rate, it is completely in accordance with the facts.

The elections were always held on the Pnyx, in the open air, even when at the end of 332 the people adopted the practice of holding their ordinary assemblies in the theatre.[5] As with all the proceedings of the Ecclesia the session opened with the reading of the *probouleuma* which authorized it (μηδὲν ἀπροβούλευτον).[6] Election was never made otherwise than by show of hands (χειροτονεῖν). When it was a question of appointing colleges of ten magistrates there were two methods of procedure: either (and this was the more frequent) they were chosen in the proportion of one from each tribe (ἀφ' ἑκάστης φυλῆς ἕνα), or else they were taken indiscriminately from the whole body of Athenians (ἐξ ἁπάντων Ἀθηναίων). As the army was divided into ten tribes (*phylai*), the first

1 *IG*, vol. II, no. 416; Arist., *op. cit.*, 44, 4.
2 Aristoph., *Clouds*, 581 *ff.* and Schol.; cf. **VI**, vol. III, ii, p. 1124.
3 Cf. *RIG*, no. 75, l. 13 *ff.*   4 Soph., *Antig.*, Hyp. I.
5 Poll., VIII, 133; cf. **CXV**, p. 1 *ff.*; **CXIII**, p. 9.
6 Arist., *op. cit.*, 44, 4.

only of these systems was applicable to the ten commanders of the infantry, the *taxiarchs*, as well as to the ten commanders and the ten recruiters of the cavalry, the *phylarchs* and the *katalogeis*, whilst the two generals of the cavalry, the *hipparchs*, each appointed for five tribes, were necessarily taken from " among all the Athenians."[1]   But the *strategoi*, at first elected according to the first system, were elected later according to the second.[2]   The change was probably effected during the epoch when Pericles was re-elected year after year.   As he could not pass for the qualified representative of his tribe, the Acamantis, but was indeed the representative of the whole city, the Acamantis obtained from time to time a second representative: this happened three times in ten years.   Force of circumstances, therefore, prevented the ancient rule from being rigorously observed, so much so that we know for the fifth and fourth centuries eleven cases in which the same tribe was doubly represented in the college.[3]   Even if, however, for one reason or another a tribe found itself thus favoured, an effort was made to give representation to the greatest possible number of tribes.

As one would expect candidates for the magistracies had recourse to all manner of contrivances.   At the time when the lot was preceded by elections in the demes corruption ran riot in these " stagnant pools," and so it was for reasons of political morality that democracy preferred the two-fold drawing of lots.   But elections always gave scope to skilful jobbery.   Every year the spectacle described by Demosthenes was witnessed: " ·Those who aspired to elective offices and the rank which they bestowed, slaves of the approval which assured them their votes, went from one to another, each dreaming of being sworn a *strategos*."[4]   Some employed pathetic devices: an old soldier would uncover his breast and display his scars;[5] others in cynical fashion would appeal to the venality of the electors: their expenses were only " advances," it was a question of spending " in order to reimburse themselves doubly."[6]   Parties organized themselves in support of their candidates; committees came into being, each with its agents and its funds; the oligarchs of the

[1] Id., *ibid.*, 61, 4-5; 49, 2; *IG*, vol. II, no. 562; Æschin., *Emb.*, 169.
[2] Arist., *op. cit.*, 61, 1; cf. 22, 2.   [3] Cf. **LXXXV**, p. 276.
[4] Dem., *Pub. Econ.*, 19.   [5] Xen., *Mem.*, III, 4, 1.
[6] Lys., *Property of Aristoph.*, 57.

fifth century were grouped in strong *hetaireiai*, which may be compared with the Tammany clubs of America.[1]

But one must not think that jobbery was a greater evil among the Athenians than among any ·other peoples of antiquity or of modern times. In many elections there was no trace of it. Intrigue could do nothing, for instance, in the recruiting of the ephebic officials. The fathers of the youths assembled by tribes, and, after having taken an oath, elected from the members of their tribe who were over forty the three citizens whom they deemed most honourable and most capable of taking care of their sons; from these three the people elected one for each tribe as *sophronistes* or censor, after which it selected from all the Athenians the *kosmetes* or principal, the head of all the *epheboi*.[2] Even in elections of a political nature the Athenians were not incapable of wise choice. One student of antiquity has investigated the social position of persons who held office in the time of Demosthenes: he has reached the conclusion that the highest functions, those which involved the greatest responsibility, were generally confided to men of high birth, rich or well-informed.[3] Plutarch[4] remarks that this people, who used the demagogues as kings their flatterers and fools, as a means of distraction, was wise enough to call to the most important positions true statesmen and, above all, to appoint the most capable to military commands. He makes that remark in connection with Phocion who, in spite of his loathing of the multitude and although he never put himself forward, was appointed *strategos* forty-five times. He might have added that a democracy capable of conferring supreme power for more than thirty years on a Pericles was assuredly lacking in neither seriousness nor clearness of purpose, but on the contrary gave a proof of it unique in the history of the world.

When they had been appointed by lot or by election, the magistrates did not enter upon their duties until they had been subjected to the test of the *dokimasia*. In the time of Aristotle this procedure was in general carried out before the tribunal, but for the nine archons there was a preliminary examination in the Council of the Five Hundred. In the

---

[1] Thuc., VIII, 54, 4. Cf. **LXXXVIII**, p. 32.
[2] Arist., *op. cit.*, 42, 2-3.
[3] **CXXI**, cf. Ps. Xen., *Rep. of Ath.*, I, 3.   [4] *Phoc.*, 8.

fifth century the Council could alone pronounce judgment;
in the fourth, however, the magistrate rejected by it could
appeal to the tribunal, which gave the final decision.[1] The
dokimasia of the archons is well known to us. It began by
questioning the future magistrate on his birth: " Who is
your father, and of what deme ? Who is your father's
father ? Who is your mother ? Who is your mother's
father and of what deme ?" By further questions it was
ascertained whether he was a member of a phratry, the issue
of a good and ancient line, whether he participated in a cult
of Apollo Patroos and of Zeus Herkeios and where were his
temples, whether he possessed family tombs and where they
were. Finally he was catechized as to his public and his
private life; he was asked whether he behaved well towards
his parents, whether he paid his contributions and whether
he had performed his military obligations.[2] When he had
answered all these questions the president ordered him to
produce witnesses in support of his statements. If one of the
witnesses turned accuser the president heard the statements
for the accusation and for the defence; after that a vote was
taken, by show of hands in the Council, by secret ballot in
the tribunal. If no accuser presented himself the vote was
immediately taken. Originally this vote was a pure formality:
a single judge gave in his voting paper. But later all the
judges were required to vote, in order that if a dishonest
candidate had succeeded in escaping accusation it might still
be in the power of the judges to exclude him.[3]

Besides all the questions of a general order which were put
to the magistrates elect, specific questions were put according
to the magistracies, since for a great number of them special
conditions were imposed. The archons were to have no physical defect; the king had to have a wife who was alive and who
had not been previously married; the *strategoi* had to have
children born in wedlock and to possess landed property in
Attica; the treasurers of " the other gods " were to belong
by their wealth to the class of the *pentacosiomedimni*.[4] The

[1] Arist., *op. cit.*, 45, 3; Dem., *C. Lept.*, 90. Cf. P. Cloché, *REG*, vol.
XXXIV (1921), p. 240.
[2] Arist., *loc. cit.*; Cratin. Jun. ap. Athen., XI, 3, p. 460 *f*.
[3] Arist., *loc. cit.*, 3-4; cf. Dem., *C. Euboul.*, 67.
[4] Ps. Dem., *C. Neaira*, 72, 75; Dein., *C. Dem.*, 71 (cf. Arist., *op. cit.*,
4, 2); Lys., *Invalid*, 13.

conditions imposed on the members of the two last colleges have an aristocratic character which at first seems surprising; but one can understand that the people should demand from magistrates who might gravely compromise the finances of the city guarantees analogous to those which we demand to-day as security. In addition, though the questionnaire was restricted in form it was not so in reality. It was easy to extend it indefinitely: the whole life of the new member was submitted to the scrutiny of all the citizens. And that was thought good, since it kept back the unworthy—undutiful sons, bad soldiers, bad tax-payers, all citizens overshadowed by the menace of *atimia*, all the enemies of democracy.[1]

III

FUNCTIONING OF THE COLLEGES OF MAGISTRATES

The majority of magistrates entered into office on the first day of the year. But during the whole of the century which followed the reform of Cleisthenes the official calendar was conformed to; this divided the ordinary year of 360 days and the intercalary year of 390 days into ten prytanies and, as a consequence, did not correspond to the civil calendar whose year had 354 or 384 days divided into twelve and thirteen months. There existed, therefore, between the two calendars a difference which sometimes amounted to twenty days. In 408-7, or rather a little earlier, when democratic institutions were reorganized after the fall of the Four Hundred, it was decided that the magistrates should henceforth enter into office at the beginning of the civil year, on the 1st of Hecatombaion. But after as before 408-7 certain magistracies commenced on the 20th of the same month, at the Panathenæa. The ten *athlothetai* who directed the games of these festivals held office for four years from one celebration of the Great Panathenæa to the next.[2] Other magistracies, though annual, began on the same day: in the fifth century, the treasurers of the goddess and those of the other gods; in the fourth century,

---

[1] Lys., *C. Philon*, 1; *C. Agor.*, 10; *Dokim. of Mantith.*, 9; *Dokim. of Evandros*, 9 ff.

[2] Arist., *op. cit.*, 60, 1; cf. *RIG*, no. 563, l. 57.

the treasurer of the military funds, the guardians of the theoric fund and the *epimeletes* of waters.[1]

All magistrates before entering upon their duties were required to take an oath of investiture. This oath varied according to the office, but it always included a promise to conform to the laws and not to allow them to be broken. The archons swore to consecrate a golden statue of their own stature if they should accept presents.[2] They took their oath twice in succession: the first time they swore standing on the " pledging-stone " erected in the agora before the royal portico; then, in company with the *strategoi* and doubtless other magistrates, on the Acropolis, before the image of the goddess and a table on which were placed the crowns of myrtle.[3] These crowns, insignia of their office, gave them sacrosanctity.[4] Thus invested they offered to the gods an inaugural sacrifice (εἰσιτήρια).[5]

Each college had its ἀρχεῖον, the building or premises where the magistrates took their meals and where the Assembly room (συνέδριον) and the offices were.[6]

Certain magistrates had assistants, *paredroi*, who were equally magistrates, since they could take the place of the officeholders, and they, too, had to undergo the examination of the *dokimasia* and render account at the end of the year.[7] Each of the three archons with special functions had two *paredroi*; he chose them himself, often from his own family, and co-operated with them in certain matters so as to form within the great college of the archons a special small college such as that of the *thesmothetai*.[8] To the ten *Hellenotamiai* were attached ten *paredroi* who could act separately in conjunction with their superior, or altogether with the *Hellenotamiai* united in a body. Since there were *paredroi* for the *strategoi*

---

[1] *IG*, vol. I, nos. 117 *ff.*; *SIG³*, no. 91, l. 27 *f.*, 58; Arist., *op. cit.*, 43, 1.

[2] Arist., *op. cit.*, 7, 1; 55, 5; Plat., *Phœdr.*, 11, p. 235d; Plut., *Sol.*, 25.

[3] Arist., *op. cit.*, 55, 5; Dein., *C. Philocl.*, 2; Lys., *Soldier*, 15.

[4] Lys., *Dokim. Evandr.*, 8; Dem., *C. Meid.*, 17, 32; Arist., *op. cit.*, 57, 4.

[5] Thuc., VIII, 70; Dem., *loc. cit.*, 114; *Emb.*, 190.

[6] Dem., *Phil.*, IV, 53; Æschin., *Emb.*, 85 and Schol., 190; Lys., *Soldier*, 6, 9 *ff.*; *RIG*, no. 116, l. 11, 29.

[7] Arist., *op. cit.*, 56, 1.

[8] Dem., *C. Mid.*, 178; Ps. Dem., *C. Neaira*, 72, 83; cf. *RIG*, nos. 634, l. 14, 18; 962, l. 2; *SIG²*, no. 587, l. 243 *ff.*

and the *euthynoi* as well, we may conclude that the institution was more or less general.[1]

In the same way as the Council, the supreme magistrature, the colleges of even the most minor officials had their " secretary-registrar," the *grammateus*. His office was annual. The secretaries of the most important colleges (those of the *strategoi*, the treasurers, etc.), and even those who were attached to the *epistatai* of public works, were citizens and had the rank of magistrates.[2] The secretary of the *thesmothetai* must be placed in a higher category. He was associated with the archons as the tenth, in order that each tribe might be represented in the college. Although in his case the *dokimasia* was not invested with such solemn formalities as in that of the *thesmothetai*, and although he had not the right of inflicting fines or of presiding over a tribunal, it was quite an adequate position by way of stop-gap.[3]

Beneath these secretaries who formed a select body, were a multitude of secretaries and sub-clerks (ὑπογραμματεῖς) attached to the magistrates.[4] Most frequently they were metics or freedmen, but sometimes they were humble citizens who had to earn their living. They had a bad reputation. By their knowledge of government departments and of the records they acquired familiarity with official documents and an experience which enabled them to direct, honestly or not, the amateur leaders appointed for a year.[5] Hence the law forbade the minor clerks to retain the same office for more than a year:[6] they passed, therefore, from one department to another in order not to lose their salary. Finally, the chief magistrates had their heralds for summonses and proclamations, and flute players to play during the sacrifices offered under their presidency.[7] All these people belonged to the category of salaried employees to whom a name little esteemed was given (ὑπηρέται).

[1] *RIG*, nos. 560, l. 3-68; 563, l. 3-69; 569, B, l. 1- 23; Arist., *op. cit.*, 48, 4; *SIG*[3], no. 305, l. 75.

[2] **LXXXVII**, p. xiv.

[3] Arist., *op. cit.*, 55, 1-2; cf. 59, 7; 63, 1.

[4] Aristoph., *Frogs*, 1083 *ff.*; Antiph., *Chor.*, 35, 49; v. **LXXXVII,** p. xv.

[5] Dem., *Emb.*, 249; *De Coron.*, 261; *RIG*, no. 572, l. 58.

[6] Lys., *C. Nicom.*, 29. There was an analogous law at Erythræ (*Abh. BA*, 1909, p. 29 *ff.*).

[7] Arist., *op. cit.*, 62, 2; cf. 64, 3; 66, 1; 68, 4; 69, 1; Aristoph., *Wasps*, 752; Ps. Xen., *Rep. of Ath.*, I, 17.

Others in great number were attached to certain administrations as servants. They were never citizens, rarely freemen, almost always public slaves (δημόσιοι).[1]   The officials responsible for the execution of criminal sentences were the object of universal loathing; recourse had to be had to slaves for the recruiting of the personnel which the Eleven required, the executioner, that unclean being who was not allowed to dwell within the city, and torturers and gaolers.[2] Public slaves served as apparitors for the *thesmothetai*, who employed them in all the material transactions necessitated by the organization and the functioning of the tribunals.[3] Others formed the gangs employed by the *astynomoi* for the policing of the streets, by the surveyors for the upkeep of the roads, by the *epistatai* for public works.[4]   We know, finally, of slaves whose administrative duties were of a higher order: book-keepers in charge of the papers of the treasurers and the *strategoi*; the archivist of the Metroon; the archivist of the Boule, who had charge of the documents necessary for the exercise of its financial functions (statistics of property let by the *poletai* and the king, containing details of rents and expirations and returns of special taxes).[5]

Democratic equality would not suffer any difference to be made between members of the same college. But the nine archons, created at different epochs and united by an artificial tie, did not form a college as the others did: the six *thesmothetai*, it is true, followed the general rule; but the archon, the king and the polemarch had their special functions and acted independently of each other; the archon properly so called might be regarded as the chief of them all, inasmuch as he gave his name to the year and had by virtue of that a moral pre-eminence over all the magistrates without exception. In the other colleges in spite of equality in principle there was usually need for a president. Sometimes he was appointed for the whole year, as in the case of the treasurers; sometimes he was chosen by turns; for example,

---

[1] *v.* Waszinski, *De Servis Atheniensium publicis*, Berlin, 1908, p. 100 *ff.*
[2] Arist., *Pol.*, VII (VI), 5, 5-7; Poll., VIII, 71; IX, 10.
[3] Arist., *Ath. Const.*, 63, 5; 64, 1; 65, 4; 69, 1.
[4] Id., *ibid.*, 50, 2; 54, 1; *SIG²*, nos. 587, l. 4 *f.*, 42 *f.*, etc.
[5] Dem., *Chers.*, 47; *Emb.*, 129; *C. Androt.*, 70.   Cf. **LXXXI**, p. 229 *ff.*, 248.

in the earliest days, each *strategos* exercised the presidency and the supreme command one day out of ten. Business was despatched either by the whole college or by one of the members acting in its name. The magistrates of a college were, therefore, collectively and individually responsible, as well in each prytany before the Assembly as at the conclusion of their office before the *logistai* and the *euthynoi*.[1] In the college of the *strategoi* the principle of collective administration and responsibility could not withstand the exigencies of war. The Assembly designated one or more *strategoi* for each expedition, allotted to each one his powers and sometimes appointed a generalissimo: it is obvious that in this case there would be either personal or partially collective responsibility.[2]

IV

POWER AND RESPONSIBILITY OF THE MAGISTRATES

The magistrates enjoyed numerous prerogatives. It is possible that the State granted them a suspensive immunity against certain actions; for we know of no instance in which a magistrate was the object of an action in civil law.[3] In any case they were assured of special protection in the performance of their duties. "Any outrage offered to them," says Demosthenes, "extends to the laws, to the crown, the symbol of public authority, to the very name of the city."[4] An insult thus became an offence liable to heavy punishment. The injured magistrate might inflict a fine on the delinquent, as was done, for example, by a *strategos* to a soldier, according to a counsel's address which has come down to us.[5] If the legal maximum of the *epibole* seemed to him inadequate he might send the offender before the courts and secure a severer sentence, such as the total deprivation of civil rights. The magistrates had, in addition, honorific privileges. They occupied a special place in processions and in ceremonies of every

---

[1] Antiph., *Chor.*, 49; Dem., *Emb.*, 211 *f.*; cf. *RIG*, nos. 563, l. 67; 569, A, l. 15-34; B, l. 3-24.
[2] *v.* Hauvette Besnault, *Les strat. ath.*, p. 52 *ff.*, 82 *ff.*; **VII**, vol. II., p. 1062, n. 1.
[3] Cf. **CVI**, vol. III, p. 802.
[4] Dem., *C. Mid.*, 32 *f.*; cf. Arist., *Probl.*, 29, 14.
[5] Ps. Lys., *Soldier*, 6-11, 16.

kind. Their seats were reserved in the theatre. In the banquets which followed the sacrifices they were offered the choicest morsels, as were the chiefs of Homeric times. One decree enumerates the number of joints to be set aside from the victims of the Panathenaeic hecatomb in honour of the *prytaneis*, the archons, the treasurers of the goddess, the *hieropoioi*, the *strategoi* and the *taxiarchs*.[1]

The democratic spirit, however, was not very conducive to a profound respect for the magistrates. The idea that the citizen ought alternately to obey and to command led each one to consider himself in all respects the equal of those who had succeeded to the command and who demanded his obedience. Such was the attitude of the majority towards the magistrates that carping critics thought it was commendable to despise them.[2] As one might expect, however, the party men who reproached the people on this account fully deserved reproach themselves: it was for their benefit that, in 426, Aristophanes in the *Babylonians* vilified Cleon, then a councillor, and, in 425, in the *Acharnians*, Lamachus, then *strategos*.[3]

It was impossible, besides, for the people to show much deference towards magistrates who were always subject to its authority. In order to provide against abuse of power the sovereign people exercised a perpetual control over its servants. Any citizen could independently superintend the activities of any official. Moreover, everything was done by order of the Council or the Assembly, or at the least, was done before their eyes. No administrative department whatever could take any initiative without seeking the advice or the collaboration of the Council.[4] The majority of the magistrates, especially those who had the management of public funds, were subjected to its penal jurisdiction, and in each prytany they had to render account to a commission of ten auditors (*logistai*) drawn by lot from the members of the Council.[5] On the recommendation of the *logistai* or on its own initiative the Council could try any magistrate on the charge of malversation; but if he were condemned the magis-

---

[1] *RIG*, no. 679, l. 10 *ff*.   [2] Xen., *Mem.*, III, 5, 16.
[3] Aristoph., *Knights*, 774 (cf. CIV, no. 8674); *Acharn.*, 593 *ff*. (cf. Zielinski, *Gliederung der altatt. Komödie*, p. 54 *ff*.).
[4] *v. supra*, p. 193.
[5] Arist., *Ath. Const.*, 48, 3; Lys., *C. Nicom.*, 5.

trate was entitled to appeal to the tribunal. It was also lawful for any citizen to bring an *eisangelia* before the Council against any magistrate who was accused of failing to conform to the laws, and, in this case again, the condemned man had the right of appeal to popular justice.[1] But the Ecclesia retained a direct and a much more far-reaching power over all those who were merely the temporary executors of its will. In the principal assembly of each prytany it proceeded to the *epicheirotonia*, that is it voted by show of hands on the question of the administration of the magistrates: it confirmed them in their power if it considered that they had acquitted themselves well; if not it deposed them and sent them before the court.[2] But even before the vote of confidence had been taken in the ordinary and customary way of procedure the Ecclesia did not hesitate to depose *strategoi* with whose conduct it was dissatisfied,[3] nor to prosecute them by means of the *eisangelia* for any offence committed in the exercise of their office;[4] and when the *epicheirotonia* was regularly inscribed in the order of the day of the chief assemblies, arraignment might either precede or follow the deposition. In the fifth century the Ecclesia itself usually judged *eisangeliai*, whilst in the fourth it sent them for preference to the heliasts.[5] If he were acquitted the deposed magistrate resumed his office; if he were condemned his punishment was arbitrarily fixed by the people, in the Heliæa as in the Ecclesia, and it was often very terrible.[6]

Save in grave cases which were almost always of a political nature, the magistrates remained in office until the end of their year; but then a searching trial awaited them. Each of them was responsible (ὑπεύθυνος), collectively with his college, and individually with his person and his property, for any crime, delinquency or fault committed in his administration. In order that this responsibility might not be rendered nugatory he was not allowed to leave the country, to dispose of his property and to pass into another family by adoption—in brief to withdraw or conceal any sum which

[1] Arist., *op. cit.*, 45, 2.
[2] Id., *ibid.*, 43, 4; 61, 2, 4; Ps. Dem., *C. Aristocr.*, II, 5; *C. Theocr.*, 28; Dein., *C. Philocl.*, 16.
[3] Thuc., VIII, 54, 3; Plut., *Lys.*, 5; Xen., *Hell.*, I, 7, 1.
[4] v. **CVI**, vol. I, p. 176 *ff.*
[5] *Ibid.*, p. 184 *ff.*
[6] Arist., *op. cit.*, 61, 2.

might in certain circumstances be claimed by the State—
before obtaining his discharge.[1] And until that formality
had been accomplished he was forbidden to initiate any
proposal for the bestowal of a reward on a magistrate in
recognition of the manner in which he had fulfilled his duties.
The whole of the action brought by Æschines concerning the
crown prematurely conferred on Demosthenes was based on
this legal prohibition.

The responsibility of the magistrates was two-fold, first
financial, and then moral and political.

Every official on relinquishing his duties had to furnish
either an account of the public funds he had administered
or a written declaration attesting that he had not had the
control of any.[2] If he evaded this obligation by illicit means
or failed to acquit himself of it within the legal period he
became liable to a public action (γραφὴ ἀλογίου) or to
eisangelia.[3] The account was called the logos and the
auditors who had to check it logistai. This college of magistrates must not be confused with the commission of the
Boule which bore the same name and which facilitated the
work of the Council by audits carried out from prytany to
prytany.[4] The logistai numbered thirty in the fifth century
and they were appointed by lot; in the fourth they numbered
only ten, but were assisted by ten synegoroi or agents, likewise elected by lot.[5] When the dossiers had been divided
among them in the chambers of accounts (λογιστήρια),
they had to be checked within thirty days.[6] They had not
only to ensure that the accounts tallied with the official
documents preserved in the archives of the Metroon, but,
if occasion should arise, they had to get from the persons
concerned explanations, with proofs. If it emerged from
the examination of the documents and from the inquiry
that an accountable official had committed a reprehensible
or indictable action the logistai charged the synegoroi to deal
with such conclusions according to law, and if the latter
accepted the charge as well-founded, in concert with the
logistai they brought before a tribunal of heliasts an action

1 Æschin., C. Ctes., 21.   2 Id., ibid., 22.
3 Poll., VI, 152; VIII, 54; Lys., loc. cit., 5, 7.
4 v. supra, p. 190.
5 IG, vol. I, nos. 32, 226, 228; Arist., op. cit., 54, 2.
6 Harp., s.v., λογισταὶ καὶ λογιστήρια.

either in respect of misappropriation (κλοπῆς δημοσίων χρημάτων), venality (δωρῶν), or offences committed in the exercise of their office (ἀδικίου). If, on the other hand, the *logistai* and the *synegoroi* found the accounts in order, they drew up an audit certificate and brought it before the tribunal, which alone had the power to grant discharge. Whether there was a suit or not, therefore, it was for a jury of at least five hundred members to pronounce the last word. In the tribunal over which the *logistai* presided the *synegoroi* acted as public prosecutor; but every citizen was entitled, on a claim being made by the herald of the *logistai*, to plead his cause with regard to the accounts under discussion.[1] There was no appeal from the decision of the tribunal. In cases of simple negligence in the administration of the public funds the guilty official had to make good the amount of which the treasury had been deprived; in case of serious error he was condemned to tenfold restitution.[2] If he were discharged he was doubly protected by the judicial sovereignty of the people and by the inviolable principle of Attic law, μὴ δὶς πρὸς τὸν αὐτὸν περὶ τῶν αὐτῶν, *non bis contra eumdem in idem*.[3]

But although he was irrevocably discharged in so far as accountability was concerned, he remained responsible for every other act of his administration. Besides the rendering of accounts in the narrow and precise sense there was in the public law of Athens a rendering of accounts in the wider and vaguer sense, the *euthyna* in the presence of the *euthynoi*. These " redressers " were ten in number, one for each tribe, and each of them had two assistants or *paredroi*. The whole thirty were drawn by lot from members of the Council. During the three days which followed the judgment rendered by the *logistai* and the *synegoroi*, the *euthynos* sat with his assistants, for the duration of the market, before the statue of the eponymous hero of his tribe. Any citizen might lodge with him against a magistrate already judged in the matter of his financial transactions a private or public suit in respect of his other actions: he inscribed on a white tablet his name, the name of the defendant, the alleged

---

[1] Æschin., *loc. cit.*, 23; Dem., *Emb.*, 2; *De Coron.*, 117.
[2] Arist., *loc. cit.*
[3] Dem., *C. Lept.*, 147; cf. *De Coron.*, 211.

injury with an assessment of the damage caused and the
required penalty, and delivered it to the *euthynos*. The latter
examined the claim, and if after investigation he deemed it
admissible, he delivered it to the competent authorities: the
private suit was transmitted to the judges of the demes
responsible for prosecution in tribal affairs; the public suit
was brought before the *thesmothetai*. If the *thesmothetai*
likewise deemed it admissible, they brought it before the
popular tribunal whose decision was sovereign.[1]

The ordinary procedure of rendering account could not
be applied to the *strategoi*: war often caused them to be
absent from Athens at the end of the year, that is in July,
and they might even have been re-elected many months before,
although they were away. They were not, therefore, compelled to render account until they relinquished their powers,
at the end of one or several years, or in the course of the
year if they had been deposed by an *epicheirotonia* which was
aimed at them in particular.[2] Moreover they had only to
justify the acts of their administration before the *thesmothetai*.
The latter in all probability went to the *logistai* for assistance
on the financial side,[3] but they did not consult the *euthynoi*
upon the remaining questions. Nevertheless they were restricted to the drawing up of a report which they introduced
before the tribunal.[4] Popular justice alone could approve or
condemn the retiring *strategoi*.

The magistrates, therefore, were subjected to an unremit-
ting and detailed supervision. They could do nothing without
the consent of the Council, instructed by a permanent directing committee. Nine times every year they had to obtain
the vote of confidence of the Assembly, under pain of being
suspended and sent before the courts. At the end of the
year all the financial documents of their administration were
examined by this court of accounts which the *logistai* formed;
every one of their actions was scrutinized, upon the request
of anyone, by the *euthynoi* acting as the grand jury. Often
even the laws and decrees whose execution was entrusted to
them contained punishments to which they were liable in case

---

[1] Arist., *op. cit.*, 48, 4-5; cf. Andoc., *De Myst.*, 78; Antiph., *Chor.*,
43; *RIG*, nos. 604, B, l. 7 *ff.*; 150.
[2] Arist., *op. cit.*, 27, 1.   [3] Id., *ibid.*, 54, 2.
[4] Id., *ibid.*, 59, 2.

of neglect.[1] They were hourly exposed to the insults and calumnies of demagogues and sycophants, they were jealously watched by the hatred of their opponents, and they saw ever suspended over their heads the terrible penalties of *eisangelia* and the action against illegality. It was inevitable that the people should adopt towards its officials the domineering attitude of a master since it meant to keep for itself all the functions of sovereignty. The very principle of democratic government demanded this control over executive power.

Thus a veritable tyranny was exercised over the magistrates. The literature and history of the fourth and fifth centuries are full of illustrations of it. There is, for instance, the characteristic scene in the *Knights* in which the Paphlagonian and the Sausage-seller contest, the one in order to retain, the other to win, the favour of Demos, as to who shall best provide for his needs. They excite his longing with promises of barley, of fine flour, of delicious cakes, of cooked meats; for they have been warned that " the control of the Pnyx will fall to the man who shall treat him the best," " to the man who shall have deserved best of the Demos and his belly." But let the one who wins the day himself beware ! Demos is ready enough " on condition that he swallows his daily mess to flatter a thief with the title of sole *prostates* "; but when he sees it come to an end he gives him the *coup de grâce*.[2] And the ruck of officials was treated no more gently than the politician who was exalted to the rank of first minister. " The cities," as Xenophon makes one Athenian say, " treat their magistrates as I treat my servants. I wish my servants to supply me with all I require in abundance and to take nothing themselves; the cities wish their magistrates to procure for them as much profit as possible and to refrain from taking anything at all."[3]

There is obviously an element of exaggeration in the buffooneries of the comedies and in the recriminations of the intellectuals. A philosopher—probably Democritus of Abdera —goes still further when he says: " In the political organization which to-day prevails, it is impossible for the governments not to do wrong, even if they are excellent in all respects; for

---

[1] Plut., *Sol.*, 24; Ps. Dem., *C. Macart.*, 54, 71; *IG*, vol. I², nos. 57, 63, 73, 94; cf. no. 58; *IJG*, vol. II, no. xxix, A; *RIG*, no. 604, B.
[2] Aristoph., *Knights*, 1100 *ff.*; 1207.   [3] Xen., *Mem.*, II, 1, 9.

their plight is that of the eagle preyed on by vermin."[1]
Nevertheless the exaggeration is only one of language. We
touch there upon the common vice of democracies. In fact
the meddling distrust of the Athenian people spared no one.
Pericles himself in the end could not escape it. He rendered
account, year by year, obol by obol, of the sums which passed
through his hands. But he required secret funds for his
diplomacy. That fact was sufficient to cause him to be accused of malversation; in vain did he declare that he had
used the money for " necessary expenses,"—he was duly
condemned.[2] Party spirit and personal rivalries multiplied
the suits which, moreover, were not always brought by
democrats: fines and capital penalties rained thick and fast.[3]
Doubtless the business of accuser had its dangers: the syco-
phant laid himself open to a lashing if he did not obtain a fifth
of the votes; the accused did not content himself with parrying
his blows, but retaliated, and we see Æschines, prosecuted by
Timarchus in connection with his financial administration,
causing his adversary to be condemned for an offence against
established customs. But this did not prevent unsuccessful
generals and ambassadors, dishonest or incapable financial
administrators, negligent governors of prisons, nay even the
officials responsible for supplies who failed to enforce the laws
dealing with the traffic in corn, from being very often treated
as criminals and sent to death.[4]

Thus exposed at all times to suspicion, people of ordinary
ability and of a timorous nature were obsessed and over-
powered by consciousness of their responsibility. The
example of Nicias shows what depressing effects fear of the
Ecclesia might have. He was a good general, but the thought
of the Pnyx paralysed him. After the first checks in the
Silician campaign he dared not give the order for retreat which
would have saved the army. We learn from Thucydides
the cause of his hesitation.[5] He was certain that the
Athenians would disapprove of a measure which they had

1 Democr., ap. Stob., *Flor.*, XLVI, 48.
2 Plut., *Pericl.*, 23; Aristoph., *Clouds*, 859 and Schol.
3 *v.* Hauvette - Besnault, *Les strat. ath.*, p. 107 *ff.*; X, vol. II, p.
971-201; P. Cloché, " Les procès des strat. ath." (*REA*, vol. XXVII,
1925, p. 97-118).
4 Antiph., *Murder of. Her.*, 69 *f.*; Isæus, *Succ. Nicostr.*, 28; Lys.,
Against the Corn-merch., 16.
5 Thuc., VII, 48.

not sanctioned, that they would pass judgment on the *strategoi* without having witnessed the situation with their own eyes, that they would believe the assertions of eloquent speakers. He told himself, too, that his soldiers, on their return to Athens, would throw the responsibility for their sufferings on their generals and would paint them as traitors, bribed by the enemy. Rather than be the victim of an unjust and ignominious accusation he chose to perish sword in hand. He pushed military bravery to the limits of temerity, because civic courage was made too difficult for him. How many magistrates must in this way have lost the spirit of initiative and the security indispensable for the proper discharging of their functions !

CHAPTER VI

JUSTICE

I

PRINCIPLES

BETTER perhaps than any other institution the judicial system reveals that perfect equilibrium between the power of the State and the liberty of the individual which was the ideal of Athens of the fifth century.

The people was the sovereign redresser of wrongs, possessing in theory absolute power over the life and property of all. Recall the declaration of Philocleon in the *Wasps* of Aristophanes—as soon as he enters the Heliæa he lifts up his head and, swelling with pride, exclaims: " Is not my power as great as that of any king ? . . . Is not my authority equal to that of Zeus ?"[1] In fact the popular courts of the Heliæa filled a prominent place in the city. It was the inevitable consequence of the advance made by democratic ideas. Previously, justice, even when it ceased to be the monopoly of the Eupatridæ, had had for organs the Areopagus and the magistrates, and even when Solon had instituted the Heliæa he had only assigned to it an appellate jurisdiction (*ephesis*) which gave it the right of supervising the judgments of the magistrates, but not those of the Areopagus. It was not until the reform of 462 that the people definitively acquired the judicial prerogative which corresponded to an historical necessity. At the same time as the powers of the Areopagus were broken the magistrates saw themselves reduced to a *hegemonia*, that is to a simple delegation in virtue of which they received suits, proceeded to investigation and presided over the competent tribunals. There was henceforth no intermediary between popular sovereignty and justiciables.

But the rights of the individual remained and were only

[1] Aristoph., *Wasps*, 549, 620.

the more surely safeguarded as a result. It seemed that each citizen could only enjoy complete security in the exercise of his rights if the whole people ensured them to him by protecting him with its omnipotence. Individualism was carried to such a point that in cases where one or other of the parties or both of them consisted of a number of individuals the action had to be brought by each of the plaintiffs against each of the defendants.[1] Moreover justice never took the initiative among the Athenians, even in criminal cases. There was no magistrate to initiate an action, no court of arraignment, no public prosecutor to uphold the cause of society. In principle it was for the injured person or his lawful representative to bring the suit, to issue the summons and to put his case before the court without the assistance of a lawyer. Even a murderer might go unpunished if no relative came forward as the champion of the victim.[2] But when it was a case of bringing an accusation in respect of an act which was prejudicial to the common interest, any citizen (ὁ βουλόμενος) might consider himself injured and come to the aid of the law. Thus two categories of suits were distinguished: private suits (dikai) and public suits (graphai). In the case of private suits the two parties deposited the expenses of justice, the prytaneia, as pœna temere litigandi; the plaintiff had always the right of withdrawal; if he won the day he might obtain in addition to the object in litigation, an indemnity, but he himself was responsible for execution. In the case of public actions the accuser alone was responsible for the expenses of justice which were then called parastasis, and if he withdrew or failed to obtain a fifth of the votes he had to pay a fine of a thousand drachmas; the condemned was liable to a penalty either corporal, infamous, or pecuniary, fines being appropriated for the benefit of the city. But in both cases the struggle, the ἀγών, was between the litigants: the magistrate in charge only assembled the declarations formulated and the proofs furnished by the antagonists; the heliasts were only jurors who played the part of umpires in the debates.

Even extraordinary prosecutions were largely set in motion by private initiative. We have seen the part it played in political actions brought before the Assembly or the

---

[1] Dem., C. Nausim., 2.   [2] **XXXIII**, p. 436 ff.

Council by way of *eisangelia* or of *probole*.[1] In cases of flagrant or notorious misdemeanour, notably when the accused was a malefactor of low birth or a foreigner who might secretly escape, the citizens had recourse to *apagoge, ephegesis*, or *endeixis*; that is they might arrest the culprit and drag him before a magistrate, or conduct the magistrate to the place where he was to proceed to his arrest, or denounce him in order that the competent magistrate might take steps in the matter. In these proceedings where *habeas corpus* was not relevant, the preliminary citation was not demanded; it was a case for summary judgment or preventive detention, which might be suspended if three citizen guarantors were furnished. Finally, in cases where material damage was caused to the State by infringement of the laws concerning commerce, customs or mines, it was again private individuals who came to the fore by means of the *phasis*, and, to induce them to do so, the State made condemnations profitable to them: they received as bounty, in the fifth century three quarters, in the fourth century a half of the fine imposed.[2]

The principle of popular sovereignty was thus distorted in judicial matters because there the survivals of the past were particularly tenacious. We shall observe this again in the organization and procedure of the tribunals.

II

TRIBUNALS AND PROCEDURE

The crime of homicide, on account of the taint which was attached to the guilty man and which threatened to infect the whole city, always retained the character of an offence against men and against the gods. Grave though it was action could not be taken by any citizen by means of a *graphe*, but only by the nearest relatives of the dead man by means of a *dike*. Nor could it be judged by ordinary citizens, but only by the semi-religious tribunals which were presided over by the head of the national cults, the king.

Of these ancient tribunals the most important was that which sat on the hill of Ares, near the cave consecrated to the Eumenides: the Boule of the Areopagus. In spite of

---

[1] *v. supra*, pp. 166-167, 225-226.   [2] **XXXIII**, p. 390, n. 5.

the fact that it was deprived in 462 of its political powers it remained a great name and preserved the prestige of its glorious past. Always composed of the ex-archons it was regarded through the centuries as " the most venerable and the most just of tribunals."[1] Its jurisdiction extended to the crimes of premeditated murder (φόνος ἑκούσιος), violence done with intent to murder, the burning of an inhabited house, and poisoning. The punishments which it inflicted were: death in case of murder, banishment and confiscation in case of violence.[2] Beneath the Areopagus were the tribunals composed, in accordance with the legislation of Draco, of fifty-one *ephetai*. There were three of these. The Palladion had competence in matter of manslaughter (φόνος ἀκούσιος) and incitement to murder (βούλευσις), if the victim were a citizen, in matter of murder intentional or unintentional in the case of a metic, a foreigner or a slave. It pronounced the penalty of exile for a term of years without confiscation; but the condemned man might not return to Attica save with the authorization of the relatives of the dead man.[3] The Delphinion had jurisdiction if the king, responsible for making investigation, decided that the homicide was excusable or legitimate (φόνος δίκαιος), which usually happened if the victim had been killed while contesting in the games, or in war by mistake, or if discovered in the act of illicit relations with the wife, the mother, the sister, the daughter or the concubine of the murderer.[4] At Phreattys on the sea-coast were judged those who, having been temporarily exiled for unpremeditated homicide, committed a premeditated murder. As they were not yet purged of their first impurity and access to Attic territory was prohibited to them they presented their defence from a boat, whilst their judges sat on the bank. If they were acquitted they returned into exile; if they were condemned they suffered capital punishment.[5] Finally, a fifth tribunal for capital offences was constituted by the king and the kings of the tribes sitting before the Prytaneum. Its function, even more than its constitution, attests to a very distant origin. It

[1] Lys., *C. Andoc.*, 14.
[2] Dem., *C. Aristocr.*, 22 *ff.*; Arist., *Ath. Const.*, 57, 3.
[3] Arist., *loc. cit.*, Paus., I, 28, 8 *ff.*
[4] Dem., *loc. cit.*, 53; Paus., *loc. cit.*, 10.
[5] Arist., *loc. cit.*; Poll., VIII, 120; cf. Plat., *Laws*, IX, p. 866d.

condemned by default the unknown murderer and solemnly
judged any animal or any object of stone, iron or wood which
had caused the death of a man, before purifying the territory
by transporting it or throwing it beyond the frontiers.[1]

The whole procedure in use in capital charges was strikingly
archaic. If the victim had granted pardon before dying
no one could bring any action against the murderer;[2] if not,
the champions of the victims were, according to the law of
Draco, the father, the brother and the sons, in default of these,
first cousins and second cousins, and in the third rank ten
members of the phratry chosen by the *ephetai*. The first
two groups might, as in the time of private vengeance,
compound with the murderer (αἴδεσις) and free him from
subsequent prosecution in return for a sum of money; but
for the transaction to be valid it had to be accepted unanimously by all the kinsmen recognized by law. If not, the
action was pursued by the kinsmen of the first group assisted
by those of the second and, further, by the kindred by marriage,
brothers-in-law and fathers-in-law, and by the members of
the phratry.[3] The metic was represented by his patron, his
prostates; the slave by his master.[4]

The action commenced with a dramatic ceremony: the
kinsmen assembled around the dead man and planted a
lance on the sepulchral mound: this was the declaration of
war. It evoked a proclamation from the king (the πρόρρησις)
which excluded the accused from sacred places and even
from the agora until the day of judgment:[5] this was excommunication. Inquiry was made in three sessions, at which
both parties were heard, held at intervals of a month.[6] The
trial was held in the open air in order that the judges and the
plaintiff might escape infection from the impurity of the
defendant.[7] On that day the king removed his crown.[8]
Before all the hearings a sacrifice was offered, in which a

---

[1] Dem., *loc. cit.*, 76 *ff.*; Arist., *loc. cit.*; Paus., *loc. cit.*
[2] Dem., *C. Pant.*, 59; cf. Eurip., *Hipp.*, 1447 *ff.*; Plat., *loc. cit.*,
p. 869a, d-e.
[3] *IJG*, vol. II, no. xxi, l. 13 *ff.*; Dem., *C. Macart.*, 57; Ps. Dem.,
C. Everg., 72.
[4] Ps. Dem., *loc. cit.*, 68 *ff.*; *C. Neaira*, 9.
[5] *IJG*, *loc. cit.*, l. 20 *ff.*; Dem., *C. Aristocr.*, 37 *f.*; *C. Macart.*, *loc.
cit.*, *C. Lept.*, 158; Antiph.,' *Chor.*, 36; Arist., *loc. cit.*, 2.
[6] Antiph., *loc. cit.*, 42.   [7] Id., *Murder of Her.*, 11.
[8] Arist., *loc. cit.*, 4.

ram, a pig and a bull were immolated; before the altar both
parties solemnly took a declaratory oath upon the facts of
the case.[1] On the Areopagus they stood upon two blocks
of stone, the " rock of offence " (λίθος ὕβρεως) and the
" rock of implacability " (λίθος ἀναιδείας).[2] They had each
the right of speaking twice. After his first pleading the
accused might still escape condemnation by a voluntary
exile and the abandonment of his goods.[3] If the votes were
equally divided between the accusation and the defence, the
accused had the benefit of what was called the vote of Athena
(ψῆφος Ἀθηνᾶς), in remembrance of the vote which, according
to tradition, Athena had given in favour of Orestes.[4] On
his way down from the hill of Ares the acquitted went to
the cave of the Eumenides to appease and give thanks to
the goddesses by a sacrifice.[5] As a general rule in order to
be absolved from the suspensive excommunication which
accusation of homicide involved and which was prolonged
by temporary exile, it was necessary to submit to the expia-
tions and the purifications fixed by the ritual and the subtle
casuistry of the *exegetai*.[6]

All the cases which did not belong to the courts for capital
charges in principle formed part of popular jurisdiction.
But this was a tremendous task. The reform of Ephialtes
had already freed the magistrates and the Areopagus from
much litigation when the increase of commercial disputes,
the development of the empire and the restrictions placed
on the jurisdiction of subject cities made Athens the city
of law-suits. It was imperative that the ordinary tribunals
should be relieved by freeing them from the hearing of trifling
affairs.

Pisistratus had previously created judges of the demes to
hear the cases of litigants from the country;[7] but the institution established by the tyrant had disappeared. It was

---

[1] *DA*, art. " Jusjurandum," p. 762.
[2] Paus., *loc. cit.*, 5. Cf. Caillemer, *DA*, art. " Areopagus," p. 398,
fig. 491.
[3] Dem., *C. Aristocr.*, 69; Antiph., *loc. cit.*
[4] Æsch., *Eum.*, 735; cf. *DA*, *loc. cit.*, fig. 491-493.
[5] Paus., *loc. cit.*, 6.
[6] Dem., *loc. cit.*, 72; Porph., *De Abst.*, 1, 9; Plut., *Thes.*, 12; Suid.,
s.v. ἐξηγηταί; cf. Plat., *loc. cit.*, p. 865c-d. v. Otfr. Müller, preface
to *Eumenides*, p. 140 *ff.*
[7] *Arist., op. cit.*, 16 , 5. v. *supra*, p. 113.

I

re-established in 453-2.[1] Thirty itinerant judges, three from
each tribe, travelled round, probably each in his *trittys*, to
try in first and final instance disputes which did not involve
more than ten drachmas.[2] Civil suits beyond that limit they
transmitted to the public arbitrators, the *diaitetai*.[3]

All Athenians of sixty and over, on being removed from
the military lists, had to enroll themselves on those of the
diaitetai to exercise the office for a year.[4] Anyone who
evaded that obligation was condemned to *atimia* unless he
held a public office or was detained abroad.[5] The *diaitetai*
were divided into ten sections, one for each tribe,[6] and each
section had a fixed seat which was a tribunal or a temple.[7]
The jurisdiction of the arbitrators was exercised by the judges
of the tribes, either directly, when they found themselves
faced with a case which was outside their competence, or
indirectly, when they served as intermediaries to magistrates
to whom appeal had been made for a private action of
moderate importance.[8] The judges of the tribes divided
suits among the *diaitetai* by lot.[9] This procedure of arbitration offered great advantages to justiciables—it was swift
and summary: the arbitrator was responsible for both the
investigation and the judgment;[10] it was cheap: each of the
parties paid a small fee, a drachma, and the same amount
as a deposit.[11] When he had been informed of the facts of
the case the arbitrator attempted to effect a reconciliation.
If he did not succeed he gave his decision, strengthened by
a solemn oath.[12] If both parties accepted it the matter was
at an end, but if one of them was not willing to abide by it
he appealed to the tribunal of the heliasts. Moreover if he
thought that he had been unfairly dealt with by the arbitrator
he could bring an action of *eisangelia* before the whole body
of arbitrators and secure his condemnation, subject to appeal,
to an *atimia* which was equivalent to a revocation.[13]

[1] Id., *ibid.*, 26, 3.
[2] Id., *ibid.*, 53, 1-2; Lys., *C. Pancl.*, 21.
[3] v. R. J. Bonner, *The Jurisdic. of the Athen. Arbitrators*, Chicago,
1907.
[4] Arist., *loc, cit.*, 4.   [5] Id., *ibid.*, 5.
[6] Ps. Dem., *C. Everg.*, 12.
[7] *Ibid.*; Dem., *C. Steph.*, I, 17; *C. Boiot.*, Il, 11; Poll., VIII, 126.
[8] Arist., *op. cit.*, 53, 2; 48, 5; 58, 2.
[9] Id., *ibid.*, 58, 2.   [10] Dem., *C. Mid.*, 84 *ff.*
[11] Harp., *s.v.* παράστασις; Poll., VIII, 39, 127.
[12] Arist., *op. cit.*, 55, 5.   [13] Id., *ibid.*, 53, 2, 6.

In spite of the relief which the judges of the demes and the *diaitetai* gave them the popular tribunals were overwhelmed with work.[1] For a century and a half the main preoccupation of Athenian democracy was to make the judicial administration adequate for the discharge of its duties. In this work, bristling with difficulties, it showed remarkable qualities of perseverance and ingenuity.

Every Athenian was able to attain to the dignity of heliast if he had reached thirty years of age and if he was in full possession of civic rights, that is he must not be a public debtor.[2] Anyone who sat in defiance of this law was prosecuted by the summary procedure of *endeixis*; he was liable to penalties determinable at the discretion of the judges, and, if a fine were inflicted, he was imprisoned until he had paid the debt which had caused his arraignment and the fine added by the tribunals.[3] The State required still further guarantees. Every year the new heliasts had to take an oath on the hill of Ardettos.[4] This oath is only known to us for the fourth century; but it is certain that the solemn formality had long been in use. In the following passage are the most important promises made by the judges:[5]

" I will vote according to the laws and the decrees of the Athenian people and the Boule of the Five Hundred. I will vote neither for a tyrant nor for an oligarch, and, if the power of the Athenian people is attacked, and if words are spoken or a vote is taken against it, I will not give my consent. I will support neither the cancelling of individual debts nor the partitioning of the lands and the houses of the Athenians. I will not recall the exiled nor those condemned to death, nor will I pronounce against those who dwell in the land banishment contrary to the established laws and the decrees of the Athenian people and the Council; I will not do it myself and I will prevent all others from doing it. I will not receive presents as heliast, neither I myself nor another for me, man or woman, with my knowledge, without deception or intrigue of any sort. I will hear the accuser and the accused with complete impartiality, and I will give my vote upon the precise matter in question. If I forswear myself, may I perish, I and my household; if I am faithful to my oath may I prosper !"

In the fifth century the number of the heliasts was fixed at six thousand.[6] It was the number which in public law

---

[1] Ps. Xen., *Rep. of Ath.*, III, 1-8.
[2] Arist., *op. cit.*, 63, 3; cf. Dem., *loc. cit.*, 182; *C. Timocr.*, 50, 123, 151.
[3] Arist., *op. cit.*, 53, 3.
[4] Harp., *s.v.* Ἀρδηττος; Bekker, *Anecd. gr.*, vol. I, p. 443, 23; Suid., *s.v.* ἡλιαστής; *Etym. Magn.*, 147, 10.
[5] *v. DA*, art. " Jusjurandum," p. 755; **CVI**, vol. I, p. 151.
[6] Arist., *op. cit.*, 24, 3; Aristoph., *Wasps*, 661 *ff.*

stood for the unanimity of the people, as the procedure of the plenary Assembly indicates, and it must not be forgotten that in many cities the name of Heliæa never ceased to be that of the Assembly. The six thousand judges were drawn by lot from the qualified citizens who presented themselves.[1] Each tribe furnished six hundred, taken probably from the demes in proportion to the number of inhabitants.[2] The drawing of lots was carried out by the nine archons and their secretary, each for his own tribe.[3]

After the taking of the oath the judges were divided by lot among the different tribunals and, consequently, among the magistrates who presided over them.[4] It was arranged in such a way that, in each of the sections, the ten tribes had an equal representation.[5] The name of *dikasterion*, therefore, signified both a tribunal and its personnel,[6] whence the name of *dikastai* usually given to the judges; the name of heliast was more specially applied to those *dikastai* who assembled on the agora, in the ancient Heliæa of the *thesmothetai*.[7] Thus the judges knew in what tribunal they were to sit and to what magistrate they were attached for the whole year:[8] one in the Heliæa under the presidency of the *thesmothetai*; another at the tribunal " near the walls," with the archon; some in the " parabyston " with the Eleven; others in the new tribunal or in the Odeum.[9] They therefore knew in advance what matters would be submitted to them, and litigants also were aware of this. One can imagine the inconveniences of such a system. A mitigating factor and one which discouraged corruption was the large number of judges who constituted a *dikasterion*.[10] There were not, it is true, six hundred, for one must take into account the absentees; but there were regularly five hundred or rather, according to the general rule which provided against equal division of votes, five hundred and one. In important cases,

[1] Arist., *op. cit.*, 27, 4.
[2] Cf. **CVI**, *loc. cit.*, p. 135.
[3] Arist., *op. cit.*, 59, 7; 63, 1.
[4] Aristoph., *loc. cit.*, 1107.
[5] Id., *ibid.*, 233 *ff.*
[6] *IG*, vol. I, nos. 37, 59; Suppl., nos. 27a, 37c; Andoc., *De Myst.*, 78.
[7] *RIG*, no. 70; Antiph., *Chor.*, 21; cf. Andoc., *loc. cit.*, 27.
[8] Aristoph., *loc. cit.*, 157, 240, 288 *ff.*; *IG*, vol. I, Suppl., no. 35b; cf. Antiph., *loc. cit.*
[9] Aristoph., *loc. cit.*, 120, 1108 *f.*; *IG*, *loc. cit.*; Antiph., *Murder of Her.*, 10 *f.*
[10] Cf. Ps. Xen., *loc. cit.*

especially in political ones, several sections were united to form a tribunal; for instance two were necessary for an affair of *eisangelia*.[1] But we have even more striking examples: Pericles appeared before fifteen hundred and one judges;[2] in 404 the Assembly decreed that certain citizens accused of conspiracy against the safety of the State should be cited before a tribunal of two thousand members;[3] Andocides even mentions an action for illegality tried by six thousand *dikastai*, that is by the Heliæa combining all the sections.[4]

It is obvious that special measures must have been necessary to fill the tribunals. Since there were practically no vacations save feast days and assembly days,[5] they functioned perhaps about three hundred days in the year.[6] It was impossible to make presence at the sessions obligatory, for then no one would have enrolled himself. In order to attract the *dikastai* the only course to be adopted in a democracy was the opposite of that adopted in oligarchic cities: instead of a fine on absentees an indemnity for those present.[7] So long as democracy was unwilling to renounce its judicial sovereignty, the *misthos dikastikos* was an absolute necessity. It was deducted by the *kolacretai*, responsible for its distribution, from judicial costs and fines.[8] The payment of two obols, and, after 425, three, was only equivalent to the earnings of half a working day, to the cost of the maintenance of one person. It was not enough to induce country dwellers, when they lived at a distance, to leave their fields and undertake a long journey in order to settle the petty differences of unknown fellow citizens: indeed, even to settle their own itinerant justices had to be sent out. The *dikastai*, therefore, were for the most part town dwellers. But the rich who had other things to do and were not to be tempted by the bait of two or three obols held aloof.[9] Hence the great majority of the *dikastai* was furnished by the middle and lower classes of the town, the port and the suburbs. Some found in the *misthos* an appreciable addition to small incomes;

---

[1] Poll., VIII, 53.
[2] Plut., *Pericl.*, 32.
[3] Lys., *C. Agor.*, 35.
[4] Andoc., *loc. cit.*, 17.
[5] Ps. Xen., *loc. cit.*, 8.
[6] Aristoph., *loc. cit.*, 594.
[7] Arist., *Pol.*, VI (IV), 10, 6-8.
[8] Ps. Xen., *op. cit.*, I, 16; Aristoph., *Knights*, 1358; cf. Lys., *C. Epicr.*, 1; Poll., VIII, 38.
[9] Arist., *loc. cit.*, 5, 5; VII (VI), 3, 4.

others the means of profitably employing a workless day. Philocleon sees in it the means of adding a dainty dish to the menu for dinner; his mouth waters in anticipation of the soufflé which his wife will serve and the kisses which his daughter will bestow on dear " papa."[1] The old men in particular were not unready to add something to the family income: those heliasts who, in the chorus of Aristophanes, happily talk over their campaigns and bring forth the reminiscences of fifty years[2] could earn easily and honourably a modest pension.   Moreover the pecuniary motive was not the only one which gave men a liking for this business. What better opportunity for incorrigible gossips than these daily meetings of acquaintances ?   And what a pleasing gratification of vulgar vanity were the cajoleries of important suitors, the flatteries of the most celebrated orators !

With judges who were for the most part only jurors, business had to be carefully prepared for the day of trial. The *hegemonia* had, therefore, great importance; for it involved, before presiding over the actual debates, the undertaking of a thorough investigation.   It belonged for the enormous majority of cases to the archons: to the king for actions pertaining to religion; to the archon for those which concerned private right; to the polemarch for those which involved domiciled or privileged foreigners; to the *thesmothetai* for those in which public interest was at stake.   The Eleven, the governors of prisons, introduced by summary procedure those which entailed imprisonment before trial. When Athens became a great maritime and commercial power circumstances demanded the creation of magistrates with special competence for suits which called for swift settlement.   The *nautodikai*, who were suppressed after 397[3] and whose heritage passed to the *thesmothetai*, had within their jurisdiction the disputes of ship-owners, transport agents and dock labourers, to which were added after 451-0 suits under the law of aliens brought against metics who masqueraded as citizens.[4]   The *eisagogeis*, who were five in number, dealt

---

[1] Aristoph., *Wasps*, 605 *ff.*
[2] Id., *ibid.*, 236, 355; cf. *Acharn.*, 875; *Knights*, 255; Plut., *Nic.*, 2.
[3] Lys., XVII, 5, 8.
[4] *IG*, vol. I, no. 29; Bekker, *Anecd. gr.*, p. 283, 3; Harp. Suid., Hesych., *s.v.* ναυτοδίκαι; Poll., VIII, 126; *v.* **CXI**, p. 95 *ff.*; **VI**, vol. III, i, p. 283, n. 2.

with commercial affairs which had to be despatched within the legal limit of a month (δίκαι ἔμμηναι), including complaints made by federated towns concerning the amount of tribute fixed.[1]

The citation was made by the plaintiff himself accompanied by two witnesses to the deed, whose deposition, in the case of the non-appearance of the defendant, authorized procedure by default.[2] Every complaint was handed to the magistrate in writing whether it was a *dike* or a *graphe*,[3] and if he accepted it the deposit for the expenses of justice was then made. For private suits the two parties deposited *prytaneia* which amounted to three drachmas, if the object in litigation was from a hundred to a thousand in value, to thirty drachmas if it were more; but the loser had to reimburse the winner. For public actions the accuser paid the *parastasis*, a small fixed sum, and, if he would benefit from any fine resulting, the *prytaneia* also. For claims of succession or for goods wrongfully confiscated the claimant deposited a tenth in the first case, a fifth in the second, the deposit being counted with the principal.[4]

The magistrate then appointed a day for investigation (ἀνάκρισις). In the interval the text of the claim was published. The inquiry opened with the taking of a declaratory oath which fixed the position of the two parties and the written formula of which was attached to the dossier (ἀντωμοσία, διωμοσία).[5] If the defendant admitted that the form of the claim was in order, the hearing proceeded finally to the substance (εὐθυδικία). If not he might oppose two exceptions to the demand, the first based on the evidence (διαμαρτυρία), the second on other objections (παραγραφή): by that he turned the tables, and in the new situation he became the plaintiff. The subsidiary action had first to be dealt with in order that the principal action might either be declared lapsed or be proceeded with.[6] On the facts of the case the means of proof were: laws, contracts, depositions of free men, declarations of slaves obtained by torture, the oath of the parties.[7] The authentic documents, originals or

---

[1] Arist., *Ath. Const.*, 52, 2; Poll., VIII, 93, 101; *IG*, vol. I, nos. 37, l. 14, 47; 38 *f.*, l. 13 *f.*

[2] **CXI**, p. 769 *ff.*

[3] *Ibid.*, p. 790 *ff.*

[4] *Ibid.*, p. 809 *ff.*

[5] *DA*, art. " Jusjurandum," p. 761 *f.*

[6] **CXI**, p. 833 *ff.*

[7] *Ibid.*, p. 865.

duly certified copies, and reports of the slightest incidents were attached to the dossier. When the inquiry was ended if it were a public action the magistrate retained the dossier sealed in a box until the appointed day of the hearing, while if it were a private action he handed it over to the arbitrator for the attempted reconciliation. If the attempt failed the arbitrator placed the documents in two separate boxes, one for the plaintiff and the other for the defendant, affixed his seal, attached the award written on a tablet and delivered the whole to the judges of the tribe of the defendant, who undertook the introduction of the case before the tribunal.[1] The litigants were forbidden to quote in the trial any piece of evidence, the text of any law, process, testimony, etc., other than those which had been brought up in the inquiry.[2]

The magistrate who had conducted the inquiry called upon the *thesmothetai* to fix the day of the trial and the number of judges who were to sit. Save in commercial cases which had to be heard within the month, the date of the hearing was often very late. In the first place the cause list was too heavily burdened;[3] and, in the second place, delays were caused by the litigants themselves who had recourse to all manner of intrigues and Fabian tactics, by means of oaths (ὑπωμοσίαι) which were vainly met by counter-oaths (ἀνθυπωμοσίαι). In this way some cases dragged on for several years. If, in the last extremity, one of the litigants failed to appear, the defendant was either condemned on the ground of contumacy or acquitted and dismissed.[4]

Finally the day of the trial came. The tribunal was surrounded by a palisade with a lattice-gate.[5] Whenever there was a case which excited public interest a mob surged outside the barrier. But, in 415, when the violators of the mysteries were on trial, out of respect for the goddesses a kind of session *in camera* was desired, and so to keep back the crowd a rope was stretched fifty feet from the barrier and was guarded by public slaves.[6] Within, the *dikastai* sat on benches of wood covered with rush matting. In the middle sat the president on a stone rostrum (βῆμα) from

---

[1] Arist., *op. cit.*, 53, 2.   [2] Id., *ibid.*, 3.
[3] Ps. Xen., *op. cit.*, III, 6 *ff.*
[4] **CXI**, p. 908 *ff.*; **CVI**, vol. III, p. 903.
[5] Aristoph., *Wasps*, 386, 552, 830 and Schol.; cf. 124 and Schol., 775.
[6] Poll., VIII, 123, 141.

whence he dominated the audience. Near him were his secretary or clerk, his herald and the Scythian archers whose duty it was to maintain order, and in front of him was the tribune from which the litigants spoke. To right and left were two other tribunes for the suitors when they were not speaking. In the intervening space was a table on which, after the vote, the count was taken.[1]

The session began early in the morning. If the *dikastai* did not wish to lose their fee they had to rise before the dawn, for, at the appointed hour, when the president gave the signal, the door was shut in the face of late-comers.[2] Those who arrived in time received on entering a token ($\sigma\acute{u}\mu\beta o\lambda o\nu$), which they exchanged when the vote was taken for another, which could be exchanged on going out for three obols.[3]

Proceedings opened, as in the Assembly, with a sacrifice and a prayer. Then, on the order of the president, the herald announced the list of cases to be tried; for in one session many private suits were despatched, though only one public suit. After that the clerk read out the claim or the writ of accusation and the declaration which the defence put forward in opposition.[4]

Speech was given successively to the plaintiff and the defendant. Everyone had to speak for himself save the incapable—women, minors, slaves, freedmen and metics—who were represented by their legal guardian, master or patron. The ligitant who did not feel equal to preparing his own speech, deputed the task to one whose business it was, a *logographos*, and learnt it by heart; but neither the one nor the other dared confess to it. Nevertheless the accused and even the accuser might ask leave of the tribunal to be assisted or replaced by a more fluent friend; permission was rarely refused on condition that the advocate (*synegoros* or *syndikos*) was not paid. In this case the person involved might either confine himself to a few words of introduction and leave the rest to his supporter, or else allow his pleading to be corroborated by a vigorous peroration or a complementary explanation. This mutual assistance was in constant use in political

---

[1] Cf. Ps. Dem., *C. Olymp.*, 31; Æschin., *C. Ctes.*, 207; Aristoph., loc. cit., 332.

[2] Aristoph., *loc. cit.*, 100 *ff.*, 345 *ff.*, 689 *ff.*, 775.

[3] Arist., *op. cit.*, 65, 3; 68, 2; 69, 2.

[4] Aristoph., *loc. cit.*, 825, 851, 860 *ff.*, 891 *ff.*, 1441.

I*

cases, and the members of oligarchic *hetaireiai* considered it one of their principal obligations.

It was customary in private suits, but not in others, for the plaintiff to have the right of reply, and the defendant the right of counter-reply (ὕστερος λόγος).[1] But the sentence had to be pronounced on the same day,[2] save when a " sign of Zeus," a storm or an earthquake, compelled the president to adjourn the session.[3] Business, therefore, had to be rapid. Except in certain suits of a sentimental character, those which concerned minors and old men for example (δίκαι χωρὶς ὕδατος), there was a strict time limit for speeches—a time regulated by the clepsydrâ.[4] In private suits, the litigants were assigned a longer or a shorter time according to the value of the case. In the fourth century, when rules were somewhat stricter than in the fifth century, each had from twenty to forty-eight minutes for the principal speech, and from eight to twelve for the second,[5] not counting the time devoted to the reading of laws, decrees and other documents of the dossier.[6] In public suits in which the penalty was not fixed, the day was divided into three parts, of which one was allotted to the accusation, one to the defence and one to the judges.

Until about 390 the depositions of the witnesses had to be oral; after that date they were drawn up in advance in writing and read by the clerk.[7] It was forbidden to each party and to his witnesses to interrupt their opponent, unless he himself formally consented to it or himself put questions to them, in which case his time limit was still the same.[8] Such incidents gave to the debates an extraordinary animation. There were others, in criminal and political cases, sometimes even in civil cases, which produced intense emotion and roused men's passions.

When the plaintiff sensed that affairs were going badly for him, he could up to the last moment withdraw his plea. In private suits he still had that right at the moment when

---

[1] *v.* **CVI**, vol. III, p. 905 *ff.*, 911.
[2] Plat., *Apol.*, p. 37b.   [3] Poll., VIII, 124.
[4] Aristoph., *loc. cit.*, 93, 857 *ff.*; *Acharn.*, 693; *Birds*, 1596; Xen., *Hell.*, I, 7, 23.
[5] *v.* **VII**, vol. II, p. 1161, n. 3.
[6] Lys., *Invalid*, 4, 8, 11, 14.   [7] **CVI**, vol. III, p. 882.
[8] Aristoph., *Acharn.*, 687; Lys., *C. Erat.*, 24 *f.*; *C. Agor.*, 30, 32; P. *Polystr.*, 11; Andoc., *De Myst.*, 55, 101.

the votes were being turned out of the urn for counting, either on his own decision, or if he agreed with the defendant on terms of a transaction or compromise by private arbitration. He incurred no penalty save the forfeiture of the deposit made for expenses.[1] In public suits the accuser who withdrew was condemned to a fine of a thousand drachmas and deprived for the future of the right of bringing any charge of similar nature. We know, however, of such agreements made, even for money, with the consent of the magistrates.[2]

Whilst the pleadings proceeded the rôle of the judges was that of silent and passive witnesses. As soon as it was at an end, they were called upon by the voice of the herald to give their vote. They voted without deliberation, and the secrecy of the vote guaranteed its freedom.[3] In the fifth century each judge received a small shell (χοιρίνη) or a pebble (ψῆφος) which he deposited according as he favoured one or other party in one of the two urns before which he passed.[4] After 390 a system was devised which better ensured the secrecy of the vote: each juror received two counters of bronze, an unpierced one for acquittal, a pierced one for condemnation; he threw the one which was to count in a brazen urn (κύριος ἀμφορεύς) and the other for the counter-vote in a wooden urn (ἄκυρος ἀμφορεύς).[5] The results of the ballot were proclaimed by the herald, and the judgment, determined by a simple majority, was pronounced by the president.

If the defendant were absolved the whole matter was at an end. It only remained to inflict on certain accusers or plaintiffs the penalties which were automatically applicable to the bringing of ill-considered actions. The accusers who did not gain a fifth part of the votes in public suits and those who withdrew their charge, were condemned to a fine and a special *atimia*. In a considerable number of private actions, such as exceptions brought into the principal actions, counter-suits, actions against trustees or against debtors, nonsuited

---

[1] **CVI**, vol. I, p. 222 *ff*.
[2] Ps. Lys., *C. Andoc.*, 12; cf. **CVI**, vol. III, p. 841.
[3] Lys., *C. Erat.*, 91; Xen., *Symposium*, V, 8.
[4] Aristoph., *Knights*, 1332; *Wasps*, 109 *f.*, 332, 349, 987 *ff*.; Xen., *Hell.*, I, 7, 9: *IG*, vol. I², no. 49, l. 18. Cf. **CVI**, vol. III, p. 924.
[5] Arist., *Ath. Const.*, 68.

accusers owed to the defendants an indemnity fixed at the sixth part of the sum in dispute (ἐπωβελία).[1]

In case of condemnation there were two possible ways of procedure. Greek law made a distinction between suits in which the damages were not fixed (ἀγῶνες τιμητοί) and those in which they were (ἀγῶνες ἀτίμητοι), that is to say the penalty was sometimes left to the discretion of the judges, sometimes determined in advance by a law or a decree of reference to the court or even by a preliminary agreement between the suitors. Thus in a suit of the second category the penalty followed automatically from the sentence of condemnation. It was only in cases where the penalty was partially determined that, on the demand of one of its members and after a special vote, the tribunal inflicted an additional penalty (προστίμημα) to the sanction laid down by the law.[2] But in a suit of the first category a new procedure was necessary in order to fix the corporal or pecuniary punishment (τιμᾶν ὅ τι χρὴ παθεῖν ἢ ἀποτεῖσαι).[3] The accuser and the accused each proposed a punishment to the tribunal: these formed the assessment (τίμησις) and the counter-assessment (ἀντιτίμησις). They were allowed a short time in which to justify their proposal; then a second vote was taken in which the judges could only pronounce for one or other of the suggestions without being able to adopt a middle course. In the fourth century the second vote was taken in the same fashion as the first, but in the fifth century wax tablets were used on which the judges traced a long or a short line according as they supported the more severe or the more lenient sentence.[4] It is this procedure, designed to limit arbitrary powers, which explains the condemnation to death of Socrates.[5]

The penal legislation applied by the tribunals was based, in popular opinion and the theories of the philosophers, on the ideas of correction (κόλασις, νουθεδία), reparation (τιμωρία) or deterrence and social defence (παράδειγμα, ἀποτροπή). The principle of responsibility was applied with increasing rigour and extended, as in the most remote times, to animals and things guilty of causing death. Cumulative

---

[1] **CVI**, loc. cit., p. 940, 937.   [2] Lys., C. Theomn., I, 16.
[3] **CVI**, loc. cit., p. 930 ff.
[4] Aristoph., Wasps, 106 and Schol., 167 ff.   [5] v. supra, pp. 253-254.

penalties were prescribed by law for crimes with definite sanctions, such as sacrilege and treason which were punishable at one and the same time by death and confiscation. But for unassessed offences corporal punishment excluded pecuniary punishment (παθεῖν ἢ ἀποτεῖσαι). Absence of intention and irresponsibility (infancy, madness, anger, passion, constraint) constituted extenuating circumstances; recidivism and offences committed during a public or sacred ceremony, on the other hand, were regarded as particularly serious. Procedure and punishment often differed according as the two parties were citizens or, either one or other or both, metics or slaves. Corporal punishments were: pain of death which was the punishment according to law for premeditated murder, sacrilege and treason, and which might be inflicted in all sorts of crimes of a similar nature to those in suits in which the penalty was not defined; banishment, which was often substituted for death; *atimia*, which after having entailed outlawry was reduced to civil degradation; penal servitude and imprisonment, reserved generally for non-citizens and for exceptional cases; flogging, inflicted only on slaves. Penalties of infamous nature were: denial of burial, which might follow upon a posthumous judgment; the forbidding of adulteresses to wear ornaments and to enter temples; the curse, launched against certain defaulters; ignominious inscription on a stele. Pecuniary punishments were: total or partial confiscation, fines and damages.[1]

Legal notice of judgment was made in writing to those who were concerned with its execution. After a public suit, the writ was delivered to the competent magistrates, for example, the Eleven, the chief gaolers and the executioner, and to the *poletai*, responsible for the sale of confiscated property. When it was of political concern it was deposited in the archives. After a private suit, it was handed over to the victorious party, the State only taking part in the execution in so far as it had an interest of its own to safeguard. The collection of fines fell to the *praktores* and, when a tithe was to be deducted from them for the benefit of Athena, it was the duty of the treasurers of the goddess to see to it. A rule common to the whole of Greece substituted for the debtor of an unpaid fine the magistrate at fault.[2]

[1] *DA*, art. " Pœna," p. 522 *ff*.   [2] *Ibid.*, p. 543 *ff*.

In principle, judgment, the expression of popular will, was irrevocable, sovereign (χύριος) and perfect (αὐτοτέλης).[1] But rescission was not impossible in criminal matters. What the people had done the people could undo, on condition that respect for the matter judged remained intact. Different means of procedure allowed this result to be attained, on the one hand juridical, on the other political. A defaulter might oppose a judgment made in default within two months, if he established on oath that his absence was justified by a flaw in the procedure. Suits against false testimony and conspiracy, and suits with no established penalty, gave the tribunals the opportunity of repairing the damage caused by a pecuniary condemnation or of furnishing the victim of corporal punishment the fresh evidence on which a plea for reversal of judgment might be based. On the other hand, the Assembly retained, in judicial matters as in all others, its supreme prerogative. It had the right of pardon. But no one could have recourse to it without having previously obtained an *adeia*, one of those bills of indemnity which had to be supported by at least six thousand votes. This procedure formed the solemn prelude to all decrees of *epitimia* or of rehabilitation. It alone gave legal validity to the collective amnesty, which was never accorded save on extraordinary occasions, as a measure of public safety. It alone protected against an accusation of illegality acts of individual indulgence, the recall of an exile, the revocation of *atimia*, the annulling of a public debt.[2] It was thus that the Athenian people found a means of safeguarding the partial sovereignty of the judges, its delegates, while conserving intact the total sovereignty which could only belong to the whole body of citizens.

III

DISTINCTIVE TRAITS OF JUSTICE AND OF LAW

The judicial institutions which we have just described have been the object of innumerable criticisms, as much with the ancients as with the moderns. What are we to think of them ?

---

[1] Lys., *Murder of Erat.*, 36; Antiph., *Tetr.*, I, ii, 13; Aristoph., *Wasps*, 512, 519; Andoc., *C. Alc.*, 9; Arist., *Ath. Const.*, 9, 1; 41, 2; Plat., *Crit.*, p. 50b.

[2] *DA, loc. cit.*, p. 536 *ff.*; **CVI**, vol. III, p. 953 *ff.*

JUSTICE 251

The fact which struck contemporaries most forcibly and which still strikes us when we read the pleadings of the orators is the presence of a spirit of unlicensed chicane, a taste for litigation which is indeed unpleasant. One opponent of democracy speculated as to whether there were as many suits public and private in the whole of the rest of Greece as there were in Athens alone.[1] It is beyond dispute that individuals went to law with a readiness which was deplorable, that the renderings of accounts and the liturgies gave rise to endless law suits, that the absence of a public prosecutor caused the swarm of sycophants to multiply. It was not without cause that the comedy writer devised the name of Dikaiopolis.

Without denying the fact it is, however, necessary to seek for an explanation of it. This eagerness to fling themselves into battle derived from the combative instinct of the Greeks and of the Mediterranean peoples in general. If one links it up with its origins and with a past still very recent, it is the mark of a great advance made in social relations. In former days antagonists rushed to arms, and throughout the whole of the sixth century we see the vendetta bathing Attica in blood. The abuse of chicanery took the place of the abuse of force and testified to the fact that citizens curbed their passions in order to subordinate themselves to the law.[2] The evil of sycophancy itself can be ascribed to the fact that Athens was still too near to the times when the jurisdiction of the State was not obligatory. And there is also another side to this evil: since there was no public prosecutor justice was at all events independent of the government, and the initiative of citizens in both private and public actions was one of the rights which resulted from this freedom.

But we will leave the litigants and turn to the judges. Here once more we see in general only subject for criticism.[3] Blame is first imputed to the *misthos*. These jurors who hurried to the tribunal in the small hours of the morning in order that they might exchange in the evening their attendance token for two or three obols, who longed for the time when " they should drink the milk of *Kolakretes*,"[4] present to minds not hypersensitive a distressing spectacle. Did not

---

[1] Ps. Xen., *op. cit.*, III, 2.
[2] Eurip., *Or.*, 507 *ff.*; Dem., *C. Con.*, 17 *ff.*; *C. Mid.*, 221; Lyc,. *C. Leocr.*, 4.
[3] Cf. **V**, p. 350.   [4] Aristoph., *Wasps*, 724.

this distribution of salaries to hundreds, to thousands of citizens turn them from productive work ? And did it not at the same time place an excessive burden on the exchequer ? Moreover, what a preposterous idea to give the mob seats in the courts ! It was to give an unlimited competence into the hands of incompetence, to permit justice to be destroyed by ignorance of the law. It was not difficult for cunning pleaders, for *logographoi* skilled in arguing beside the point, to cite texts falsely, to indulge in fallacious interpretations. And there was something still worse. Summoning to its aid *ethos* and *pathos* eloquence attempted to touch the heliasts upon their weak spot, to excite their passions. Defendants surrounded themselves on the tribune with their kinsmen, their wife and weeping children, in order to soften the hearts of the judges.[1] On all sides play was made with patriotism or devotion to democracy; a litigant would ransack the past life of his adversary in order to hurl at his head the vilest insults, the basest calumnies. As soon as a case touched upon politics the tribunal was transformed into a public assembly: the judges no longer restrained themselves from yielding to the influence of party, and partiality disguised itself as justice. Moreover, law can do nothing when the feeling of professional responsibility is replaced by pride in irresponsible sovereignty.[2] It was besides completely silent in a great number of cases in which arbitrary power was left to the judges in the determination of penalties. The system of assessable cases thus permitted the court, as, for instance, the one for *eisangeliai*, to treat in the same way offences of widely differing nature. And there was no appeal. We can see why Athens was able, by her condemnation of Socrates, to commit the greatest of judicial crimes.

To these charges, which we have in no way exaggerated, there are many replies to be made. Once more it is necessary for a true appreciation of the institutions of the fifth century to observe them in the light of the past and not to place implicit faith in the criticisms of the opponents of the regime.

The *misthos dikastikos* had its origins in the remote past: even so far back as the Homeric city the *gerontes* required litigants to make a deposit of golden coins as the price of the arbitration which they sought, and at a later date the " de-

[1] *v.* **XXXIII**, p. 552 *ff*.   [2] Aristoph., *loc. cit.*, 622 *ff*.

vourers of presents " who held sway in Bœotia did not administer justice gratuitously. Why should democracy adopt a different practice when the sacrifice of a day was a much greater burden for men of small means ? The rate of the *misthos* was, moreover, extremely low: about the time when it was established at Athens at the rate of two obols, at Halicarnassus it was a *hemiecton* which was worth seven times as much.[1] It was certainly not enough to encourage laziness in the citizens, nor were even the three obols, which merely permitted them to add a delicacy to the evening meal and, if they were old, saved them from being regarded by their families as so many useless mouths. As to the public treasury it was in no way affected since the payment was made out of a special fund from the revenues of justice: the judges lived by giving justice. In short the payment of the jurors in no way merited the reproaches which were one day to be heaped, with some appearance of reason, upon the payment of citizens attending the Ecclesia.

Undoubtedly it would have deserved it still less had the number of judges been smaller. But one must remember that it could not well have been smaller at the epoch when the Heliæa was instituted. Solon aimed at marshalling the whole people against arbitrary sentences of the magistrates by giving it the right of amending them in appeal. In the Heliæa, as in the plenary Assembly, the legal people had, therefore, to consist of six thousand citizens. All that one could and ought to do when the Heliæa judged in first instance —and naturally, therefore, in the last—was to divide it into as many *dikasteria* as were necessary to fit it for its task, and to it was applied, as to other institutions, the rule of decimal division. These enormous juries had their inconveniences, their dangers even: that is an undeniable fact. They were without juridical knowledge and they often allowed themselves to be swayed by reasons irrelevant to strict justice.

Again we must not exaggerate criticism nor allow it to lead us to false conclusions. The condemnation of Socrates was the tragic consequence of a procedure specifically designed, by compelling the judges to choose between the penalties proposed by the plaintiff and the condemned man, to prevent them from arbitrary assessment of penalties. The accusers

[1] *IJG*, vol. I, no. 1, l. 26 *f.*

had experienced great difficulty in obtaining a verdict of
guilt even though the accused had scorned to make use of any
appeal ill-befitting his dignity.[1] He could easily have saved
his life by opposing to the proposal put forward by Meletus,
which demanded the penalty of death, a counter-proposal
which might have resulted in a less stringent punishment.
But he was not willing at his time of life to give the lie to his
past, to his mission. Without bravado, with an ironic pride,
he declared that a man such as he deserved to be nourished
in the Prytaneum for the remainder of his days.[2] The condemned man demanded the most coveted of rewards. Grudg-
ingly he consented, as a concession to the urgent appeals of
his friends, to propose to pay a fine of thirty *minai*.[3] But
the judges could not go back on their first vote and impose
an almost nominal penalty. He wished for death, and so
he died.

One must not, therefore, infer too much from that example,
nor from those which the political suits of the fifth century
furnished, and believe that the people sitting in the tribunals
always exhibited the caprices of a tyrant. At all events there
is one reproach which cannot be brought against it, namely
that of venality: the judges were too numerous to be bribed.
On this point we have valuable testimony. An Athenian
oligarch turns down the idea of reducing the personnel of
the tribunal. " It would be too easy, he thinks, to intrigue
with a small number of judges, and, by means of corruption,
decisions far less equitable would be obtained."[4] According
to Aristotle the first Athenian who gained acquittal by means
of bribery was Anytus in 409, one of the future accusers of
Socrates.[5] All things being considered, democratic prejudice
did not involve miscarriages of justice more glaring than those
which political and social prejudices have been and still are
guilty of under no matter what system of government. Here
again we have the testimony of the same oligarch: he deplores
the fact that no hope for a revolution is to be looked for in
the discontent of citizens punished with *atimia*, because
condemnations of this order were in Athens so rarely unjust.[6]

[1] Plat., *Apol.*, p. 34b *ff*.   [2] Id., *ibid.*, p. 36d.
[3] Id., *ibid.*, p. 38b.   [4] Ps. Xen., *loc. cit.*, 7.
    [5] Arist., *Ath. Const.*, 27, 5; Diod., XIII, 64, 8; Plut., *Coriol.*, 14;
v., however, Aristoph., *Knights*, 1358 *ff*.
    [6] Ps. Xen., *loc. cit.*, 12.

Striking homage rendered by an enemy to the regime which he abhorred !

Of the criticisms brought against Athenian justice there remains the charge concerning the instability and insecurity of the law which it applied. In current opinion Athens is regarded as the country of art, of letters and of philosophy, but a country which never possessed juridical sense. But is it possible that she should have failed to give to her laws and jurisprudence, as to everything else, the stamp of her reason and practical sense ? In estimating it as one does, one compares Attic law, consciously or not, with Roman law; fundamentally one is reproaching the law of a transitional period for not being completely developed. The criticisms which are brought against it are its praises. This absence of unity, this lack of systematic spirit, this inconstancy of principles and rules which flowed therefrom, would not have existed if Athens had remained superstitiously attached to ancient customs and ancient laws, instead of continually distinguishing between what ought to be conserved intact and what ought to be renovated. It is her glory to have been in the fifth century a flaming furnace from whence issued day by day ideas which poets and philosophers fashioned and forged. In the theatre, in the schools of the sophists, questions of fundamental law were thrashed out. Æschylus in the *Oresteia* shows us the people passionately discussing the question of penal responsibility and the powers of the Areopagus. Protagoras, for the first time in history, sought for the rational basis of the right of punishment, and at the outset he expounds all the ideas, in order that he may repudiate or establish their validity.[1] Antiphon composed series of speeches which are less exercises in judicial rhetoric than models of juridical argumentation, worthy indeed of the man whom Thucydides styled a profound thinker.[2] These were the great ancestors of the *jurisprudentes*. Moreover they were not content to be mere theorists. Protagoras in particular exercised a great influence. When a pan-Hellenic colony was established at Thourioi he was commissioned to amend for it the laws of Zaleucus.[3] He was counted among the intimates of Pericles,[4] and we know

[1] *DA*, art. " Pœna," p. 523.   [2] Thuc., VIII, 68.
[3] Diog. Laert., IX, 50.   [4] Plut., *Consol. to Apoll.*, 33, p. 118d.

that the statesman and the philosopher passed an entire day in discussing like subtle casuists a question of penal responsibility.[1]

The system of assessable actions and *eisangeliai* had at least the advantage of familiarizing judges who were not professionals with all the subtleties of jurisprudence. It led them to continual assimilations, and so permitted, for example, all sorts of crimes and delinquencies to fall within the range of the ancient law against sacrilege and treason, and in consequence to render them liable to capital punishment. But, on the other hand, it allowed traditional pains and penalties to be mitigated in accordance with new ideas and more civilized customs. Armed with an arbitrary power the people, the sovereign justiciary, admitted of no restriction either upon its severity or upon its mercy; but it placed its omnipotence more often at the service of its constant humanity than of its sudden and short-lived passions. Above all it freed itself from the tyranny of forms and fixed rules in order that individual rights might prevail and equity be discovered.[2]

The whole penal code of Athens was dominated by the desire to assure full and complete freedom of person, and this produced one of its peculiar aspects. No reproach has been more frequently brought against Athenian judges than that of abusing their power of inflicting pecuniary penalties, and it has often been insinuated that it was done from interested motives with a view to filling the exchequer of the *misthos*. As a matter of fact there were in Athenian history critical moments when no stone had to be left unturned in order that the needs of the exchequer might be met,[3] and even in normal times confiscations and fines were of a frequency which readily lends itself to unfriendly interpretations. But one must see things as they really were. Pecuniary penalties took the place of corporal penalties which modern tribunals are so free with, and of which many would have appeared intolerable to Athenians. At the end of the fifth century confiscation was no longer added to the penalty of death; it became the price of ransom and thus saved many heads. As to fines they were only so numerous because since Solon

---

[1] Stesimbr. ap. Plut., *Pericl.*, 36.
[2] Cf. G. M. Calhoun, " Greek Law and Modern Jurisprudence " (*California Law Review*, vol. XI, 1923, p. 295 *ff.*).
[3] Lys., *C. Nicom.*, 22; *C. Epicr.*, 2.

the dignity of the citizen seemed irreconcilable with penalties which deprived men of their liberty. Imprisonment, as well as preventive detention, might be suitable for metics; flogging for slaves; they were not punishments applicable to Athenians. " Only in the last extremity," says Demosthenes, " ought one to lay hands on the person of a free man. . . . Do you wish to know the difference between servitude and liberty ? The most remarkable consists in this, that all the misdeeds of the slave are visited upon his body, while the free man, though he be in the last degree of wretchedness, at least remains master of that."[1]

But there was another spirit which animated Athenian justice and which led to the accomplishment of great reforms: the humanitarian spirit. The Greeks in general were merciful in comparison with the barbarians their neighbours: they did not carry torture to a high degree of refinement as did the Asiatics; their violence was that of anger, not of drunken brutality, as was that of the Thracians. More than all other Greeks the Athenians won for themselves the reputation of exhibiting in all circumstances that sympathy for misfortune which in their eyes was the privilege of civilized men, that all-embracing love of humanity to which they were the first to apply the name " philanthropy."[2] The Bœotians might be hard and vindictive, but the Athenians must be just and merciful. They desired that in the furthest extremities of the barbarian world, if a law protecting the weak were mentioned, homage should be rendered to the benignity of their customs.[3] This mercy extended even to the guilty, even to those condemned to death: unless they were base malefactors they were not delivered over to the executioner; they were allowed to escape this fate by way of suicide; they might demand from their gaoler the cup of hemlock which assured to them a swift and painless death.[4] And still more did the judges show pity for innocence.

Constant amendments of the law went concurrently with its application. In general the laws of the Athenians were undoubtedly mild and indulgent, " made beautiful by kindness "; such was their advantage for the majority and

[1] Dem., *C. Timocr.*, 167; *C. Androt.*, 55.
[2] Eurip., *El.*, 294 *f.*
[3] Dem., *C. Lept.*, 109; *C. Mid.*, 48 *f.* Cf. **XXXIII**, p. 243 *f.*
[4] *DA*, art. " Kôneion."

especially for the lower classes.[1]   But the laws did not meet
all cases; and in addition there were some which had been
neither abrogated nor amended, and which burdened the
families of certain criminals with formidable responsibilities.
How were innovations possible in the case of laws which
antiquity and the name they bore made sacred ?   It was
clear that innovations were necessary, and reason demanded
that the laws should not be immutable.[2]   The Athenians,
quite simply, fulfilled their duty as judges with the hearts
of men.   They were ever ready to pardon, and plaintiffs
habitually sought to warn them against excess of mildness.
If a woman and her children, threatened with a life of misery,
were but to place themselves near the defendant and begin
to weep, the tribunal was moved.   " What else can we
do ?" says Philocleon.   " We feel the violence of our anger
melting away."[3]   And so it was with them all; they preferred to absolve a guilty man rather than condemn with
him his innocent dependants.   In this way jurisprudence
never ceased to amend the law and to be amended itself by
" philanthropy."

Throughout the whole of the fifth century the last traces
of family responsibility were being progressively abolished.
In 479 a councillor who was suspected of being a traitor was
stoned with his wife and his children.   Somewhere between
465-460, in a law imposed on the Erythræans, Athens demanded that the traitor should be put to death with his
children, " unless the children had given proof of devotion
to the people," that is to say unless they obtained letters
of remission which were only refused in cases of personal
guilt.   In 411, when the oligarchs Archeptolemus and
Antiphon were condemned to death, the sentence did not
mention the children.[4]   Under the law of ostracism all the
kinsmen of Pisistratus had been menaced, since 508, with
banishment.   In 471, on the other hand, the children of the
proscribed Themistocles remained unmolested in Athens for
as long as they wished.[5]   *Atimia*, the deprivation of civil
rights, was still hereditary in a decree of 444-3, but in 410
we find a plaintiff saying to the tribunal: " We see you,

---

[1] Dem., *C. Timocr.*, 190 *ff.*; *C. Mid.*, 57.
[2] Arist., *Pol.*, II, 5, 11 *ff.*   [3] Aristoph., *Wasps*, 574.
[4] **XXXIII**, p. 456 *ff.*   [5] *Ibid.*, p. 473 *ff.*

Oh judges, softening your hearts at the thought of the infamy which threatens the children at the same time as their guilty fathers, and acquitting the fathers for the sake of the children."[1] A decisive circumstance enabled the people to assure here once more the principle of personal responsibility: the amnesty which, in 403, brought an end to the civil war extended to the sons of the thirty tyrants, and, when their personal enemies attempted to violate it, the people refused to follow them.[2] It is true that frequent recourse to confiscation, inevitably a collective punishment, as is all pecuniary punishment to a certain extent, remained; but we have seen in what spirit the Athenians multiplied punishments of this order: they laid hands on men's property in order that their persons might remain free. Moreover, they felt keenly the unjust repercussions of confiscation in certain cases and did their utmost to allay them: they always left some resources for those whom they struck indirectly.[3]

Whilst Athenian justice assured the benefits of liberty and fraternity to its citizens, it applied in a certain measure the principle of equality to those even who seemed excluded from it by nature, to the slaves. Logically the conception of the city made the slave a chattel of the citizens, a tool without name, without family, without property, without rights. By a consequence no less logical the democratic principle, always favourable to the bottom dog, was to lead the people to see that this chattel had a human form, that this tool had a soul, that the slave himself deserved to be treated with philanthropy. The sophist Antiphon clearly reveals by what steps rational men arrived at this subversive conclusion. A fragment of papyrus enables us to follow his reasoning. He lays down as a principle that men of good family have no greater right to respect than others: " we are all and in all respects of the same birth." But then there is no distinction between the Greek and the barbarian: " we all breathe in the air through the mouth and the nostrils. And . . ."[4] Here the papyrus is mutilated; but we have the conclusion in the pathetic lines spoken by a character in one of the comedies: " Though a man be a slave, my master, he is none the less a human being as thou art; he is

---

[1] Lys., *P. Polystr.*, 34. [2] *Ibid.*, p. 493 *ff.*; **XCII**, p. 320 *ff.*
[3] **XXXIII**, p. 515 *ff.*, 544 *ff.* [4] Antiph., *De Ver.*, 5.

made of the same flesh. No one is a slave by nature; it is destiny which enslaves men's bodies."[1]

Economic necessities tended in the same direction. Servile labour assumed less severe forms.[2] Certain masters, in order not to allow the " bodies " to remain unproductive, hired them out to employers in search of labourers. It very soon happened that men bought labour simply in order to hire it out and receive the rent for the day or the month. As one would expect the bonds which attached slaves bound to the soil to their owner grew more and more relaxed. Then men began to think that it was very much simpler to leave to the slave who had learned a trade the business of exercising it where and when he wished, on condition of paying to his master, thus become a *rentier*, the return which alone interested him. Thus was formed a class of slaves " separately domiciled " (χωρὶς οἰκοῦντες): they differed from free workmen only in the obligation to deduct from their earnings the master's share, one or two obols per day. Finally the State itself had recourse to servile labour, especially for the construction of buildings and upkeep of roads, as well as in its administrative departments. Whence a new class of slaves, and highly privileged ones, arose: not only had they necessarily the right of separate domicile without paying any due, but, thanks to their accounts, their knowledge of the archives, and their administrative experience, they were able to guide the magistrates who were elected by lot and who changed every year; they exercised over their ostensible masters a secret power, and thus succeeded in playing an influential part.

What need for surprise that the Athenians should have left to their slaves a liberty which the poorer citizens of many an oligarchic State might have envied ? Obviously it was to the interest of the masters to accord to their slaves the right of free speech which was thought proper for the amelioration of their condition;[3] it was to the interest of the city not to exasperate them since they constituted a formidable body. But there was yet another motive: simply the democratic fervour which possessed the Athenians. The oligarchs were indignant at what to them appeared " the consummation of

---

[1] Philemon, fr. 94, Kock.   [2] **XXXV**, p. 249-257.
[3] Menander, fr. 370, Kock.

licence."[1]   What an indignity that one could not strike slaves,
nor even demand that they should yield place in the road,
for the sad reason that, dressed as citizens, they were indis-
tinguishable from them !   It is this, " the anarchy of slaves,"
which, for Aristotle, is a characteristic trait of democracy.[2]
Of this reproach the Athenian people made for itself a
virtue.

It did not admit that the right of corporal correction[3]
might be exercised in any way upon a slave by anyone other
than the master, nor that, for the master, it extended to the
power of life and death.   The victim of arbitrary and continued maltreatment might even seek refuge in certain
sanctuaries and demand to be sold to another master.[4]   The
murder of a slave not only involved a claim for payment of
damages; his master, his champion, might cause the murderer
to be exiled by the Palladion.[5]   The slave's honour was even
protected by the same public action as the citizen's (γραφὴ
ὕβρεως).   There was another provision, even more noteworthy
than the preceding one on account of the reasons which
Æschines, in agreement with Demosthenes, gives for it: " It
is not for the slaves that the legislator has such tender
solicitude; he has realized that any man who, in a democracy,
outrages anyone no matter whom, is not fitted for the
communal life of the city. . . .   It is his conviction that he
ought to consider, not the status of the injured person but the
act committed; . . . for it is the city which he judges to have
been attacked."[6]   But the boldest and most novel idea of
Athenian law was that of giving the slaves guarantees against
the magistrates, against the very representatives of the city.
Throughout the whole of Greece police regulations inflicted
a fine on the free-man and a flogging on the slave.   But
whilst everywhere else the severity of the flogging was left to
the discretion of the magistrates or the executioner, at Athens
a maximum was established for corporal as well as for

---

[1] Ps. Xen., *op. cit.*, I, 10; Plat., *Rep.*, VIII, p. 563b.
[2] Arist., *Pol.*, VII (VI), 3, 12.
[3] Aristoph., *Knights*, 5; *Peace*, 452, 746; *Plout.*, 21; Lys., *Murder of Erat.*, 18; Xen., *Mem.*, II, 1, 16; Theophr., *Char.*, XII, 12.
[4] Poll., VII, 13; Plut., *Thes.*, 36; *De Superst.*, 4, p. 166d; Aristoph., *Knights*, 1312 and Schol.; *Thesm.*, 224 and Schol.
[5] Eurip., *Hec.*, 291 *ff.*; Arist., *Ath. Const.*, 57.
[6] Æschin., *C. Timocr.*, 17; Dem., *C. Mid.*, 45 *ff.*; cf. Athen., VI, 92, p. 266 *f.* to 267a.

pecuniary penalties: fifty drachmas, fifty stripes.[1]   A small detail in the whole body of legislation, but a most significant assault upon its principles.   Not only did the law place on the same footing, within the limits of the possible, the man who could be punished only with his body and the man who could be punished only with his goods; but the city, in restricting the right of its representatives, bestowed on a creature denuded of all juridical capacity a right opposable to itself.   Here we have the most typical of those beneficent contradictions, those fine inconsistencies which were due to the introduction of democratic ideas into the old legislation, and which inspired in the Athenians a noble pride because they saw in them the mark of their moral superiority over the rest of the Hellenes.[2]

So long as the Greek cities were concerned with establishing their power upon the ruins of the family regime, with replacing private vengeance by obligatory recourse to justice, and with individualizing responsibility for personal delinquencies they had advanced together with more or less equal steps along the road of law.   But ever since Solon had attempted to give an absolute value to the principle of personal liberty and had instituted public actions for the protection of the weak, and Cleisthenes and Pericles had strengthened popular justice, Athens, carried forward on a wave of democratic fervour, had marched along the road to which her traditions bound her, far ahead of all the other cities.   At the end of the fifth century she alone granted the individual the right of free disposition of his property by will; she alone had abolished the State privilege of collective responsibility; she alone had carried philanthropy so far as to sap the rational basis of the institution of slavery—an institution without which it seemed that the city must perish.

---

[1] v. " Les esclaves et la peine du fouet dans le droit grec " (*CRAI*, 1908, p. 571 *ff.*).
[2] Eurip., *loc. cit.*; Dem., *loc. cit.*, 48 *f.*; *C. Lept.*, 109.

CHAPTER VII

EXPANSION OF THE CITY IN THE FIFTH CENTURY

I

ALIENS AND CITIZENS

THE old conception according to which the stranger ceased to be an enemy (ἐχθρός) only if he were received as a guest (ξένος) had left many traces in the Greece of classical times.[1] The right of a city to lead foraying expeditions (συλᾶν), carrying off persons (ἄγειν) and property (φέρειν) from the territory of another city, remained intact so long as there existed no formal and bilateral convention as obstacle. It was exercised without scruple among the savage tribes of the North-West;[2] nowhere did peoples hesitate to have recourse to it when a claim deemed legitimate failed to receive a satisfactory answer, especially when they considered that justice called for reprisals and there was justification for the seizing of pledges (ῥυσιάζειν). Within each city aliens had only very limited rights, even if their position were established not only by law but also by a treaty, and even if they were permanently domiciled in it as metics. These principles persisted to the end; but their severity was tempered, in international and public law alike, without, however, infringing the sovereignty of the State.[3]

Customs which were ranked among the " unwritten laws,"[4] the " common laws of the Hellenes,"[5] and which

---

[1] v. in general, **XXIX**, bk. III, ch. XII.

[2] Thuc., I, 5, 3; 6, 1.

[3] v. Rod. Dareste, *REG*, vol. II (1889), p. 305 *ff.*; Ch. Lécrivain, " Le droit de se faire justice soi-même et les représailles dans les relat. intern. de la Grèce " (*Mém. de l'Ac. de Toulouse*, vol. IX, 1897, p. 277 *ff.*); **XLIII**, p. 38 *ff.*; Hitzig, " Der griech. Fremdenprozess " (*Sav. Z.*, vol. XXVIII, p. 220 *ff.*); Ad. Wilhelm, *Jh. AI*, vol. XIV (1911), p. 195 *ff.*; **LXI**, vol. I, p. 353 *ff.*

[4] Arist., *Rhet.*, I, 10, 13; v. R. Hirzel, Ἄγραφος νόμος (*Abh. SG*, vol. XX, 1900, p. 1 *ff.*); **LXI**, vol. I, p. 43 *ff.*; Glotz, " Le droit des gens dans l'antiq. gr." (*MAI*, vol. XIII, 1915).

[5] Thuc., III, 58, 3; 59, 1; 67, 6; IV, 97, 2; Eurip., *Or.*, 495.

consequently were placed under the protection of the gods,[1] regulated the right of war. The heralds, who were rendered inviolable by the caduceus, played an important rôle therein:[2] a war was not legitimate unless it was declared by them,[3] they alone could pass between the belligerents as truce-bearers, and they gave sacrosanctity to the negotiators sent into the ranks of the enemy.[4] After the battle the conquerors erected a trophy on which were suspended the arms of the conquered. This trophy usually took the form of a stake or simply the branch of a tree; it was held that it should not be of stone or bronze in order that hatred might not be perpetuated.[5] It was a fine application of the Greek adage: "Treat thine enemy as if he ought to become thy friend." The conquered as a general rule recognized their defeat by demanding an armistice for the burying of their dead.[6] The victors might not refuse that request unless it came from a sacrilegious army,[7] and, when it was not made involuntarily, it was for them to bury the fallen enemy.[8] When a town surrendered itself, its fate was determined by the terms of the capitulation; but the general rule was that in war the lives of suppliants should be spared.[9] When a city was taken by assault, everything—persons and property—was at the mercy of the conquerors:[10] the men were put to the sword, the women and children were reduced to servitude.[11] As for the prisoners, first of all exchange was effected;[12] those who were left over were usually bought back by their city or by individuals,[13] but otherwise they were sold as slaves.[14] In the division of booty a tradition dating from Homeric times was followed, while at the same time the deduction of the tithe reserved for the gods was regarded as an absolute duty.[15]

[1] Soph., *Antig.*, 454; Xen., *Mem.*, IV, 4, 5 *ff.*, 19.
[2] Her., VII, 133 *ff.*; Eurip., *Suppl.*, 121.
[3] Her., V, 81; VII, 9, 2; Thuc., I, 29, 3.
[4] Thuc., *loc. cit.*; 53, 1; 146; IV, 38, 3; 97, 2; 99; VII, 3.
[5] Diod., XIII, 24; Plut., *Qu. rom.*, 37, p. 273d; Cic., *De Inv.*, II, 23; 69.
[6] Plut., *Nic.*, 6; Xen., *Hell.*, III, 5, 25; cf. VI, 4, 14; VII, 5, 26.
[7] Thuc., IV, 97 *ff.*; cf. Diod., XVI, 25.
[8] Her., IX, 79.   [9] Thuc., III, 58, 3; 66, 2; 67, 5.
[10] Xen., *Cyrop.*, VII, 5, 73.   [11] Thuc., III, 86, 3; V, 3; 32.
[12] Thuc., II, 103; V, 3.   [13] Her., V, 77; VI, 79.
[14] Thuc., VII, 85.
[15] Her., VIII, 121 *ff.*; IX, 80 *ff.*; Thuc., III, 50, 114.

As one might expect the rules of clemency and moderation were often violated, especially in the case of a people which had been guilty of disloyalty. But, on the other hand, even when the Peloponnesian war was at its height the Athenian and Spartan generals refused, for example, to avail themselves of their right of reducing Greeks to servitude.[1] Religion, too, had its influence on the laws of war. The inviolability of temples was recognized, provided they were not used as military bases.[2] The " Truce of God " ($\dot{\epsilon}\kappa\epsilon\chi\epsilon\iota\rho\dot{\iota}a$) proclaimed by the *spondophoroi*,[3] protected pilgrims travelling to pan-Hellenic festivals against all acts of hostility, even in a country occupied by a belligerent army. Moreover the Dorians of the Peloponnese agreed never to embark upon a campaign during the sacred month when the Carnea was held. They also refrained from marching against a city in the interval which elapsed between the announcement and the celebration of its festival: a scruple which certain cities sometimes abused by tampering with their calendar in such a way that they were able to demand the remission of hostilities which they feared to meet.[4]

So much did war seem the natural state of affairs between cities that treaties of peace were only suspensions of arms, and even treaties of alliance did not offer very substantial guarantees.[5] A progressive step was taken when definite duration was assigned to treaties, a duration which might, it is true, be only of five years,[6] but which was more frequently thirty,[7] fifty,[8] or even a hundred years.[9] It was for the most part a Utopian vision to think of a state of perpetual peace ($\epsilon\dot{\iota}s$ $\tau\dot{o}\nu$ $\dot{a}\epsilon\dot{\iota}$ $\chi\rho\dot{o}\nu o\nu$).[10]

Attempts, however, were made to settle disputes by pacific means. Differences between cities were sometimes

[1] Thuc., VIII, 41, 2; 62, 2; Xen., *Hell.*, I, 6, 14; cf. Plat., *Rep.*, V, p. 469*b*.
[2] Thuc., IV, 97 *f*.
[3] *SIG²*, no. 587, l. 4, 106, 227; *IG*, vol. II², nos. 1235, 1236; *REG*, vol. XXXII (1919), p. 190 *ff*., l. 25 *ff*., 35 *ff*.; cf. Æschin., *Emb.*, 133 *f*.
[4] Her., VII, 206; VIII, 72; Thuc., III, 56, 2; 65, 1; V, 54, 2; Xen., *Hell.*, IV, 7, 2; V, 1, 29; 3, 27; Hesych., Suid., Harp., *s.v.* ἱερομηνία.
[5] *v.* **LXI**, vol. II, p. 1 *ff*.; Br. Keil. " Eirene " (*Abh. SG*, vol. LXVIII, 1916, p. 1 *ff*.
[6] Thuc., I, 112.   [7] Id., I, 23, 4; 87, 6; 15; II, 2, 1; V, 14, 4.
[8] *IO*, no. 10; Thuc., V, 18; 23; 79; cf. *SIG³*, no. 135.
[9] *SIG³*, no. 9; Thuc., III, 114, 3; V, 47.
[10] Thuc., IV, 63, 1; *SIG³*, no. 71 (doubtful restoration); cf. no. 122.

submitted to arbitration.[1] As early as the end of the seventh century or the beginning of the sixth the Athenians and the Mitylenians appealed to Periander, the tyrant of Corinth, to settle their dispute on the subject of Sigeum.[2] The Corinthians and the Corcyræans entrusted to Themistocles the task of deciding between their pretensions to Leucas.[3] Conflicting cities usually took as arbiter, not an illustrious individual, but a third city (πόλις ἔκκλητος) or, in certain cases, the priesthood of Delphi.[4] Athens and Megara, who were squabbling over Salamis, called upon Sparta to give a deciding vote; five Spartans pronounced in favour of Athens.[5] As a general rule the treaties of peace and armistice concluded in the second half of the fifth century between the Lacedæmonians and the Athenians stipulated that in case of disagreement they should have recourse to judicial methods of settlement, they themselves and their allies.[6] By the treaty of 418 the Lacedæmonians and the Argives bound themselves to submit all disputes, of any nature whatsoever, to the judgment of a third power.[7] Unfortunately, since the arbiter had not any means of constraint at his disposal, the defeated party was not always ready to yield. Thebes, after having appealed to the Corinthians to settle its difference with Athens on the subject of Platæa, rejected the award which went against it.[8] We see, too, the Eleans refusing to accept a settlement proposed by Lepreon on a question of debts.[9] Facts of this sort explain perhaps why international arbitration disappeared in the fourth century and did not reappear till the Hellenistic epoch.

One must at any rate recognize the permanent efficacy of conventions of a less ambitious nature whose object was to put an end to the vexations of all kinds which harassed traders when they ventured into a strange town without guarantee. Thus, as late as the fifth century, a certain

---

[1] v. E. Sonne, De arbitris extern. quos Græci adhibuerunt, etc., 1888; V. Bérard, De arbitrio inter liberas Græcorum civitates, 1894; Hitzig, loc. cit., p. 244 ff.; **LXI**, vol. II, p. 127 ff.; **LXVI**; **LXXV**.
[2] Her., V, 95; Arist., Rhet., I, 15; Strab., XIII, 1, 38, p. 600.
[3] Plut., Themist., 24; cf. Thuc., I, 136.
[4] Thuc., I, 28; Diod., XV, 18, 2.
[5] Plut., Sol., 10.
[6] Thuc., I, 78, 4; 140, 2; 144 f.; IV, 118, 8; V, 18, 4; VII, 18.
[7] Id., V, 79.   [8] Her., VI, 108; cf. Thuc., III, 55.
[9] Thuc., V, 31.

city was obliged to conclude a treaty with a neighbouring city in order to protect the people from it against violence and to assure to them in case of need a right of recourse to the magistrates and tribunals. It was what was called a treaty of *asylia*. There is extant a document of this kind, in which two towns of Western Locris, Chaleion and Oianthea, in about 450 brought to a close a time-honoured system of reprisals.[1] The agreement, instead of being made directly between the two cities concerned, seems to have been due to the intervention of a third city acting as a common capital: it is comparable with the case of Argos reconciling Cnossus and Tylissus.[2] At the beginning of the century, the injunction of a satrap was required to curb the cities of Ionia and to assure to them the benefits of mutual security:[3] there is perhaps no fact in the whole history of the Greeks which illustrates more strikingly their love of autonomy and the conception which they clung to even under foreign domination.

Through these rudimentary treaties of *asylia* the Greek cities learnt to conclude veritable treaties of international civil law, *symbolai* or *symbola*.[4] Great difficulty arose from the fact that the right of judicial action was, in principle, one of the privileges reserved to citizens. Men found themselves faced with this difficulty as soon as strong colonies of metics began to be formed in the commercial cities. Then it had been solved by placing the metics under the jurisdiction of a special magistrate, a *kosmos* in Crete, the polemarch in Athens. But, if it was impossible to place metics as justiciables on the same footing as citizens, it appeared no more desirable to place foreigners who stayed just long enough to carry through a business transaction, to disembark or embark a cargo, on the same footing as metics who were permanently established in the country. Trading cities realized that they had a common interest in filling that gap.

Hence arose those conventions (σύμβολα) whose essential object was to regulate the procedure applicable in certain specific cases (δίκαι ἀπὸ συμβόλων), namely: (1) commercial suits arising between subjects of the two contracting parties or rather between one and the citizens of the other; (2) offences which involved as plaintiff and defendant subjects of the

---

[1] *v.* Dareste, *loc. cit.*; **XLIII**, p. 39.   [2] *SIG*[3], no. 56.
[3] Her., VI, 42.   [4] *v.* **XLIII**; **LXI**, vol. I, p. 198 *ff.*

two cities. These conventions, of which we have good examples for the fifth century,[1] treated, therefore, of special matters, one might say of professional matters;[2] and so the Ecclesia of Athens, although it usually deliberated on foreign affairs, contented itself with considering them only as a matter of form and sent them for close examination to a tribunal of heliasts sitting under the presidency of *thesmothetai*.[3] As a general rule the case went before the tribunal of the city to which the defendant belonged. The Athenians of the fifth century were thus often compelled to plead in cities unfavourable to them; but they enacted by ordinary decrees that commercial suits between Athenians and subjects of the empire should henceforth be settled by Athenian tribunals under the presidency of the polemarch, if they arose out of contracts which had been concluded at Athens.[4] Save for this exception, which is explained by political circumstances and by the supremacy of Athenian commerce and commercial law, it is true to say that the rules in use in the *symbola* and in the procedure which they instituted reveal a broad-minded and truly international spirit.

Instead of availing themselves of treaties applicable to all the citizens of two cities, aliens might see their position improved by individual and unilateral measures. Each town in fact with more or less liberality conferred on foreigners privileges more or less advantageous. There were decrees as well as conventions of *asylia*,[5] and *asylia* was supplemented by *asphaleia*, that is to say inviolability of person by that of property. The right of acquiring immovables, lands or houses (*enktesis*),[6] exemption from taxes and imposts falling specially on aliens (*ateleia*) or the right of paying imposts and contributions in kind on the same conditions as citizens (*isoteleia*)[7] were obtained only as rewards for services rendered. But the greatest honour which could fall to an alien was the *proxenia*[8] although throughout its whole history it was at

---

[1] Thuc., I, 77.
[2] See the agreements between Athens and Phaselis (*RIG*, no. 6; cf. Photiades, 'Εφ., 1922, p. 62 *ff*.), between Athens and Trœzen (*IG*, vol. II², no. 46; cf. **XLIII**, p. 60 *ff*.
[3] Arist., *Ath. Const.*, 59, 5.   [4] Thuc., I, 77; cf. *RIG*, no. 6.
[5] *v. SIG*³, no. 55; cf. nos. 168, 187, 189.
[6] *IG*, vol. I, no. 44; *SIG*³, no. 108.   [7] *v.* **VII**, vol. I, p. 299 *ff*.
[8] *v.* P. Monceaux, *Les proxénies grecques*, 1885; **XXVI**, p. 169 *ff*.; J. D. André, *La proxénie*, 1911; **LXI**, vol. I, p. 145 *ff*.

the same time a burden. The men of one city individuals or ambassadors, when they were passing through another wanted someone to give them advice and assistance. To this public host, this kind of consul, the city showed its gratitude by bestowing on him the title of *proxenos*, which it supplemented when the person in question was a great man, by adding that of *euergetes* or benefactor. Since the title was hereditary, since it was accorded subsequently to a number of citizens of the same town and since its bearer often settled in his second country the *proxenia* became little more than an honorific distinction. Nevertheless it played an important rôle in international relations, and it never ceased to assure to a few outstanding aliens the highest position which men could have in a Greek city of which they were not citizens. And the *proxenoi* could become citizens more easily than any others.

What then was the precise boundary which separated aliens of every condition, whether metics or not, from citizens ? How could citizenship be conferred upon those who did not possess it by birth ?

One often sees apparent contradictions in the conduct of the Greeks, and especially of the Athenians, in matters concerning the possession and bestowal of civic rights. In the Homeric epoch, when moreover there were still so many survivals of primitive hostility towards the foreigner, the king and the chiefs had no reason to oppose unions of nationals and aliens, because they themselves eagerly sought matrimonial alliances with noble and rich houses, whatever their origin, and they saw no reason to prevent the common people, deprived of political rights, from marrying as they pleased. The great families for long preserved this tradition, even in democratic cities. Thus it happened that even the most illustrious citizens of Athens were born of foreign mothers (μητρόξενοι). The law-giver Cleisthenes, son of the Alcmæonid Megacles, bore the name of his maternal grandfather, the tyrant of Sicyon. Pisistratus had two sons by the Argive Timonassa. Cimon, born of a Thracian princess, married most probably an Arcadian. Thucydides had for wife one Hegesipyle who bore the same name and came from the same family as the mother of Cimon. Themistocles' mother was either a Thracian, an Argive or an Acarnanian, in any

K

case a foreigner. In spite of this propensity towards mixed marriages the oligarchs were, in principle, vigilant guardians of the right of citizenship: since they sought to diminish its value, they were not disposed to extend freely its benefits. After the fall of the Pisistratidæ, the chief of the oligarchic party, Isagoras, expunged from the list of citizens all those whom the tyrants had illegally enrolled.[1] Sparta, who was ever ready to expel aliens, practically never granted letters of naturalization; Herodotus only knew of two examples.[2] In the fourth century also Ægina, Megara, Lacedæmon and even a small town such as Oreus, adopted in this matter a fiercely uncompromising attitude.[3] In democratic cities, on the contrary, tradition was favourable to aliens, at least before the middle of the fifth century. Even in his time Solon had attracted craftsmen into Attica by granting citizenship to them;[4] Pisistratus was no less liberal,[5] while Cleisthenes included in the list expurgated by his opponents a great number of metics and even of slaves.[6]

Thus it remained until the commercial prosperity of the Piræus and the strength of the empire made the title of citizen very profitable. Then the people found it more expedient to restrict the number of participants. We have seen that Pericles himself passed a law according to which only those whose parents were both Athenians could be citizens. Citizenship became a privilege the concession of which was rendered difficult and hedged in with formalities of the most solemn nature. But even this was not a sufficiently secure safeguard. On great occasions the Ecclesia decreed a general revision (διαψήφισις) of the civic registers in the demes: this was what was done in 445-4 in order to prevent interlopers from participating in a special distribution of corn.[7]

The people was, therefore, in no way tempted in the fifth century to abuse the right, which was its monopoly, of conferring on foreigners the title of citizen. It bestowed it either on individuals or on classes, but always for good and sufficient reasons. Pericles demanded it for the son whose exclusion

---

[1] Arist., *op. cit.*, 13, 5; *v.* **XXXVI**, vol. I, p. 467.
[2] Her., IX, 35.   [3] Dem., *C. Aristocr.*, 211 *ff.*
[4] Plut., *Sol.*, 24.   [5] Arist., *loc. cit.*
[6] Id., *Ath. Const.*, 26, 3; Plut., *Pericl.*, 37; cf. Aristoph., *Birds*, 1660.
v. supra, pp. 128, 152. Same law at Oreos (Dem.. *loc. cit.*, 213), at Rhodes (*IG*, vol. XII, 1, n. 766), at Byzantium (Ps. Arist., *Œcon.*, II, 4).
[7] Plut., *loc. cit.*; Philoch., fr. 90 (*FHG*, vol. I, p. 398).

he had caused by his own law, the child of Aspasia the Milesian.[1] Thrasyboulus of Calydon obtained it in 409 in recompense for so meritorious an act as the murder of Phrynichus, one of the most hated of the Four Hundred.[2] In 406 all the metics who had taken part as rowers in the victorious expedition to Arginusæ[3] were promoted to the rank of citizens; and in 401-0 all those who had rushed to Phyle to join forces with the liberators of democracy.[4]

The bestowal of civic rights on all the members of a foreign community or at least on all those who applied for them was of much greater importance. This occurred, however, only in exceptional circumstances. In the middle of the sixth century the Delphians, in recognition of the magnificent gifts which Crœsus had sent, conferred the right of citizenship on all Lydians who should in the future ask for it;[5] this was merely a nominal offer which was to have little result. It was not so when Athens, in the fifth century, from motives of political interest allowed deviations from the law of 451-0 in favour of certain cities. To the Eubœans she granted not citizenship but one of the most essential parts of it, *epigamia*: she thus recognized the validity of marriages between Athenians and Eubœans, whether of an Athenian man with a Eubœan woman or *vice versa*, and consequently gave the right of citizenship to the issue of these unions.[6] During the Peloponnesian war she went still further: she received with open arms the inhabitants of those cities which had suffered for her sake. In 427, after the destruction of their town, the Platæan refugees in Athens received civic privileges: after the judicial authorities had verified their claims in each individual case, they were divided out among the demes and tribes and placed on a footing of equality with the Athenians, save for access to the archonship and the priesthoods.[7] In

---

[1] Plut., *loc. cit.*; Suid., *s.v.* δημοποίητος.
[2] *RIG*, no. 1435; Lys., *C. Agor.*, 70-72. [3] Diod., XIII, 97.
[4] Arist., *Ath. Const.*, 40, 2; Æsch., *C. Ctes.*, 187 and Schol.; *SIG*[3], no. 120 (cf. Ad. Wilhelm, *Jh. AI*, vol. XXI-XXII, 1922-1924, p. 159 *ff.*, no. V); cf. Ps. Plut., *Lives of Ten Orat., Lys.*, 8, p. 853 *f.*; *P. Oxy.*, vol. XV, no. 1800, fr. 6-7.
[5] Her., III, 1, 54; cf. *BCH*, vol. V (1892), p. 383 *ff.*; *v.* **LXXIII**, p. 97-99.
[6] Lys., XXXIV, 3.
[7] Ps. Dem., *C. Neair.*, 104 *ff.*; Isocr., *Panath.*, 74; Lys., *C. Pan.*, 2; *v.* **VI**, vol. III, ii, p. 1038. This decree was put in force again after the second destruction of Platæa, in 373 (Diod., XV, 46, 6).

405, after the defeat of Ægospotami, Athens wished to reward Samos for her fidelity: hence the Samians were raised to the rank of Athenians, while at the same time retaining their constitution, their judicial system and their autonomy.[1] Thus was inaugurated a policy which would have wrought a fundamental transformation in the Athenian confederation and perhaps have changed the course of history, if, instead of being dictated at the last moment by a hopeless situation, it had been adopted earlier and applied more extensively.

But enough has been said of the measures which the Greeks of the fifth century took to mitigate, in international and public and private law, the traditional hatred for the foreigner while at the same time preserving unimpaired the autonomy of the cities. Let us now see how they were able, without fear of encroaching upon that, to group towns hitherto sovereign into durable leagues and federations.

II

THE GREAT LEAGUES (*Symmachiai*)

In the fifth century two leagues were formed which were serious attempts to put an end to the isolation of the cities. With Lacedæmon and Athens at their head they might have entered upon a great work of unification had not their rivalry brought them into conflict and so perpetuated division.

1. *The Lacedæmonian League*

The Lacedæmonian league, which played so important a rôle for two centuries, never had, however, a really strong organization.[2] It owed its foundation to Sparta towards the middle of the sixth century, after the conquest of Messenia and the defeat of Argos, and it always retained the essentially military character and oligarchic spirit which it derived from its origins. When it had been extended to Corinth

---

[1] *RIG*, no. 80; *v.* P. Foucart, *REA*, 1899, p. 196 *ff.*; **VI**, *loc. cit.*, p. 1627 *f.*; **LXXIII**, p. 95 *f.*
[2] *v.* **XXXVIII**, p. 211 *ff.*; L. Pareti, " Elementi formatori e dissolvente della egemonia spartana in Grecia " (*Atti. d. Accad. di Torino*, vol. XLVII, 1912); **XLVII**, vol. I (1922), p. 26 *ff.*, 81 *ff.*, 267 *ff.*, 311 *ff.*, 336 *ff.*; **VII**, vol. II, p. 1320 *ff.*

after the fall of the Cypselidæ, to Megara after the fall of Theagenes and perhaps at one point to Athens after the fall of the Pisistratidæ, Sparta gained enormous strength from it, although she did not dare to encroach upon the autonomy of the cities or even to place their contingents under the command of her own officers. At the time of the Persian invasion all the cities which were preparing for resistance turned towards the league, which was thus transformed into a pan-Hellenic league which entrusted supreme command on land and sea to the Spartans.[1]   But this new league, which appeared to unite the greater part of Greece, was even less suited than the old one for centralization. The delegates or *probouloi* who assembled on the Isthmus,[2] were only empowered to discuss the questions of contingents to be furnished, embassies to be sent to the colonies,[3] oaths to be administered[4] and anathemas to be hurled against the cities which were unfaithful to the national cause.[5]   Then they dispersed and the only indications which remained to remind the Greeks that they were acting as a common body were the councils of war at which the *strategoi* deliberated under the presidency of the Spartan commander-in-chief.[6]   After the victory the Athenians were able, without violating any obligation, without breaking any promise, and without seceding from the league, to found a rival league.[7]   Shrinking once more without regret within the confines of the Isthmus Sparta desired at least to establish a better control over her Peloponnesians.   It was probably about the middle of the fifth century that the reform was accomplished the results of which we see some twenty years later.

Οἱ Λακεδαιμόνιοι καὶ οἱ σύμμαχοι, " the Lacedæmonians and their allies " or rather " the Lacedæmonians and their confederates," such was the official name of the league.   It implies a dualist regime and the subordination of the anonymous cities to the directing city; it implies also the existence of *symmachoi* who were not only bound to Sparta by a bilateral contract, but were bound to each other by reciprocal

---

[1] Her., VII, 148, 235; VIII, 2; Plut., *Them.*, 7.
[2] Her., VII, 145 *f.*, 148, 153, 169, 172.
[3] Id., *ibid.*, 145.   [4] Id., *ibid.*, 132.
[5] Xen., *Hell.*, VI, 5, 35; Diod., XI, 3, 2.
[6] Her., VII, 49; VIII, 19, 50, 56, 58 *ff.*, 71.
[7] Thuc., I, 102, 4.

bonds.   It was not a simple alliance nor was it a federal State,
but a league of cities agreed upon the permanent necessity
of common action with regard to other cities and recognizing
the supremacy, the *hegemony*, of the most powerful of their
number.   There was no federal citizenship, nor did the
league exercise authority over citizens, but only and then in
duly specified cases, over the governments of the contracting
cities.   Autonomy was guaranteed to these cities;[1] they
retained their constitution, their laws, their administration,
their justice; and further they directed their own foreign
policy as towards each other, often a hostile policy.   Sparta
tried in vain to make the principle of arbitration prevail in
the settlement of their difficulties; resort was had to arms,[2]
and hence the league was compelled to forbid any federal
city to enter the field against any other member during a
federal campaign.[3]   Moreover, although in theory Sparta
had no power to interfere in local politics, she was constantly
exerting pressure in the direction of oligarchy, whether by
her own example, by moral suasion or even by open force.[4]
But the ostensible object of the league was common defence.
It can even be said of the Council, its principal organ, that it
was never convoked save to confer upon the declaration of
a war, a truce or proposals for peace.   It had not, therefore,
a   permanent   existence.   When   circumstances   demanded
Sparta invited the cities to send their delegates to discuss
matters of common concern.[5]

The way in which war was declared against the Athenians
in 432[6] brings out clearly the respective rights of the Lacedæmonians and the allies.   The Corinthians took the initiative
and sent their representatives to Sparta to accuse the
Athenians of having violated their treaties; but the Council
could not be brought into being by this act: it was to an
assembly of Spartans that the Corinthians unfolded their
grievances, and the Athenian ambassadors came there to
reply to them.   It was essential that the outsiders should
retire before this extraordinary reunion ($\sigma\acute{v}\lambda\lambda o\gamma o\varsigma$) could be

[1] Id., V, 77, 5; 79.
[2] Id., I, 103, 4; IV, 134; V, 29, 33; cf. Xen., *Hell.*, V, 2, 7; 4, 36.
[3] Thuc., I, 27 *ff.*; Xen., *loc. cit.*, 4, 37.
[4] Thuc., I, 19, 76, 144; cf. Xen., *op. cit.*, VI, 3, 14.
[5] Her., V, 91; Thuc., I, 87, 119, 125, 141; IV, 118; V, 17, 36, 82.
[6] Thuc., I, 67 *ff.*

transformed into a regular assembly (ἀπέλλα): the Spartans deliberated among themselves and voted for war. But this decision was only valid for the Lacedæmonians; the concurrence of the allies had still to be obtained. Sparta summoned their delegates, who naturally came with specific instructions. They sat under the presidency of the ephors. Each city, whatever its strength, commanded only one vote,[1] and the small ones inclined, as always, to vote with the controlling power. A large majority voted for war. This time the decision was accepted, and the Council forthwith began to make preparations for mobilization.

Thus the resolutions of the allies could not prevail against those of the Lacedæmonians; but common resolutions had the force of law and were binding upon all the cities. An ancient oath bound them to conform to the decisions of the majority, " unless the gods or heroes stood in the way."[2] As soon as the Council had given its vote its work was finished: there was nothing for it to do save dissolve, nor did it even leave behind an executive committee.

The Lacedæmonians alone were responsible for ensuring the execution of measures which had been agreed upon. They were even authorized in cases of emergency, in order to defend a city against a sudden attack, or to proceed against a disloyal city, to put an army into the field and to summon such contingents as they judged necessary, without previous consultation with the Council.[3] But the case of absolute necessity had to be well established; for the spirit of autonomy was sensitive, and the obligation to lead out troops at the bidding of an alien chief dangerously resembled the most humiliating of subjections. In normal times the Lacedæmonians sent messengers to announce to each town the number of men it had to furnish and the date when they had to be put into the field;[4] everything relating to them was regulated by the Apella and the ephors. During the Persian wars the contingents were placed under the command of leaders named by the cities; but during the Peloponnesian war they had at their head, from the day of their assembly, officers of the

---

[1] Id., ibid., 125.
[2] Id., V, 30; cf. Xen., op. cit., IV, 2, 16; V, 2, 2 (sacred truce); II, 4, 3 (counter-agreement).
[3] Her., V, 74; Thuc., V, 57; cf. Xen., op. cit., III, 5, 4-6; IV, 6, 3, etc.
[4] Thuc., II, 10; V, 17, 54.

Spartan staff, " commanders of the foreigners " (*xenagoi*).[1] Since the principle of autonomy was opposed to the institution of a federal tribute, each town provided for the upkeep of its troops and paid, if there were need, only voluntary contributions.[2]

In conclusion, the organism controlled by Sparta was one to which historians are justified in applying sometimes the name Lacedæmonian league, sometimes Peloponnesian league; for the powerful hegemony of Sparta succeeded in imposing itself on the cities in matters diplomatic and military, but in everything else it left them complete independence.

2. The Athenian Confederation

The Athenian confederation, which was formed within the pan-Hellenic league in 478 and only officially detached from it after 464, offered to the Greeks, much more than did the Lacedæmonian league, an example of what the political unity of a great number of cities under the supremacy of a single city might be.

After the victory of Mycale the islanders who had thrown off the Persian yoke were received into the pan-Hellenic league; but the Lacedæmonians, weary of the naval war, left the Athenians to provide for the protection of the Ionians of the continent. The contrast between the services rendered by the Athenian fleet to the common cause and the treacherous ambition of the Spartan Pausanias led the *strategoi* of the towns of the Ægean littoral outside the Peloponnese to offer to the Athenians the hegemony, the chief command, for the duration of the war.[3] This alliance of maritime cities was soon converted into a confederation which had for centre the temple of Delian Apollo.[4] It embraced Eubœa, the Cyclades, the islands of the Asiatic coast, the ports of Ionia and Æolis, of the Hellespont and the Propontis, a little later the Greek ports in Thracian land and, later still, those of Caria.

In the beginning the maritime confederation of Athens resembled in many characteristics of its institutions the continental league of the Peloponnese. Its official name,

[1] Id., II, 75, 3; cf. Xen., *op. cit.*, III, 5, 7; IV, 2, 19; 5, 7, etc.
[2] Thuc., I, 19, 80, 141 *f.*; cf. *SIG*³, no. 84.
[3] Her., VIII, 3; Thuc., I, 95 *f.*, 130; Arist., *Ath. Const.*, 23, 4.
[4] Thuc., I, 96, 1.

" the Athenians and their allies,"[1] indicates its dualist nature; it also had no common right of citizenship and exercised its authority over individuals only through the medium of the cities, declared autonomous;[2] and its chief organ was a Council in which all the delegations had an equal voice.[3] But from the start it had its distinctive mark. Since its object was not war against any aggressor whatsoever, but solely war against the Persians,[4] and since it was composed only of maritime cities, it required a great fleet. Now though it was easy and advantageous to demand homogeneous squadrons from great towns, it would have been pure folly to require of towns of the second or third rank one or even many ships, because these units would have been too scattered and disparate to be of any use. All the towns, therefore, which did not discharge their federal obligations by furnishing ships had to do so by payment of money. Thus the confederation always had a treasury, supplemented by an annual tribute, the *phoros*. It was the great work of Aristides, and a very miracle of political wisdom, to make an inventory of the resources at the disposal of this large body of cities, to estimate their ability to pay and to divide out the total of the 460 talents required—all this in such a way as to satisfy everyone.[5]

But when once the Persians had been expelled from the Ægean sea the confederate cities began to ask why they still continued to fulfil their obligations. Between them and the supreme city divergence of interests was soon rapidly to increase. There were soon to be very few cities to furnish ships, and, in proportion as the naval resources of the confederates were to diminish, Athens was to increase her own.[6]

[1] *RIG*, no. 1428, l. 20 *ff.*, 29 *ff.*; *IG*, vol. I, no. 11; Thuc., IV, 119; V, 18.
[2] Thuc., I, 97, 1; 98, 4; III, 10, 4; 11.
[3] Id., III, 10, 5; 11, 3.   [4] Id., I, 96; III, 10, 3; VI, 76, 3.
[5] Id., I, 96, 2; Plut., *Arist.*, 24; Diod., XI, 47, 2; Arist., *loc. cit.* Many attempts have been made to explain this total of 460 talents; only approximate results have ever been obtained. By the following method the exact number is reached. The confederation had every year to equip 200 triremes manned by 200 men each for seven months: each man receiving 2 obols per day. But, in the Attic calendar, seven months did not make 210 days; with four months of 30 days and three of 29 days the number was 207. With these data a very simple operation (2 ob. ×200× 200 ×207) gives us the necessary sum, 460 talents.
[6] Thuc., I, 99.
K*

The tribute was rarely to rise higher and usually remained lower than the total fixed by Aristides, although it was paid by a greater number of cities; it was none the less protested against. Athens had no desire to intervene in the intestine quarrels of cities, to encroach upon their autonomy. But when they fell into civil war and when the partisans of oligarchy negotiated with Sparta, she had to respond to the appeal of the democrats, and, if hostility went as far as defection, it was essential after the revolt had been repressed to take precautions for the future. When arrears of payment became a subject for scandal she was compelled to use force. It was in this way that the Attico-Delian confederation (συμμαχία) was transformed into an Athenian empire (ἀρχή).[1] In the language of diplomacy Athens still continued to talk of allies or confederates (σύμμαχοι), or else she employed the customary and vague term of cities (πόλεις);[2] but in plain language it was now a question of subjects (ὑπήκοοι)[3] and of tributaries (ὑποτελεῖς).[4] The transformation began in 469 when Naxos furnished the first example of disloyalty. It was an accomplished fact in 454 when it was decided that the treasure, until then administered by Athenian officials (the *Hellenotamiai*) but deposited in the sanctuary of Delian Apollo, should be transferred on to the Acropolis of Athens and placed under the protection of Athena.[5] This measure was adopted on the proposal of the Samians; it was doubtless the last act of the federal Council, for henceforth nothing more is heard of it.

From being federal all the institutions of the league became imperial. Formerly the position of the cities had been determined by bilateral treaties; general measures had been adopted by resolutions of the Council while the Ecclesia of Athens had probably restricted itself to the ratification and execution of these acts. Henceforth it controlled everything. If a rebellious town were compelled to capitu-

[1] Id., I, 76, 2; 77, 3; II, 63, etc.; Ps. Xen., *Rep. of Ath.*, I, 14; II, 2-4; Aristoph., *Knights*, 1114; *Peace*, 619. Official expressions: Thuc., V, 18, 7; *RIG*, no. 73, l. 2, 14.
[2] Aristoph., *Ach.*, 192, 506, 636, 643; *Knights*, 802; *IG*, vol. I, nos. 31, 37, 40; vol. XII, v, no. 480. A comedy of Eupolis was entitled *The Cities*.
[3] Thuc., I, 19, 98, 99; III, 10, 4; VII, 57, 4; cf. VI, 69, 3; 85, 2.
[4] Id., II, 9, 4; VII, 57, 4.
[5] Plut., *Pericl.*, 12; Theophr., *ibid.*, 25.

late, if a town harassed by internal dissensions should furnish the ruling city with an excuse for interfering in its affairs, in short in no matter what circumstances and under no matter what pretext, the Athenians drew up for their allies the articles of their constitutions, regulations for internal administration, terms of compromise between the conflicting parties. We have a whole series of documents showing them legislating for rebel or suspect towns.[1] As soon as the central authority had trained the towns to receive its orders, it found it more convenient to group them by districts: in 446-5 it created five of them, the Islands, Caria, Ionia, the Hellespont and Thrace. It had no hesitation then in taking decisions applicable to a whole district.[2] It finished by legislating for the whole empire: it promulgated general ordinances on internal administration, on the payment of tribute, on the first-fruits due to the goddesses of Eleusis, on monetary unity.[3]

A characteristic change was introduced into the formula of the oath in which the confederate towns swore to remain loyal: in 465 they bound themselves still to " the Athenians and the allies ";[4] after 450 they promised fidelity and obedience to the " Athenian people " (πείσομαι τῶῶῶωι δέμῶῶῶωι τῶῶῶωι 'Αθεναίῶῶῶων).[5] For the confederate towns it was no longer a case of lending each other support against the Persians; the subject cities were required to have the same friends and the same enemies as the mistress city, to furnish her with contingents for fighting in the Ægean, at Samos, against the Peloponnesians, against Syracuse.[6] It was no longer a case of paying to Delos a contribution to ensure common defence; it was rather a tribute which was sent to Athens. Each town was taxed by the Athenian Boule, according to the estimates of Athenian officials (the *taktai*), and claims were presented by other Athenian officials (the *eisagogeis*) before Athenian judges.[7] The allotted sums were

---

[1] Thuc., I, 98 (Naxos); 101, 2 (Thasus); 117, 3 (Samos); *SIG³*, no. 41 (Erythræ); *IG*, vol. I, Suppl., n. 22a (Miletus); *SIG³*, no. 52 (unknown town), 64 (Chalcis), 107 (Neapolis).   [2] *SIG³*, no. 75.
[3] *Ibid.*, I, 42 *ff.*; *IG*, vol. I, nos. 37, 38; Suppl., no. 27b; vol. XII, v, no. 480.
[4] *SIG³*, no. 41; cf. n. 64; *IG*, vol. I, no. 13.   [5] *SIG³*, nos. 52, 64.
[6] Thuc., I, 105, 2; 116; 117, 2; II, 9, 56; III, 3, 4; IV, 13, 2, etc.
[7] It was in affairs of this kind that Antiphon delivered his speeches for Samothrace and for Lindos.

brought by the delegates of the towns at the Great Dionysia,[1] placed in the hands of the *apodektai*, and finally transmitted to the treasurers of the goddess, the ever-watchful guardian who was rewarded for her pains with a first-fruit of a sixtieth part.[2] Remission of payment was a privilege which could only be conceded by the Ecclesia. Unjustified delay in payment involved the addition of a fine to the *phoros*, an *epiphora*.[3] In order to receive her due the creditor people sent out bailiffs who acted as tax-collectors (*eklogeis*);[4] if any resistance were anticipated she deputed execution to the *strategoi* at the head of a squadron.[5] This compulsion was made intolerable by the fact that the money paid as tribute was no longer used solely for the construction and maintenance of the fleet. Pericles laid down in principle that the sums paid by the cities constituted a contract under which Athens undertook to ensure their defence with her navy: as soon as they were living in complete security she could dispose as she wished of the federal exchequer[6]—a theory which was often contested by the parties concerned and by the oligarchs of Athens, but which nevertheless triumphed. The administrators of the *phoros*, the *Helleno-tamiai*, had to subsidize in part the expenses of monuments erected on the Acropolis. Even though they were never called upon to pay out large sums for this purpose[7] the principle involved in making the cities contribute to the sumptuary expenses of Athenian democracy was still of great moment.

One can imagine what, in these circumstances, became of the autonomy promised to the confederates in the beginning. It no longer existed save in those few cities which were in a position to escape from the *phoros* by contributing ships.[8] To the others Athens allowed it only when com-

---

[1] Aristoph., *Ach.*, 378, 502 *f.* and Schol.; cf. *IG*, vol. I, no. 38c-d.
[2] *v.* **XC**, Ad. Wilhelm, " Urkunden des att. Reichs " (*Anz. WA*, vol. XLVI, 1909, p. 41 *ff.*); **XXV**, p. 99 *ff.*
[3] *IG*, vol. I, no. 37t-v.; 240 *ff.*
[4] Harp. Suid., *s.v.*, ἐκλογεῖς; *IG*, vol. I, no. 38c.
[5] These *strategoi* and these ships were called ἀργυρολόγοι; *v.* Thuc II, 69; III, 79; IV, 50, 75; VIII, 107 *f.*; Aristoph., *Knights*, 1070; Plut., *Alc.*, 30; cf. Xen., *Hell.*, I, 1, 8.
[6] Plut., *Pericl.*, 12.
[7] Perhaps 1/60 of the *phoros* for the Parthenon and seven talents a year, in all 35 talents, for the Propylæa (*v.* P. Foucart, *RPh*, vol. XXVII, 1903, p. 5 *ff.*; **XC**, p. 87; Dinsmoor, *AJA*, 1913, p. 53 *ff*).
[8] Arist., *Ath. Const.*, 24, 2.

pelled by events.[1] In the cities where there was no pretext for intervention oligarchic government was able to maintain itself for a long time: Miletus, for example, preserved it until 450.[2] But as soon as Athens was called upon to re-establish civil peace, especially after she learnt that concessions to oligarchic cities did not make them any more favourably disposed towards her, she showed herself openly and vigorously the champion of democracy.

Even as early as 465 the Athenians sent to Erythræ, after a revolution, a garrison commanded by a *phrourarch* and commissioners of surveillance or *episkopoi*. Without delay they organized the Boule of Erythræ on the model of their own and drew up the formula of the oath which the councillors were to take in promising to exercise their office with a view to the common good of the Erythræans, the Athenians and the confederates. On the first occasion the Boule was to be elected by lot and installed under the direction of the *episkopoi* and the *phrourarch*; for the future it was to be elected every year by the *phrourarch* and the retiring Boule.[3] If the cities were controlled to this extent by Athens in the days when they still had obligations to the confederation as a whole, one can imagine how much more stringent that control would be when they were subject to Athens alone. Everywhere there were permanent garrisons with a *phrourarch* who combined military and political authority.[4] The *episkopoi* who were drawn by lot from the Athenians and remunerated by the cities in which they functioned, were invested with judicial powers, sometimes supplemented by armed force, in order that they might settle on the spot suits arising from the application of the treaties: Aristophanes gives them two urns for insignia.[5] In other circumstances Athens intervened by sending officials or extraordinary delegates, such as the *eklogeis*, whose function we know, or certain commissioners who were entrusted, after a civil war, with the task of holding an enquiry and taking

[1] Thuc., V, 18; *SIG*³, no. 112, l. 5 *ff.*
[2] Ps. Xen., *Rep. of Ath.*, III, 11; *SIG*, no. 58; *IG*, vol. I, Suppl., no. 22a.
[3] *SIG*³, no. 41; cf. *IG*, vol. I, no. 10.
[4] *IG*, vol. I, Suppl., no. 22d-e (Miletus); Eupolis, fr. 233, Kock (Cyzicus); Aristoph., *Wasps*, 237 (Byzantium); Thuc., IV, 7, 108, 113; V, 39 (Thrace). Cf. Isocr., *Areop.*, 65.
[5] *SIG*³, no. 76; Aristoph., *Birds*, 1022, 1032, 1053.

necessary measures.[1] It ended quite simply by placing at
the head of the government in a good number of cities one
or more Athenian magistrates, an archon or a college of
archons, that is to say a mayor or leading officials representing
the central power.[2]

Amongst all these marks of subjection, there were few
which appeared more infamous, and perhaps not one which
was so prejudicial to the material interests of the cities, as
the duty of granting landed property to the cleruchs sent
from Athens.[3] This was a direct attack upon citizenship,
since it robbed it of its essential and exclusive privilege of
landed property. It was a spoliation the more odious in
that the victims continued to live near the land from which
they had been ejected or continued to work there while
paying dues to the men who were quartered on them and
who kept them in submission; for sometimes the cleruchs
settled on their estate and cultivated it themselves; sometimes the old proprietors were reduced to the position of
tenants and were compelled to pay two hundred drachmas
each year to a cleruch who, in virtue of this income, became
a *zeugites* owing hoplite service. Land-owners or *rentiers*,
the cleruchs constituted a section of the Athenian people
detached from the main body; they were " the Athenian
people dwelling in Scyros," " the Athenian people of Imbros,"
" the Athenians dwelling in Hephæstia," etc. They had their
Ecclesia and their Boule, subordinated for all important
decisions to the Ecclesia of Athens. They formed a colony
charged with the surveillance of a city, while they made it
pay with interest the price for such surveillance.

At the same time the judicial sovereignty of the cities
was reduced to a shred.[4] At first the Athenian people reserved
to itself the right of judging all crimes and delinquencies
against the federal pact or against the imperial government—

[1] *IG, loc. cit., a*; cf. Ps. Xen., *loc. cit.*, 15.
[2] *SIG*³, nos. 54, 107, 114; Ps. Xen., *op.·cit.*, I, 19; Aristoph., *loc. cit.*,
1050; Antiph., *Murder of Her.*, 47; cf. *RIG*, no. 86, l. 22.
[3] *v.* P. Foucart, " Mém. sur les col. ath. " (*MAI*, vol. IX, 1878,
p. 323 *ff.*); **VII**, vol. II, p. 1271 *ff.*
[4] *v.* A. Fraenkel, *De condicione, jure, jurisdictione sociorum Atheniensium*, 1878; **CXXIII, CVI**, vol. III, p. 969 *ff.*; Hiller von Gaertringen,
GN, vol. CLXXXIII (1921), p. 62 *ff.*; H. Grant Robertson, " The
Admin. of Justice in the Ath. Emp. " (*University of Toronto Studies*,
vol. IV, no. 1, 1924); cf. P. Cloché, *REG*, vol. XXXV (1925), p. 123 *ff.*

acts of high treason, disloyalty, hostile intrigues, or failure to meet the prescribed obligations. Pleas of this order had to be brought to Athens and sent before special *epimeletai*. It was this procedure which, in 425, sanctioned the decree for doubling the *phoros*.[1] Then a further step was taken. Since in political cases Athens felt apprehensive of sentences hostile to democracy or the empire being given, she deprived most of the cities of the right of hearing almost all suits which involved capital penalties.[2] In 446-5, after the submission of Chalcis, a decree of the people laid down rulings for the trial of the guilty: it made no mention of any other competency save that of the Boule and the Heliæa in first resort; it maintained the sovereignty of the Ecclesia for all decrees inflicting loss of civil rights without trial, for all cases of condemnation to banishment, to prison, to death or to loss of property. An amendment of a general order recognized in principle the penal jurisdiction of Chalcis, but with the reservation of obligatory recourse to the popular tribunals of Athens for any condemnation to *atimia* or death.[3] Finally, having once embarked on this course, the Athenian people encroached even upon jurisdiction over private affairs within the town of the empire. This usurpation might, it is true, have its good side, as for instance when the litigants were of two different towns, and it was perhaps to this type of private suit (and again only if the value of the suit exceeded a certain limit) that the sacrifice demanded of the towns was confined.[4] One must recognize, moreover, that when commercial suits were being heard this great firm which was Athens conducted itself with scrupulous fairness. Whether she negotiated with federal cities or with other towns for conventions of private international law ($\delta i\kappa a\iota$ $\dot{a}\pi\dot{o}$ $\sigma v\mu\beta\dot{o}\lambda\omega\nu$), or whether she adhered to traditional relationships, she sought to make the principle of consular law prevail—namely, that the plaintiff should plead in the town to which the defendant belonged.[5] But, since the Athenians were bad

---

[1] *IG*, vol. I, no. 38; cf. Ad. Wilhelm, *Anz. WA*, vol. XLVI (1909), p. 56.
[2] Ps. Xen., *loc. cit.*, 14, 18; Aristoph., *Wasps*, 287 *ff.*; *Peace*, 639; Thuc., I, 77, 1; VIII, 48, 6.
[3] *SIG*³, no. 64. *v.* the oration of Antiphon on the *Murder of Herodes.*
[4] Ps. Xen., *loc. cit.*, 16-18; cf. *IG, loc. cit.*, l. 25.
[5] Ps. Dem., *Halonn.*, 12.

merchants,[1] they found themselves compelled to restrict the application of this principle, by requiring that the Athenian tribunal alone should be considered competent in cases of contracts concluded at Athens.[2]

Pushing her policy of unification to the extreme limit Athens aspired to impose on the empire her system of weights, measures and coinage. The small towns had ceased, after their entry into the confederation, to strike any other coins than the copper coinage needed for the local market. Many great towns which had been guilty of defection saw themselves deprived of a prerogative pertaining to sovereignty. In fact the " owls " of Laurium were practically the only silver pieces of money which the sailors of the fleet brought into the towns and which the towns sent back in the form of tribute; the Athenian talent and foot were familiar to the merchants of all ports. A decree proposed by a man named Clearchus ordered the exclusive use of Athenian standards in all the cities of the empire and forbade them to strike silver money. It seems that it met with serious resistance, for a second one had to be issued (before 420) to order individuals to exchange foreign money for Attic money.[3]

Because of its complete contempt for all the attributes of autonomy, the Athenian empire seemed to its subjects a tyranny. The Athenians were the first to recognize it, but they justified their policy either by referring with Pericles to the services they had rendered and were continuing to render, or else by declaring with the brutality of a Cleon that there could be no retracing of the steps which had been taken, but only a marching forward and a crushing of all obstacles. Thus the cities which had united in order to assure their liberty felt themselves enslaved, and an Athenian could indignantly declare that they were treated like slaves at the mill.[4] They paid tribute for the adornment of Athens and the enrichment of her goddess. They were compelled to send delegates to the Dionysian festivals to deliver their tribute, to the Panathenæa to offer costly victims, to the festivals of Eleusis to consecrate to the goddesses the first-

---

[1] Thuc., I, 77, 1.　　　　　　　　　　[2] *RIG*, no. 6.
[3] *SIG*³, no. 87; Aristoph., *Birds*, 1040. *v.* Weil, *ZNu.*, vol. XXV (1905), p. 52 *ff.*; vol. XXVIII (1910), p. 351 *ff.*; **XC**, p. 179 *ff.*; Babelon, *RNu.*, vol. XVII, p. 457 *ff.*
[4] Aristoph., *Lysistr.*, 571 *ff.*

fruits of the yearly harvest.[1] They were confined within the strait way of democracy, forced to obedience and fidelity by archers and hoplites encamped on their acropolis, by triremes stationed in their port, by the cleruchs established in thousands on their soil. Discontent smouldered in all parts of the empire. For long it was impotent: for isolated cities, separated by great distances, all collective effort against the mistress of the sea was impossible. At last the Spartans gave the signal for the great struggle against Athens; from the beginning they proclaimed it a war of deliverance. In actual fact the empire was to fall less as a result of the furious attacks launched against it from without than of the work of undermining ceaselessly carried on by its enemies within.

Autonomy avenged itself upon a centralization odious to the Greeks. This autonomy of the small cities was so intractable that it did not admit as easily as one might think international solidarity of parties. Cleon did not realize that among the rebel Mitylenians there was a distinction between democrats and oligarchs: for him they were all equally guilty.[2] And when the Athenian people was asked as a measure of public safety to permit the allied towns a change of constitution in favour of oligarchy, Phrynichus opposed the demand. What good could come of it ? " It would be neither a motive of submission for the revolting cities, nor a pledge of fidelity in those who remain with us; for rather than be slaves of either oligarchy or democracy they prefer to be free under no matter which of these governments."[3]

The imperialism of the Athenians, however, was only premature and not entirely fruitless. The great mistake of Athens—an inevitable mistake at this epoch—was her failure to understand that if she assailed the rights of other cities she must make her own more accessible to them. Under the blow of defeat bolder spirits thought of this, but it was already too late and they were to wait for the coming of overwhelming disasters before making an exceptional and despairing application of an idea which Rome was to make so fruitful.[4] At all events the experiment of Pericles and his successors had great results, not only for Athens, which would not have left so great a name had she not been the capital of

[1] *SIG*³, no. 83.   [2] Thuc., III, 39.
[3] Id., VIII, 48.   [4] *RIG*, no. 80.

so great an empire, but for the empire itself and for the whole of Greece. It is always the defects of the system which attract attention because the ancients only saw and in their turn the moderns have looked at little else than the political side of events. But from other points of view, and even from that one, the Athenian empire rendered great services by giving birth to precious elements of unity. Through the medium of the confederate cities democracy, in spite of everything, supplied the mass of Greeks with an example which never lost its influence. Thanks to the commercial liberalism which even in the midst of war the Athenians did not abandon save to ensure their subsistence and to procure materials for naval constructions, the basin of the Mediterranean formed a single market the benefits of whose exploitation were not confined to the Piræus.[1] And, moreover, the allies who came each year to the plays of the Greater Dionysia and the processions of the Panathenæa carried away with them and diffused everywhere a love for great literature and art. Finally, just as the vanquished France of 1815 bequeathed to her conquerors the Code Napoléon, so Athens, before being crushed, spread the principles of her law among the confederates whom she brought before her courts, and this so effectively that many of them permanently adopted not merely her legal technique but her conceptions of personal liberty and personal responsibility.[2] Thus, as a result of the domination which she exercised for three-quarters of a century, Athens contributed greatly to the political, economic, intellectual and juridical unification of the Greek race.

III

THE FEDERATIONS (*Sympoliteiai*)

As a reaction against the menacing ambition of the leagues with their imperial outlook we see in all parts of Greece neighbouring and kindred cities seeking to give each other mutual guarantees and for that purpose uniting in larger communities. From a similar need were born con-

---

[1] *IG*, vol. I, no. 41; cf. Ad. Wilhelm, *loc. cit.*, p. 57 (commercial freedom); *SIG*[3], no. 75; *IG*, vol. I, Suppl., no. 42; Ps. Xen., *op. cit.*, II, 12 (restrictions). *v.* **CXVI.**

[2] Isocr., *Pan.*, 104. *v.* **CXXIII; XXXIII**, p. 345, 528 *f.*

federations of the most diverse nature. Two words usually serve to designate them, namely, *sympolity* and *synœcism*. They were for long synonymous, and hence the union of Attica around its capital has retained the name of *synœcism* in history. But after a certain time the Greeks differentiated between the two terms. Union was accomplished in all cases by the adoption of a common constitution, in all cases men continued to apply to it the same name of sympolity; but when it was accomplished by a total or partial transference of the population into the most important of the cities which were uniting or, if they were of equal importance, into a new town, to this concentration, at once geographical and political, the henceforth specialized term of synœcism was attached.

But the sympolities which are known to us present so many forms, so many gradations, that it is often puzzling to know how to define them: not only are there cases in which one hesitates for the appropriate name, but one cannot always see at what point an alliance, a *symmachia*, substituted for the sovereignty of the contracting cities a superior sovereignty or, on the other hand, at what point it begins to constitute, still under the same name, an authentic confederation.[1] In theory the sympolity created a State embracing many groups by depriving them of part of their autonomy. Its conditions were: citizenship, which was, moreover, something more than a formality and belonged implicitly to all the citizens of the individual units; a constitution, which might be merely the assembly of clauses by which the cities were bound one to another; a government provided with a Council and usually with an Assembly; a jurisdiction responsible for the application of the laws relating to the general welfare; an administration allowing of only a few magistracies. Synœcism implied, in addition, local union, suppression of frontiers between a number of districts, and concentration of the inhabitants in a capital which was often founded for that purpose.

Certain parts of the Peloponnese which wished to secede from the Spartan hegemony began to organize themselves in 471. They acted under the influence of Athens and perhaps, in the beginning, upon the advice of Themistocles in person.

[1] *v.* **XXI, LXXIII, XXIII.**

The small rural cities of the Eleans had for a long time formed an aristocratic State loosely bound together, when the democrats, having come into power, decided to centralize the country by incorporating the subject cantons. They divided it into ten local tribes, each of which was represented by a *Hellanodikas* and fifty members of the Council. At the same time they built the town which they needed: Elis became the seat of the plenary Assembly and a large population settled within its walls.[1]

About the same time Arcadia made two analogous attempts. The shepherds of these plateaux had always lived scattered in hamlets, villages or independent towns (κατὰ κώμας).[2] In certain naturally isolated cantons the inhabitants of these scattered districts did little more than bear a common name and meet together on special occasions: there were, for example, nine villages of Heræans, the same number of Tegeans, five of Mantineans, ten of Mænalians, at least six of Parrhasians and four of Cynurians. Each of these small groups had its own nationality: when an Arcadian was victor in the Olympic games he was proclaimed as a Stymphalian or as a Mænalian.[3] Each one had its own policy: in the fourth century, for instance, the Heræans concluded with the Eleans a truce for a hundred years,[4] and the Tegeans, as soon as they were at peace on the Lacedæmonian side, fought with the Mantineans. Here and there, sooner or later, however, slightly more important centres arose: in the North Orchomenus was of importance during the wars of Messenia,[5] while in order to be in a better position to resist their enemies the nine *komai* of Tegeans built the town of Tegea.[6] And besides the memory of their common origin was not forgotten:[7] the Arcadians came to Parrhasia to sacrifice together to a pre-Hellenic Mother-Earth, the Despoina of Lycosoura,[8] and to celebrate the feast of an Achæan god

---

[1] On the institutions see *RIG*, no. 196; Thuc., V, 47; Hellanicos and Aristodemos, ap. Schol. Pind., *Ol.*, III, 22. On synœcism, Diod., XI, 54, 1; Strab., VIII, 3, 2, p. 336 *f.*; Paus., V, 4, 3. Cf. **VI**, vol. III, i, p. 117; Swoboda, *RE*, art. " Elis "; **XXI**, p. 129-137.
[2] Cf., Strab., *loc. cit.*, p. 337.   [3] *P. Oxy.*, vol. II, no. 222.
[4] *RIG*, no. 1.   [5] *v.* **XXXVI**, vol. I, p. 371.
[6] Strab., *loc. cit.*; Paus., VIII, 45, 1.
[7] Xen., *Hell.*, VII, 1, 23; Paus., V, 27 (offering of an Arcadian-Mainalian). Cf. Hiller von Gaertringen, *IG*, vol. V, ii, p. ix-x.
[8] Paus., VIII, 27, 6; 35, 2; 37, 1 *ff.*; 42, 1.

worshipped on Mount Lycæus, Zeus Lycæus.[1] In the long run this feeling of ethnic solidarity produced its effect.

In the sixth century Tegea struggled single-handed against the Spartans; all the Arcadians suffered its fate and were compelled to recognize the hegemony of the conquerors.[2] In 473 practically all of them made common cause and they soon organized themselves in a confederation. The coins, from which we learn of this political union, tell us also of its extension: federal money was struck which bore on the one side the image of Zeus Lycæus and, on the other, the head of Despoina with the legend Ar, Arca or Arcadicon; at the same time Heræa, unlike Mantinea and some other refractory cities, ceased to strike money of its own.[3] Twenty years later Tegea, conquered by the Spartans, entered the Lacedæmonian league. This was sufficient to make Mantinea break with the league with which, up to that time, she had allied herself. By a pact of synœcism she annexed the population of four surrounding villages, offering them a safe citadel in which to take refuge in case of invasion.[4] From this time the Arcadian confederation ceased to be of importance. When the Peloponnesian war broke out it, too, was forced in its turn to enter the Lacedæmonian league.[5] Compelled as guarantee of its fidelity to give hostages who were massacred,[6] rent by the supporters of Mantinea and those of Tegea,[7] it faded out of existence, and the cities began once more to strike their own money.[8] As for the synœcism it was only able to maintain itself by virtue of a truce for thirty years which was granted to it by Sparta in 418.

After the confederations whose very birth-right was hostility to the Peloponnesian league, others were formed whose principal or sole *raison d'être* was resistance to Athenian imperialism.

The first of these confederations was formed on the frontier of Attica, like that of the Arcadians on the frontier of Laconia. The Bœotians gave themselves a soundly con-

[1] Id., *ibid.*, 2, 1; 38, 5; Pind., *Ol.*, IX, 95; XIII, 107; *Nem.*, X, 48.
[2] Her., I, 65-68; VII, 202; VIII, 72; IX, 28, 77; cf. *SIG*³, no. 31.
[3] R. Weil, *ZNu.*, vol. XXIX (1911), p. 139 *ff.*; Boelte, art. "Heraia," *RE*, vol. VIII, p. 414; **XL**, p. 368; **VII**, vol. II, p. 1398; *contra* **I**, vol. II, p. 843 *ff.*
[4] Cf. **XXII**, p. 372 *ff.*; **VI**, vol. III, i, p. 119.
[5] Thuc., II, 9.   [6] Id., V, 61, 77.
[7] Id., IV, 134, 1.   [8] Cf. **XLI**, p. 447 *f.*; **I**, *loc. cit.*, p. 838.

structed constitution, which was the product of a considerable period of time. Since their settlement in the country
they had been dispersed in a large number of small towns.
They kept alive the memory of their common origin, however,
in the annual festival which reunited them at the temple of
Poseidon at Onchestus[1] and in the Pambœotia celebrated in
honour of Athena Itonia at Coronea.[2]   In addition the small
independent towns were all similarly governed by oligarchies
of land-owners.   Moreover one can discern even in the first
half of the sixth century the embryo of confederation: local
coinage bore a federal emblem, the Bœotian buckler,[3] and
the hoplites of the towns formed on occasion a common army
under the command of the *Bœotarchs*.[4]   Thebes, the most
important centre of the country, was in a fair way to become
the capital when its attitude during the second Persian war
frustrated its ambitions: after the battle of Platæa the confederation was dissolved upon the orders of Sparta (479).[5]
But in 457 Sparta went back on its decision in order to
encircle Attica.   For ten years the revived confederation
was the bone of contention in the struggles to which the
Lacedæmonians, the Bœotians and the Athenians surrendered
themselves, as in those which brought the oligarchs and
democrats of Thebes to blows.   In 447 the defeat of Athens
at Coronea gave permanency to the federal institution.[6]

The constitution then drawn up by the Bœotians is not
only remarkable in itself; it has besides the supreme interest
of being one of the Greek constitutions of which we are most
fully informed, since it was described in detail by an historian
who saw it at work, the " Anonymous " of Oxyrynchus.[7]
In contrast with the Lacedæmonian and Athenian leagues
the Bœotian confederation determined the rights and the
obligations of the constituent cities in proportion to their
population and wealth.   There was no hegemony as of

¹ Strab., IX, 2, 33, p. 412; cf. *Iliad*, II, 506.
² Strab., *loc. cit.*, 29, p. 411; cf. *IG*, vol. VII, nos. 2858 *ff.*; 3087,
3172.
³ I, vol. II, i, p. 936 *ff.*; **XLI**, p. 343 *ff.*
⁴ Compare Her., IX, 15 with VII, 202, 205, 222, 233.
⁵ Diod., XI, 81, 2 *f.*; Just., III, 6, 10.
⁶ Thuc., I, 108, 3; 113, 2-3; III, 62, 4; 67, 3; IV, 92, 6; Ps. Xen.,
op. cit., III, 11.
⁷ *P. Oxy.*, vol. V (1908), no. 892, col. xi, 2 *ff.* *v. BCH*, vol. XXXII
(1908), p. 271 *ff.*; **LIX**, p. 315 *ff.*; **LXXI**, p. 256 *ff.*; Walker, *The Hellenica
Oxyrh.* (1913), p. 134 *ff.*

right; that which Thebes was to exercise was in fact assured to it solely by a common rule, and there was no question of a Theban league but of a Bœotian confederation. Since federal institutions had as their framework districts comprising a variable number of autonomous cities, they were closely connected with the institutions of these cities. At first there was no federal citizenship outside and above local citizenship. Afterwards, the spirit of the confederation was inevitably that of the cities, since they all alike were ruled by a moderate oligarchy. Consequently the whole ordering of the confederation could be based on the organization of the cities.

In each the necessary qualification for active citizenship was the possession of landed property reaching a legal minimum, probably fixed sufficiently high for service as a hoplite to be possible.[1] Commerce was, therefore, derogatory.[2] All the qualified citizens were divided in equal numbers among the four sections of the Council, the four *Boulai*. Each of the four sections in turn exercised the functions of a Council; the four together formed the Assembly. The section in office prepared motions and submitted them to the three others; to have the force of law a decree had to be adopted by all four.

The cities were divided into eleven districts ($\mu\acute{\epsilon}\rho\eta$). Thebes, after the destruction of Platæa, found herself placed at the head of four districts, of which one was divided into five small cities; Orchomenus and Thespiæ each had two; Tanagra, one; Haliartus, Coronea and Lebadea together had cne, as had Acræphia, Copæ and Chæronea. All the districts had the same rights and the same obligations, distributed equitably among the communes. The federal Council was composed of 660 members so that the eleven districts should have equal representation, that in each district all the cities should be represented in proportion to their importance and that in each city the four sections of citizens should have in their turn equal representation. In this way Thebes, with all the districts in its territory, had the right to 240 delegates; Orchomenus to 120, etc.

The Council sat at Thebes and its members received a

---

[1] Xen., *Hell.*, V, 4, 9.
[2] *v. BCH, loc. cit.*, p. 276; cf. **VII**, vol. I, p. 353, n. 5.

daily salary out of the federal treasury. As each delegation represented more specially one of the four sections of its city, so the members of the federal Council, in their turn, divided themselves naturally into four sections, into four *Boulai*.[1] Just as in the cities, each in turn did the work of the Council, and decrees had to be issued by all the sections together in order to have statutory power in all the cities. The judicial power of the confederation was organized in the same way as the legislative power: the High Court, which tried offences against the federal pact, acts of disobedience and perhaps disputes between cities, was composed of judges taken in equal number from the districts and in a proportionate number from the towns. Executive power was in the hands of the *Bœotarchs*. They were elected by the *Boulai* of the cities to the number of eleven, one from each district: thus four from Thebes, two from Orchomenus, two from Thespiæ, one from Tanagra and one furnished in turn by each of the three cities of the other two districts. Their principal function was the command of military forces. When all of them were in the field the supreme command was usually exercised by one alone, either in rotation, or at the request of his colleagues, or on the designation of the Council.[2] As leaders of the army they represented the confederation in dealings with foreign States, received or despatched ambassadors, conducted negotiations and then made their report to the Council, which made a decision.[3] The army was composed of contingents furnished by the eleven districts and fixed for each one at a thousand hoplites and a hundred knights. A federal treasure was required for the expenses of war and the payment of councillors: it was supplied by the *eisphorai*, entrance fees, which were the same for all the districts. The contingent and the contributions were divided among the cities in the district according to the constitutional ratio.

Thus nothing could be done in the confederation save through the agency of the cities, and the importance of each city in the confederation was determined by the number of its active citizens. The influence of Thebes was based solely

---

1 Thuc., V, 38, 2.
2 Id., IV, 91; cf. Diod., XV, 52, 1; 53, 3; 62, 4; 68, 1.
3 Thuc., V, 37-38; Xen., *Hell.*, III, 4, 4.

on the fact that it contained twice, four times, twelve times, twenty times as many landowners possessing the legal minimum as such and such a city, and that, in the same proportions, it had the right to a greater number of representatives in the Council and of Bœotarchs; but, on the other hand, it was required to furnish more men for the army and to contribute more to the treasury. Officially its superiority was marked only by two signs: the Council sat on the Cadmea, and the federal money which alone had currency bore in addition to the emblem of the buckler the legend Th, The or Theba.[1] There was nothing in common between this Bœotian *sympolity* and the leagues subjected to the hegemony of Sparta or Athens.

Such was the confederation which was formed in a spirit of hostility to Athens during the first Peloponnesian war. At the time of the second the same spirit gave birth to two synœcisms, one on the frontiers of Macedonia, the other on the coast of Asia Minor.

In 432, when the Athenians besieged Potidæa, almost all the Greeks of Chalcidice took its part. On the advice of King Perdiccas the inhabitants of the small maritime towns decided to abandon them, to raze the walls and to take refuge in the interior, in the stronghold of Olynthus. From this synœcism a sympolity was born, with Olynthus for capital.[2] The new State soon assumed all the attributes of sovereignty: it treated with foreign powers, sent ambassadors to them, issued decrees of *proxenia*,[3] and had its own army.[4] All the surrounding towns which abandoned the Athenian confederation entered this one.[5] Olynthus rapidly became the most important city of the Thracian coast.[6]

In 408 the Rhodians wishing to put an end to the rivalries which had for long separated their three cities, Ialysus, Camirus and Lindus, built a common capital, Rhodes, a town destined to have so glorious a future. The neighbouring isles of Chalcia and of Syme threw in their lot with the great island; Telus, Carpathus and Casus also joined it at a later date. In spite of the rapid development of the new town

[1] **XLI**, p. 349.   [2] Thuc., I, 58, 2.
[3] Id., V, 31, 6; 38, 1; IV, 83, 3; 78, 1.
[4] Id., II, 79, 3 *ff.*; IV, 7.   [5] Id., V, 82.
[6] Xen., *Hell.*, V, 2, 12.

the ancient communities, great or small, remained, but as tribes and demes of the city. There was but one Rhodian *demos* which united in a general Assembly and which was represented by a Boule; but the " Lindians," the " Camirians," the " Ialysians " continued to issue decrees and to nominate *mastroi*.[1] Here, as formerly in Attica, the synœcism gave birth to a truly unitary State, and the old cities degenerated almost to the position of mere municipalities.

One can see, even in those instances where the passion for autonomy was more or less quelled, how repugnant this repression of local sovereignty was to the spirit of the Greeks. The idea of political concentration might triumph over small areas, when a common danger menaced neighbouring towns or villages incapable of defending themselves; but it never went beyond vaguely federal institutions which one by one succumbed, less often as the result of the attacks of foreign foes than of the ungovernable power of a centrifugal force.

[1] Diod., XIII, 75; Strab., XIV, 2, 11, p. 655. *v.* **LXXIII**, p. 140 *ff.*; **XXIII**, p. 195 *ff.*

PART III
THE CITY AND ITS DECLINE

CHAPTER I
NEW MANNERS AND IDEAS

I
PRIVATE LIFE

THE just balance which Greece in its greatest days had succeeded in establishing between public power and the rights of the individual could not be maintained indefinitely. After having helped the city to triumph over the patriarchal family, individualism for some time suffered itself to be kept within bounds, on the one hand by the still solid organization of the small family, and still more on the other hand by the apparently immutable law of the State. But the right of the individual was to degenerate into egoism. By steady encroachments, by increasingly exacting demands, it was to undermine the family and ruin the city.

At the close of the fourth century the great towns experienced what has been justly called the " marriage crisis," and the " reign of the courtesans."[1] This does not mean that in an epoch when men were looking for happiness in private life they were not alive to the charm of well-matched marriages. The works of Aristotle—who himself rejoiced in having married the niece of his friend Hermias—are full of passages in which marriage appears, not as a simple business proposition nor yet as an alliance having for end the propagation of the race, but as a communion of souls designed to satisfy all the moral needs of existence, to bestow on husband and wife the advantages and blessedness of mutual love.[2] What

---

[1] O. Navarre, art. " Meretrices," *DA*, vol. III, p. 1824.
[2] Arist., *Nic. Eth.*, VIII, 14, 7-8; *Eud. Eth.*, VI, 10, 7; VII, 9, 4; cf. Ps. Arist., *Econ.*, I, 4, 1-3. *v.* G. Guizot, *Ménandre*, p. 309 *ff.*; **LXVIII**, vol. II, p. 165 *ff.*

was new and indicated a serious change in custom was the fact that marriage was no longer considered as a strict duty of the individual, bound in his turn to hand on the life he had received in trust from his ancestors; it came often to be regarded as an artificial institution, a mere convention. In the opinion of devisers of Utopian societies it could be replaced by community of women; in the eyes of the common people it was simply one of the alternatives offered to each man in his search for personal well-being and pleasure. A suitor could say in open court: " We have wives that our name may be perpetuated, concubines that our needs may be cared for, courtesans that we may be diverted."[1]

Undoubtedly concubines and *hetairai* were always prominent in Greece; husbands there never prided themselves upon conjugal fidelity. The laws of Draco mentioned without any reprobation certain concubines,[2] and the liaison of Pericles with Aspasia was publicly known. But the concubinage to which ancient legislation accorded a sort of legitimacy had at least for object the procreation of natural children in case of a sterile marriage, and it is well known that the great statesman, in spite of his prestige, failed to secure recognition for his beautiful and learned Milesian in Athenian society. Now everything was allowed without the necessity of pleading excuses and without causing scandal. Illicit unions no longer shocked men. The hardy bachelor and the courtesan became the normal and often pleasing characters of the comedy. In a comparison between free love and the state of marriage one of the characters of the poet Amphis does not hide his preferences: " Is not a concubine more desirable than a wife ? . . . The one has on her side the law which compels you to retain her, no matter how displeasing she may be; the other knows that she must hold a man by behaving well or else look for another."[3] This was no pure tirade, effective on the stage; it was a current maxim. Men of letters and artists conformed to it for the most part: Praxiteles openly took for mistress his model, Phryne; Menander lived with Glycera, Diphilus with Gnathæna. Thus the demi-monde shone in highest circles; it set the tone. It was not only hot-blooded youth which invited concubines to its symposia. Socrates,

¹ Ps. Dem., *C. Neair.*, 122.   ² Dem., *C. Aristocr.*, 53.
³ Amphis. ap. Athen., XIII, 7, p. 559*a-b*.

the passionate admirer of beauty, sentimentalized over
Theodote.[1] Phryne created no more scandal when she dedicated her statue in gold at Delphi or when she placed her
image by the side of Aphrodite in the temple of Eros at
Thespiæ, than did her lover and defender Hyperides when he
brought her forth naked in full court.[2]

A Plato nevertheless could find much to condemn in these
customs: he who was not married would gladly have forbidden
all intercourse with a woman other than a legitimate wife;
but one has to live with one's times, to resign oneself to
necessary concessions, and the statesman tolerated the unions
which displeased the moralist, on condition that they were
concealed.[3] As to the philosophers who propagated the
doctrine of pleasure they did not trouble about appearances,
and rendered this kind of homage to virtue neither by their
precepts nor by their example; they were openly opposed
to marriage: Aristippus preferred to be the lover of Lais, as
Epicurus later was that of Leontion.

When such ideas on marriage prevailed what happened
to the birth-rate ? In Greece, where the land was not
fertile and where it was naturally divided, the rule of equal
inheritance was no sooner established than it inspired in
fathers of families fears for the future of their children and
inclined them towards Malthusianism. The poet Hesiod,
a small proprietor of Bœotia, even in his day wished to have
only one son (μουνογενής).[4] Moreover some of the old laws
urged the upper classes to limit the number of their children,
one of the Cretan by prescribing the seclusion of women
and homosexual relations, those of Lycurgus at Sparta and
of Philolaus at Thebes by constituting a fixed number of
inalienable and indivisible entailed estates.[5] At the close of
the fourth century men evaded as much as possible the duties
of fatherhood. "There is no one so unhappy as a father,
unless it is a father who has more than one child "; "there
is no need to have children":[6] such were henceforth the maxims

[1] Xen., *Mem.*, III, 11.
[2] Paus., IX, 27, 5; X, 15, 1; Athen., *loc. cit.*, 59, p. 591.
[3] Plat., *Laws*, VIII, p. 841.
[4] Hes., *Op. et Dies*, 376. *v. supra*, p. 26.
[5] Arist., *Pol.*, II, 7, 5; 9, 7; cf. Plat., *Laws*, p. 836*b*; Heracl. Pont.,
fr. 3, 5 (*FHG*, vol. II, p. 211).
[6] *v.* Stob., *Flor.*, LXXVI, 1 and 15; cf. LXXXIII, 20; LXXXIV, 21.

of current wisdom. Daughters were not wanted at all; more than one son was too many. One son—that was the ideal if one wanted to leave posterity. As justification they had recourse to the sophism of paternal solicitude: the man of moderate means declined to produce a line of paupers, the rich man thought it his duty to prevent the division of his patrimony after his death; they did not wish for many children, they said, because they loved children too dearly. In reality the parents were most often obeying the promptings of egoism: they were repelled by the daily trials and troubles which a numerous family causes, by the expense which children entail until their education is finished.[1]

All methods were good which restricted birth or offered a way of ridding oneself of the newly born. Abortion was punishable only if it were practised by a woman against the wish of her husband or by a third person who had seduced her; provided that the head of the family had ordered it justice did not interfere.[2] If efforts to prevent a child from coming into the world failed, a way remained which also was not considered criminal: it might be killed or exposed.[3] Exposure was a very frequent practice: the child abandoned by its parents and rescued by some kind-hearted soul became a popular character in the new comedy. One might think that the practices devised by individuals and tolerated by the State would at least call forth the protests of philosophers. But this by no means happened: by reason of their theories, because they wished to preserve the city from a fatal over-population, they countenanced all restrictions upon birth ($\epsilon\pi\iota\sigma\chi\epsilon\sigma\epsilon\iota\varsigma$ $\gamma\epsilon\nu\epsilon\sigma\epsilon\omega\varsigma$).[4] Plato, in order to maintain the purity of the race and to prevent licentiousness from carrying the number of citizens beyond 5,040, proposed that all weakly children or those born of base or elderly parents should be killed. Aristotle, in order to prevent the growth of an indigent class, could think of no better scheme than that public authorities should issue an edict recommending abortions and exposures.[5] One can see in what direction

---

[1] v. art. " Expositio," DA, vol. II, p. 931 f.
[2] **XXXIII**, p. 351-353.
[3] v. DA, art. " Infanticidium " and " Expositio."
[4] Plat., Laws, V, p. 741d.
[5] Id., Rep., V, 459d-e, 460c, 461b-c; Arist., Pol., IV (VII), 14, 10; cf. 6 and 11; II, 3, 6; 4, 3.

the State would have acted if it had attempted to interfere. Malthusianism had free play.

In certain parts of Greece egoism made such ravages that a complete disorganization of the family resulted. Very characteristic in this respect is the spectacle afforded by Bœotia towards the end of the third century, according to the description which Polybius gives:

" People who had no children, in place of leaving their property to their collaterals, as was formerly the custom, spent it on banquets and drinking parties and bestowed it on their friends as common property; a good number of those who had children reserved the major part of their wealth for such convivial parties; so much so that many Bœotians held more supper parties in the month than the month had days." [1]

The same Polybius examines the question in a more general fashion; he shows us the gravity of an evil which reached its climax in his time, but which had raged for two centuries. *A propos* of this he makes some very illuminating remarks:

" We see in our time throughout the whole of Greece such a shrinking of the birth-rate and, in a word, such depopulation, that the towns are deserted and the fields lie waste, although there are neither continual wars nor epidemics. . . . The cause of the evil is manifest. . . . From vanity, from avarice or from cowardice men are unwilling either to marry or to bring up children without marrying; at the most they will have only one or two in order that they may leave them a fortune and ensure for them a luxurious existence: thus the plague has rapidly assumed dangerous proportions. If once war or sickness comes to claim its tribute in these families of one or two children, the line inevitably dies out and, just as with swarms of bees, the cities, becoming depopulated, quickly lose their power." [2]

Whilst the philosophers still clung to the belief that there was a danger of an excessive birth-rate, actually the excess of deaths over births was proving the efficacy of Malthusian practices. Population diminished alike in democratic and in aristocratic cities. Athens, which numbered 30,000 citizens at the time of the Persian wars, had more than 40,000 in the time of her greatest prosperity.[3] Although the Peloponnesian war caused her to lose again what she had gained,[4] voluntary restrictions cost her as much in the fourth century as pestilence and war combined in the preceding century: the census ordered by Demetrius of Phalerum

[1] Pol., XX, 6, 5-6.
[2] Id., XXXVI, 17.
[3] Her., V, 97; VIII, 65; Thuc., II, 13.
[4] Aristoph., *Ass. of Women*, 1132 *ff.*; Ps. Plat., *Axioch.*, p. 369a.

placed the number of citizens at 21,000.[1] At Sparta the situation was even worse. By making the patrimonial *kleros* an indivisible entail and by forbidding citizens to engage in a trade, the law compelled the family to restrict birth as rigidly as possible. The best thing was to have only one son; if by some misfortune one had more then the younger ones settled down in common on property other than the *kleros* and took only one wife between them.[2] This involved alarming depopulation.[3] The State attempted to counteract this by imposing a moral slur on the bachelor and by according certain advantages to the fathers of three or four children.[4] But what result could it hope to obtain by such superficial palliatives ? It neutralized the effects itself by the restrictions which it placed upon entry into the upper class. Moreover, it even required that the newly-born, whom the father wished to rear, should be brought before a council of inspection, before their right of succeeding to the *kleros* was recognized, and, if they were considered unfit for their duties, they were sent to the Apothetai, to death.[5] The dearth of men (ὀλιγανθρωπία) was at Sparta, therefore, an evil which could only be remedied by a change, not merely in manners, but in the constitution itself. That was not to be thought of. Thus the Spartans qualified to bear arms saw their ranks grow sparser with a disastrous rapidity. In 480, they numbered more than 8,000; in 371, they numbered only 2,000; forty years or so later Aristotle computed the number of " Equals " as 700. Doubtless the decline in the numbers of the supreme class did not represent pure loss to population, for an appreciable number of " Equals " were relegated, because of inadequate incomes, to the class of " Inferiors "; but, on the whole, the diminution was constant and remained considerable.

The countryside in particular suffered from depopulation, for the town exercised a strong attraction. It had not always been so. Until the time of the Peloponnesian war

---

[1] Ctesicles, fr. 1 (*FHG*, vol. IV, p. 375); cf. Ps. Dem., *C. Aristocr.*, I, 51.
[2] Tim. in Pol., XII, 6, 8.
[3] *v.* **XXIX**, Cavaignac, " La popul. du Pél. aux Vᵉ et IVᵉ siècles " (*Klio*, vol. XII, [1912], p. 270 *ff.*); **XXXVI**, vol. I, p. 367-369.
[4] Plut., *Lyc.*, 15, 1; Arist., *Pol.*, II, 6, 13.
[5] *v.* art. " Expositio," *loc. cit.*, p. 937.

the landowners of Attica, rich or poor, had for the most part continued the practice of living in the country. In those days a Strepsiades " led a delightful peasant life—all in a muck, careless of dress, free from care, abounding in bees and sheep and grapes "; sniffing eagerly the smell of " new wine, and cheese and wool and fertility "; but he had only to marry a woman of high birth, a niece of Megacles, to be dragged off to the town and to lose all hope of seeing his son " bringing in the goats as he himself had done, leaping over the rocks in his leather jerkin."[1] When Pericles concentrated the population in the town, in order to leave a gap between the enemy and themselves, it was a heartbreaking, bitter thing for the country dwellers to abandon the houses and temples to which all their family traditions bound them: " they were called upon to change their habits of life and to bid farewell to what each regarded as his native city."[2] Now however the city had become a magnet. The prosperous farmers were lured towards it by a desire for comfort, a taste for society or for politics. Ischomachus, the type of great landowner who required a steward to manage his labourers, lived in the town and went every day to his estate in the early morning, by foot or by horse.[3] As for the small peasants, resistance became more and more difficult. Either they were evicted by pitiless creditors or in a bad year they would listen to the tempting offers of land dealers and abandon their land. In districts where the sole resource was cultivation or breeding, as for instance in Arcadia and Achæa, there was nothing to do but to emigrate and attach themselves to some band of mercenaries; elsewhere they went into the town and engaged in commerce.[4] Thus, at the same time as the population was diminishing, the exodus from the country was changing its distribution.

II

ARTS AND LETTERS

In societies in which unbridled individualism is destroying the communal spirit arts and letters inevitably reflect the change. From whatever angle one looks one notices in

[1] Aristoph., *Clouds*, 43-72.   [2] Thuc., II, 16.
[3] Xen., *Econ.*, XI, 15; cf. *C. Callicl.*, 3.
[4] Xen., *Revenues*, IV, 6.

L

Greece between the fifth and fourth centuries great differences in these two domains.

A crisis which shook the very foundations of Greece necessarily modified the material and moral conditions of art. Men no longer thought in terms of common work for the embellishment of the city: the weakening of patriotism, even more perhaps than the impoverishment of the public treasury, made that impossible. Orders came from individuals whose wealth permitted them to satisfy their desire for beautiful things, their love of luxury or their vanity; they came more often still from Greek or Oriental princes who, in Cyprus, at Halicarnassus, at Sidon, at Pella, at Syracuse, wished to adorn their capital with monuments destined to perpetuate their memory. In this new world the masters, in order to advance themselves, cast away the old traditions like so much useless matter and demanded freedom to develop their own qualities according to their inspiration and the fashion of the moment.

Until the fourth century architecture had been solely concerned with the building of temples which, from one town to another, rivalled each other in splendour. The houses were of a rustic appearance, small, badly built, inconvenient, scattered in haphazard fashion along narrow and tortuous little streets.

" The edifices which their administrations have given us," said Demosthenes, " their decorations of our temples and the offerings deposited by them, are so numerous and so magnificent, that all the efforts of posterity cannot exceed them. Then, in private life, so exemplary was their moderation, their adherence to the ancient manners so scrupulously exact, that, if any of you ever discovered the house of Aristides, or Miltiades, or any of the illustrious men of those times, he must know that it was not distinguished by the least extraordinary splendour."

To this patriarchal simplicity of the great days of old the orator opposes " private houses whose magnificence surpasses that of certain public buildings."[1] Doubtless he exaggerates the contrast, advocate as he is. In the fifth century wealthy Athenians lived on their estate, and, though they usually neglected the *pied-à-terre* which they possessed in the town, the house which they inhabited in the country was sometimes

[1] Dem., *Ol.*, III, 25 *f.* (trans. Leland); *Pub. Econ.*, 29 *f.*; *C. Aristocr.*, 206 *f.*

beautiful and well appointed.[1] In the town itself at that epoch there were mansions remarkable for their lodge, their painted vestibule, their pillared halls, their bath-rooms, and whose chambers, with their ceilings covered with arabesques, with their sculptured wainscotting, with their walls decorated with paintings, were adorned with gay tapestries, with Milesian beds, with vases of earthenware, of bronze, of precious metals.[2] But this luxury was exceptional and reserved for a few great families. Later it spread. Timotheus built for himself a house which testified to his riches and which was called his " tower "; the house of Midias at Eleusis shadowed the whole neighbourhood; Phocion's house was regarded as quiet and yet it had walls covered with bronze.[3] Anyone who had a comfortable income wished to have rooms to offer to his guests, to extend the ground-floor by a garden, to surround the peristyle with higher galleries, to have the walls painted by artists of renown. During this time the monuments of the Acropolis remained unfinished; the people found money only for military works, for fortifications, for an arsenal, or for constructions which ministered to its pleasure or its convenience—a theatre of stone and a colonnaded walk, the portico of Philon. . . . Where were now those happy years in which Pericles, Ictinus, and Pheidias with united efforts strove to raise for the glory of Athena a sanctuary which should be worthy of her ?

Monumental sculpture had now perforce to restrict its sphere, save in remote Caria where an opulent dynast wished it to make the Mausoleum one of the wonders of the world. Statuary took its place and assumed an essentially individual character. In art, as in literature, the predominating form was the portrait: what subject could better please the Mæcenases who wished to have good value for their money, or the public which was solely interested in the illustrious men of the present and the past ? In place of the bas-reliefs which depicted religious myths, the exploits of heroes and the ceremonies of national festivals on pediments and friezes, one now saw in public places, in palæstræ and gymnasia, in the parks dedicated to the Muses, in mansions

---

[1] Thuc., II, 65; Isocr., *Areop.*, 52; Xen., *Econ.*, III, 1.
[2] P. Monceaux, art. " Domus," *DA*, vol. II, p. 343 *ff.*
[3] Aristoph., *Plut.*, 180; Dem., *C. Mid.*, 158; Plut., *Phoc.*, 18.

and palaces, the heads and busts of prosperous merchants
and concubines, of *strategoi* and *hipparchs*, of poets and
philosophers, of *kosmetai* and benefactors, and kings.[1]
Leochares even consented to engrave in marble the features
of Lykiskos, a slave merchant. After the end of the fourth
century practically all sculptors, and the most illustrious
ones, Scopas, Praxiteles, Lysippus, were "makers of men."[2]
Even the gods were transformed into men; their majesty
was tempered in *scènes de genre* which showed Hermes carrying the divine child or Apollo killing lizards; preference was
given to those which symbolized joy, intoxication and
voluptuousness, to Dionysus and Aphrodite. Sculptors were
individualists in the subjects they treated and still more in
their manner of treating them. They tried, each in his turn,
to express states of mind and to merge their own with that
which emanated from their model. Whether pathetic or
voluptuous, their works breathe forth a sentimentality and
a sensuality which are entirely personal. The history of art
had reached a point when, being no longer attached to a
collective idea, it dissolved into a history of the artists.

Painting, since it is more fitted to realistic expression,
outstripped plastic art. It was besides given scope for
executing vast decorative compositions, such as those which
were painted by Euphranor in the temple of Zeus the Deliverer
at Athens and by Zeuxis in the palace of Archelaus at Pella;
but, in general, the fresco was supplanted by the easel-piece
which was suitable both for wealthy individuals and for
sovereigns. To whatever school they belonged painters gave
to mythology the human aspect which it assumed in the
theatre, transformed current ideas into allegories, painted
the battles of the epoch, sought in common life scenes for
genre pictures and, inclining more and more to precise observation, affected above all the portrait. They were also
sons of their times in the prices which they demanded for
their works: we are told that Zeuxis received from Archelaus
400 minæ (about £1,500), that Aristides paid 10 minæ for
each figure in a military scene which grouped a hundred of
them (about £4,000) and that Apelles obtained from the

---

[1] No statue was erected to Miltiades after Marathon, nor to Themistocles after Salamis (Dem., *Pub. Econ.*, 21).
[2] *v.* Ch. Picard, *La sculpt. ant.*, vol. II, p. 60 *ff.*

Ephesians for a portrait of Alexander 20 talents of gold (about £5,000).[1] There was the same development in literary forms.

The drama, born in Athens, spread throughout the whole of Greece which was covered with theatres; but if it was to continue to produce fine work it was more than ever essential that it should remain faithful to its past. The very organization of the contests and plays revealed a new state of mind. In the fifth century the theatre brought the whole city to worship before the altar of Dionysus. The dithyrambic and dramatic contests were held between tribes or between *choragoi* chosen by the archon: in the lists of victors and on the votive offerings dedicated in commemoration of the victories the name of the tribe appeared first, before that of the *choragos*, for the prize for the dithyramb; the name of the *choragos* preceded that of the poet for the prizes for comedy and tragedy. In the fourth century, although the organization of the theatre retained its public character, the name of the *choragos*, the delegate of the State, disappeared, and was replaced by those of the poet and the principal actor; soon also in the dithyrambic contests, the name of the executant, of the *auletes*, prevailed over that of the author.[2] Collective, anonymous effort was almost completely a thing of the past. Individuals who formerly had been kept in the background now attempted to thrust themselves into the limelight: so much so and so successfully that eventually the audience was more interested in the acting than in the merits of the play, and the virtuosity of musicians was ranked higher than the merit of the composers.

Nor did the spectators look to the theatre for the same kind of pleasure as formerly. Tragedy was *démodé* ; men were content with revivals which exalted as classics the three great poets of the fifth century. But though men had a respectful admiration for Æschylus and Sophocles who remained faithful to the religious and patriotic conception of the old legends, they raved about Euripides. What a sign

---

[1] Ælian., *Var. Hist.*, XIV, 17; Pliny, *Nat. Hist.*, XXXV, 99, 92.
[2] Cf. *RIG*, n. 879, 881, 915. *v.* Capps, *The Introd. of Comedy into the City Dionysia at Athens*, 1904; " Epigr. Problem in the Hist. of Attic Comedy " (*AJP*, vol. XVIII, 1907, p. 179-199); Ad. Wilhelm, " Urkunden dramatischer Aufführungen in Athen " (*Sonderschriften d. österr. arch. Inst.*, vol. VI, 1906); P. Foucart, " Documents pour l'hist. du théâtre ath." (*JS*, 1907, p. 468 *ff.*, 545 *ff.*, 590 *ff.*).

of the times ! Here was a poet who, by his loathing for public life, his mobile and restless nature, his passion for reasoning and subtle psychology, his tendency to exalt passion and to make his persons speak in character, stood outside his century: he achieved his first victory at the age of forty, after fifteen years of struggle, and was victorious only five times in his whole life, so true is it that to the very end he had to beat down the resistance of the public ! After his death he enjoyed an extraordinary vogue: his plays were so completely in harmony with the new spirit that they were played over and over again in preference to all others. They gave rise to imitations which Aristotle criticized severely: " Formerly," he says, " poets made their characters speak like citizens; to-day they are made to speak like rhetoricians."[1]

An even more remarkable transformation took place in comedy. With Aristophanes it sought its subjects in public life, and in the parabasis subjected the spectators to a political harangue on the events of the day. Since it was reserved to Athenians by birth the Old Comedy could not have metics for authors. Metics, on the contrary, were the authors of plays of the Middle Comedy, and they took as characters popular types, craftsmen.[2] Soon in the New Comedy even the representation of a social milieu was abandoned and the plot was centred on an incident of private life and was confined to the portrayal of character.

These changes were manifestations of a most important fact: it was no longer to poetry that the new generations looked for the expression of their ideas and the satisfaction of their intellectual needs, but to prose. As realists and individualists they needed a language free from all constraint, the language of everyday life. In the schools, where formerly only the poems of Homer were recited, the art of speaking was now learnt under the direction of rhetoricians; at banquets where in earlier days elegies and *skolia* had been sung, men turned to political and philosophical discussions; in the great panegyrics where the rhapsodes used to declaim the epics, we see for the first time a Gorgias delivering, in pompous fashion, a discourse on questions of national interest. Plato, the greatest prose writer of his century and perhaps of all time, banished from his republic the greatest of all poets.

[1] Arist., *Poet.*, VI, 8.   [2] Cf. **XXXV**, p. 228.

It was in the schools where sophists taught the art of disputation that minds were henceforth formed. Men went there to learn how to uphold a cause in the Assembly or the courts. Eloquence erected itself into a literary *genre* and a profession. Pericles was considered in his day the most perfect orator whom men had ever heard; of his speeches, however, there remain only a few of those superb thoughts and brilliant images which earned for him the nickname of the Olympian, a few rare specimens of those oratorical flashes which lingered in men's memories.[1] After his day speeches were written down either before or after they were delivered. Eloquence aimed at stimulating æsthetic emotions in the reader and the delights of *amour-propre* in the writer. It had, moreover, a practical utility; *logographoi* and orators lived by the speeches which they sold and the harangues which they had just uttered.

Since it was all-powerful in public life individualism necessarily influenced the conception of history. Isocrates claimed for prose writers the right, hitherto reserved for poets, to compose panegyrics on great men.[2] Biographies multiplied, not only for the glorification of men who had actually been of importance, as for example Agesilaus or Euagoras, but even for the rendering of pious homage to young men of brilliant promise, such as Gryllus, son of Xenophon.[3] In the hands of Philistus the history of Sicily was converted at one point into a history of Dionysius the Tyrant. Xenophon did not confine himself to weaving a crown in honour of his hero Agesilaus; he centres the incidents of the *Anabasis* upon Cyrus the Younger, Clearchus and himself; even in such a connected story as that of the *Hellenica* he freely introduces personal elements. Character sketches, which in Thucydides were only rare and suggestive outlines, filled a large place in the work of his successors.[4]

Even philosophy ceased to be impersonal in form and became essentially concerned with upholding the rights of personality. By his method of discussion with the sophists, and his maieutic mode of inquiry applied to ordinary people, Socrates led his disciples to bring out his own ideas and their

---

[1] Plat., *Phædr.*, p. 270; Eupolis ap. Schol. Aristoph., *Acharn.*, 529.
[2] Isocr., *Euag.*, 9 *ff.*   [3] Diog. Laert., II, 54.
[4] *v.* **LVII**, vol. V, p. 361 *ff.*

own in the dialogues, where the character of the disputants appears as in a play. Xenophon, no less as a philosopher than as an historian, is a portrait painter. Plato is it to perfection. When the Socratic doctrine substituted a practical study of the human soul in place of abstract speculations and ambitious theories of the universe it aimed at subordinating the desires of the individual to the good of the city, but it facilitated the spread of very different ideas. The schools of the sophists prepared the way for individualism. Thanks to them it was to be enabled to advertise itself in deed and to justify itself in theory. It was to bring about a fundamental revolution in men's minds, to oppose the immutable and inevitable order of nature to the variable and contingent order of law, to reduce the law of the city to the position of pure convention and to authorize the philosopher to ignore it.[1] " The useful, as it is determined by the laws, is a brake upon nature; the useful according to nature is unfettered ":[2] that was the principle. Callicles, in the *Gorgias*, follows out the consequences. In nature the strong man raises himself above other men: what the law considers an injustice is absolute freedom for any man capable of rising above the common level. Law is made for the weak and in their interest; but a single reasonable man is superior to a million irrational men, and it is for him to command and for them to obey. Since there are souls of masters and souls of slaves the only law which is legitimate is that which recognizes the superiority of the one over the other; true morality is the morality of the masters.[3] To justify the domination of the powerful was, logically, to emancipate all individuals, to detach them from the State, to assign to them as the sole end of life the search for happiness; Aristippus of Cyrene and Diogenes the cynic only gave a general application to the ideas of a Callicles. Individualism sweeping all before it was to leave standing none of the conceptions from which the city derived its strength: it was tending already to legitimize the sovereignty of one man, tyrant or monarch, and to foreshadow the triumph of cosmopolitanism.

[1] Antiph., *De Ver.*, 4; Plat., *Protag.*, p. 337c; *Gorg.*, p. 484d. v. **LXXVII**, p. 25 *ff.*
[2] Antiph., *loc. cit.*   [3] Plat., *Gorg.*, p. 483b-d, 490a.

CHAPTER II

TRANSFORMATION OF SOCIAL AND POLITICAL LIFE

I

CLASSES

As soon as family and national sentiment began to grow weaker, communal interests necessarily took on new forms and impelled individuals and even cities themselves into new combinations.

There had always existed in Greece a very considerable number of private societies. Between the great community which included all families and the small community which was the family itself, there were free associations of a utilitarian or sentimental character. Some had an aristocratic stamp; others made their appeal to the lower classes. Since Homeric times certain warriors, and those the most illustrious, had been united by special bonds, took their meals together and considered it their duty to have the same friends and the same enemies: they were called among themselves *hetairoi*.[1] Later the rich or the well born formed *hetaireiai*, clubs whose members gave each other mutual support in elections and law suits,[2] or else met together for festive banquets, to throw ridicule upon popular beliefs or to discuss philosophy and politics.[3] Completely different in recruitment as in purpose were certain fraternities, the oldest of which bore the name of *thiasoi*. These had united since pre-Hellenic days the humbler folk who wished to maintain the worship of divinities excluded from the official pantheon. In earlier times they had done much to spread belief in the mysteries, the dogma of the passion and the resurrection, the doctrine of personal survival and posthumous justice.

[1] *v.* **XXXIII,** p. 88.   [2] Thuc., VIII, 54; Plat., *Theæt.*, p. 178*d*.
[3] Thence came the literature of *Symposia* (Plato, Xenophon, Plutarch, Lucian, Athenæus, etc.) and the works of political science (Pseudo-Xenophon, Critias, etc.).

Whether aristocratic or popular all these societies had a special attraction for generations imbued with individualist ideas. What became of the *hetaireiai*, as they multiplied in order to satisfy the love of material pleasures, we have seen above in the example of the Bœotians who disinherited their collaterals and often even their children and devoted their wealth to feasting and drinking fraternities.[1] As for the confraternities they found an increasingly favourable field in commercial towns, especially in the ports and suburbs where the metics attracted unceasingly new influxes of strangers. As freedom of association was unrestricted group-ings by nationalities, by professions, by religions—by religions especially—were very easily made. Old pupils of gymnasiums formed little republics with their magistrates and their assemblies. Philosophers, who in the old days had poured forth their ideas anywhere, in the street or on the agora, in a palæstra or in a shop, were now heads of schools and shut themselves up with their disciples in private gardens, such as the Lyceum or the Academy. Merchants in foreign costume together with common slaves assembled in chapels where ceremonies, moving the whole audience to a profound degree, were celebrated. The gods of the barbarians had always been well received: since the fifth century the Great Phrygian Mother and the Egyptian Ammon had had their disciples, not only in Asia Minor and in Cyrene, but in numerous cities of Greece proper; Plato went to the Piræus with the Athenian crowd to take part in the procession of the Thracian Bendideia. There was a very different state of affairs when the public cults, with their cold ritual, had become incapable of satisfying religious cravings, of firing men's imagination and stirring their hearts. Men and women sought exaltation in the moving festivals of the Orientals, in the exotic mysteries of the Egyptian Isis and the Syrian Adonis. Upon the heights of their acropolis the city deities felt themselves deserted and saw their people thronging into the confraternities where each one, no longer turning his thoughts towards the terrestrial world, strove to assure his salvation in the world to come.

Dangerous in another way was the responsibility which bound citizens to a party. This was the special vice of the

[1] *v. supra*, p. 299.

Greeks. It had always existed, but never had it raged with so complete a disregard of the common interest as in the fourth century. Athens had still a certain discipline in this respect, because, in spite of everything, after a century and a half of democratic tradition she preserved some principles of civic loyalty, while the remnants of material prosperity, outliving political supremacy, prevented hatreds from becoming too bitter. But in Greece as a whole there existed almost everywhere a glaring contrast between the equality promised by the constitution and the inequality created by social and economic conditions.

The power of money was spreading and corrupting morality.[1] Those who had just enough to live on wished to be rich; the rich wished to be still richer. It was the triumph of that insatiable passion for gain which the Greeks called πλεονεξία. There was no longer a profession which escaped the clutches of capitalism, of *chrematistike*. Agriculture was commercialized to such an extent that by the progressive eviction of small peasants and the concentration of estates in the same hands the system of large estates was recreated.[2] Rhetoricians, advocates and artists, who had formerly reckoned it a dishonour to commercialize their talent, now felt no scruples in selling their goods as dearly as possible. Everything could be bought, everything had its price,[3] and wealth was the measure of social values.[4] By gain and by extravagance fortunes were made and unmade with equal rapidity. Those who had money rushed into pleasure-seeking and sought every occasion for gross displays of luxury. The newly rich (νεόπλουτοι) were cocks of the walk.[5] Men speculated and rushed after money in order to build and furnish magnificent houses, to display fine weapons, to offer to the women of their family and to courtesans jewels, priceless robes and rare perfumes, to place before eminent guests and fashionable parasites fine wines and dishes prepared by a famous chef, or to commission some popular sculptor to carve their bust.[6]

What happened to public affairs when " love of money

[1] *v.* **LXIII**, vol. I, p. 236 *ff.*   [2] *v.* **XXXV**, p. 298 *f.*
[3] Menander, fr. 337, Kock (vol. III, p. 160); cf. Ps. Xen., *Ath. Rep.*, III, 3.
[4] Arist., *Pol.*, III, 5, 9; *Rhet.*, II, 16.   [5] Id., *Rhet.*, loc. cit.
[6] Xen., *Revenues*, IV, 8; Plat., *Rep.*, II, p. 373a.

left no one the smallest space in which to deal with other things, to such an extent that the mind of each citizen, passionately absorbed in this one purpose, could attend to no other business than the gain of each day "?[1] Politics also was a business concern; the most honest worked for a class, the others sought for themselves alone the profits of power and barely concealed their venality.[2] We are dealing with a time when " riches and rich men being held in honour virtue and honest men are at a discount," when " no one can become rich quickly if he remains honest."[3] Were these merely the capricious outbursts of a philosopher in love with the ideal or of a character in a comedy ? Listen to the terrible words uttered before a tribunal: " Those who, citizens by right of birth, hold the opinion that their country extends wherever their interests are, those obviously are people who will desert the public good in order to run after their personal gain, since for them it is not the city which is their country, but their fortune."[4]

What was there beneath this class which flung itself so eagerly into its business and its pleasures ? In the declining city the distress of the exchequer and the development of capitalism resulted in the extension of pauperism over a great part of the population. The peasants laboured with the sweat of their brow without winning a yield sufficient to keep them alive.[5] In the towns free labour was crushed by the competition of slavery. Innumerable were those who relied upon the fee for attendance at the tribunals, who on festival days jostled before the temples in order to receive a handful of barley meal.[6] Thousands of Athenians could recognize themselves in the unfortunate wretch described by Plato, " who dwells within the city without falling into any of the categories of the city, whom one can call neither trader nor artisan, neither knight nor hoplite, but only poor or indigent."[7] Their next meal depended upon the drawing of lots for juries at the gate of the tribunals, and a man who

---

[1] Plat., *Laws*, VIII, p. 831c.
[2] Arist., *Pol.*, III, 4, 6; VIII (V), 6, 5; Dem., *Phil.*, III, 39.
[3] Plat., *Rep.*, VIII, p. 551a; Menander, fr. 294, Kock (*loc. cit.*, p. 84); Aristoph., *Plout.*, 29 *ff.*, 36 *ff.*
[4] Lys., *C. Philon*, 6.   [5] Aristoph., *loc. cit.*, 28 *ff.*, 224.
[6] Id., *ibid.*, 627; cf. Isocr., *Areop.*, 52.
[7] Plat., *loc. cit.*, p. 552a.

danced in the theatre in robes of cloth of gold shivered in winter beneath his rags.[1] Unceasingly from this proletariat came groans ready to change into cries of revolt. The percentage of those who possessed nothing increased with an alarming regularity. About 431, they numbered from 19,000 to 20,000 out of a total of more than 42,000 citizens (about 45 per cent.); about 355, they were already a majority;[2] forty years or so later, they numbered 12,000 out of 21,000 citizens (57 per cent.).

Although colonization was no longer a way of escape for down-and-outs, they still emigrated. " They wandered in strange lands with their wives and children, and many of them, forced by their daily needs to hire themselves out as mercenaries, died in fighting for their enemies against their fellow-citizens."[3] It was useless to send these voracious bands off to foreign countries; new ones always formed in their stead. In the East, after the Peloponnesian war, Cyrus the Younger took into his service more than a thousand mercenaries drawn for the most part from Achæa, Arcadia, Crete and Rhodes; the Spartan Thibron threw himself upon Asia Minor with the remnant of the Ten Thousand; finally, the Great King and the rebel satraps, the king of Egypt and the princes of Cyprus made unceasing appeals to the Greek condottieri. In the West Dionysius the Tyrant raised a great army by appealing particularly to the Peloponnesians. That was only a half-evil: Greece was ridding itself of a plethora of starvelings. But she kept more than enough of these formidable adventurers for herself. Jason of Pheræ followed the example of Dionysius; the Phocian chiefs for ten years procured with the gold of Delphi as many veteran soldiers as they wanted; and all the cities filled the gaps in their armies by means of foreign contingents. Here, there and everywhere roamed savage bands whose increasing force was becoming a danger to the whole of Greece.[4]

As for the multitude which remained in its native city it only too often justified the dictum: " Poverty's sister is Mendicity."[5] Poverty exhibited at every street corner was the disgrace of the towns.[6] It gave the lie direct to the

[1] Isocr., *Areop.*, 54.
[3] Id., *Paneg.*, 168; cf. *Phil.*, 96; *Peace*, 24.
[5] Aristoph., *Plout.*, 549.

[2] Id., *ibid.*, 83.
[4] Id., *Phil.*, 121.
[6] Isocr., *Areop.*, 83.

noble principles upon which democracy prided itself. The
title of citizen is sorry consolation indeed for the man who
has nothing to eat. He was assured that the government
was based upon liberty and equality, that there existed no
distinctions save those established by talent, that poverty
was no disgrace for the man who attempted to escape from
it.[1] But what is that liberty which allows only those who
have the means of leisure to take part in politics ? What
is that equality which places workers in dependence on those
who control the purse-strings ? Liberty ? It has not the
same value for the weak as for the strong: through it the
latter become rich to excess, and the former completely desti-
tute;[2] and in consequence while annihilating itself it destroys
equality. To these purely theoretical rights was opposed,
therefore, a disillusioning reality. In this *demos* which was
called sovereign there was a majority in subjection to masters,
bound to a sort of servitude, more wretched than the serfs
under an oligarchy.[3] For a large proportion of the king-
people to go to the Assembly, to sit in the Council or the
tribunal was less the fulfilment of a duty or the exercise of
a right than the means of earning a livelihood.[4] What a
contrast between political theory and the social system !

The contrast was exacerbated by the glaring opposition
between luxury and indigence. On the one hand the rich,
grasping and voluptuous, but refined by education, displayed
an insulting arrogance and sought to justify their attitude
by the ignorance and the grossness of the vile mob.[5] On the
other hand, the proletariat, in whose eyes all wealth was
unjustly acquired, envious and embittered, refused to exert
themselves, on the ground that it was useless to suffer and to
labour in order that another might reap the benefit and act
the great lord. In small towns where contacts were perpetual and comparisons inevitable, " the poor man when he
sees the leisured man able to spend all his life in doing nothing,
realizes in a flash how hard and wretched existence is for

    1 Thuc., II, 37 *ff.*
    2 Plat., *Rep.*, VIII, p. 552*a ff.*, 556*a*.
    3 Arist., *Pol.*, I, 5, 10; III, 2, 8; Dem., *C. Euboul.*, 45; Isocr., *Peace*,
125.
    4 Isocr., *loc. cit.*, 130; cf. *Areop.*, 24.
    5 Arist., *Rhet.*, II, 16; Aristoph., *loc. cit.*, 614 *ff.*; Ps. Xen., *Ath. Rep.*,
I, 55.

himself."[1] Democratic sentiment had to endure so violent
and so constant a trial in this that the harmony necessary
for the working of the constitution was necessarily strained.
Aristotle gives a good description of this state of affairs:

> " By reason of the luxury in which they are brought up they never
> learn, even at school, the habit of obedience. On the other hand, the
> very poor, who are in the opposite extreme, are too degraded. So that
> the one class cannot obey, and can only rule despotically; the others
> know not how to command and must be ruled like slaves. Thus arises a
> city, not of free men, but of masters and slaves, the one despising, the
> other envying; and nothing can be more fatal to friendship and good
> fellowship in states than this. . . ."[2]

The philosopher was right. With those who are humili-
ated by life, consciousness of personal dignity produces an
exaggerated moral sensibility, a morbid susceptibility. Love
of liberty and equality may therefore become a sort of collective hysteria. It ends by no longer tolerating even
subjection to the social contract. " The main result of all
these things," Plato tells us, " is that it makes the souls of
the citizens so sensitive that they take offence, and will not
put up with the faintest suspicion of slavery that anyone
may introduce. For finally you know they set entirely at
naught both unwritten and written laws, so afraid are they
of any kind of master."[3] To have no master—this conception
of personality is so tender, this pride rejects so completely
the slightest suggestion of subordination, that a friend of
Socrates, Eutherus, who was reduced to poverty in his old age,
yet refused the position of steward, which would have made
him a free man, and preferred to live from hand to mouth on
the proceeds of manual labour.[4] As for egalitarian susceptibilities everything excited and wounded them. Deinarchus
reproached Demosthenes for having been carried to the
Piræus in a litter and insulting in this way ordinary pedes-
trians; and a law of Lycurgus forbade women to go to the
feast of Eleusis in carriages, in order that the poor women
should not be offended by the great ladies.[5]

There was thus a class psychology because there were
class interests; and this psychology and these interests
opposed with increasing intensity the wider spirit which

[1] Menander, fr. 405, Kock (vol. III, p. 118).
[2] Arist., *Pol.*, VI (IV), 9, 5-6; cf. III, 2, 9.
[3] Plat., *Rep.*, VIII, p. 563d.   [4] Xen., *Mem.*, II, 8, 4.
[5] Dein., *C. Dem.*, 36; Ps. Plut., *Lives of Ten Orat.*, *Lyc.*, 14, p. 842a.

the solidarity of the city had long inspired. Aristotle, who defined man as " a political being," himself observed that man is also " an economic being."[1] As soon as the two classes into which the city was divided clearly recognized that truth a gulf was created between them: latent antagonism or open conflict. Neither of them after that admitted any restriction upon the principle which it judged most advantageous for its cause: the one wished to extend to the economic sphere the constitutional rules which conferred supremacy on the majority in the political sphere; the other persuaded itself that wealth ought to confer power upon it.[2] Let us hear what Aristotle has to say about this:

" Justice is thought by them to be, and is, equality, not, however, for all, but only for equals. And inequality is thought to be, and is, justice; neither is this for all but only for unequals. . . . The reason is that they are passing judgment on themselves, and most people are bad judges in their own case. . . . Because both the parties to the argument are speaking of a limited and partial justice, but imagine themselves to be speaking of absolute justice . . . and any who are equal in one respect, for example freedom, consider themselves to be equal in all."[3]

These two conceptions developed side by side in contrary directions, for ever incapable of meeting. An insoluble conflict was the result. The city was henceforth composed of two opposing and antagonistic sections, of two enemy cities.[4]

This was no new situation in Greece, but never had it been so dangerous. Formerly, in the days when a bad system of landed property had brought creditors and debtors into violent conflict, on the one hand were men " gorging themselves with wealth to the point of satiety," and on the other men " rushing to the plunder, full of rich hopes." Only then a Solon had been able to throw himself between the extreme factions, " to arise and cover both parties with his solid buckler," " to stand, a staunch pillar, between the two armies."[5] He could do this because he rested upon the support of a middle class.[6] In the fifth century, too, the State was in a position to support, assist and preserve this

---

[1] Arist., *Nic. Eth.*, VII, 10.   [2] Id., *Rhet.*, II, 16 *ff.*
[3] Id., *Pol.*, III, 5, 8-9.
[4] Id., *ibid.*, VI (IV), 3, 15; VIII (V), 7, 19; 9, 19; Plat., *Rep.*, IV, p. 422*e*; VIII, p. 551*e*.
[5] Solon in Arist., *Ath. Const.*, 5, 3; 12, 3, 5.
v. **XXXVI**, vol. I, p. 429.

class of self-sufficing landowners. Living was not dear, and Athens found sufficient wealth in her empire to relieve the necessities of the poor, and even to enable the *thetes* to ascend in the social scale to the rank of *zeugitai*. At that time she sent thousands of citizens as cleruchs into the lands of the federal domain; she made liberal distributions of meat and corn; she provided for the payment of rowers and officials; and she paid good wages to the artisans and workmen continually engaged upon works of public utility or adornment.

But in the fourth century the middle class was steadily declining. There was no longer anything which approximated to a third party. There still appeared, however, a few isolated men to adopt on occasion the attitude of conciliators. Here for example is the cry of an orator, with the eloquence of reason impassioned by the imminence of the danger which threatened all:

" We ought to find out some other means of supplying their necessities. If the rich proceed on these principles, they will act agreeably, not to justice only, but to good policy; for to rob some men of their necessary subsistence is to raise a number of enemies to the commonwealth. To men of lower fortunes I give this advice: that they should remove those grievances of which the wealthier members complain so loudly and so justly (for I now proceed in the manner I proposed, and shall not scruple to offer such truths as may be favourable to the rich). Look out, not through Athens alone, but through every other State, and, in my opinion, you will not find a man of so cruel, so inhuman a disposition, as to complain when he sees poor men, men who even want the necessaries of life, receiving these appointments. Where then lies the difficulty? Whence this animosity? When they behold certain persons charging private fortunes with those demands which were usually answered by the public . . . then it is that their indignation is raised; for justice requires, Athenians, that the advantages of society should be shared by all its members. The rich should have their lives and fortunes well secured; that so, when any danger threatens their country, their opulence may be applied to its defence. Other citizens should regard the public treasure as it really is, the property of all, and be content with their just portion; but should esteem all private fortunes as the inviolable rights of their possessors. . . ."[1]

The same counsels of moderation are naturally found scattered in the *Politics* of Aristotle, always the supporter of the happy mean. According to him, the city, whatever it may be, procures for man the benefit of satisfying the social instinct which is natural to him; the perfect city would be that which assured to all the greatest sum of happiness; a city which understands its duty, which acquits itself of its

[1] Dem., *Phil.*, IV, 41-45 (trans. Leland).

choregia, is one which at the least ensures their subsistence, and if it has the means, their well-being. Though he does not agree with community of property on an obligatory basis Aristotle recommends community of usufruct as a voluntary measure. Though he declaims against the demagogues who distribute to the people the surplus from receipts, a measure which does no one any good, he nevertheless desires that the sincere union of the people shall prevent the excess of property which perverts democracy, that it shall devote all its efforts to the spreading of comfort, and that all surpluses shall be placed in a reserve fund from which money may be borrowed for the purchase of land, for the establishing of a business or for agricultural improvements.[1] But, since he was an observer as well as a theorist, Aristotle was compelled to recognize that he was a voice crying in the wilderness, that oligarchs and democrats committed everywhere the same mistake in looking always solely to their own interests, and that the element in society which had been capable of reconciling extreme passions was now in a state of decay. He saw clearly that a return to that mixed constitution which he called " constitution " *par excellence* (πολιτεία) was impossible, because it required a middle class sufficiently numerous and sufficiently strong to balance the proletariat, and possessing a sufficiently large proportion of the public wealth to counterbalance the share held by the rich—two conditions necessary in order that the " constitution " should not be converted into a democracy or an oligarchy.[2]

II

CONFLICT OF CLASSES

The organization of property, the distribution of wealth, this, therefore, was the major problem of internal policy, the source of intestine struggles and revolutions. In many cities the poor demanded the redistribution of land and the cancellation of debts[3]— when a people has reached that point the recognition of duties towards the State is very near disappear-

---

[1] Arist., *Pol.*, III, 4, 3; IV (VII), 12, 2; 4, 2, 9, 6; II, 4, 1 and 6.
[2] Id., *ibid.*, VIII (V), 7, 8, 11-12, 19; VI (IV), 10, 1-4.
[3] *v.* XXXIX, p. 195 *ff.*; LXIII, vol. II, p. 333 *ff.*

ing. Each party exploited power for its own ends and crushed all opposing factors. Democracy thought only of favouring the poor, oligarchy recognized only the rich, and the two factions, closing their eyes to the needs and interests of the city, worked towards its ruin.[1] Finally, social conflicts became so bitter that they no longer had for object merely the acquisition of material advantages, but the satisfaction of vile hatreds. The oligarchs in certain towns took this terrible oath: " I will be an adversary of the people and in the Council I will do to it all the evil which I can."[2] The democrats were in a state of open or secret hostility to all those whose fortune rendered them suspect; when they despoiled them it was as much for the pleasure of impoverishing them as for the purpose of enriching themselves.[3] Isocrates epitomizes these reciprocal attitudes in a sentence which throws much light on the Greece of his day:

" Instead of securing general conditions of well-being by means of mutual understanding, the anti-social spirit has reached such a pitch that the wealthy would rather throw their money into the sea than relieve the lot of the indigent, while the very poorest of the poor would get less satisfaction from appropriating to their own use the property of the rich than from depriving them of it."[4]

Led on by the logic of principles and passions, some of the democrats came to desire complete equality, a ruthless levelling. For a long time no privilege had been accorded to birth. The sophist Lycophron said that nobility of blood was a mere word: the people whom a foolish convention calls well born are born as other people are.[5] Men took this to mean that all distinctions of person among citizens should be abandoned. On this point the feeling of the people was at one with the reasoning of thinkers. But on others there was divergence, because the principle of equality was pushed to its extreme in two different directions. For the sophists, since men are of identical birth, the barbarian is of the same stuff as the Greek, " nature does not make slaves," and the power of the master is founded solely on the right of might consecrated

[1] Arist., *Pol.*, III, 5, 4 and 7; VI (IV), 3, 8; 9, 9-10; 10, 5; VIII (V), 6, 4-5.
[2] Id., *ibid.*, VIII (V), 7, 19; cf. Plat., *Rep.*, VIII, p. 566c.
[3] Ps. Xen., *op. cit.*, I, 13.   [4] Isocr., *Archid.*, 67.
[5] Lycophr., ap. Ps. Plut., *For Nobl.*, 18, 2, p. 969; cf. Antiph., *De Ver.*, 5.

by law:[1] cosmopolitanism and the abolition of slavery, such were in the eyes of certain intellectuals the consequences of equality. The multitude, however, attacked another kind of superiority, which was precisely that represented by the sophists, a superiority born of education. Good style, culture? —what is all that to people who " think themselves equal in all things "? Simply another means of rising above the commonalty! It is a by-word that education has envy for its companion.[2] As early as the fifth century Cleon saw nothing superior to unassuming ignorance and proudly asserted that " States are better governed by mediocrities than by the finest brains."[3] Aristophanes seized upon this maxim joyfully. And he did not forget it; the Sausage-seller who, in his comedy, wishes to take the place of the Paphlagonian in power, knows his letters, but " very slightly and very badly "; yet the servitor of Demos finds that even this is too much.[4] Thus, without taking into account the native or acquired differences which exist between men from an intellectual point of view, men came to desire the establishment of " an equality which shall give the same share to those who are equal and to those who are not."[5] In brief the notion of quality was lost, and all grading of social values tended to disappear. In wishing to convert equality of right into equality in fact the inequalities of nature were regarded as null and void.

Minds so Utopian as to contemplate the levelling of intelligence would be still more apt to contemplate the levelling of fortunes. The fourth century saw the birth of innumerable theories of communism and socialism in Greece.[6] But, in a country which knew nothing of big industry and where the mass of the population lived on agriculture, these theories, of necessity, assumed a special form.

The philosophers who elaborated them were, in general, full of contempt for merchants and artisans as well as for workmen: they saw in equality of wealth the best means of returning to the patriarchal regime of old times or at least of procuring for cities perverted by democratic pre-

---

[1] Antiph., *loc. cit.*; Alcidamas ap. Arist., *Rhet.*, vol. I, 13; Arist., *Pol.*, I, 2, 3.
[2] Arist., *Rhet.*, II, 23.
[3] Thuc., III, 37.
[4] Aristoph., *Knights*, 189 *ff.*
[5] Plat., *Rep.*, VIII, p. 558c.
[6] Arist., *Pol.*, IV (VII), 9, 6.

judices the advantages of Laconian institutions.[1] Plato
thought by this system to suppress egoism, to prevent divisions, to realize justice by sacrificing the individual to the
State. In the *Republic* he is still full of illusions in spite
of his first voyage to Sicily. He hoped to establish an immutable order by means of communism; but this communism,
which was to extend to women and children as well as to
material things,[2] was only to apply to the two superior classes
of philosophers and soldiers, and not to the inferior class of
producers, whose duty it was merely to provide for the needs
of the two others: his postulates were privilege and servitude.
In the *Laws*, disillusioned by two further attempts in Sicily
and now very old, the idealist, in order to render his ideal
more practicable, strikes a bargain with prejudices and
modifies his scheme with elements borrowed from Sparta.
Property shall be private, granted; but it shall at least belong
to the family and not to the individual; in order that it shall
remain inalienable and indivisible it shall belong to a fixed
number of citizens, the 5,040; and strict precautions shall be
taken to prevent the people, by an abuse of its legislative
and judicial power, from assailing these fundamental principles.[3] The communist ideals of the philosophers seem to
have had a moral rather than an economic character: they
disdained mere observation of facts and proceeded by an
a priori method; they seemed made to gratify aristocratic
coteries.

But when they descended into the market-place the same
ideas, the same words took on a very different colour. Let
us take our stand in the years of distress when the State
had been compelled to abolish the salaries of officials and the
fees of the heliasts, to put a stop to the public works which
provided work for craftsmen, to abandon at the command
of the victor the naval constructions which gave wages to
so many workmen and rowers. Heads were raised in protest,
suffering caused discontent to grow rife, imaginations grew
hot with desires and cherished insensate hopes. A fine
subject for comedy, when conditions had improved. In 392

---

[1] *v.* **LXIII**, vol. II, p. 1-339; **XII**, p. 215 *ff.*; **XXXV**, p. 186-192.
[2] Plat., *Rep.*, III, p. 416d *ff.*; V, p. 457 *ff.*; cf. Arist., *Pol.*, II, 1, 2 *ff.*;
2, 11 *ff.*
[3] Plat., *Laws*, V, p. 739c, 740a-b, 737e, 772c, 767c.

Aristophanes seized upon it. In the *Assembly of Women*
Praxagora expounds the system:

> " All goods must be held by all in common, so that all live from an
> equal portion. It must not be allowed that one should be rich and
> another wretched, that one should have a great farm and another not
> enough ground to bury him, nor that one should have a whole army of
> slaves and another not a single servant. No, I shall make one common
> life for all, the same for all. . . . The women shall belong to all the
> men and they shall have children by anyone they wish. . . . The
> children shall regard as their fathers all men older than themselves."[1]

The placid husband of this impassioned virago found of
course many objections to bring forward, but Doña Quixote
easily overrules Sancho Panza. One of her replies, however,
is worth noting. If everyone spends his time going from
banquet to banquet and no one is compelled to work, who
then will cultivate the land ? Slaves. Thus communist
democracy itself was nothing more than an aristocracy
which was to be maintained by means of a class bound to
the soil. The principle was always the same: no city is
possible without slavery. But Aristophanes goes still further.
In 388, when the maritime strength of Athens was being
reconstituted and when tolls levied on ships coming from the
Euxine supplemented the treasury, he came to grips with
the problem. In the *Plutus* he attacks the foolhardy men
who wished to give sight to the blind god of Riches and to
drive out Poverty. If Plutus should recover his sight and
share himself among all equally, there would remain no one
to ply a trade or learn an art; for it is to Poverty, the sole
author of all wealth, that everyone owes his subsistence.[2]
It is by the sacred law of labour, whose celestial origin and
splendid dignity Hesiod affirmed,[3] that individuals ought to
be stimulated and society regenerated.

When a comic poet ceases to utter large obscenities and
adopts the tone of the preacher without fear of being howled
down, his counsels must be in accord with the profoundest
convictions of his hearers. There was, indeed, a great gulf
between the numerous cities which allowed themselves to
be dragged into all the horrors of social wars and Athens,
preserved from the worst excesses by her comparative wealth
and her traditions. Let us see the difference.

---

[1] Aristoph., *Ass. of Women*, 590 *ff.*, 614 *f.*, 636 *f.*
[2] Id., *Plut.*, 510-512, 468-470.   [3] *Op. et Dies*, 303 *ff.*

When Polybius, following the example of Aristotle, drew a picture of revolutions he described the Greece of the fourth century as well as that of his own day.

" When they have made the populace ready and greedy to receive bribes, the virtue of democracy is destroyed, and it is transformed into a government of violence and the strong hand. For the mob, habituated to feed at the expense of others, and to have its hopes of a livelihood in the property of its neighbours, as soon as it has got a leader sufficiently ambitious and daring, being excluded by poverty from the sweets of civil honours, produces a reign of mere violence. Then come tumultuous assemblies, massacres, banishments, redivisions of land." [1]

Examples of such revolutions are innumerable.[2] Let us take three of them in the East, the centre and the West of the Greek world. At Mitylene the debtors massacred their creditors wholesale and then pleaded in excuse passion and the absolute necessity created by their financial position.[3] The democrats of Argos, in 370, using the pretext of conspiracy, threw themselves upon the rich and important citizens; carried away by reckless madness, they butchered more than twelve hundred of them and confiscated their property. Then calm ensued once more, whilst the whole of Greece, though accustomed to incidents of this kind, resounded with a great cry of indignation.[4] In Sicily landed property was the bone of contention in the civil wars. Previously Dionysius the Elder had deprived the knights of their estates and divided them in equal lots among his veterans and the serfs: it was by this measure that he had consolidated his power.[5] After the expulsion of Dionysius the Younger (356) the liberator Dion had to struggle against the extreme party which, incited by a man named Hippon, was clamouring for a new distribution of lands. " For the disinherited," the demagogue violently asserts, " equality is the beginning of liberty, as poverty is of servitude."[6] A decree of spoliation was voted and Dion left Syracuse; only Hippon's fall, after the recall of Dion, prevented the application of this decree. After lying dormant for the space of a generation, the social problem woke to terrible life. In

[1] Pol., VI, 9, 7-9; cf. VII, 10, 1; XV, 21.
[2] Cf. Arist., Pol., VIII (V), 4, 2-3.
[3] Ælian., Var. Hist., XIV, 24.
[4] Diod., XV, 57 f.; Isocr., Phil., 52; Plut., Prac. ger. reip., 17, 9; Dion. Hal., VII, 66.
[5] Diod., XIV, 7, 4.   [6] Plut., Dion., 37 ff.

317 Agathocles hurled his soldiers and the mass of the people against the Six Hundred and their partisans. A man-hunt began. At the end of two days four thousand citizens had perished and six thousand had taken the road of exile. Agathocles was then able to seize absolute power and to put a stop to the shedding of blood; he knew how to win over the people: he went to the Assembly to promise the cancellation of all debts and the distribution of land to the poor.[1]

At no time did the history of Athens present such sights. In a city which held economic domination in the Mediterranean world, democracy, the mistress of power, had no reason for allowing itself to be embroiled in social revolution. It was content to effect from day to day in the Assembly and the tribunal a fragmentary and piece-meal revolution. Let other cities decree the division of landed property, of capitals and revenues, or let them content themselves with seizing inheritances for the exchequer;[2] in Athens there were no measures of that kind. Every year the archon, on his entry into office, proclaimed that, whilst he was in power, every man should enjoy full and complete possession of his property.[3] But acquired wealth was subject to a variety of taxes, and in particular sumptuary expenditure. In a very great number of suits the heliasts delivered what were essentially class sentences. Even in the fifth century they were unfavourably disposed towards the rich. They felt the joy of kings or gods when they were making " great personages of four cubits in stature " tremble before them, or listening with a malicious glee to their supplications and their flatteries.[4] Everything goes to prove, however, that for a long time they had too high a conception of their mission to allow themselves to rejoice in miscarriages of justice, since even in the time when Aristophanes represented Philocleon assuming the airs of Zeus, an oligarch complained that the number of unjust sentences was not sufficiently great to swell the body of malcontents.[5] But at the close of the fourth century, especially in the unhappy years which followed the Peloponnesian war and the " social " war, men who had grown degenerate

---

[1] Diod., XIX, 6-9; Justin., XXII, 2, 9-12.
[2] Arist., Pol., VIII (V), 7, 11; Ps. Arist., Alex. Rhet., 3.
[3] Arist., Ath. Const., 56, 2.
[4] Aristoph., Wasps; 548 ff., 550 ff., 575 f., 620 ff.
[5] Ps. Xen., op. cit., III, 12 f.; cf. Isocr., Areop., 31-35.

as a result of the universal distress found it difficult to keep themselves within the limits of impartiality.

" It is a known fact," says the orator Lysias with a naïveté which borders upon impudence, " that the annual Council does not commit injustices when it has resources sufficient for administration, but that in years of distress it is simply compelled to welcome denunciations, to confiscate the property of citizens and to obey the suggestions of the most dishonest of the rhetoricians."[1]

Sycophants found the system to their liking; they had a fine opportunity for exciting jealousy against the great and for demanding judgments in favour of the small.[2] And one hears certain plaintiffs excusing their wealth or recalling how much of it they have devoted to the service and amusement of the people; others in a cynical fashion plead their poverty as a claim upon the benevolence of the judges.[3] If an occasion offered itself for the infliction of a heavy fine or a total confiscation, the plaintiff did not hesitate to point out that the treasury was empty and that it must be restored to a condition in which it would be able to pay salaries.[4] It was of course partisan exaggeration to assert that it was more dangerous at Athens to appear rich than to be criminal; it was merely a witty flash to deplore the misfortune of the rich man who is a slave, and to vaunt the happiness of the poor man who is a king.[5] Nevertheless, at certain moments the mass of fiscal edicts, the too frequent incidence of " liturgies," the heaviness of the taxes which weighed upon the members of *symmoriai*, the perpetual fear of seeing oneself compelled by another tax payer to an interchange of fortune, gave some appearance of reasoned foundation to these apparent paradoxes.[6]

Athens, therefore, had a place apart in the class struggles. She was none the less carried away by the general agitation. The gravest danger to the regime of the city in the fourth century lay in the fact that party spirit reared itself above patriotism. We have already noted many instances of exiles

[1] Lys., *C. Nicom.*, 22; cf. *C. Epicr.*, 1; *On the Prop. of Aristoph.*, 11, 39, 45, 49 *ff.*
[2] Arist., *Pol.*, VII (VI), 3, 2-3; Isocr., *C. Lochit.*, 19 *ff.*
[3] Lys., *On the Prop. of Aristoph.*, 10, 61; Isocr., *Antid.*, 142.
[4] Arist., *loc. cit.*; Lys., *C. Epicr.*, I; cf. Aristoph., *Knights*, 1358 *ff.*; Ps. Xen., *op. cit.*, I, 13.
[5] Isocr., *Antid.*, 160; Xen., *Symposium*, IV, 31.
[6] Isocr., *Peace*, 128.

seeking foreign help in order to return to their native country and regain power there. Athens had undergone that bitter experience twice in the course of the fifth century, when ambition and the desire for vengeance turned the Pisistratid into the ally of the Great King and led Alcibiades into placing himself successively at the service of the Spartans and the Persians. The novel fact was that individuals who had no injury to avenge armed themselves against their native city simply from sympathy with the institutions of another city, that factions would rather see the loss of national independence than the triumph of the opposing faction.

Xenophon is the perfect type of the Greek who was completely detached from his native country,—a Laconian by political and social prejudice. He began by making himself known as the leader of the countryless men lost by the death of a pretender in the heart of Asia. When he returned to Europe he felt not the slightest scruple, Athenian though he was, in fighting against the Athenians at the side of his friend Agesilaus. Then, worn out, he retired to a beautiful estate at Scillus in Elis to live on the fruits of his plunder, peacefully, gloriously, as the hunting squire steeped in piety. Finally, when he had been driven out by war, he rejected the offers of his countrymen who, forgiving everything, recalled him, and established himself at Corinth where he died.

The cold indifference of a Xenophon is even more significant than the resentment of an Alcibiades. What is even more so is the solidarity of whole parties from town to town. It did not merely create moral bonds; it tended towards the effective suppression of frontiers. Since the fifth century democrats everywhere had fallen into the habit of appealing to Athens for help, and Athens had been dragged, in spite of herself at first, into restricting by her intervention the autonomy of the federal cities. Then Lysander set himself the task of grouping the oligarchies of the whole of Greece under the hegemony of Sparta. His attempts were premature and too ambitious for his day. But soon a particular incident shows clearly how political passion might work against the city. In 393 Corinth was torn asunder by civil strife: the democrats wished for war against Sparta in line with Thebes, Athens and Argos; the oligarchs were supporters of peace and the Spartan alliance. The oligarchs prepared a surprise attack; but the democrats forestalled them, surprised them during a banquet and massacred a great number. After that, despairing of saving the independence of the town without help from without, they decided to unite with Argos in a single State. Frontier lines between the two countries were destroyed; the name of Argos alone appeared on official documents. Corinth of its own consent disappeared from the list of Greek cities. It is true that the fury of the surviving oligarchs soon destroyed the revolutionary work; but by what means ? They opened a gate in the long walls to the Lacedæmonian army.[1] Corinth, placed between Argos and Sparta, could only maintain its autonomy by some sort of balance between parties, a matter which they no longer troubled about.

[1] Xen., *Hell.*, IV, 4, 5 *ff*.

CHAPTER III

CORRUPTION OF DEMOCRATIC INSTITUTIONS

Since human institutions are always only what men make of them a change in social ideas leads necessarily to profound changes in political organization. Greece of the fourth century went through that experience. Whilst other cities were being thrown into confusion by revolutions bearing in their train massacres, banishments and collective confiscations, Athens, in the midst of struggles which at least involved only individual condemnations, was working out new implications of the democratic principle.

I

THE ASSEMBLY OF THE PEOPLE IN THE FOURTH CENTURY

The Assembly of the people could not remain what it had been before the Peloponnesian war and the oligarchic *coups d'état*. In so far as history admits of such lines of demarcation the archonship of Euclides (403-2) marks, from all points of view, a beginning and an end. From this moment the Ecclesia was to exercise a power more and more " tyrannical," but by making private interests prevail more and more over general welfare: in such a way that the city was never to have appeared so powerful as in the time when individuals, by exploiting it, were preparing its destruction.

Popular sovereignty presented a curious spectacle in the fourth century. It was constantly vacillating between the absolutist tendency which was natural to it and an hereditary craving to oppose the laws to the caprices of decrees.

The public action against illegality, the *graphe paranomon*, had been in former days the principal defence of the democratic constitution. A double experience had shown that the partisans of oligarchy could only seize power by overthrowing this obstacle. Their decisive defeat placed the institution above attack. But at the time when it became unassailable, under the archonship of Euclides himself,[1] a general revision of the laws made it less necessary. Thenceforward it suffered abuse in the struggle of parties. In place of assuring by direful threats supreme protection to the constitution, it became merely a common-place weapon in the hands of the antagonists who met on the Pnyx; soon it became blunted and bent. It was still capable of inflicting death,[2] while it could also be used to inflict an ordinary fine of twenty-five drachmas.[3] Here is a very characteristic instance: a party leader, Aristophon of Azenia, had to defend himself against the accusation of illegality seventy-five times. The result was that the *graphe paranomon*, without preventing the Ecclesia from legislating at random, was an obstacle to wise innovations as well as to foolish, a shackle on that liberty of speech of which the citizens were so proud.[4]

Another process, it seems, might have been able to supplement the *graphe paranomon*: viz. the *eisangelia*, but it too underwent the same degradation.[5] In the fifth century it was intended to repress crimes not provided for by the laws and dangerous to the safety of the State, treason and high treason, including attempts to overthrow democratic government by words or deeds. Laws being lacking the tribunals could not take direct cognizance of these: it was for the Assembly of the people and the Council to take necessary measures for public safety. It involved such severe penalties that the accused did not wait for judgment before exiling themselves.[6] The people clung to this institution, which it attributed to Solon,[7] and which gave a terrible efficacy to its power of supreme justice. It was abolished at the same time as the action against illegality by the Four Hundred,[8] and probably by the Thirty. Not only was it restored under the archonship of Euclides,[9] but a law was then promulgated (the νόμος εἰσαγγελτικός) which, without formally defining it, enumerated the cases in which it was applicable according to

---

[1] Cf. Arist., *Ath. Const.*, 40, 2.
[2] Dem., *C. Timocr.*, 138; Dein., *C. Aristog.*, 2.
[3] Hyper., *P. Euxen.*, 18.
[4] Æschin., *Ambass.*, 6; cf. 194.
[5] Cf. Caillemer, *DA*, art. " Eisaggélia "; **CXI**, p. 312 *ff.*
[6] Hyper., *loc. cit.*, 2.   [7] Arist., *op. cit.*, 8, 4.
[8] Id., *ibid.*, 29, 4.   [9] Id., *ibid.*, 43, 4; 59, 2.

precedents.[1] This apparent limitation was to no purpose.
By a series of assimilations the Athenians came to treat as
attempts against the republic crimes, delinquencies or simple
contraventions which bore no relation to the acts legally
susceptible to process by *eisangelia*. Hyperides protested
against such abuses and quoted examples which he rightly held
up to ridicule: Lycophron was accused by *eisangelia* for
having persuaded a woman to be unfaithful to her husband;
Agasicles for having been enrolled in a deme not his own;
Diognis and Antidorus for having hired out some flute players
at more than the legal rate; Euxenippus for having made a
false statement as to a dream he had in a temple.[2] Here
again a part of the framework of the city was deranged by
political hatreds.

What means, then, were to be adopted to prevent illegal
proposals from flooding the city ? Men remembered the
commissions of *nomothetai* who had restored the laws of
democracy after the disturbances of 410 and 403. They had
been invested with extraordinary powers because of exceptional circumstances; they were now made a regular institution.[3] The existence of this new type of *nomothetai* is proved
for the period from the speech of Demosthenes against
Leptines in 355-4 to an inscription which bears the date 329-8.
In this case we see the people deliberately stripping itself of
legislative power, in order to escape the temptation of abusing
it. The principle is plain: " no existing law may be abolished
save by the authority of the *nomothetai*."

In the first session of the year, therefore, on the 11th of
Hecatombeion, the Assembly had to vote on all the laws
($\epsilon\pi\iota\chi\epsilon\iota\rho\sigma\tau\sigma\nu\iota\alpha$ $\tau\hat{\omega}\nu$ $\nu\acute{\sigma}\mu\omega\nu$) to ascertain if there was need to
abrogate any of them. In this vote the people made its
decision on the reports of the magistrates, pointing out any
defect, lacuna or contradiction which had been revealed in

---

[1] Hyper., *loc. cit.*, 21 *ff.*
[2] Id., *ibid.*, 3; *P. Lycophr.*, X, 5 *ff.*; cf. **XCV**, p. 135 *ff.*
[3] On the *nomothetai* v. Dem., *C. Timocr.*, 18, 20-27, 33, 47 *f.*; *C. Lept.*,
88 *ff.*, 93, 98 *f.*, 146; Æschin., *C. Ctes.*, 38-40; *RIG*, nos. 1459, 1462, 1465,
107, 108; *IG*, vol. II, Suppl., no. 128*b*.   Cf. R. Schoell, " Ueb. att.
Gesetzgebung " (*Sb. MA*, 1886, p. 83 *ff.*). P. Foucart, *JS*, 1902,
p. 177 *ff.*; A. Elter, *Ein att. Gesetz üb. die Eleusinische Aparche*, Bonn,
1914, p. 8 *ff.*; **CVI**, vol. I, p. 383 *ff.*; J. H. Lipsius, " Zur att. Nomothesie "
(*Bph. W*, 1917, p. 909 *ff.*); W. Bannier, " Zu den att. Gesetzünder-
ungen " (*ibid.*, 1918, 1215 *ff.*); **VII**, p. 462 *ff.*, 1011 *ff.*

the course of the past year in the legislation in force. If the majority voted for a revision every citizen was free to propose new provisions in the matter in dispute, on condition that he placed his proposal on the pedestals of the eponymous heroes and recognized his responsibility by attaching his name to it. At the fourth ordinary session of the first prytany a decree fixed the number of *nomothetai* called upon to sit, the duration of their office, the procedure they were to follow, the salaries they were to be paid, and drew up their programme, indicating the provisions to be modified or completed eventually. The Assembly then gave its instructions to the *nomothetai*; further, it named four or five *synegoroi* or *syndikoi* whose business it was to defend before them the laws in question. But, once having appointed its representatives, its rôle was finished, its power exhausted.

Henceforth the legislative people was no longer the Ecclesia but the tribunal of *nomothetai*. They were chosen, to the number of five hundred and one or a thousand and one, from the sworn heliasts, men of age and experience. They were summoned by the *prytaneis* and had their own standing orders. Their committee was constituted, like that of the Assembly, by the *proedroi* whose president, the *epistates*, changed with each session and their procedure was similar to' that of the Heliæa. It was not a question of deliberating among themselves, but of hearing a suit which was tried in their presence and of which they were the judges. The *synegoroi* took the defence for the law impugned, while the author of the new law demonstrated its superiority. After that the *epistates* put first the one law and then the other to the vote of the tribunal. The one which obtained the most votes was *ipso facto* valid. Without further formalities, without any further intervention of the Boule or the Ecclesia, it was transcribed by the public secretary of the archives, to be classed among the documents having the force of law.

In the texts which have come down to us *nomothesia* was applied in two cases: it legalized decrees which, in the past year, had sanctioned expenses not provided for in the budgetary law;[1] and it authorized changes made in the sacred laws, for example in the ordinances relating to the first-

---

[1] *RIG*, nos. 1462, 108; *IG, loc. cit.*

fruits of Eleusis and the feast of Amphiaraus.[1]   But there
seems no reason why it should not have been applied to many
other classes.   It is to be presumed that the procedure had
a general application.

What is the reason for Aristotle's total neglect of it in his
description of the Athenian constitution ?   Was it, as has
been maintained,[2] because the master left everything concerning legislation to his disciple Theophrastus, who did,
indeed, write a treatise on the *Laws* ?   No; for in that case
he would have been guilty of wittingly falsifying the picture
which he was drawing, for the lack of a word, which would
have sufficed to bring it into focus.   Moreover, in the *Politics*,
not only does he include legislative power in sovereignty, but
also he frequently criticizes Athenian democracy for legislating
by decrees.[3]   The reason must, therefore, be that *nomothesia*
in his eyes was of no very great importance and that the
decisions of the *nomothetai*, dignified though they were by
more complicated formalities, were of the same order as the
decrees of the Ecclesia.   The best intentions, the justest ideas
avail nothing against habits of license and arbitrariness.   *Quid
leges sine moribus ?*

This people, so proud of its sovereignty, nevertheless
expected to be paid in hard cash for the trouble it expended
in exercising it.   We see here one of the most striking differences between the Athenians of the old and those of the new
age.   In the fifth century citizens were so interested in public
affairs that they appeared in the Ecclesia in considerable
numbers; at the beginning of the fourth, everyone was so
preoccupied with his own affairs that the Pnyx was deserted.
One must not think that abstention was particularly notable
in the case of the leisured classes, although it has often been
maintained that the rich, disgusted at seeing themselves
defeated in all the discussions, retired from political life.   The
poor to an equal extent neglected the assemblies.[4]   It became
necessary to drag them there if the very character of the
regime were not to be changed and if democracy, the government of all, were not to be turned into oligarchy, the govern-

---

[1] *RIG*, nos. 1465, 107; cf. *IG*, vol. II, no. 162.
[2] Cf. H. Usener, *Preussische Jahrbücher*, vol. LIII (1884), p. 22;
Haussoullier, edit. of Arist., *Ath. Const.*, p. xxvi.
[3] *v.* p. 165.   [4] Isocr., *Areop.*, 38.

ment of the few. In the terrible years which followed the fall
of Athens and the tyranny of the Thirty, when the staunchest
defenders of the constitution, the artisans, could hardly keep
themselves alive and could not afford to lose several days'
work each month, "the *prytaneis* devised all manner of
expedients in order to obtain the number necessary to give
decrees validity."[1] They resolved once for all to supply a
remedy for the disease of abstention. It was not possible, as
in certain oligarchies, to inflict a fine upon the absent;[2] by an
inverse method remuneration was given to those present.
They simply extended to the Ecclesia the system of *misthophoria* which had prevailed for sixty years in the Heliæa.
Agyrrhius first established a payment of one obol; a little
later Heracleides of Clazomenæ increased it to two, and
Agyrrhius, returning to office, to three.[3] Since the cost of
living went up considerably in the course of the fourth century
they did not keep to this scale: in the time of Aristotle the
tally became worth a drachma for ordinary sessions and a
drachma and a half for principal sessions.[4]

The three obols of the *ekklesiastes*, and still more the
drachma, have evoked much criticism. In antiquity the
enemies of democracy alleged that it made the people idle,
gossiping and grasping;[5] and many modern writers have
condemned it in the same way. To these criticisms reply is
easy. We have seen the reasons of a material and moral
order which justified the institution: it was to assure to the
worst placed citizens the leisure necessary for taking part in
political life.[6] It would, nevertheless, have been a deplorable
device, if it had ruined the State. But its financial consequences were not so serious. In a time when the daily earnings of a workman were a drachma and a half, the three obols
were merely an indemnity. They were not, moreover, given
to all citizens: a total sum, fixed in advance in the budget,
was divided between the different sessions of the year, and
the sum allotted to each session determined the number of
counters to be distributed to the first arrivals. In order to
receive payment one had to arrive very early, at the " second

[1] Arist., *op. cit.*, 41, 3.　　[2] Id., *Pol.*, VI (IV), 10, 6.
[3] Id., *Ath. Const., loc. cit.* The complete reform was accomplished
in 392 (Aristoph., *Ass. of Women*, 184 *ff.*, 300 *ff.*, etc.).
[4] Arist., *op. cit.*, 62, 2.
[5] Plat., *Gorg.*, p. 515e.　　[6] Arist., *loc. cit.*, 5, 5.

M

crow of the cock,"[1] and to wait until the end of the session to exchange the counter for money.   In brief, great results were achieved at little cost.

But though the *misthos ekklesiastikos* does not deserve the censures which have been heaped upon it, it is nevertheless a remarkable indication of the change in social life and public spirit which had come about in the fourth century.   The time was no longer when the citizen consecrated himself to the city, without other reward than the satisfaction of duty accomplished and the feeling of contributing to the common good.   Now the city had to remember that it existed only on condition that it looked first to the interests of the individuals who did its business: to secure the necessary co-operation of citizens it had to pay.

The direction of the Assembly in the fourth century also suffered changes which we must now consider.

Since the time of Cleisthenes the committee of the Boule and the Ecclesia had been composed of the *prytaneis*, whilst the presidency belonged to an *epistates*, elected by lot for each session.   After a date which cannot be precisely fixed by any test the committee was composed quite differently: before each session the *epistates* of the *prytaneis* drew by lot nine *proedroi*, one from every tribe except the one which was exercising the prytany, and from these *proedroi* another *epistates*: to them he remitted the order of the day and the task of conducting the debates.[2]   What was the reason for substituting the *proedroi* for the *prytaneis* ?   It has often been attributed to the habitual suspicion of democracies, which are always eager to divide and weaken powers in order to rule more securely.   Support for this point of view can be adduced from the fact that no councillor was allowed to be a *proedros* more than once in each prytany, nor *epistates* of the *proedroi* more than once each year.[3]   This explanation, however, does not hold.   The *proedroi* had in reality semi-oligarchic antecedents, since they had existed for some months in 411-0 under the regime of the Five Thousand.[4]   If on the other hand one examines closely the formulæ of the decrees issued in the first quarter of the fourth century one is led to the conclusion that

---

[1] Cf. Aristoph., *loc. cit.*, 282 *ff.*, 289 *ff.*, 380 *ff.*, 390 *ff.*, 548.
[2] Arist., *Ath. Const.*, 44, 2-3.   [3] Id., *ibid.*, 3.
[4] Id., *ibid.*, 30, 4; Thuc., VIII, 67, 3; *IG*, vol. II, Add., p. 396, no. 1c.

the committees of *proedroi* were created during the winter of 378-7.[1] It was the moment when Athens was remodelling her institutions in order to adapt them to those of the new confederation which was being evolved. The Boule became the liaison agent between the Ecclesia of Athens and the Synedrion of the other cities; the permanent section of the Boule and its president had other things to do than to show themselves off in the "cabinet" and the presidency of the assemblies. It was far better to designate for these ceremonial functions persons who had more leisure, a representative from each of the non-prytanic tribes. This system offered in addition the advantage of placing at the head of the deliberating bodies a more complete representation of the republic. There is, therefore, no necessity for adducing the prejudices of domestic policy to explain a reform determined by foreign policy.

But if one turns away from forms and principles and looks at actual fact the true leaders of the assembled people frequently present a displeasing spectacle. They were not great landowners who had been elected *strategoi*, as was Pericles, for progress in the division of political labour had for the most part relegated the *strategoi* to purely military functions; nor were they merchants and traders: the tanner Anytus, whose career extended from 410 to 399, was the last demagogue of this type. Politics had become a special profession admitting of a variety of employments. It had its *élite*, the rhetoricians or orators,[2] often of rich and respected families,[3] almost all intelligent and some remarkable, who divided offices among themselves and fiercely disputed for power. Eubulus and Lycurgus were veritable ministers of finance and public works; Callistratus of Aphidna and Demosthenes, ministers of foreign affairs. Beneath the statesmen swarmed a despicable mob: second-rate rhetoricians, "supreme masters of tumults and uproars,"[4] politicians who zealously fostered the passions of the crowd and satisfied their lusts in exciting those of others, fishers in troubled waters, demagogues, sycophants. They called themselves the "watch dogs of the people,"[5] boasted of defending it

[1] *v. REG*, vol. XXXIV (1921), p. 1-19.
[2] Cf. **CXIII**, p. 63-74.   [3] Cf. **CXXI**.
[4] Hyper., *C. Dem.*, p. 102*b*.
[5] Ps. Dem., *C. Aristocr.*, I, 40; Theophr., *Car.*, 29, 3; Aristoph., 1023; cf. Xen., *Mem.*, II, 9, 1.

against the wolves, and grew fat at its expense. As soon as they scented a rich man they snarled and tried to bite him. Benevolent spies and accredited informers, they took to themselves a general right of prosecution in the name of the State, a sort of public prosecutorship. On the Pnyx as in the Heliæa they skilfully fostered mistrust and jealousy, outbidding legitimate demands and even excessive claims. Their supreme end was not to procure resources for those who lacked them, but rather to pull down those who possessed something to the level of those who had nothing; for in order to prosper they had to keep the open sore of wretchedness constantly festering and to maintain the division which was their *raison d'être*.[1]

Great or small, these men who lived by politics were continually brought into conflict by party differences and professional rivalry. They inevitably came to seek personal successes rather than the good of the State. One remembers the passage in which Plato rails against the competition of the incompetent who wish to grasp the tiller, that amusing passage in which the sentences reel in drunken fashion like the ship whose tempestuous progress he describes:

" Conceive something of this kind happening on board ship, on one ship or on several. The master is bigger and stronger than all the crew, but rather deaf and short-sighted. His seamanship is as deficient as his hearing. The sailors are quarrelling about the navigation. Each man thinks that he ought to navigate, though up to that time he has never studied the art, and cannot name his instructor or the time of his apprenticeship. They go further and say that navigation cannot be taught, and are ready to cut in pieces him who says that it can. They crowd round the solitary master, entreating him and offering him every inducement to entrust them with the helm. Occasionally when they fail to persuade him and others succeed better, they kill those others and throw them overboard, overpower the noble master by mandragora or drink or in some other way, and bind him hand and foot. Then they rule the ship and make free with the cargo, and so drinking and feasting make just such a voyage as might be expected of men like them. Further they compliment anyone who has the skill to contrive how they may persuade or compel the master to set them over the ship, and call him a good seaman, a navigator and a master of seamanship; any other kind of man they despise as useless. They have no notion that the true navigator must attend to the year and seasons, to the sky and the stars and the winds, and all that concerns his craft, if he is really going to be fit to rule a ship. . . . If ships were managed in that way, do you not think that the true navigator would certainly be called a star-gazer and a useless babbler by the crews of ships of that description ?"[2]

---

1 Isocr., *Peace*, 129 *ff*.
2 Plat., *Rep*., VI, p. 288 (trans. Lindsay).

The caustic criticism of the idealist doctrinaire must of course be greatly tempered. It is actuated by an ulterior motive, namely that philosophers alone ought to be allowed to undertake the task of governing men; and, more than that, it should not lead one to ignore the aptitude which the Athenian people so often displayed for making wise choices. It is none the less justified in many cases from the conflicts in the Ecclesia, as they appear in the speeches of orators. Though in the battle of principles eloquence on the Pnyx sometimes reached the level of the sublime, in personal discussions it descended to a deplorably low level. The greatest, Demosthenes along with the others, took a malicious pleasure in hurling against their opponents the vilest insults, the most infamous imputations, the most atrocious calumnies, without sparing their private lives nor even those of their family. So much mud would not have been thrown had general reprobation been feared. But these duels to the death excited, apparently, the same emotions as the fights of pugilists. There must have been few people sufficiently dispassionate to realize that such practices, by degrading both orators and auditors, dishonoured the tribune and even the city.

One of the most usual and one of the gravest accusations of which party men availed themselves, and which readily aroused public animosity, was that of corruption or venality. Here we come to one of the weaknesses of the Greeks. Already in the fifth century we saw the most eminent men of Sparta, even kings themselves, stretching out their hands for the sacks of gold offered by foreign powers, and, among the Athenians, not only was liberty of speech in debates on external policy paralyzed by too easily aroused suspicions,[1] but the management of public funds, and especially of secret funds, was dangerous for those responsible for it. But at this time precise details were at any rate necessary to lend substance to suspicions. In the fourth century, however, when men made a business of politics, when a great number of them, starting out poor, displayed a vulgar luxuriousness of life and had their own houses, what else could people think of these scandalous fortunes ? At intervals they grew angry, they flourished the arms with which the arsenal of

[1] Thuc., III, 42.

penal law furnished them—*eisangelia*, actions against pecu-
lation of public funds or against bribery and corruption
(γραφὴ κλοπῆς χρημάτων δημοσίων, δώρων, δωροξενίας). But
those whose consciences were not easy took refuge in
hypocrisy or cynicism and made an expiatory victim of some
one of those *logographoi* who earned their living by writing
speeches for others,[1] as if the profession which these writing
advocates followed were not the most reputable to which
the necessities of political and judicial life had given birth.
Launched on false tracks, and hardly knowing where to turn,
universal suspicion wavered between anger and scepticism.
Always disposed to " philanthropy " the people applied in its
own fashion the laws which forbade orators to derive profit
from their interventions in the tribune. It admitted that
liberty of thought and speech implied the right of accepting
money for upholding an opinion, provided that a man were
sincere and not wittingly injuring the country.[2] An interpretation which went far when money was sent in from
outside. Here was a great opportunity for Æschines. The
ass laden with gold that the Macedonian sent into the
towns so calmly could walk through the walls of Athens in
the full sight and knowledge of everybody. This was not
one of the least causes of the ruin of the regime of the city.

Thus directed by men who too often bartered their talents
without thought of the common interest, the multitude
exploited its sovereignty in such a way as to derive material
profit from it, even though it might be to the detriment of
the exchequer. The principle which Athenian democracy
worked upon was, however, peculiar neither to Athens nor
to democracy. In all times, in all the cities of Greece and
under all governments, political sovereignty had carried with
it economic advantages. It had always been admitted, for
example, that certain extraordinary revenues of the State,
such as those from mines, might be divided among the citizens:
this is what the Siphnians did in the sixth century.[3] But
the different fashion in which the Athenians applied this
rule a hundred and forty years later throws a revealing
light on the transformation of the public outlook: in 483,
on the instigation of Themistocles, selfish suggestions were

---

[1] Æschin., *Emb.*, 165; cf. Dein., *C. Dem.*, 111.
[2] Hyper., *loc. cit.*, p. 110b.   [3] Her., III, 57.

rejected in order to consecrate the silver of Laureion to the
construction of a fleet, the fleet which was to achieve the
victory of Salamis;[1] a little before the defeat of Chæronæa,
when the orator Lycurgus had caused the sentence of death
and confiscation to be pronounced against a person who
had accumulated a vast fortune by the illegal exploitation
of a concession, they divided the wealth of the condemned
man between them at the rate of fifty drachmas per head.[2]

The party in power found it quite natural to appropriate
all the perquisites accruing from such sources. But why rest
content with contingent profits of this sort ? Could not old
institutions be transformed in such a way as to bring them
in line with new needs ? Since the time of Pericles the State
had granted, to those who applied, the two obols collected
at the gates of the theatre: this was the *diobelia* of the plays,
the *theorikon*.[3] Later, after the Sicilian disaster and the
occupation of Decelea by Spartans, on the proposal of
Cleophon, the State made to the indigent a daily grant of
two obols which was also called the *diobelia*.[4] Moreover at
all times it had regularly offered hecatombs to the gods and
sometimes it received from foreign princes cargoes of grain
as diplomatic gifts:[5] these were so many occasions for making
liberal distributions of meat and corn. Why not give a
definitive and permanent organization to public measures of
relief, in such a way as to help needy citizens or, at the least,
to regale and amuse them on feast days ? To what better
use could budgetary surpluses be put ? Thus the *theorikon*
was to have its special fund, supplemented year by year and
each time as generously as possible: for surely the people
ought to be assured of its bread and its theatre, *panem et
circenses.*

In the fifth century, when men were still trying to reconcile
the rights of the citizen with those of the city, they saw in
the system of *misthophoria* the essential element of democratic
government, so much so that the first act of triumphant
oligarchy had been to suppress it.[6] When once the mob

[1] Id., VII, 144, Arist., *op. cit.*, 22, 7.
[2] Ps. Plut., *Lives of Ten Orat., Lyc.*, 34, p. 843d.
[3] Plut., *Pericl.*, 9; Philoch., fr. 85 (*FHG*, vol. I, p. 397).
[4] Arist., *op. cit.*, 28, 3; *RIG*, no. 569.
[5] Plut., *loc. cit.*, 37; Aristoph., *Wasps*, 716 and Schol.
[6] Thuc., VIII, 67; Arist., *op. cit.*, 30, 1.

began to think of nothing save the satisfaction of its egoistic impulses the theoric fund became the dominant feature of the regime. There were still of course patriots who tried to make men realize the needs of national defence, to oppose the *stratioka* to the *theorika*: budgetary surpluses became the stake in the game which was played on the Pnyx: the pitiful struggle of individual interests and the common interest, this drama upon which the fate of Athens depended, was epitomized in the opposition of two funds. But even the champions of the city, realizing that an entente between rich and poor was a condition of its existence, were compelled to proclaim the quasi-constitutional importance of the theoric money: they would not allow it to be criticized, to be " blasphemed," and demanded that all should regard it as sacred.[1] The demagogues took pride in endowing the cherished fund with new resources won from fortune hunting or financial juggling. In order that everyone might see the three performances of a tragedy, a drachma, if the necessary means were available, was given in place of two obols.[2] Then the theoric money was increased to five drachmas and distributed, not only at the Dionysia and the Panathenæa, but at all festivals.[3] Still more: Demades boasted of having secured for every citizen a half *mina* in order that they might celebrate in proper style the joyous Day of Pots.[4]

It needed no very scrupulous moral code to condemn the system. It condemned itself by its failure to achieve its end in spite of excessive grants. Careful analysis of facts and figures verifies these pessimistic reflections of Aristotle: " The avarice of mankind is insatiable; at one time two obols was enough, but now, when this sum has become customary, men still want more and more without end; for it is of the nature of desire not to be satisfied, and most men live only for the gratification of it. . . . The poor are always receiving and always wanting more and more, for help of this sort is like water poured into a leaky cask."[5] Demades himself, who knew all about demagogic distributions, called the *theorikon*

---

[1] Dem., *Phil.*, IV, 36 *ff.*; cf. Arist., *Pol.*, VII (VI), 3, 4.
[2] Suid., *s.v.* δραχμὴ χαλαζωσα; Dem., *De Cor.*, 28.
[3] Hyper., *loc. cit.*, p. 110c.; Dem., *Ol.*, I, 20; *C. Leoch.*, 37.
[4] Plut., *Præc. ger. reip.*, 25, 1, p. 818 *f.*
[5] Arist., *Pol.*, II, 4, 11; VII (VI), 3, 4.

the bird-lime of democracy.[1] Always inadequate and always being increased, the funds for public grants corrupted the regime, dissipated in alms the resources necessary for essential services and dragged to the abyss the treasury and the city.

And it is the Ecclesia which was responsible for the evil. We have on this point an unexpected witness, Æschines, the adversary of Demosthenes. In a moment of indignation, less righteous than interested, the skilful rhetorician found a sentence which strikes home. He is speaking of the sessions at which politicians contrive to have all sorts of honour paid to them by the people: " They proceed," he says, " not as deliberative assemblies, but rather as meetings of shareholders after a distribution of surpluses " (ὥσπερ ἐκ τῶν ἐράνων τὰ περιόντα νειμάμενοι).[2] It was true: the republic had really become an *eranos*, meaning by that a society for mutual help which demanded from one class the wherewithal to furnish another with the means of subsistence. By a strange reversal of the relations which once had seemed natural it was no longer the citizens who were called upon to render filial duty to the city, but the city which had to accept the duty of maintaining its citizens, as parents do their children.[3]

II

JUDICIAL, FISCAL AND MILITARY OBLIGATIONS

The whole of national life is inter-related. This preponderance of personal interest, which changed the very conception of the city, could not weigh on the deliberations of the Ecclesia without disorganizing the administrative system which derived its strength from civic spirit. It had inevitably a prejudicial effect upon the recruiting of judges and, above all, it disorganized the army and finances.

In the first years of the fourth century, when the empty state of the exchequer made it impossible to re-establish judicial payment, the heliasts made themselves so scarce that they had to be authorized to enroll themselves in several sections. That expedient could be abandoned when they were given the *triobelia*, but even then the *dikasteria* could not be

---

[1] Plut., *Plat. Quæst.*, 4, 4, p. 1011*b*.   [2] Æschin., *C. Ctes.*, 251.
[3] Plat., *Crit.*, p. 50*d ff.*; Dem., *Phil.*, IV, 41.

M*

supplied with the same ease as formerly. Whereas before it had been necessary to limit the number of jurors to six thousand, now it was found necessary to allow all citizens who were eligible to be enrolled and sworn as *dikastai*. Instead of dividing them by tribes, as was done in all other administrative departments, they had to be classified in approximately equal sections, having consideration only to the requirements of the work. We have a document, moreover, which gives us precise information as to the unwillingness of the Athenians in the second half of the fourth century to discharge their duty as judges. In the list of public arbitrators who sat in 325-4 103 names occur. It ought to have contained the names of all citizens who, during the year, had reached the age of sixty, that is to say about one in every hundred of the 23-25,000 citizens of Athens.[1] We see from this example that more than half of the people who had an obligatory function to perform contrived to evade its performance.

The Athenians of the fourth century were still more reluctant to accept their financial responsibilities. The fiscal history of this epoch presents a most singular spectacle. The State, reduced to a perpetual condition of penury by the perpetual wars, struggled hard to find new resources: it doubled indirect taxes, the hundredth on imports and exports, the hundredth on sales of real estate;[2] it resorted as frequently as possible to extraordinary war taxes, so that it made them almost ordinary taxes; it organized the trierarchy in such a way as to convert a prestation into a direct impost; it appealed for voluntary contributions; as a last resort it multiplied confiscations and ordered its generals to sustain war at the expense of the enemy or even of a friendly country. Thus the statesmen who remained longest in power were financiers of the first rank. Callistratus of Aphidna organized the exchequer of the second confederation; Eubulus saved Athens from bankruptcy after the Social War; Lycurgus solved all the difficulties caused by the disaster of Chæronæa. Learning from experience Athenian democracy even abandoned in the case of high financial officials the principles of appointment by lot, yearly tenure and collegiate responsibility: the administrators of the theoric fund and the single treasurer

[1] *RIG*, no. 1028; cf. **XXXII**, I, p. 435.
[2] Ps. Xen., *Rep. of Ath.*, I, 17; *RIG*, nos. 564 *ff.*

of the military funds were elected for four years.[1] Whilst philosophers and publicists were led by the general distress to lay the foundations of the science of economics, individuals were racking their brains to find ways of filling the public treasury: they proposed that the State should build inns, shops, merchant ships, that it should hire out slaves in thousands for the working of the mines, that it should create a salt tax or a monopoly of lead.[2] What valiant efforts to save the country ! There was only one difficulty—taxpayers vied in escaping payment and taxable material melted away.

It is this conflict between the exigencies of public interest and the evasions of refractory taxpayers, a conflict moral even more than economic, which explains the successive transformations of the *eisphora*.

Since the time when the intervention of Persian gold had changed the Peloponnesian war into a war for money, whether she would or no, Athens was forced to have frequent recourse to this extraordinary tax. When in 378 she decided to reconstitute the maritime confederation, she wanted to raise as much as possible from it. Was it in the black years which brought the fifth century to its close or thirty years or so later, that she increased the number of people liable to it ? We do not know. However that may be the property qualification which marked off the *zeugitai* from the *thetes*, the taxpayers of the lowest rank from the tax free, was lowered from 200 drachmas to 150:[3] the lists of taxpayers and hoplites grew longer accordingly. It was then also, since the *eisphora* was being levied upon a greater number of citizens, that, in accordance with the dictates of equity, it was made progressive or rather regressive. At a time when it was held that a man's capital was the equivalent of twelve years' income, incomes were capitalized at the rate of 12 annuities for the *pentacosiomedimni*, 10 for the knights, $6\frac{2}{3}$ for the *zeugitai*, while fortunes less than 1,800 drachmas were not taken into account. Taxable capital ($\tau i\mu\eta\mu a$), therefore, was identified with real capital for the first class, but for the second it was reduced by a sixth and for the third by a third. According to the class the minimum was 6,000, 3,000 or 1,000

[1] Arist., *Ath. Const.*, 43, 1.
[2] Xen., *Revenues of Ath.*, III, 12-14; IV, 13 *ff.*; Aristoph., *Ass. of Women*, 814 and Schol.; Ps. Arist., *Econ.*, II, 2, 3, and 36.
[3] Ps. Dem., *C. Macart.*, 54.

drachmas.[1] Since it was proportioned to taxable capital and admitted of exemptions at the bottom, the impost was, therefore, markedly regressive; on the other hand, in spite of being ostensibly a tax on capital, it was, in reality, a tax on income. We know that the amount on the registers was, at the first assessment which was made in 378-7, 5,750 talents; throughout the fourth century it remained round about 6,000 talents.[2] Even with a moderate assessment the *eisphora* could, with this organization, assure ample resources to the city.

But evasions, more or less fraudulent, had to be taken into account. For the compiling of the registers (διαγράμματα), the State trusted to the declarations of the taxpayers. Statements as to landed property could be sufficiently carefully checked by the demarchs who held a kind of cadastral survey (ἀπογραφή) and were able to estimate returns. The value of buildings could be reasonably determined according to rent. Similarly live-stock and slaves could be valued according to their number and their physical condition.[3] But what guarantee had the fisc of the truth of declarations with regard to personal property, to " invisible " wealth (ἀφανῆ)? It was just because men did not hesitate to dissimulate (ἀφανίζειν, ἀποκρύπτεσθαι) that litigants so often cited as a virtue the regularity with which they paid their taxes.

In 378-7, however, perhaps at the time same as the change in the property qualification, a vigorous measure was passed to facilitate the gathering in of the *eisphora* and to improve its distribution. The taxpayers were grouped into twenty *symmoriai*, in such a way that all the *symmoriai* had to pay for the same fraction of taxable capital the same share of the tax. Each of them was made responsible for its collection, each being responsible for its own share. The State thought that it had only to fix a sum and it would receive it, provided that the *symmoriai* were reorganized from time to time in accordance with changes of fortune and divisions of inheritances. It was for the *symmoriai* to manage as best they

---

[1] Chief authority; Poll., VIII, 130. Cf. Lécrivain, *DA*, art. " Eisphora "; P. Guiraud, *Ét. écon. sur l'ant.*, p. 77 *ff.*; **XXV**, p. 25 *ff.*
[2] *Pol.*, II, 62, 7; *De Symmor.*, 19, 30; Philoch., fr. 151 (*FHG*, vol. I, p. 409).
[3] Cf. *RIG*, nos. 1354, l. 24 *ff.*; 1351, l. 7 *ff.*; 1355, l. 25 *ff.*

could. But it was not an easy matter: the small taxpayers always found good reasons for securing exemption; the great were obliged to give proof of public spirit by paying more than they were legally called upon to do. Timotheus, who was exceedingly wealthy, undertook to pay a fifth of his income, and the guardians of Demosthenes, in a fit of generosity which cost them nothing, did the same in the name of their ward.[1] In spite of all this there were recalcitrants who had to be brought to justice, insolvents whom their *symmoria* abandoned to personal responsibility. In short arrears dragged on hopelessly from year to year.

In 362 at the latest, it was found necessary to reorganize the institution in order to safeguard the State against all risk of deficit. Of the 12,000 citizens who were grouped in the 20 *symmoriai* in the proportion of 60 to each, the richest, to the number of 300, were divided out among them in the proportion of 15 to each. The 300 were called upon to pay in advance to the treasury the whole of the *eisphora*, and to recoup themselves in the course of the year from the taxpayers of the second category: thus an extraordinary " liturgy," the *proeisphora*, analogous to the trierarchy, was imposed upon them. This time the State felt certain that by a fixed day it would receive the amount it demanded. But once more it suffered disillusionment. In 355 it had to appoint a commission, at the head of which it placed Androtion, to collect the arrears which had accumulated since 378. At the head of the police Androtion hunted down the debtors, broke into their houses, seized their goods and threw them into prison, unless they succeeded in concealing themselves under their beds or escaping by the roofs.[2] But it was in vain that the financial administration racked its brains and employed violence: the reluctance of the contributors proved the stronger force. Demosthenes, in 354, exclaimed despairingly:

" Look at our whole city. In the wealth it contains it is equal, or very nearly so, to all the other cities combined: but those who possess wealth are so constituted that even if all the orators in unison were to proclaim the terrible news that a king was about to establish himself, that there was no means of averting the catastrophe . . . not only would they not pay the *eisphora*, but they would conceal their wealth and deny its existence."[3]

---

[1] Dem., *C. Aphob.*, I, 7.   [2] Id., *C. Androt.*, 49 *ff.*
[3] Dem., *C. Aphob.*, II, 17.

This deterioration of civic morality is particularly obvious in the history of the institution which involved both fiscal and military obligations—namely the trierarchy.

Originally the burden of trierarchy was imposed on a single citizen for each ship, and it could only be reimposed after an interval of two years. But, during the war for Decelea, the trierarchs were authorized to group themselves in twos to bear the heavy cost: this was what was called *syntrierarchy*.[1] The system of ordinary trierarchy and syntrierarchy functioned simultaneously; it was the business of the taxed to regulate according to broad conventions questions of equipment and command.[2] Actually the relief was not great for them; for when it was divided into two, the burden recurred twice as frequently. It was endurable so long as the fleet consisted only of a hundred vessels and armaments were few; but when Athens reconstituted the maritime confederation in 378-7, she had to build on a large scale and decree annual consignments. In 357-6, when the Social War broke out, she possessed 283 triremes, perhaps even 383. In vain did she appeal for good citizens prepared, like Demosthenes, to volunteer out of their turn; willing helpers melted into thin air. The majority tried to get out of it as cheaply as possible. Speculation was mixed up in it. *Entrepreneurs* contracted for the obligations of the trierarchs; if they profited out of it, it was because they furnished bad tackle. We know, for example, that Demosthenes was forced by cunning intrigues to endorse a contract of this kind.[3] Even more serious was the fact that trierarchs found substitutes in time of war: in 361, Aristophon of Arzenia accused several of them of treason and cowardice and demanded that they should be put to death.[4]

The institution needed to be overhauled. It was decided to augment the number of those liable by demanding a proportional share from more modest fortunes. Such was the object of a law proposed by Periander. This law applied to the trierarchy the system of the *symmoriai*, as it had existed since 362. There were, therefore, trierarchic *symmoriai*.

---

[1] Id., *C. Mid.*, 80, 155.
[2] Id., *C. Everg.*, 21 *ff.*, 44, 78; *De Coron.*, 103; *IG*, vol. II, nos. 793b, 795f, 803c, 804b.
[3] Dem., *C. Aphob.*, II, 17.   [4] Id., *C. Mid.*, 80, 155.

Each contained sixty members, ranged in classes according to their wealth, with fifteen heading the list. Each had its chief or *hegemon*, whose name it bore, its administrator or *epimeletes*. A commission of Twenty (the twenty *hegemones* or *epimeletai*) collaborated with the *strategoi* in the work of dividing trierarchic duties among the various *symmoriai*. The ships, which formerly the State had assigned directly, one by one, to one or two trierarchs, were henceforth distributed by the *symmoriai* as they thought best. The effort required to be made varied according to the importance of the armament decreed: for one ship, especially in time of peace when the outlay was not very heavy, the *symmoria* might appoint a single trierarch; for another, especially in time of war, it might appoint a varying number of associates (συντελεῖς), a number which we see rising as high as sixteen.[1]

At the first glance the reform of Periander seems to mark a financial step forward, since it divided among several the burden which formerly had fallen upon one or two, since, in brief, it converted a " liturgy " into a direct tax. Even from the fiscal point of view, however, the result of the system fell far beneath expectations. Of the twelve hundred enrolled a great number enjoyed temporary dispensations, for instance widows, only daughters on whom the continuation of their line depended (*epikleroi*), cleruchs, and joint inheritors of property. Demosthenes calculated that there were 480 dispensations of this kind.[2] Others petitioned to be struck off the list because of reverses of fortune. In fact, the list was never complete and hundreds of names only appeared there for record. But the system was accompanied by many other disadvantages. From the political point of view, it relieved the richest class by burdening the most prosperous part of the middle class, while from the national point of view it had still graver consequences. Responsibility, by being divided, was nullified and unceasing conflicts were created. In place of being animated, as in former days, by a patriotic spirit of emulation, which made each man proud of his task, the trierarchs were guided only by the basest motives of self-interest.

---

[1] Id., *C. Everg.*, 21 *ff.*, 44, 78; *De Coron.*, 103; *IG*, vol. II, 793*b*, 795*f*, 803*c*, *e*, *f*, 804*b*.
[2] Dem., *De Symm.*, 16.

The history of the trierarchy alone would suffice to show what difficulty Athens experienced in the fourth century, because of the decline of public spirit, in seriously organizing her defence. But this is such an important fact that it must be examined in greater detail.

The education given to the young no longer fostered in the State the military strength required. As early as the fifth century the Athenians, contrasting themselves with the Spartans, had boasted of relying less on long years of military training than on their natural courage. A dangerous confidence. It was more or less justified in an epoch when the cultivation of the mind went hand in hand with love of action and the cultivation of the body.[1] Yet even then Aristophanes broke out into bitter complaints against the customs introduced by the sophists and sighed for the times when children used to go coatless to school beneath the falling snow, when young folk played among the olive trees of the gymnasium, smelling sweetly of smilax and the buds of poplars, and won for themselves strong chests, fresh complexions and broad shoulders.[2] The developments of later days were much worse.

The Socratic school made valiant efforts to react against them. The master tried to arouse a war-like spirit in his compatriots, insisting on the qualities and attainments essential for the officer and the general, appealing to the politician to study the material resources of the different States, exhorting individuals to make themselves physically fit, that they might be able to come to the aid of the city.[3] His disciples believed that the very root of the evil ought to be attacked, namely the freedom left to the father of a family to direct as he wished the education of his children. Plato, who held that all individual elements should be eliminated from the ideal, nay even from the merely healthy, republic, stood for compulsory education with or without the consent of the parents;[4] Aristotle declared that it was the business of the law to regulate questions of education, and wanted the single and public school, of which he was an advocate, to be modelled on the principles of the constitution.[5] Both of

---

[1] Thuc., II, 39, 40.   [2] Aristoph., *Clouds*, 965, 1002 *ff.*; cf. *Frogs.*
[3] Xen., *Mem.*, III, 1-6.   [4] Plat., *Laws*, VII, p. 804c-d.
[5] Arist., *Pol.*, V (VIII), 1, 1-3: " Since the city has only one and the same object, education ought to be the same for all; it ought, therefore, to be the business of the State, and not of individuals "; VIII (V),

them attached the highest importance to physical exercises and demanded that they should be devised with a view to a thorough preparation for military service;[1] for " it is education which brings victory."[2]

But, to the profound regret of the philosophers, the liberty of families was unrestricted. They used it to give education an exclusively utilitarian character, against which Aristotle protested.[3] Isocrates' defence of the system of private education was actuated by motives of personal interest: " It is impossible to prescribe the same training for all because of the inequalities of wealth; each, therefore, must receive an education proportioned to his means; the humbler must be directed towards agriculture and commerce; the sons of the rich ought to learn riding, gymnastics, hunting and philosophy."[4] Actually physical culture was neglected by all classes of society, and Isocrates was the first to disdain it.[5] It became more and more the concern of specialists and professionals (ἀθληταί) as opposed to amateurs (ἰδιῶται).[6]

The decline of the military spirit and of physical culture was not confined to the Athenians; it was perceptible throughout almost the whole of Greece, for the simple reason that in all societies it is the inevitable result of economic and intellectual development. Long ago the Ionians, spoilt by prosperity, had resigned themselves to servitude rather than suffer fatigue and the heat of the sun; it was a well-known fact that their troops were not to be relied upon.[7] The other Greeks despised them then; soon they imitated them. In 383, at the time when Sparta was again struggling for hegemony, the Peloponnesian league was obliged to allow the towns to buy themselves out of military service, and to exact a fine from them for every man lacking from their contingent.[8]

7, 20: " The essential thing for the stability of the State, although it is totally neglected in our day, is to bring education into conformity with the constitution."
  [1] Plat., loc. cit., p. 794c, 804c; Rep., p. 429e, 537b; Arist., Pol., VIII (V), 3, 3.
  [2] Plat., Laws, I, p. 641e.   [3] Arist., Pol., V (VIII), 1, 4-3, 2.
  [4] Isocr., Areop., 44.
  [5] Xen., Mem., III, 5, 15; Isocr., Paneg., 2.
  [6] Xen., Mem., III, 7, 7; Hiero., IV, 6. Cf. Norman Gardiner, Greek Athletic Sports and Festivals, p. 130 ff.
  [7] Her., VI, 12; Thuc., I, 124; V, 9; VI, 77; VIII, 25; Xen., Hell., III, 2, 17.
  [8] Xen., Hell., V, 2, 21.

Gymnastics, national art though it was, was no longer practised save in poor or isolated lands: though a crowd collected from all parts of the country at the Panhellenic contests, the victors of Olympia were all Arcadians or Thessalians. The evil thus became general; but it was in the centre of commerce and letters that it was most deeply rooted and, in any case, most visible.

When Athens, after a period in which she had been compelled under the hegemony of Sparta to suspend all military activities, found herself obliged by political events to reconstitute her army, the results of her efforts were pitiable. The mass of citizens jeered at those who made themselves conspicuous by trying to make themselves fit. Hoplites and knights loved their comfort too dearly to submit to discipline.[1] Any pretext was good enough to escape from military obligations. Men boasted of doing it, as though it were a praiseworthy act. Æschines, in the peroration of his apology, mentions his two years of service as an exceptional qualification, and, by implication, contrasts himself with Demosthenes who could not say as much for himself.[2] In proportion as the number of citizens in the army diminished, that of mercenaries increased. The whole of Greece was then swarming with vagabonds and exiles who hired themselves out to the highest bidder; they followed with enthusiasm the condottieri who promised them not only regular pay, but also lucrative victories.

Athens, like other cities, availed herself of their services. Many protests were raised against such a state of affairs. When the Athenians had for the second time lost their empire Isocrates pointed out to them the principal cause of their misfortune: the replacement of a national army by a mob of expatriates, deserters and criminals, the lavishing of pay on foreigners from an exchequer incapable of relieving the poverty of the people. As remedy the rhetorician proposed a return to tradition: let the citizens defend their country with their bodies, instead of disgracing themselves by serving as rowers and leaving others to do the fighting. About the same time Xenophon even went so far as to propose that metics should be freed from serving as hoplites, since an infantry in which citizens were not mingled with a heterogeneous mob

[1] Id., *Mem.*, III, 5, 15 and 19.   [2] Æschin., *Emb.*, 167.

could not but be better, while it was to a people's honour if it relied less on alien help than on its own valour. Demosthenes spent his life in clamouring for this reform, but as a statesman forced to take into account facts and opinions: from his knowledge of the necessities of war and the number of men it required, he realized that henceforth it would be impossible to dispense entirely with the services of professional soldiers and to create again a purely national army; he wished to have a solid, well-trained, well-paid nucleus of citizens, to which could be added, when necessary, mercenary troops.[1] Since then, as we have seen, the great question with which the conscience of every man was faced and which brought political parties into conflict was whether budgetary surpluses should be appropriated for the theoric fund or for the army, devoted to the petty pleasures of the people or to defence. Demosthenes did not succeed in time to prevent the disaster of Chæronæa. Only when she was trembling on the very brink of the precipice did Athens seek salvation in a strong organization of the *epheboi*, in a return to physical training and apprenticeship in arms.[2] It was too late.

[1] Isocr., *Peace*, 43-48; Xen., *Reven. of Ath.*, 6, 11, 3-4; Dem., *De Symm.*, 15; *Phil.*, IV, 46; *Ol.*, I, 20; III, 11, 19.
[2] Arist., *Ath. Const.*, 42, 2-5. The earliest ephebic inscription (*RIG*, no. 603) is for the year 334-3.

CHAPTER IV

THE UNIFICATION OF GREECE

I

THE IDEA OF UNITY

WITH the general transformation of men's outlook the cities of Greece were led to lend themselves more readily than in former days to change, to regulate their relations with other Greek cities in accordance with ideas less narrow and less jealous. Towns in which commerce and industry had developed to any considerable degree attracted a heterogeneous collection of people—craftsmen in search of a livelihood—and sent out their sailors to visit all the shores of the Mediterranean. By this coming and going a constant interchange of men, of merchandise and of ideas was effected. Blood was intermingled and prejudices disappeared one by one. In the interior of each country, citizens and metics alike, from being continually brought together, generation after generation, by the same necessities of economic and social life, felt the same love for their common country: the ports in particular were melting pots where day by day lasting fusions were made. From one country to another, more and more clearly, more and more consciously, the conception of Hellenic unity was being formed.

It was this which had in former days allied the combatants of Salamis and Platæa, of Himera and of Cumæ against the Persians, the Carthaginians and the Etruscans. The brotherhood of arms which had saved Greece was sung enthusiastically by contemporary poets. Pindar, although the son of a town unfaithful to the national cause, found magnificent strains in which to salute Athens " enwreathed with violets, the rampart of Hellas," and associated with her in glory Ægina, Sparta and Syracuse.[1] In the *Persians* of Æschylus the sublime pæan which preludes victory is

[1] Pind., *Pyth.*, I, 73-80.

a call to the " children of the Hellenes " united to deliver the temples of their gods and the tombs of their ancestors.[1] All these memories Herodotus transmitted to posterity in order above all to render homage to the Athens which he cherished as a foster mother, but also to show that the object at stake in the struggle had been the destiny of a race, of a language, of a religion, of a whole civilization.[2]

In the midst of the Peloponnesian war when Grecian hands were freely shedding Grecian blood, voices were raised protesting that these were fratricidal struggles, that honour demanded that instead of emulously begging for Persian gold, all should march out united against that people. If Aristophanes never wearied of imploring for peace, it was not only because he believed it to be essential for the peasants of all the belligerent cities, but also because he remembered the kinship of the " Panhellenes " which asserted itself before the sanctuaries of the Amphictyonies and which ought to unite them against the barbarians.[3] Thucydides probably shared these ideas, at least as far as the Persians were concerned: this man, who kept before his eyes so lofty a conception of historic veracity and the duties which it imposed, did not dare, doubtless from feelings of patriotic shame, to mention the peace of Callias, and, whilst he recounts the humiliating conduct of the Lacedæmonians at the court of the Great King,[4] he is silent concerning the negotiations, equally dishonourable, which the Athenians in their turn engaged upon. Even on the opposite side one sees Callicratidas, one of the noblest figures of the time, blushing for the Persian alliance, opposing to the inexpiable hatreds of the cities the idea of Greek solidarity, working for a general reconciliation.

In spite of the innumerable conflicts which followed the great Peloponnesian war, the idea of Panhellenic unity made enormous progress in men's minds during the fourth century. As in the past, but with a precision which the vague beliefs had never had and which the reasoned theories attained to, Hellenism was defined in contrast to barbarism. It was recognized that, by its very climate and its conception of the

---

[1] Æschyl., *Persians*, 402 *ff.*   [2] Her., VIII, 144.
[3] Aristoph., *Lysistr.*, 1128 *ff.*
[4] Thuc., II, 67; IV, 50; VIII, 18, 39, 43, 57 *ff.*, 80, 99 *ff.*

city, Greece enjoyed an essential superiority over the monarchies of torrid countries and the tribes of cold regions, that
Nature had placed between Greeks and barbarians a gulf
as great as that between men and beasts, that, moreover,
she had created a race of masters and races of slaves, thus
giving to all that was Greek obvious rights over all that was
not.[1] But even those who based their conception of Hellenism
on a physical principle, unity of race, added to it a loftier
principle, education (παιδεία), manner of thought (διανοία),
in short, civilization.[2]

Consequently the Greek must not think of himself as the
member of a single city, but as forming part of a community
embracing all cities of Greek origin and customs. Plato
wanted to see his projects of political reform realized by the
tyrants of Sicily. Isocrates, looking round for someone to
whom to expound his, failing Athens and Sparta, turned to
a prince of Cyprus, before admitting that a Macedonian was
also a Greek. Extensive though Greece was when thus
defined, the ethnical and moral unity of the men who inhabited
it made every war between cities seem a civil war; a disease,
said one,[3] madness, said another,[4] a fratricidal war. There
must be no more of it. Such was the language that the most
famous orators used before the assembled crowds at the great
Olympic gatherings (panegyris). Gorgias of Leontini set
the example in 392: he exhorted the Greeks to put an end to
the struggles which weakened them all and, united, to undertake in the East the only one which was worthy of them.
Developments of this sort converted the " panegyric " speech
into a literary genre, practised in turn by Lysias and Isocrates.
Gorgias did not fear to let the Athenians know what he
thought: in a speech devoted to the memory of citizens who
had fallen on the field of honour, he regrets that they should
have paid with their lives for victories less glorious than those
of Marathon and Salamis,—praises and regrets which find
expression again in another Epitaphios delivered by a contemporary of Lysias.

It was impossible for the ideal of unity not to be translated

    1 Arist., Pol., IV (VII), 6, 1; Isocr., Antid., 293; Panath., 150 ff.;
Phil., 124.
    2 Isocr., Paneg., 50. Cf. LVI, p. 41 ff.
    3 Plat., Rep., V, p. 470.   4 Isocr., Phil., 126.

in certain spheres into reality.   From the beginning literature
and art had constituted a sort of common patrimony of the
Greeks.   That community grew more intimate.   In the old
days schools of sculpture had been distinguished by local
peculiarities; henceforth there was a general evolution marked
only by individual characteristics.   We know how diverse
alphabets had been up to that point; the Ionian alphabet,
the most complete of all, triumphed over the others: in Attica
in the last quarter of the fifth century it began to dominate
in private usage and to penetrate into official documents;
under the archonship of Euclides (403-2) it was officially
adopted.   But it was Athens which, uncontested, stood at the
head of Hellenism.   Even in the time of Pericles she boasted
of being the school of Greece[1] and proclaimed herself on the
tomb of Euripides as " the Hellas of Hellas."   In the writings
of Isocrates she justified her claims.   She is the " capital "
of Greek civilization ($ἄστυ τῆς Ἑλλάδος$)[2] because she embodies
all its elements in a magnificent form, because she concentrates
in herself all which gives it grandeur, humanity, wisdom,
reason, and diffuses it among the others.[3]   An admirable
panegyric, confirmed by the facts.   The Attic dialect became
the language of culture for all Greeks.   Other dialects continued to serve for local purposes: the Ionian of Hippocrates
is preserved in his books on medicine, the Dorian of Pythagoras in numerous mathematical works; but Attic was the
literary language, the language common to all cultured people,
the *koine*.   In order to strengthen the connection between
their country and the Greek world the kings of Macedonia
employed it as the language of State.

    Could the idea of unity spread from the intellectual and
moral to the political sphere ?   Here, unfortunately for
Greece, it was for a long time faced with insurmountable
barriers.   We have seen that it was tending to bring the
Greeks into alliance against the rest of the world.   Why did
it happen, however, that barely a quarter of a century after
the Persian wars the Greek cities began, never to cease, to
make appeals to the Persians for help against each other, and
that, in the spring of 386, an edict issued from Susa became
law for all of them, imposing on them for many years the

[1] Thuc., II, 41.   [2] Isocr., *Antid.*, 299.
    [3] Id., *ibid.*, 293 *f.*, 300; *Paneg.*, 47-50.

" King's Peace "? The reason lay in the fact that deeply embedded in the hearts of the Greeks was a passion which counterbalanced pride in the Hellenic name and contempt for the barbarians: an invincible love of autonomy. The purest patriotism could not reconcile itself to the idea that the city, founded by the gods and maintained by their ancestors, should cease to be a free and independent community, absolute mistress of its constitution, its laws, its army, its finances. We must not forget that the greatest minds, in metaphysical speculations as well as in realist theories, did not consider that political science could be applied to a State other than the *polis*. Thus two forces were ready to clash: moral unity and the passion for particularism.

Alone, Greece was incapable of securing the triumph of centralization. Only an impetus from without could overthrow the barriers which bristled everywhere; she was to be unified only by conquest. Greece had to be defeated before the political regime of the city could disappear. But before disappearing it was to suffer change as the result of new ideas and new needs. We shall see small societies, once so exclusive, opening their gates more freely to individuals. We shall see them, compelled by the necessity of defending themselves against a powerful enemy, renouncing a part of their sovereignty and lending themselves to tentative efforts towards limited union and federalism.

II

BESTOWAL OF CITIZENSHIP AND *ISOPOLITEIA*

When one knows what citizenship of Greek towns meant in theory and then sees what it was in fact in the fourth century, particularly at Athens, one realizes that legal enactments are of no avail against the force of customs.

Immediately after the democratic restoration of 403 the Athenians re-established the law of Pericles which protected the body of citizens against the intrusion of metics. This law had been constantly violated or side-tracked during the last years of the Peloponnesian war, as a result of military exigencies and political disorders. On the proposal of

Aristophon, amended by Nicomedes, it was decided that it should be once more enforced, though it was not to operate retroactively.[1] For the future all conceivable precautions were taken. From a consultation of legislative texts only it would seem that never had the bestowal of the privilege of citizenship been so hedged in with formalities or so difficult. The decree which conferred it had to be justified by exceptional services rendered to the people; it had to be confirmed in full assembly by at least six thousand votes; finally, it could be attacked by a public action against illegality.[2] Usurpation of the right of citizenship fell beneath a very serious indictment, to which no less severe a penalty than slavery and confiscation of property was attached (γραφὴ ξενίας).[3] From time to time, when it became evident that many cunning evaders were slipping through the meshes of the law, attempts were made to strengthen the defences by means of control of the registers. The books of the demes, which were equivalent to our municipal registers, were subjected to a general revision in 346-5,[4] as they had been a century earlier. Those of the phratries, which might also serve as evidence, were liable to similar revisions.[5]

But it was all useless: this plethora of precautions and certain outbursts of popular indignation[6] imply persistent frauds. Rich and influential metics had no difficulty in hunting out a suitable little deme where, at not too excessive a price, their names would be enrolled without questions being asked. The rotten borough of Potamos had a well established reputation in this respect.[7] There or in a similar one, the demarch himself might undertake the business and secure the necessary accomplices, at the rate of five drachmas a head.[8] Failing the deme there was the phratry to fall back upon, and a clever man could insinuate himself into a family of lawful citizens by the subterfuge of adoption or slip into a batch of legitimate naturalizations.[9] Thus con-

---

[1] Schol. Æschin., C. Timocr., 39; Isæus, Succ. of Philostr., 47; Succ. of Cimon, 43; Dem., C. Euboul., 30.

[2] Ps. Dem., C. Neaira, 88-91; Andoc., De Redit., 23.

[3] v. CVI, vol. II, p. 416 ff.   [4] v. CII, p. 38-51.

[5] IJG, vol. II, no. xxix, A, l. 13 ff.

[6] Dem., C. Euboul., 49.

[7] Id., C. Leoch., 35 ff.; Harp., s.v. Πόταμος.

[8] Dem., C. Euboul., 59 f.; Hyper., C. Euxen., 3; Harp., s.v. Ἀγασικλῆς.

[9] Isæus, Succ. of Euphil., 1-2; Lys., C. Agor., 64, 73.

tinually forming and reforming was a class of illegally registered citizens, the παρέγγραπτοι.[1]

Two or three times in a century the anger of the people would burst out, but nevertheless they themselves were not above extending and debasing the right of citizenship by the ever increasing number of honorific decrees. Even by the end of the fifth century this kind of abuse was a butt for jokes or a subject for tears: comedy did not treat very tenderly the instrument maker Cleophon, a vulgar and ignorant demagogue, the offspring of a Thracian mother and an unknown father.[2] Very soon orators began to fulminate as violently and as frequently against easy naturalizations as against illegal enrolments. Isocrates laments that so noble a title, which ought to inspire respect and pride, should be dragged in the dust. Demosthenes, in one of those tirades which he knew by heart and which he brought into one speech after another, contrasts the time when the most glorious recompense which foreign sovereigns could win was a nominal exemption from taxes, with these degenerate days when citizenship has become merely base merchandise offered to slaves, the sons of slaves: " It is not," he says to the Assembly, " that you are by nature inferior to your fathers; but they possessed pride in their name, and this pride you have lost."[3]

Lovers of the past, of course, very easily become despisers of the present. And again we do not see in the fourth century, as we do in the Hellenistic epoch, bankers accumulating as many nationalities as they have branches and cities officially selling at a fixed rate letters of naturalization. Isocrates is obviously exaggerating when he goes on to say that foreigners take the place of citizens in war.[4] Nevertheless there was much truth in these exaggerations. The evidence which orators and inscriptions give us strongly suggests that decrees conferring citizenship increased in number and diminished in value. The emergency decree proposed by Hyperides after the defeat of Chæronæa, which promised the status of Athenians to metics who armed themselves for the defence

---

[1] Æschin., *Emb.*, 76; 177; Harp. Suid., *s.v.* διαψήφισις.
[2] Aristoph., *Frogs*, 679 ff., 1504, 1532 and Schol.; Plat. Com. fr. 60, Kock (vol. I, p. 617); Æschin., *loc. cit.*, 76.
[3] Isocr., *Peace*, 50; Dem., *Pub. Econ.*, 23-25; C. *Aristocr.*, 210 ff.
[4] Isocr., *loc. cit.*, 88.

of the State, was likewise in line with tradition.[1] But Athens showed herself less and less parsimonious of individual privileges. She awarded the title of citizen for services of all kinds: to a politician such as Heracleides of Clazomenæ, to a mercenary leader such as Charidemus, a simple metic of Oreus, to bankers of servile origin such as Pasion, Phormion, Epigenes, Conon, to merchants such as Chærephilus and his three sons.[2] She even made citizens *honoris causa* by decrees which could be very useful to friends of Athens driven from their country (Astycrates of Delphi, Peisitheides of Delos), but which were often merely honorary distinctions, foreign decorations almost (Storys of Thasus, Dionysius the Elder, Tharyps and Arybbas, kings of the Molossians).[3] A curious fact, well fitted to arouse the anger of Demosthenes, shows how lightly honours of this kind were bestowed: citizenship was accorded successively to Cotys king of Thrace and to his murderers.[4]

The Athenians were not blind to the fact that they were violating principles which they professed to respect: so far as they could they multiplied and rendered more complicated the formalities and still more the actual papers of naturalization and their wording.[5] But the constant pressure which new ideas and new customs exert cannot be counter-acted by methods of procedure and declarations.

Characteristic as was the tendency to multiply naturalizations it was only one sign of the times. A practice which was to be of the greatest value in the future for modifying the system of petty sovereignties was the admission *en masse* of one city into another. Even in the fifth century the example of the Samians and the Platæans, who were made citizens of Athens, had not remained unique. In the same epoch two towns of Asia opened their gates to the inhabitants of two Sicilian towns: Antandrus, to the Syracusans; Ephesus, to the people of Selinus.[6] It was really simply a way of honouring soldiers who had come to the aid of their allies;

---

[1] Ps. Plut., *Lives of Ten Orat.*, *Hyper.*, 8-9, p. 849*a*; Lyc., *C. Leocr.*, *s.v.* ὑπεψηφίσατο.
[2] **CIV**, nos. 6489, 15380, 11672, 14951, 4782, 8700, 15187.
[3] *SIG³*, nos. 175, 226, 127, 159, 228.
[4] Dem., *C. Aristocr.*, 118 *f.*
[5] *v.* A. Wilhelm., *AM*, vol. XXXIX (1914), p. 266 *ff.*; **VII**, p. 964.
[6] Xen., *Hell.*, I, 1, 25; 2, 1041; *v.* **LXXIII**, p. 96 *f.*

but the general form given to this distinction indicated, never-theless, a tendency towards the indefinite extension of citizen-ship. In the fourth century there were similar cases, and these were of potential political significance. The Cyreneans strengthened the ties which bound them to Thera by recog-nizing as brothers the sons of their old mother country.[1] For the first time we see, not merely one town conferring civic privileges upon another by a unilateral convention, but two towns reciprocally conferring citizenship by a bilateral convention: a treaty concluded about 365 between Ceos and Histiaia stipulates that each of the contracting States shall accord to the citizens of the other freedom of trade and, to individuals making application, civic rights.[2] This exchange of citizens between States which remained on a footing of equality, retaining each its sovereignty, its constitution and its laws, was later to be known in Greek public law by the name of *isopoliteia*.

III

LEAGUES AND FEDERATIONS

Another institution marks a further advance: namely the association of cities in wider communities. In the fifth century we saw a number of leagues and federations coming to birth, developing or declining. The fermentation at work in Greece in the fourth century multiplied these attempts at political concentration in which elements of the repre-sentative system made their first appearance. Whilst Elis and Rhodes were maintaining more or less peaceably the unity which they had established by synœcism, and whilst the sympolities of Arcadia and of Chalcidice were leading a troubled existence, a great number of groupings, till then amorphous, were beginning to take shape. At the same time Lacedæmon, Athens and Thebes were making vigorous efforts to reconstitute on new lines the leagues and federations which they had ruled during the Peloponnesian war and were attempting to find in them the power which would give them dominion over the Greek world.

[1] S. Ferri, *Abh. BA*, 1925, fasc. v, p. 4 *ff.*; *Notiziaro arch. d. Minist. delle Colonie*, fasc. iv (1927).
[2] *SIG²*, no. 172.

Immediately after her victory over Athens Sparta strengthened her position in the Peloponnesian league. She had at her command all the might which the authority of her harmosts and the organization of the *dekadarchoi* gave her throughout Greece. She exacted from all the cities which she had compelled to secede from the Athenian empire the tribute which they had previously paid; and from Athens herself she exacted tribute.[1] Moreover the weight of her influence was felt among the Peloponnesians. Decisions continued to be made conjointly by the Council of the confederate towns and the Spartan Assembly; but the Council no longer deliberated separately before voting; it took part only in the debates of the Assembly—a procedure which deprived it of its full liberty.[2]

During this time any attempt towards a synœcism, a sympolity or a confederation made outside the Lacedæmonian league met at once with the opposition of the oligarchic parties, who could only hope to maintain traditional privileges within the narrow framework of the autonomous cities, and with the systematic hostility of the Spartans, who wished at all costs to prevent the formation of States sufficiently extensive and powerful to stand against them. Not until the war against Corinth, the first attack directed against the hegemony of Sparta, were the Peloponnesians in a position to develop such projects. In 393, Corinth, having fallen into the power of democracy, decided to incorporate herself in Argolis. About 390, the cities of Achæa—which had always taken advantage of the festivals celebrated in the sacred wood of Zeus Homarios to come to a general understanding on foreign policy—converted this kind of amphictyony into a federation, which extended its civic privileges to an Acarnanian town.[3] Sparta did not fail to take action. Summoned to their aid by the oligarchs of Corinth she re-established the duality favourable both to their interests and her own.[4]

But what steps were to be taken against Thebes whom the confederation of 447 was making more and more powerful ?

[1] Diod., XIII, 70, 4; XIV, 10, 2; Xen., *loc. cit.*, 6, 12; II, 2, 20; Lys., *C. Nicom.*, 22; Isocr., *Paneg.*, 132; *Panath.*, 67; Arist., *Ath. Const.*, 39, 2.
[2] Xen., *Hell.*, V, 2, 12, 18.
[3] Id., *ibid.*, IV, 6, 1; cf. **XLI**, p. 416. *v.* **VII**, p. 1535, n. 1.
[4] Id., *ibid.*, 4, 5 *ff.* *v. supra*, p. 289..

What checks could be brought against Athens who was leading up to the reconstitution of her empire by treaties of defensive alliance and who was already taking it upon herself to interfere in the domestic policy of the allied cities, to change their constitutions, to impose garrisons and governors upon them, to demand contributions from them, to forbid them to give refuge to men banished from Athens ?[1]

The treaty of Antalcidas (386) was a master stroke for Spartan policy. By imposing autonomy on all Greek cities as an absolute obligation the King's Peace not only crushed the reviving Athenian empire which disturbed the Persians even more than the Spartans, but it also put an end to the Bœotian confederation, brought Corinth, detached for ever from Argos, back into the Lacedæmonian league, and, finally, made possible the dissolution of all synœcisms as contrary to the new right of the peoples.

In Bœotia the eleven federal districts were suppressed; the towns became isolated units, governing themselves as they thought best, that is according to the military dictates of Sparta.[2] All the dependencies of Thebes were taken from her[3] and, as a check against her, Platæa was reconstructed. No longer was there common money: once again every city struck its own, which, though it might have on one side the Bœotian shield as a geographical indication, on the other had its own device and its own name.[4] A series of individual treaties swelled the Peloponnesian army with new contingents.[5]

To the great joy of the oligarchs the population of Mantinea was, in 384, scattered to its five villages once more: it is chiefly from information given about this *dioikismos* that we learn of the earlier *synoikismos*.[6]

Remote Chalcidice thought itself secure. For half a century its institutions had been firmly consolidated, and, from being a sympolity, it was in a fair way to becoming a unitary State.[7] Without formally creating a federal citizen-

---

[1] Id., *ibid.*, 8, 27; *IG*, vol. II, nos. 24, 28.

[2] Xen., *op. cit.*, V, 1, 33, 36.   [3] Cf. **XLI**, p. 344 *ff.*

[4] *Ibid.*   [5] Xen., *loc. cit.*, 2, 4, 25, 29 *ff.*

[6] Id., *ibid.*, 2, 1-7; Ephor., fr. 138 (*FHG*, vol. I, p. 272); Diod., XV, 5, 12; Paus., VIII, 8, 7 *f.* Cf. *supra*, p. 289.

[7] **XXVII**, p. 149 *ff.*; **LXXIII**, p. 118-150; Swoboda, *AEM*, vol. VII (1884), p. 1 *ff.*, 47 *ff.*; **LXXI**, p. 212 *ff.*; A. B. West, *Cl. Ph.*, vol. IX (1915), p. 124 *ff.* Cf. *supra*, p. 293.

ship, a general law offered its equivalent to all Chalcidians:
if a man had civic rights in one city he automatically had
the right of marriage and the right of property in all the
others.[1] Civil equality was thus guaranteed, independently
of political equality, throughout the whole community.
Such an arrangement, binding on all the towns, in itself
implied a considerable restriction of autonomy—a restriction
equal for all, at any rate in theory. In fact the republic
officially styled itself " *koinon* of the Chalcidians."[2] It had
the exclusive right of striking money, and the cases in which
coins bear the name of Olynthus as well as that of the Chalcidians are exceptional.[3] But though ostensibly on the same
footing as the other towns, the real hegemony which the
capital exercised was barely dissimulated. The federal
Assembly sitting at Olynthus scarcely differed at all from
the Olynthian Assembly. Its powers were considerable. It
concerned itself with foreign affairs, with political treaties
and commercial agreements, it superintended military affairs,
including the direction of campaigns, chose the *strategos*, the
first magistrate of the confederation and, finally, voted the
federal contributions, which consisted of customs duties
levied in the ports and the emporia.[4] Thanks to its organization the Chalcidian State attained a comparatively strong
position. Its alliance was bought by Macedonia at the price
of commercial advantages and territorial concessions.[5] It
extended its power by drawing the peninsulas of Pallene and
Sithonia into its sphere of influence by means of the towns
of Potidæa and Torone. Success was rewarding its efforts
on all sides when two towns, called upon to enter the confederation, appealed to Sparta for help. The Spartans rushed
to their assistance (382). After three years of fighting the
sympolity was compelled to dissolve.

Sparta had worked well. In Arcadia, in Bœotia, everywhere on the continent where associations of enemy cities
were to be feared, she had re-established autonomy. But her
very triumph intensified the desire for unification wherever

---

[1] Xen., *Hell.*, V, 2, 19; cf. 12, 14.
[2] *RIG*, no. V.   [3] **XLI**, p. 208.
[4] Xen., *loc. cit.*, 15-17; Dem., *Phil.*, III, 56, 66; *RIG, loc. cit.*; *SIG*,
no. 143.
[5] *RIG, loc. cit.*

she had suppressed it.   The march on Olynthus had begun
the occupation of Thebes; in 379 Thebes was delivered by a
night attack.   At day-break the hastily summoned Assembly
appointed four Bœotarchs.[1]   It was a proclamation that the
Bœotian confederation was about to be reborn : a declaration,
too, that it could only be reborn by the consent of the whole
people, that this time it was to be democratic.   Much work
had to be done before it could reassume its former proportions : Platæa had once more to be destroyed, Thespiæ reduced
to the position of a subject State, Orchomenus to be brought
to submission, and, as it eventually turned out, razed to the
ground and its whole male population massacred.

In form and in law the new confederation resembled the
old;[2] its basic principle was the autonomy of the towns: their
privilege of citizenship was not debased into a collective
citizenship,[3] they were left the task of leading their contingent
in the army,[4] but the right of striking money was taken
from them.[5]   But, in reality, the Bœotians approached much
more nearly than before to a unitary regime, thanks to a
more powerful hegemony.   The suppression of the districts
of Thespiæ and Orchomenus and the annexation of their
territory reduced the number of Bœotarchs from eleven to
seven;[6] since Thebes kept four of them, she commanded by
herself a majority in the governing committee.   She consequently controlled foreign policy, and her representatives
at international congresses claimed that the name of Thebans
was equivalent to that of Bœotians.   There was another
important change tending strongly in the same direction: the
damos formed by the mass of the citizens was no longer
represented in the Council by a number of delegates proportioned to the importance of the towns; instead it sat in
Assembly on fixed days.[7]   Since the Assembly met at Thebes
it consisted in large part of Thebans.   All affairs and, in
particular, foreign affairs, were thus treated of directly

[1] Plut., *Pelop.*, 13 *f.*; *Ages.*, 24.
[2] Cf. **XXVII**, p. 134 *ff.*; **LXXIII**, p. 156 *ff.*; **LXXI**, p. 262 *ff.*; **VII**,
vol. II, p. 1426 *ff.*; J. H. Thiel, " De Synœcismo Bœotio post annum
379 peracto " (*Mn.*, 1926, p. 19-29).
[3] *v.* **VII**, *loc. cit.*, p. 1427, ɪ . 1.
[4] Diod., XV, 79; Paus., IX, 13, 8.   [5] *v.* **XLI**, p. 351 *ff.*
[6] *IG*, vol. VII, nos. 2407 *f.*; Diod., XV, 52, 1; 53, 3; Paus., *loc. cit.*,
6-7.
[7] Diod., *loc. cit.*, 80, 2; Paus., *loc. cit.*, 1, 5.

between the people and the Bœotarchs; for the official head
of the confederation, the eponymous magistrate, the archon,
had no power whatsoever. The Bœotarchs who formerly
had convened the Council now convened the Assembly; they
presented to it their reports, prepared its decisions and
executed them; they negotiated with the outside world and
commanded the military contingents of the seven districts.
But they were constantly in dependence on the Assembly:
they were elected by it and might be re-elected; not only did
they present their accounts to it at the end of the year, but
throughout their period of office they were responsible to it
and might be deposed.[1] Although the Assembly was competent to deal with offences violating the federal pact, side
by side with it, as previously, there operated a High Court
whose members were chosen by lot and who sat in judgment upon magistrates accused of jobbery.[2] This constitution might have led Bœotia, by a wisely prudent progression,
to a more complete unity. Unfortunately Thebes saw in it
only an excellent instrument for strengthening her foreign
policy, only a means to power.

Bœotia could never have regained her unity in 378 had
she not been covered on her southern frontier. But Athens,
similarly provoked by the perfidy and violence of Sparta, had
similarly reorganized her confederation. At the first opportunity the two countries concluded a treaty against the
common enemy,[3] and Athens, reviving the system of alliances
which she had inaugurated in 389 and had been forced to
abandon in 386, concluded analogous treaties with Chios,
Mitylene, Methymna, Rhodes and Byzantium.[4] These bilateral agreements between one city and six others were
immediately converted into a mutual pact between the seven,
and new adherents were added to the original nucleus during
succeeding years. The maritime confederation of Athens
was once more coming into being.[5]

First and foremost it was agreed that all the participating
cities should remain autonomous and enjoy equal rights in

[1] Diod., *loc. cit.*, 71, 7; 72, 2; Nep., *Epam.*, 7.
[2] Plut., *loc. cit.*, 25; Corn. Nep., *loc. cit.*, 8; Paus., IX, 14, 7.
[3] Xen., *Hell.*, V, 4, 20 *ff.*, 34; Diod., XV, 28, 3 *ff.*; 29, 6; Plut., *loc.
cit.*, 14 *f.*; *Ages.*, 24, 26.
[4] *RIG*, no. 86, A, l. 24 *ff.*, 79 *ff.*; *IG*, vol. II², nos. 40-43.
[5] *v.* CVIII.

N

the federal Council: thus the King's Peace was respected and Athenian hegemony was restricted in advance. In order completely to still the fears of those who were apprehensive of a return to the methods of the first confederation the Athenians promulgated, in February or March 377, the decree of Aristoteles. They guaranteed the autonomy promised to the cities. They undertook to interfere in no way in domestic affairs, to impose neither a governor nor a garrison upon any of them, to exact no tribute and to respect local jurisdictions. Very special guarantees were given against the establishment of cleruchs: the Athenians not only renounced all property previously acquired in federal territory, but, in addition, deprived themselves of the right of acquiring it in the future, whether under public or private claim, by purchase, mortgage or any other method. These provisions were to be valid and obligatory for ever: the author of any proposal designed to change them was to suffer *atimia* and confiscation before trial, before being condemned to death or exile.[1]

It was inevitable, however, that the new confederation should subject the autonomy of the cities to the hegemony of Athens.[2] In it were involved two principles which had to be reconciled. The association implied a dualism clearly shown in the official title which it assumed: " the Athenians and the allies " (οἱ 'Αθηναῖοι καὶ οἱ σύμμαχοι). The federal party had, therefore, to organize a conjoint mode of activity. It brought into co-operation and harmonious working the deliberative organs of Athens and a federal Council, the " Synedrion of the allies " (συνέδριον τῶν συμμάχων), in which the Athenians were not represented, but which sat permanently at Athens.[3] Thus were made " the resolutions of the allies and the Athenian people," the *dogmata* which determined the federal constitution (τὰ δόγματα τῶν συμμάχων καὶ τοῦ δήμου τῶν 'Αθηναίων).[4] Each city might send one or several *synedroi* or representatives,[5] but it had only one vote: since the ballot was taken on a simple majority principle, Athens was fairly well assured of the

---

[1] *RIG, loc. cit.*, l. 51 *ff.*
[2] Diod., XV, 28, 3; 29, 6; Xen., *Rev.*, V, 6.
[3] *IG, loc. cit.*, nos. 96, 103; Isocr., *De Pace*, 29; *Plat.*, 21; Æschin., *Emb.*, 86.
[4] *IG, loc. cit.*, no. 96; cf. nos. 43, 44, 123.
[5] Single delegates: *IG, loc. cit.*, nos. 124, 232; several: nos. 96, 107.

co-operation of the small cities. Obviously such a system, which aspired to secure equilibrium between a great power and a group of small independent powers, could endure so long as common safety was in danger, but not indefinitely. All went well till 371. The relations of the Synedrion and the Athenian Ecclesia and Boule were in conformity with the provisions of the federal pact. Athens possessed the initiative and control in foreign affairs, but she did nothing decisive without consulting her allies. Since it was she who had created the confederation by separate treaties, she continued to treat with cities who wished to enter it, and admission was announced by a decree of the Assembly issued on the recommendation of the Council.[1] But the matter was of vital concern to the Synedrion, since it involved the introduction of a new member with a right to vote and since all the confederates were bound, in case of aggression against one of their number, to lend assistance by land and by sea with all their resources and all their power. Moreover, the exchange of mutual pledges, without which admission was not complete, entailed the assembling of the allies, the parties to the oath and, consequently, the consent of the Synedrion.[2] But treaties which were concluded with States which were and remained outside the confederation were submitted to the Athenian Assembly alone by a *probouleuma* of the Boule based on a *dogma* of the Synedrion,[3] and did not become binding on any city unless it pledged itself to it. Again, in 371, at the congress of Sparta, whilst the Lacedæmonians took the oath both for themselves and their allies, the Athenian confederates swore separately, town by town, after Athens had done so.[4] It was exactly the opposite of what took place at the peace of Nicias,[5] and nothing shows better the path followed by Sparta and Athens for half a century. In short, all the decisions which concerned the confederation were made at this time in the same way as the constitutional *dogmata* had been: the Synedrion could do nothing without the Ecclesia, nor the Ecclesia without the Synedrion. There resulted a *modus vivendi* which established a division of powers between Athens and the confederates.

[1] *SIG*[3], nos. 146, 148. [2] *Ibid.*, nos. 149, 150.
[3] Again after 371; *ibid.*, nos. 159, 181; Æschin., *loc. cit.*, 60 *ff.*; C. Ctes., 69 *ff.*, 74.
[4] Xen., *Hell.*, VI, 3, 19; cf. *SIG*[3], no. 159. [5] Thuc., V, 18, 9.

N*

The hegemony of Athens consisted essentially in the control of foreign affairs, in the command of the federal army and in the free disposition of the fleet, which was almost exclusively composed of Athenian ships. Over everything else the Synedrion had supreme control. By the very fact that the federal pact forbade the levying of a *phoros* the confederation could only raise money with the consent of its members. The common treasure did not belong " to the Athenians and the allies," but to the allies alone. There was no tribute, there were no contributions (συνταξεις).[1] Assessed, allotted, collected and administered by the Synedrion they neither could nor ought to be used save for common expenses, in particular for war.[2] If they rapidly increased it was because the majority of the cities soon sought to buy themselves out of military service, which originally had been the most important of their obligations. In this way fines imposed by federal jurisdiction accrued to the common treasury. The confederation had, in fact, a right of supreme jurisdiction. Before the Synedrion sitting as a high court appeared individuals or persons accused of violation of the federal pact. In accordance with the decree of Aristoteles, the guarantee of this pact, the Synedrion received denunciations against Athenians guilty of acquiring land in the territory of the confederate towns, confiscated the property in question and divided the proceeds of its sale between the informer and the common treasury.[3] In accordance with the same decree any citizen or magistrate who should propose or put to the vote a motion whose object was the rescission of any clause whatsoever, " should be judged before the Athenians and the confederates as guilty of seeking to dissolve the confederation, and should be punished by death or banishment from Athenian and confederate territory," without prejudice to the preliminary confiscation of his goods.[4] These were provisions of the highest importance. They indicate so compliant an attitude on the part of Athens towards her confederates that they call for certain modifications in order not to appear improbable. It must be recognized that in a case

[1] Theop., fr. 97 (*FHG*, vol. I, p. 294); cf. *IG, loc. cit.*, no. 126, l. 13 *ff.*
v. **CVIII**, p. 38 *ff.*
[2] Isocr., *Antid.*, 113; Xen., *loc. cit.*, 2, 1; cf. *IG, loc. cit.*, nos. 123, 207.
[3] *RIG*, no. 86, A, l. 44 *ff.*   [4] *Ibid.*, l. 51 *ff.*

where the Synedrion was both judge and party Athens did not deliver her citizens to it bound hand and foot. The Synedrion, which, in general, was on the same footing as the Athenian Boule, doubtless could not, any more than the latter, give executory force to all its judgments: beyond certain penal limits the condemned man, if he were an Athenian, had to be allowed the right of appeal to Athenian jurisdiction. Nevertheless the pact of the second Athenian confederation marks a wholly remarkable step forward in international law.

Sparta was forced to accept all these developments, though she made some attempt to stand against them. She employed at first the same methods as her adversaries. She wished to oppose to the Thebans and the Athenians a league stronger than theirs by strengthening her hegemony: but, military city that she was, she could only think in terms of her army. Already in 383-2, just as she was entering upon the war against Chalcidice, she had authorized the Peloponnesian States, at a congress which was held, to buy themselves out of service: a serious innovation, which enabled professional soldiers to be recruited, but which disaccustomed the citizens to fighting. In 378, in order to outwit Thebes and the Athenian confederation, she divided all the countries dependent on her into ten recruiting divisions: (1) Lacedæmon; (2 and 3) Arcadia; (4) Elis; (5) Achæa; (6) Corinth and Megara; (7) Sicyon, Philus and the coast towns of Argolis; (8) Acarnania; (9) Phocis and Locris; (10) Chalcidice.[1] But, in 375, the sympolity of the Chalcidians, which Sparta had just destroyed, was reconstructed and, to protect itself against retaliatory attacks, incorporated in the Athenian confederation.[2] The Acarnanian population was scattered in villages and for long they had come together only for purposes of war. They had resolved, however, to create a common representative body at Stratos and to strike common money,[3] but, in 390, they had been compelled to accept Spartan domination.[4] At the same time as the Chalcideans they took a similar step.[5]

In 371 Sparta decided to adopt other tactics. She convoked representatives of all the powers to a congress at which

[1] Diod., XV, 31, 2.   [2] RIG, loc. cit., l. 80.
[3] Xen., Hell., IV, 6, 4; **XLI**, p. 328 ff.
[4] Xen., loc. cit., 7, 1; Ages., II, 20.
[5] RIG, loc. cit., B, l. 5; SIG³, no. 150.

a general peace, based on the King's Peace, was to be concluded. Everyone was in agreement on that score, but it remained to be seen what were their conceptions of autonomy and
how they reconciled them with federal law. On the day appointed for the oath the Lacedæmonians swore as such in the
name of all their allies; no one objected. With the Athenians
all the allied States swore in succession. The Thebans
were of the number. They swore to and counter-signed the
instrument of peace, while adding to the name of " Thebans "
a note specifying that their oath and their signature were
valid for all the Bœotians. Protests were raised against this
interpretation. The Thebans then asked that the name of
Bœotians should be substituted for that of Thebans. This
would have meant the formal recognition by the whole of
Greece of the federal State. The Lacedæmonians declined
absolutely to agree to this change; the Thebans stuck to their
last proposal and rejected a treaty which would have nullified
in one day the efforts and the successes of eight years.[1] It
was the definitive rupture with Sparta and with Athens.
A month later the power of Sparta was shattered on the plain
of Leuctra (August, 371).

A new epoch began for all the associations of cities.
Thebes had a free hand not only in Bœotia but also beyond
her northern frontiers. On top of the confederation on
which she could rely, she erected another and a vaster one,
which she created in central Greece. The Phocians, the
Locrians and the Heracleans, detached from the Lacedæmonian league, united with their neighbours the Malians and
the Ænianians and were joined by a section of the Acarnanians,
by the Eubœans and soon by the Byzantines, the latter having
seceded from the Athenian confederation. All these peoples
undertook to defend each other in case of aggression; they
sent their delegates to a Synedrion which sat at Thebes and
recognized the obligatory force of decisions made by their
representatives in concert with the Bœotian representatives.[2]

But it was too much to ask of the good will of the ones
and the moderation of the others. The Phocians never

---

[1] Xen., *Hell.*, VI, 3, 19 *f.*
[2] Diod., XV, 57, 62, 85; Xen., *loc. cit.*, 5, 23; VII, 3, 11; 5, 4; *Ages.*,
II, 24; *RIG*, no. 617.

agreed with the Thebans, and when they were accused of sacrilege by their enemies before the Amphictyonic Council and sentenced to an enormous fine, they rushed to arms (356) and re-established a confederation which had had a vague existence for at least two centuries.[1] The citizens of their twenty-two towns met in an Assembly to exercise power of war and peace and to appoint or, if necessary, to depose magistrates.[2] During the Sacred War the chief of these magistrates were the *strategoi*.[3] One of these, the *strategos autokrator*, had the supreme command of the army; he was invested with the powers of a dictator and on the coins his name replaced that of the Phocians which formerly had been there:[4] he had even the right of naming his successor, a right which, in fact, placed the country under the domination of a dynasty. In 346 Phocis, defeated, disarmed and more than half deserted, was placed under archons, while her federal obligations were confined to paying the victors every six months a crushing war tax.[5]

Among the Arcadians the defeat of Sparta justified all hopes. Hardly had Epaminondas appeared in the Peloponnese (Spring, 370) than they took their revenge. The Mantineans of the five villages rebuilt their town and re-established their synœcism;[6] they set up a government of limited democracy which suited peasants too busy to frequent the Assembly and who preferred to leave everyday business to the elected magistrates.[7] Immediately afterwards, in response to the appeal of the Mantinean Lycomedes, all the Arcadians, save those of the North, decided to form a State on the model of the Bœotian confederation.[8] A capital was needed, and, in order to avoid competition between Mantinea and Tegea, the two age-long rivals, a commission of ten *oikistai* was appointed to undertake the foundation of a new city. In 369 the great town of Megalopolis arose. The dimensions of its walls were such that in case of need it could house all the Arcadians of the South-west and the Centre, along with their flocks.

---

[1] Cf. **VII**, vol. II, p. 1447.
[2] Diod., XVI, 23, 6; 24, 1; 27, 2; 32, 2-4; Paus., X, 2, 3 and 7.
[3] Diod., *loc. cit.*, 35, 1; 56, 3, 7.   [4] Cf. **XLI**, p. 339.
[5] *SIG*³, nos. 230-235; cf. p. 320.
[6] Xen., *Hell.*, VI, 5, 3-5. Cf. p. 338, 423. *v.* **XXII**, p. 596 *ff.*
[7] Arist., *Pol.*, VIII (VI), 2, 2.
[8] Xen., *loc. cit.*, 6-22; VII, 1, 23; Diod., XV, 59, 1; 67, 2.

Its population was to be recruited immediately from the Mainalians, the Eutresians, the Parrhasians, the Cynurians, the people of Ægytis, Skiritis, Tripolis, etc., and it was to absorb at least forty districts.[1]

The new State, " the Arcadicon,"[2] thus formed by a synœcism, was given a federal regime. The cities retained their autonomy, their old institutions, their Council, their magistrates and they continued to have their own coinage side by side with the common coinage.[3] There was no federal citizenship above local citizenship: men were Arcadians with the names of Tegeans, Mantineans, etc. But the sympolity was the more able to restrain the sovereignty of the cities in that they were very soon divided into political districts after the Athenian fashion. The federal constitution was strongly reminiscent of limited democracy. It recognized no hegemony, but gave the cities representation in proportion to their population. The citizen body was constituted by the Ten Thousand,[4] that is to say probably by property owners in a position to serve as hoplites at their own expense, to the exclusion of the poor. All these, but only these, had access to the Assembly or Ecclesia.[5] An immense building, the Thersilion, was constructed at Megalopolis for the Assembly. Its powers extended to all important affairs: it concluded treaties of peace and alliance, declared war, sent and received ambassadors, regulated the pay of the troops, fixed the entrance fees of the cities, conferred honorific distinctions. To its deliberative power it added judicial power: it passed sentences on federal or civic magistrates or on ordinary citizens convicted of infringement of the federal statutes or of resistance to federal decrees, and it arbitrated in disputes which arose between cities.[6] Since the Assembly sat only at intervals and since it was too numerous to prepare legislative work, it had for auxiliary a Council or Boule. But the only

1 Parian Marble, 73; Paus., VIII, 27, 3 ff.; Diod., XV, 72; 4. v. **XXIII**, p. 115.
2 Xen., *loc. cit.*, VI, 5, 6, 11 f., 22, etc.
3 Id., *ibid.*, 4; VII, 4, 33; *BCH*, vol. XXXIX (1915), p. 55, l. 3 ff.; IG, vol. V, ii, nos. 351-357; **XLI**, p. 444, 449.
4 *SIG*³, no. 183; Harp., *s.v.* μύριοι; Diod., XV, 59, 1; Xen., *Hell.*, VII, 4, 35 ff.
5 Phylarch., fr. 65 (*FHG*, vol. I, p. 354).
6 Xen., *loc. cit.*, 4, 33; 5, 38; *BCH*, *loc. cit.*, p. 53 ff.; IG, *loc. cit.*, no. 343, A, l. 9 ff.

body which functioned permanently was an executive committee of fifty members. It represented the towns unequally, having five delegates per town from seven of them, two and three from two others, and ten from Megalopolis. They were officially called *demiourgoi*; but since they shared among themselves the different administrative functions and thus formed colleges of magistrates, they were often called *archons*.[1] Since military and diplomatic affairs were of primary importance the chief magistrate of the confederation was the *strategos*,[2] who had at his command a permanent army-corps, the *eparitai*.

Such an attack on the immemorial principles of autonomy and isolation, the compulsory transfer of a considerable mass of men and the necessary re-allotments of land, created many difficulties and provoked much resistance. Some small towns furnished Megalopolis with only a part of the contingent demanded and existed as more or less free communities; the inhabitants of some flatly refused to abandon their houses and their lands, and had to be compelled by force, the *eparitai* being marched out against them. We know of one, Trapezous, whose population was massacred or emigrated to the Euxine. As early as 363 the old animosities of cities were reviving, exacerbated by bitter disagreements on domestic policy. There was a scission. Mantinea reverted to oligarchy and began to make advances to Sparta; Tegea, supporting the capital, remained faithful to democracy and the Theban alliance. In the battle of Mantinea (362) the Arcadians fought among themselves, either for or against Epaminondas. A reconciliation was effected, but it was neither general nor permanent. In 361 the peasants returned *en masse* to their old homes, and in order to make them return to the capital a Theban army had to accomplish a systematic destruction of the villages.[3] So difficult was it for the Greeks to renounce their local independence in favour of even a limited union !

And yet the formation of the Megalopoliticon marked a notable advance in the struggle against centrifugal forces. For the first time Arcadia possessed its " great town," and one whose area covered a third of the federal territory. Moreover

---

[1] *SIG*³, *loc. cit.*, l. 9 *ff.*; Xen., *loc. cit.*, l. 24; 4, 33 *ff.*
[2] Xen., *loc. cit.*, 3, 1; Diod., XV, 62, 2.
[3] Diod., XV, 94; Paus., VIII, 27, 7.   *v.* **VII**, vol. II, p. 1404.

her example influenced the surrounding districts, even those which had stood apart from the movement. The villages of Triphylia united at Lepreon and henceforth adhered to the Arcadian confederation.[1] The canton of Heræa, midway between Arcadia and Elis, was converted into a city with nine demes.[2] Since three localities neighbouring upon Orchomenus had joined the confederation the Orchomenians, to counteract the weakness resulting from their isolation, annexed the Euaimmians by synœcism, by concluding with them a very curious agreement with clauses concerning religion, marriage, justice, the division of lands and common liability for public debts.[3]

The Athenian confederation could not escape from repercussions of the great events which had distinguished the year 371. The congress of Sparta was for it the beginning of the breach with Bœotia, while the battle of Leuctra removed the Spartan menace. Like Thebes, Athens immediately sought to turn the situation to account. All the cities who wished to maintain the King's Peace and, consequently, autonomy in its narrowest sense, were invited to send plenipotentiaries to Athens. This meant the exclusion of the Thebans. Whilst the latter consoled themselves with creating the confederation of central Greece the congress of Athens resolved upon the formation of a Hellenic league which was to embrace in one large unity Lacedæmon with its league and Athens with its confederation.[4] A spectacular conception and superficially full of promise, but in reality it was no more than a paltry diplomatic success, doomed to die as soon as it was born. Sparta being no longer formidable and Thebes becoming day by day more hostile, the members of the Athenian confederation very soon found irksome the bonds which tied them to the latter. Discontent was to lead to defection, and the struggle against defection was to justify and intensify the discontent. The hegemony of Athens, light, on the whole, from 378 to 371, was going, therefore, to weigh heavily upon the federal constitution and to distort its originally equitable provisions.

Henceforth mutual distrust characterized the relations of

---

[1] *SIG*[3], *loc. cit.*; *Fouilles de Delphes*, vol. III, i, no. 3; Xen., *loc. cit.*, 1, 33.

[2] Strab., VIII, 3, 2, p. 337.   [3] *BCH*, *loc. cit.*, p. 98 *ff*.

[4] Xen., *Hell.*, VI, 5, 1-3.

the Synedrion and the Ecclesia. Athens had the right to treat alone with powers outside the confederation, provided that the latter was not involved, but it was very difficult for the undertakings made by the principal city not to become binding upon the others indirectly, and, on the other hand, it was very easy for Athens to abuse her right by concluding alone treaties which directly concerned her associates. The fact that certain decrees, relating to alliances binding only upon Athens, were nevertheless adopted only after consultation with the confederate States was merely a pandering to the *amour-propre* of punctilious partners. All that the Synedrion could do now when it really took part in negotiations of federal interest was to present its *dogmata* to the Ecclesia through the medium of the Boule or, at the very most, if the Boule consented, bring them before the Ecclesia itself.[1] In any case the decrees of the people alone had force, whether they were in accordance with or opposed to the *dogmata*: the *synedroi* were compelled to take with the Athenian jurors the customary oath,[2] and if one of them were to be included in an embassy sent for further negotiations, it was the Ecclesia which chose him.[3] Sometimes, moreover, the Synedrion did not even bother to conceal the real state of affairs: a *dogma* might declare in advance that whatever was decided by the Athenian Assembly would be regarded as " a common resolution of the allies."[4] In short, in place of being a legislative organ on the same footing as the Ecclesia, the Synedrion had degenerated into a consultative body like the Boule.

Was it likely that, under these conditions, the other guarantees given to the confederates would stand against the encroachments of a hegemony which became the more exacting the more it was contested ?

The financial system was completely upset. In principle, the *syntaxis* was only paid by towns which did not furnish a naval contingent,[5] but, in fact, the defection of the large towns, who alone were in a position to have a navy, resulted in all the towns which remained faithful paying in specie, and thus the contribution strongly resembled tribute. A correlation was established between the right to sit in the Synedrion and

---

[1] *SIG*³, no. 181; cf. no. 184.
[2] Æschin., *Emb.*, 60 *ff.*; *C. Ctes.*, 69 *ff.*, 74.
[3] Id., *Emb.*, 21, 97, 126.
[4] Id., *ibid.*, 20.   [5] Isocr., *Peace*, 2.

the obligation. to send the *syntaxis*.[1] Nor did the Synedrion any longer fix the sums to be paid: the Athenian Assembly directed foreign policy, therefore it was for her to estimate the cost. Even if a town made an agreement with a *strategos* as to the proportion which was to fall to it, the agreement was only valid after ratification by the Ecclesia.[2] It was Athens alone who gave orders to each town either to send funds to the federal treasury or to hand them over to such and such a *strategos* for such and such a purpose, or to send them to the commander of its garrison for the payment of his men.[3] If there were delay once more it was the Athenians who elected officials to undertake the collection of arrears, by force if necessary.[4]

As to the judicial power of the Synedrion one might almost say that it had ceased to exist. In 357-6 certain members of the confederation had taken part in an attack upon the confederate town of Eretria. Here was an occasion, if ever, for federal jurisdiction to intervene. But it was the Ecclesia which took action. A decree ordered the Boule to prepare rules of penal procedure for prosecuting the guilty and laid down that, for the future, the taking of arms against Eretria or any other town of the confederation would entail the penalty of death and total confiscation for the benefit of the federal exchequer.[5]

Even the autonomy of the towns suffered rude assaults after defections had made counteraction necessary. Athens despatched everywhere garrisons and governors to superintend affairs. She interfered in internal conflicts in favour of democracy and demanded high payment for her services. After having established peace at Ceos she permitted insurgents to appeal from local justice to her tribunals, then extended that ruling to all sentences, while at the same time she obtained for herself a monopoly for the exportation of red-lead.[6] On one point, however, Athens respected the promises made in 378-7: she did not send cleruchs into federal territory. But

---

¹ Id., *ibid.*, 29; Æschin., *C. Ctes.*, 93.
² Cf. *RIG*, no. 1463, *b*; Ps. Dem., *C. Theocr.*, 37.
³ Plut., *Phoc.*, 7; Isocr., *Antid.*, 113; Ps. Dem. *C. Timoth.*, 49; *IG*, vol. II², nos. 123, 207.
⁴ *RIG*, nos. 95, 600, 1463; cf. Dem., *On the Aff. of Chers.*, 26.
⁵ *RIG*, no. 1455.
⁶ *Ibid.*, nos. 95, 401; cf. *IG*, vol. II², no. 179.

at the close of 366-5 she did not hesitate to post them on strategic points which were not amenable to the confederation or had been reconquered after defection: at Samos,[1] at Potidæa,[2] in Chersonesus.[3]   There was much to disquiet even those who were not themselves menaced.

The general transformation of an hegemony which ill concealed its weakness by its violence was inevitably to provoke resistance and revolt.   At first there were partial risings which were suppressed.   Then the cities formed local unions.   To enable themselves to secede the four towns of Ceos, Carthæa, Poiessa, Ioulis and Coressus formed a sympolity.   Each retained its Council and its Assembly which continued to confer local citizenship:[4] but they had a joint Council, a joint Assembly, a common privilege of citizenship and the prerogative of supreme sovereignty, a common coinage.[5]   About the same time Byzantium conceded its privilege of citizenship to two towns of lesser importance, Selymbria and Chalcedon.[6]   Finally the Social War, the war of secession, broke out.   In two years (357-355) the confederation was shattered.   The Athenians retained only fragments, which were soon to be taken from them by the Macedonian conquest.

IV

THE LEAGUE OF CORINTH

In the face of these multifarious attempts to introduce a little unity into the anarchic relations of the cities, attempts which almost invariably ended in the violent clashing of groups, one is at first bewildered as at the sight of innumerable waves rising, crashing and annihilating each other.   If, however, one ignores the historical contingencies which produced and destroyed this welter of associations two great currents can be distinguished.

---

[1] Crater, fr. 15 (*FHG*, vol. II, p. 622); Philoch., fr. 131 (*ibid.*, vol. I, p. 405).

[2] *SIG*³, no. 180; Diod., XV, 108, 113; Dem., *Phil.*, II, 20.

[3] Dem., *ibid.*, III, 15; *On the Aff. of Chers.*, 6.

[4] Cf. *RIG*, nos. 403, 404, 406.

[5] *v. IG*, vol. XII, v, p. xxxvi; **LXXIII**, p. 138 *f.*; Swoboda, *Sb. WA*, CXCIX, ii (1926), p. 38 *ff.*

[6] Dem., *De Rhod. Lib.*, 26; Theop., fr. 65 (*FHG*, vol. I, p. 287).

On the one hand there was the system of federal leagues, such as the Lacedæmonian league and the Athenian confederation. They grouped together allied cities widely separated, giving them the minimum of common government, without general citizenship, without any means of direct control over individuals. In theory they left to each city almost complete autonomy in all that concerned domestic policy, and their sovereignty consisted solely in the control of diplomatic and military affairs. Having for nucleus a State much more powerful than the rest, they acknowledged the hegemony of that State. They were, therefore, subjected to a dualist regime whose balance was inevitably precarious. Since the principal organ of the league was a Council in which all the cities had an equal voice and whose decisions were binding upon all, the dominant city was successful for a longer or shorter period in grouping round herself a majority. But when the purpose for which the league had been founded had been achieved (the struggle against the Persians or Sparta, the struggle against Athens), the hegemony no longer rendered the services which were its justification, it appeared and became oppressive; in order to maintain itself it supported a party in each city, until the moment came when the principle of autonomy took its revenge and gained once more the upper hand.

On the other hand there sprang up a mass of federal leagues which bound together neighbouring and congeneric cities (Bœotians, Chalcidians, Arcadians, etc.). These were the sympolities. They respected in the mass the anterior privileges of the cities: and even though they never attained to complete unity, they did not fall far short. They had a federal citizenship which was based on local citizenship; that is to say every citizen of any one of the towns was a citizen of the confederation: being a Theban made a man a Bœotian; by the very fact that a man was a Tegean he was also an Arcadian. From one town to another the articles of the confederation assured civil rights, but not political rights: it is probable that in the majority of sympolities, as in those of the Chalcidians and the Orchomenians, a citizen of the confederation had the right of free residence, of lawful marriage, and of property on all federal territory. This provision is sufficient to show that, in certain cases, the activity of the confederation extended to the individuals of particular towns without the intermediary of local authorities. It is evident, moreover, that its institutions led of themselves towards unification by their political colour, by favouring either democracy or oligarchy. However varied federal sovereignty might be in regard to its constitution and its particular treaties, it had always for symbol the right of striking money, which further implies a common system of weights and measures, for principal functions the direction of foreign policy and the administration of the army, for guarantee a supreme jurisdiction. According as the government was oligarchic, democratic or semi-democratic deliberative power pertained to a Council, to an Assembly or to both: but executive power was never exercised save by high magistrates o a diplomatic or military order, *Bœotarchs* or *strategoi*. That fact alone forbids one to rate too highly the progress realized by the sympolities in the direction of centralization. Fundamentally it was still a question of alliance, of common defence, of opposing groups, and the ideal was not the attainment of Hellenic unity but the formation of a small State on the model of Attica or Laconia.

Hellenic unity was only realized after the catastrophe of Chæronea, and then by Philip of Macedon and at the point of the sword. The conqueror was not content with having subjugated the Greeks of Europe; he wished to pose as the champion of the Panhellenic idea in order to extend his authority over those of Asia. If the forces of his old friends and his old enemies were to be amalgamated, a general peace and a mutual understanding were essential. He convoked delegates of all the cities to Corinth. To this constituent assembly he gave his instructions—instructions which were commands. In this way a league was formed which recalled in many respects the hegemonic leagues of the past, but which was differentiated from them by certain essential traits: the unlimited authority of a sole head and definitive intervention in the domestic policy of the cities.[1]

[1] The principal sources are: Diod., XVI, 89; Just., IX, 5; *SIG*³, no. 260; cf. Ps. Dem., *On the Treaty with Alex.*, 4 *ff.*; *IG*, vol. II², no. 329. *v.* A. Wilhelm, " Urkunden d. korinth. Bundes " (*Sb. WA*, vol. CLXV, ii, 1911); U. Wilcken, " Beitr. z. Gesch. d. korinth. Bundes " (*Sb. MA*, 1917, fasc. x); Id., *ibid.*, 1922, p. 142 *ff.*; **XLVI**, p. 268 *ff.*, 526 *ff.*; cf. **VII**, vol. II, p. 1389 *ff.*

The official name of this league of Corinth was very simple: " the Hellenes " (οἱ "Ελληνες); it was only in common speech that it was spoken of as " the confederation of the Hellenes " (τὸ κοινὸν τῶν Ἑλλήνων). The Macedonians did not form part of it, for general opinion did not recognize them as Hellenes; but their king, with all his power, was the chief, the *hegemon*, of the league. At the beginning of the federal charter came the inevitable bait: all the cities are free and autonomous; they shall not receive garrisons nor shall they pay tribute. But in this one there are unusual restrictions upon the principle postulated: the league must resist any attempt made to overthrow existing constitutions (constitutions which were for the most part oligarchic, thanks to a vigorous pressure exercised by Philip for several months). In addition, it prohibited unlawful executions and banishments, confiscations, any new divisions of lands, all wholesale emancipation of slaves. In short, it was its privilege and duty to interfere everywhere where the need was felt, to protect the propertied classes against revolution. Consequently every city was bound to prevent exiles from preparing on its territory armed attacks against any other city of the league. In a more general fashion, the cities in their relations with one another had to remain faithful to the sworn peace, to place no shackles on the freedom of the seas and to settle their differences by judicial methods, that is by means of the arbitration of a third party. All were bound not only themselves to refrain from machinations against peace, but to assist with their contingent in repulsing attacks upon any one of them, and to consider the violator of the treaty as excluded from the peace, as a common enemy.

The organ of the league was the Council, the " Synedrion of the Hellenes " (συνέδριον τῶν Ἑλλήνων or κοινόν).[1] It was representative of the cities. The delegations of which it was composed, however, had not all an equal voice as in the earlier constitutions of the Peloponnesian league and the Athenian confederation, but one or more votes in proportion to the population represented, in accordance with the principle adopted by the Bœotians and the Arcadians.[2] Usually it

[1] *RIG*, nos. 14, 33; Just., *loc. cit.*, 2; Æschin., *C. Ctes.*, 161, 254; cf. *P. Oxy.*, vol. I, p. 25, col. III, l. 27; Diod., *loc. cit.*, 3; XVII, 73, 5.
[2] *SIG*³, *loc. cit.*; *v.* A. Larsen, " Representative Govern. in the Panhellenic Leagues " (*Cl. Ph.*, vol. XX, 1925, p. 313 *ff.*; vol. XXI, 1926, p. 52 *ff.*).

sat at Corinth and concerned itself with all federal affairs, with questions of peace and war principally, but also with all questions relating to the political and social control of the cities. In order to maintain legal order and to secure arbitration upon differences which arose among them, it worked in conjunction with special magistrates. It acted as a supreme Court to deal with all violations of the federal pact and with acts of high treason: it might, for instance, sit in judgment upon a citizen of a federated town who took service in a foreign army against the league or its chief, and could condemn him to exile or confiscate his property.[1] But the Synedrion of the Hellenes was merely a tool in the hands of a master. It was the *hegemon* who convoked it or ordered it to be convoked by a mandatory; it was he probably who appointed, like *missi dominici*, persons whose duty it was, together with the Council, to watch over suspect cities. He was omnipotent, because his name was Philip, because his name was to be Alexander, because he was and remained, as his title indicates, the commander of the army, the leader in war. As a first move he ordered a census to be made in all the cities of men in a position to bear arms, in order to establish a percentage for the determining of contingents to be demanded: he needed 200,000 foot-soldiers and 15,000 horsemen.

Such was the unity achieved at the bidding of the Macedonian. No longer leagues which split Greece into two, no longer small confederations, but the whole of Greece organized in a *koinon* and proclaiming compulsory concord.

But we must see what, in reality, this peace was and what the political and social value of the union which was effected. What was this peace? The first act of the newly born league was a vote for war against the Persians and the appointment of Philip as *strategos autokrator*. Without gaining a respite from internal dissensions Greece was constantly to be exposed to repercussions of the tempests which were shattering the world. And the principles which were to guide the coming generations? We have a foretaste of these in reading the clause of the federal pact which, desiring to maintain for ever the existing order, forbade the emancipation of slaves as a revolutionary measure.

[1] *RIG*, no. 33, l. 10 *ff.*; Æschin., *ll. cc.*; Hyper., *P. Euxen.*, 20; Dem., *De Coron.*, 201.

CONCLUSION

THE END OF THE GREEK CITY

THE victory of Philip at Chæronea and the formation of the Panhellenic league mark an epoch in the history of the world: they give a specific date to that outstanding event, the end of the Greek city. The death of the system was not un-announced: for long years it had kept itself alive only with difficulty: nor was it so complete as to prevent the survival of time-honoured institutions in the new regime. But it was at the close of 338 that the Greek cities really ceased to be free and that the whole of Greece became a mere dependency of a foreign country.

Was this a good thing or a bad ? It is a question which historians are only justified in asking if an objective method of solving it can be found.

Most of them have no doubts whatsoever: by the sweeping away of innumerable frontiers Greece attained to a certain degree of territorial unity, and, by the conquest of Asia, opened up a vast field for her civilization. Since the end of the nineteenth century German scholars have agreed in this interpretation; but they have given the question a particular bent: they are for Philip against Demosthenes, for the military monarchy and against the *Advokatenrepublic*.[1]   In earlier days, one of them has said,[2] one might have been mistaken on this point, but to-day we know how tremendously important to antiquity was the northern power which imposed unity on Greece by fire and the sword and sealed it by its war against the *Erbfeind*. " It is natural," concludes the same author, " that an epoch such as ours, which reverences the will of authority, which justifies the violation of political rights by a higher right, which endeavours to extend national policy into world policy, should find its own characteristics

---

[1] Cf. Drerup, *Aus einer alten Advokatenrepublic*, 1916.
[2] Lenschau, in Bursian, vol. CXXII (1904), p. 254-256, 268; see other quotations of the same kind in **LVI**, p. 54, 221.

in the work of Philip and his glorious son and should place itself unreservedly on the side of Macedonia." Perhaps we shall not find here the objective criterion we are looking for.

It is, nevertheless, true that after 338 the field of Greek history has different dimensions than before. That is one stable point. At first glance—and too often one limits oneself to that—it seems a sign of an enormous advance. But one must look more closely. It is the wrong approach to estimate things in the light of figures. We cannot answer the question simply by comparing the area and the population of the new State with those of the old, for the progress of civilization is to be measured neither by the square mile nor by so many thousands of inhabitants. The quantitative point of view, however, is by no means negligible when it throws light upon the vast extension of a superior civilization. And it is certainly true that in the Hellenistic epoch new fires were kindled in all parts, giving to Greek civilization a radiation which it had never known before.

Undoubtedly the bonds between Greece and the East had multiplied long before the Macedonian conquest. Throughout the fourth century Lydia, Caria, Phœnicia, Egypt and Persia had felt the influence of Hellenism. As in the time of the Philhellenic Mermnadæ, Sardis was more than half Greek. The dynasts of Halicarnassus employed western architects to adorn their capital with magnificent monuments; the most illustrious of them commissioned Scopas and Praxiteles to embellish the " Mausoleum." In the Phœnician ports there was a craze for Cyprian and Ionian dancing girls;[1] while the kings of Sidon brought in artists of the West to carve for them magnificent sarcophagi. On the banks of the Nile Alexandrian art dawned before the foundation of Alexandria;[2] throughout the whole empire the last monuments raised by the Achemenidæ and the beautiful darics which the satraps, the princes and the king lavished on their mercenaries, testified that Greek art had passed that way. The presence of the physician Ctesias at the court of Artaxerxes and the permission given to this foreigner to collect the documents of the country in order to write a history, proclaimed the fact

[1] Theop., fr. 126 (*FHG*, vol. I, p. 299).
[2] *v.* W. Schur, " Zur Vorgesch. des Ptolemäerreiches " (*Klio.*, vol. XX 1920, p. 270 *ff.*).

that the Greek world and the Oriental world were ready to bow down together in the worship of the arts and sciences. These developments were rich in promise. Greek civilization was ripe for universality.

But the civic system could not provide the necessary political conditions. A different organization was needed before Greece could fulfil its mission, and this Macedonia supplied. Henceforth Hellenism had for centre countries which hitherto had marked its extreme limits and had felt its influence only intermittently. From India to the gulf of Liguria, from Istria to Ethiopia, there was but one market, everywhere swarming with Greek traders. The moral barriers which separated Greek from barbarian were broken down, and the philosophers whose one thought had been to strengthen them were succeeded by cosmopolitan theorists.

We have yet to see whether Greece obtained from unity all the advantages which she might expect and whether her civilization did not lose by its extension some of its essential qualities.

The centuries which followed the Macedonian conquest were not blessed with that peace which the league of Corinth had promised. The cities had experienced to the full unending rivalries, interminable wars which went on in an unbroken chain like the old family vendettas. But they were in no better position now when they formed part of great States and were reduced to a sort of municipal autonomy; they continued to quarrel among themselves, to form sympolities which, in their turn, were dragged into incessant conflicts, and the two leagues which, at the end, divided practically the whole of Greece between them, embarked on a struggle which culminated for both in the total and definitive loss of independence. The great difference from the past was that the wars in which the Greeks now engaged among themselves were, in addition, entangled with wars in which the Diadochi, the heads of the great States, sought to aggrandize themselves still further. A perpetual shedding of blood, but henceforth over immense areas, such was the " peace " of Corinth. One can apply to it the words which in Xenophon follow the account of the battle of Mantinea and bring the *Hellenica* to a conclusion: " And afterwards there was greater anarchy and turmoil in Greece than before."

But if we look at the internal affairs of the States we see an entirely new world. Political forms are radically different. To the republican city monarchy has succeeded.

Here again we are faced with a change which could not have been brought about at one stroke had not men's minds and the facts paved the way for it. It had been in preparation, indeed, since the end of the fifth century. Even then class solidarity was, if we may use that term, a collective egoism. The feeling was: make way for those who feel themselves strong enough to rise above parties and to seize absolute power. Tyranny died in Greece as soon as the cities found constitutional equilibrium, almost always through the victory of democratic government. It was to return, thanks to the new ideas which recognized for sole guide personal interest, for sole proof of merit that unmistakable sign of divine protection —success. Since the ideal for man was to lead a life of self-indulgence and to sate himself with pleasure, what better means of attaining it was there than to rise above the common law and to assume the position of lord over men's bodies and their souls ? When Polyarchus, a courtier of Dionysius the Elder, was discussing this question with Archytas of Tarentum, he unequivocally declared that the greatest felicity which could fall to a human being was that which the Persian king enjoyed in his palace.[1] Think of the enormous place which " great men," Alcibiades, Lysander, Agesilaus, held in their city and one realizes that " supermen " were beginning to prevail. Nietzschean ethics ended in Machiavellian politics. The State was swallowed up in forceful personalities, in dominating characters who armed ambition with cunning and violence; thus rose Dionysius of Syracuse, Euagoras of Cyprus, Hermias of Atarnea, Lycophron and Jason of Pheræ, Clearchus of Heraclea, and a multitude of others.[2] In the striking words of Aristotle: " It has now become a habit in cities not even to want equality; all men are seeking for dominion, or, if conquered, are willing to submit."[3]

These customs, which the greatest observer of antiquity is content merely to note, the theorists justify and laud. The

---

[1] Aristoxenus of Tarentum, fr. 15 (*FHG*, vol. II, p. 276).
[2] We may mention in addition Philiscus and Iphiades of Abdera, Neogenes of Oreos, Themison of Eretria, the Phocian leaders, Timophanes of Corinth, Euphron of Sicyon, Chairon of Pellene.
[3] Arist., *Pol.*, VI (IV), 9, 12.

idea of monarchy was in the air. So much the better thought the greatest minds of the day: enlightened despotism would be able to put in force well-regulated systems, to realize sublime dreams. Xenophon looks for the man capable of " governing men's caprices "; he shows such a one in the Cyropædia in his portrayal of a type by that time legendary; he gives a living presentation of him in the characters of Cyrus and of Agesilaus; though he depicts in the portrait of Hiero the evil which the oppressive tyrant was capable of, it was to contrast it with the good which the wise and benevolent tyrant could do. Plato wanted to do more than write; he sought for a monarch who would champion his Republic. Three journeys to Sicily and disappointments, humiliations and sufferings innumerable were required to convince him that he would not find at the court of Syracuse the man who, possessing the " royal art," was worthy to impose his absolute authority upon all and to found the model State. Even after countless disillusionments, when, in his old age, he had resigned himself to seeking from the laws what he had wished to obtain from a personal will, he still retained a lingering affection for the tyrant, young, learned, courageous and of noble spirit.[1] More than all others the rhetorician Isocrates was full of admiration for the heroes, the defenders and propagators of Hellenism, and, in general, for the great men whom the deity brought forth to accomplish its designs. Without quitting his school, pen in hand, he sought unremittingly for half a century for the resolute man who should bring Greece to unity by leading her out against the Persians. Deceived in the hopes which he centred on the Athenian Timotheus, he abandoned thoughts of anything save an absolute monarch: was he not the friend and counsellor of the Cyprian princes Euagoras and Nicocles ? Had he not for disciple the tyrant of Heraclea ? So there we see him endeavouring successively to push to the fore Jason and Alexander of Pheræ, Dionysius of Syracuse, Archidamus son of Agesilaus, until, despairing of his cause, he appealed to Philip of Macedon.[2]

Men called for a leader. Even those who did not wish to

---

[1] *Laws*, IV, p. 709*e*; cf. *Rep.*, V, p. 473*d*; VI, p. 499*b*; *Polit.*, p. 293*c*, 296 *ff*, 300*e ff*.

[2] *v.* **XLIX**; Pohlmann, " Isokrates und das Problem der Demokratie " (*Sb. MA*, 1913, p. 2 *ff*.); **LVI**, p. 44 *f.*, 95-100, 133 *f.*, 155 *ff*.

see a single man ruling the whole of Greece, and that man a foreigner, nevertheless saw clearly what the strength of the Macedonian was accomplishing: he made a decision, he carried out his decision; his power did not dwindle away in formalities but concentrated itself upon commanding and acting. That was the opinion of his greatest adversary who himself was compelled to make superhuman efforts to convince those whom he wished to save. And in later days Hyperides, when he pronounced the funeral oration for the soldiers who had given their lives for Athens, and at the same time that of Athens herself, said: " Our city had need of one man, and the whole of Greece of one city, capable of taking the lead."[1]

Thus, desired, expected and proclaimed necessary, was born the political system which was to prevail throughout the Hellenistic world, before spreading to the Roman world. The great States which absorbed the chaotic welter of autonomous cities could only exist under a monarchical form of govern-ment. Monarchy alone could give substance to the confused aspirations and urgent entreaties of several generations.

Men's dreams were being fulfilled. It was of divine right. The Greeks had always regarded the founders of the towns as heroes. The oligarchs at the beginning of the fourth century had worshipped Lysander as a saviour and had erected statues to him as to a god. Isocrates compared in anticipation the mission of Philip to that of Heracles and the other demi-gods, and, in the letter which he addressed to the victor of Chæronea, he definitely promised him that the conquest of Asia would be rewarded by apotheosis.[2] The Greek spirit was ready to join with the Oriental to give birth to king-worship.

In exchange for these divine honours monarchy was expected to establish not only peace between the cities but also order in each. The classes perpetually disturbed in the peaceful enjoyment of their property were exhausted by the tyranny of the people. Obviously turmoil and danger were not everywhere the same: democratic Athens, for example, was sufficiently sagacious to protect public offices from the shortcomings of election by lot, and, on all occasions, in the oath demanded from the heliasts and in the annual proclama-tion of the archon, she forbade any infringement of the right

[1] Hyper., *Epitaph.*, 10.   [2] *v.* **LVI**, p. 216.

of property. But in many places the rich, whether their
wealth consisted in landed property, in movable securities or
in slaves, felt day by day an ever increasing danger of revolution. Philip knew what he was doing when in the federal
pact of Corinth he forbade any change of constitution, any
political reprisals, any social transformation. He conceived
of the mission of a king exactly as the teacher of his son
defined it: " It is the duty of a king to be the protector of the
rich against unjust treatment and of the people against insult
and oppression." [1]

With the coming of the military monarchy, therefore, the
conservative element triumphed; oligarchy secured a victory
over democracy. Demosthenes had long realized what was
at stake in the struggle with Philip. When he made un-
wearying appeal to national honour, when in the fervour of
patriotic pride he swept from the pathetic to the sublime,
his reasoning was free from sentiment: he was convinced
that to fight for Athens was to defend democracy.

" Let it also be considered that you, my fellow-citizens, have waged
many wars against States of both popular and oligarchical government.
Of this you are not to be informed; but perhaps you have never once
reflected what were the causes of your several wars with each other.
With popular States your wars arose from particular complaints which
could not be decided in a national council; or from disputes about
districts and boundaries; or from love of glory and pre-eminence. But
of your wars with oligarchies, there were different causes: with those
you fought for your constitution, your liberty. So that I should not
scruple to avow my opinion that it would be better for us to be at war
with all the States of Greece, provided that they enjoyed a popular
government, than to be in friendship with them all, if commanded by
oligarchies; for with free States I should not think it difficult to conclude
a peace whenever you were inclined; but with oligarchical governments
we could not even form a union to be relied on; for it is not possible
that a few can entertain an affection for the many; or the friends of
arbitrary power for the men who choose to live in free equality." [2]

No more than monarchy proved able to secure the reign
of peace could oligarchy, its ally, succeed in assuring order.
Never had Greece been so cruelly rent by intestine strife as
she was in the two centuries between the Macedonian conquest
and the Roman conquest. In those years class conflict raged
in all its horror. To give some indication of what it was in
the fourth century we have already quoted the description

[1] Arist., *Pol.*, VIII (V), 8, 6; cf. 2.
[2] Dem., *De Rhod. Lib.*, 17-18 (trans. Leland, *Orations*, p. 275-277).

which Polybius gave.[1] Instead of citing the innumerable examples mentioned by the historian in the course of his work, we will confine ourselves to saying that they helped Fustel de Coulanges to discern the fundamental causes of the final catastrophe, the reduction of Greece to a province of Rome.[2]

The regime which destroyed the autonomy of the cities did not succeed in re-establishing social equilibrium, but it was sufficiently powerful to arrest a development which was rich in the promise of good things.

In her law Athens had advanced far ahead of the rest of Greece. The principles of Draco and Solon, applied by Pericles' contemporaries in a way which tempered public authority with liberty, had produced individualistic and democratic laws which recognized only personal claims and responsibilities and looked for the realization of equity through philanthropy. Since the beginning of the sixth century the Athenian State had prohibited enslavement for debt and consequently penal servitude; in the property system it had opposed to the system of entail the right of bequest. Later it abandoned the practice of invoking the collective responsibility of the family against authors of political crimes, and assured legal protection to slaves.

In law as in everything else Athens had become the school of Greece and became it increasingly. Demosthenes, ever ready to improve upon the claims of his country, did not fail to mention it: " Innumerable Greek towns have times without number decided to adopt your laws. It is for you a just subject of pride: for . . . the laws of a town are its way of life."[3] We do in fact find in the islands (in Amorgus, Ceos and Cos) and in Asia Minor (at Erythræ and at Zela) the same organization of the courts and the same classifications of public suits as at Athens. Three at least of the laws of Solon enjoyed an extraordinary popularity; his law relating to funerals, which was copied by the Bœotians and imitated at Ioulis, Gambreion in Mysia and at Rome; his law relating to plantation, building and excavation, which was reproduced by many legislators[4] before being included in the code of

---

[1] *v. supra*, p. 323.
[2] Fustel de Coulanges, *Polybe ou la Gr. conquise par les Rom.* (1858).
[3] Dem., *C. Timocr.*, 210; Isocr., *Paneg.*, 104.
[4] Plat., *Laws*, VIII, p. 843e.

Alexandria and in the law of the Twelve Tables; finally, his law relating to wills, which no other city was sufficiently bold to imitate before the fourth century but which thenceforward gradually won universal adhesion. The other cities had shown themselves most willing to profit by the experience of Athens in some cases where she had discovered a means of facilitating the work of justice, of perfecting procedure, of imposing practical, wise and convenient civil laws and police regulations. But the provisions which best illustrated the spirit of Athenian legislation, which caused vigorous individualism and a fine philanthropy to flourish, these encountered resistance even in democracies. Of the cities which fell under the direct influence of Athens, however, some ventured along the road which she had so boldly embarked upon: in the island of Amorgus deprivation of civil rights ceased to be hereditary; the democrats of Ceos no longer allowed the punishment of death and confiscation to be combined in political sentences. The path of evolution was clearly marked out; was it going to be pursued in the Hellenistic epoch ?

In the new societies where races mingled, where a great number of citizens were citizens of several towns, where corporations were federated from State to State, where cosmopolitanism and syncretism dominated philosophy and religion, where all cultured men spoke the same language, law ought equally, so it seems, to have become unified in a *koine*, after the Attic model. The technical organization of justice still continued, indeed, to be modelled on Athens: such reforms were well fitted to a monarchical regime. But, since the regime was based on social inequality, it rejected any change which savoured of the principle of individualism and of democratic philanthropy. Not one of the cities which had retained collective punishment abandoned it. Athens stood alone, absolutely alone, in guaranteeing personal liberty by a virtual *habeas corpus*. Though she herself continued to forbid creditors to lay hands on the persons of their debtors, to confine imprisonment before trial and likewise the penalty of imprisonment to exceptional cases, to limit in favour of the very slaves the powers of coercion with which the magistrates were invested, yet here she made no proselytes.

To-day we know what the Alexandrian law was.[1] So far

[1] *v. JS*, 1916, p. 21 *ff.*

as judicial administration was concerned progress was incontestable. Specialization of courts, establishment of appellate jurisdiction, separation of the presidency from the preliminary investigation, the creation of officials responsible for execution, greater precision in the definition of delinquencies and the determination of offences: in all these matters Alexandrian law drew extensively upon Athenian law and improved upon it. If, however, we turn from its material aspect and consider its spirit, we see a distinct retrogression. What became of personal liberty ?   " No citizen may be thrown into servitude ": this was always the principle; but how was it applied ? For Athenian democrats it was inviolable under all circumstances; for the Alexandrians, as for all other Greeks, it was combined with imprisonment before trial, with the possibility of bail, execution being made on the person in case of insufficiency of property. The liberty of the citizen was no longer inviolable. There was another characteristic which distinguished the Athenians: we have seen that, without fearing to contradict the principles which deprived the slave of all juridical capacity, they had given him legal protection. With them the slave was protected against his master, against a third person, against the State itself. The magistrates were forbidden to inflict more stripes on the slave than they would exact drachmas from the free man, while everywhere else the slave might be flogged at discretion. Alexandrian law made a pretence of adopting the rule of converting drachmas into lashes; but since the fine was raised to a hundred drachmas the penalty of flogging was similarly stiffened, and, whilst at Athens the slave might receive fifty stripes " at the most," at Alexandria he received a hundred " at the least." Under a system which no longer recognized equality liberty declined and humanitarian sentiments disappeared.

Thus it is clear that Greek civilization, in passing from small cities to great monarchies, gained in extent but lost in value. Athens had traced a programme of political and social reforms which could have led the whole of Greece to a work of splendid liberation. Doubts were already being felt as to the lawfulness, if not the necessity, of slavery. The path of development was marked out and the end visible. But the Macedonian phalanx arrested everything. One of the first steps which the victor took was to prohibit the emancipation of the slaves. Athens fell before she had fulfilled her mission; with her nobly conceived laws on personal liberty she was henceforth merely an exception to the common rule. Driven everywhere else from public law, the noblest ideas which she had launched into the world had to find refuge in the teachings of philosophers in order to have, at least indirectly, some influence on human societies.

Such are the facts. It was not, therefore, the Macedonian who, in the decisive struggle, represented progress; and the Athenian could assert that the vanquished of Chæronea had no more failed in defending the moral patrimony of their country than had the victors of Marathon, of Salamis and of Platæa.

BIBLIOGRAPHY

I.—SOURCES

I.—EPIGRAPHIC AND PAPYROLOGICAL SOURCES

	ABBREVIATIONS
Corpus Inscriptionum Græcarum, 4 vol., 1827-77	*CIG*
Inscriptiones Græcæ, 1873 ss......................	*IG*
Inscriptiones Græcæ, editio minor, 2 vol., 1913-24	*IG*, I² or II²
LEBAS-WADDINGTON, *Voyage archéologique en Grèce et en Asie Mineure*, 3 vol., Paris, 1846-76............	LEBAS
DITTENBERGER-PURGOLD, *Inschriften von Olympia* (*Olympia Ergebnisse der Ausgrabungen*, vol. v), Berlin, 1896...................................	*IO*
BOURGUET-COLIN, *Inscriptions de Delphes* (*Fouilles de Delphes*, vol. iii), Paris, 1909...................	*ID*
LATYSCHEV, *Inscriptiones antiquæ oræ septentrionalis Ponti Euxini*, Petersburg, vol. i-ii-iv, 1885-1901; vol. i, 2nd edit., 1912	*IGPE*
PATON-HICKS, *Inscriptions of Cos*, Oxford, 1891	*IC*
O. KERN, *Inschriften von Magnesia am Mœander*, Berlin, 1910.......................................	*IMa.*
M. FRAENKEL, *Inschriften von Pergamon* (*Altertümer von Pergamon*, vol. iii), Berlin, 1890-95	*IPe.*
HERBERDEY, *Forschungen von Ephesos*, vol. ii-iii, Vienna, 1912-13	*IE*
HILLER VON GAERTRINGEN, *Inschriften von Priene*, Berlin, 1906	*IPr.*
REHM, Milet, *Ergebnisse der Augsgrabungen*, fasc. iii, Berlin, 1914....................................	*IMi.*
H. ROEHL, *Inscriptiones Græcæ Antiquissimæ præter atticus in Attica repertas*, Berlin, 1882	*IGA*
COLLITZ-BECHTEL-HOFFMANN, *Sammlung der Griechischen Dialekt-Inschriften*, 4 vol., Göttingen, 1884-1915.......................................	*GDI*
DARESTS-HAUSSOULLIER-Th. REINACH, *Receuil des Inscriptions Juridiques Grecques*, 2 vol., Paris, 1891-1904	*IJG*
VON PROTT-ZIEHEN, *Leges Græcorum Sacræ e titulis collectæ*, 2 fasc., Leipzig, 1896-1907	*LGS*
Supplementum Epigraphicum Græcum, Leyden, 1923 ss..	*SEG*
DITTENBERGER, *Sylloge Inscriptionum Græcarum*, Leipzig, 2nd edit., 3 vol., 1898-1901; 3rd edit., 4 vol., 1915-24	*SIG*

o*

		ABBREVIATIONS
MICHEL, *Receuil d'Inscriptions Grecques*, 1 vol., and 2 supplements, 1899-1927		*RIG*
B. P. GRENFELL-A. S. HUNT, *The Oxyrhynchus Papyri*, London, 1898 ss................................		*P. Oxy.*

II.—LITERARY SOURCES

BERGK, *Pœtœ lyrici Grœci*, 4th edit., 3 vol., Leipzig, 1878-82		BERGK
KINKEL, *Epicorum Grœcorum fragmenta*, Leipzig, 1877 ..		KINKEL
KOCK, *Comicorum Atticorum fragmenta*, Leipzig, 1880-88..		KOCK
C. MULLER, *Fragmenta Historicorum Grœcorum*, 5 vol., Paris, 1841-84		*FHG*

II.—PERIODICALS AND DICTIONARIES

I.—PERIODICALS

Abhandlungen der Preuss. Akademie der Wissenschaften zu Berlin, Philos.-hist. Klasse..............	*Abh. BA*
Abhandlungen der Bayer. Akad. d. Wiss. zu München, Philos.-philol.-hist. Klasse.................	*Abh. MA*
Abhandlungen der Gesellschaft. d. Wiss. zu Göttingen, Phil.-hist. Klasse...............................	*Abh. GG*
Abhandlungen der Sachs. Gesellschaft d. Wiss., Phil.-hist. Klasse......................................	*Abh. SG*
Archaeologisch-Epigraphische Mittheilungen eus Oesterreich-Ungarn....................................	*AEM*
American Journal of Archæology	*AJA*
American Journal of Philology.....................	*AJP*
Mitteilungen des Deutsch. Archaeol. Instituts in Athen..	*AM*
Anzeiger de Wiener Akad., Phil.-hist. Klasse	*Anz. WA*
Archaeologischer Anzeiger	*Arch. Anz.*
Archiv für Papyrusforschung und Verwandtes	*Arch. Pap.*
Bulletin de Correspondance Hellénique	*BCH*
Berliner philologische Wochenschrift	*Bph. W*
Annual of the British School at Athens	*BSA*
BURSIAN, Jahresbericht über die Forstchritte der klass. Altertumswissenschaft..........................	BURSIAN
Classical Journal	*Cl. J*
Classical Philology...............................	*Cl. Ph.*
Classical Review.....................................	*Cl. R*
Comptes rendus de l'Académie des Inscriptions et Belles-Lettres	*CRAI*
Ἐφημερὶς ἀρχαιολογική	*Ἐφ.*
Glotta	*Gl.*
Göttingische Gelehrte Anzeigen	*GGA*
Nachrichten von der Universität und der Gesellsch. d. Wiss. zu Göttingen	*GN*

BIBLIOGRAPHY

	ABBREVIATIONS
Hermes..	*Herm.*
Historische Zeitschrift............................	*HZ*
Jahrbuch des Deutsch. Archaeol. Instituts............	*Jb. Al.*
Jahreshefte des Oesterreich. Archaeol. Instituts........	*Jh. AI*
Journal of Hellenic Studies	*JHS*
Journal international d'Archéologie numismatique	*JIANu.*
Journal of Philology..............................	*JPh.*
Journal des Savants	*JS*
Klio. Beiträge zur Alten Geschichte	*Klio.*
Monumenti antichi pubblicati per la cura dell' Accademia dei Lincei..............................	*MA*
Mémoires présentés par divers savants à l'Académie des Inscriptions et Belles-Lettres....................	*MAI*
Mnemosyne.......................................	*Mn.*
Musée Belge	*Mu. B*
Neue Jahrbücher für das klassische Altertum	*NJbb.*
Nouvelle Revue Historique de Droit français et étranger	*NRHD*
Philologus.......................................	*Phil.*
Πρακτικὰ τῆς ἀρχαιολογικῆς Ἑταιρίας	*Πρ*
Revue Archéologique	*RA*
Revue des Études Anciennes	*REA*
Revue des Études Grecques........................	*REG*
Revue Historique.................................	*RH*
Rheinisches Museum...............................	*Rh. M*
Rivista di Filologia classica........................	*Riv. Fil.*
Rivista di Storia antica	*Riv. St.*
Revue Numismatique	*RNu.*
Revue de Philologie, de Littérature et d'Histoire anciennes	*RPh.*
Revue des Questions Historiques	*RQH*
Zeitschrift der Savignystiftung für Rechtsgeschichte, Romanistische Abteilung	*Sav. Z*
Sitzungsberichte der Preuss. Akad. d. Wiss. zu Berlin ..	*Sb. BA*
Sitzungsberichte der Bayer. Akad. d. Wiss. zu München, Philos.-philol.-hist. Klasse	*Sb. MA*
Sitzungsberichte der Akad. d. Wiss. zu Wien	*Sb. WA*
Wiener Studien	*WSt.*
Zeitschrift für Numismatik	*ZNu.*

II.—DICTIONARIES

DAREMBERG-SAGLIO-POTTIER-LAFAYE, *Dictionnaire des Antiquités grecques et romaines*, 5 vol., Paris, 1873-1919..	*DA*
PAULY-WISSOWA-KROLL, *Real-Encyclopädie der klassischen Altertumswissenschaft*, Stuttgart, 1894 ss.......	*RE*
ROSCHER, *Ausführliches Lexicon der griech. und röm. Mythologie*, Leipzig, 1882 ss.	ROSCHER

III.—GENERAL WORKS

BABELON (Ernest), *Traité des monnaies grecques et romaines*. Part I, *Théorie et Doctrine*, vol. i, 1901. Part II, *Description historique*, vol. i, 1907; vol. ii, 1910; vol. iii, 1914; vol. iv, fasc. 1, 1926. Part III, *Album de planches*, pl. i-cclxxvi, 1907-26 I

BELOCH (Julius), *Die Bevolkerung der griechischrömischen Welt*, Leipzig, 1886................................ II

— *Griechische Geschichte*, 2nd edit., Strasbourg-Berlin, 4 vol. each in 2 parts, 1912-27 III

BOURGUET (Émile), *L'Administration financière du sanctuaire pythique au IVe siècle avant J.-C.*, Paris, 1905 IV

BURY (J. B.), *A History of Greece to the Death of Alexander the Great*, 2nd edit., London, 1913 V

BUSOLT (Georg), *Griechische Geschichte* (Handbucher der alten Geschichte), vol. i, 2nd edit., Gotha, 1893; vol. ii, 2nd edit., 1895; vol. iii, 1, 1897; 2, 1904 VI

— *Griechische Staatskunde* (Handbuch der klassischen Altertumswissenschaft hgg. von Iwan VON MULLER, vol. iv, 1, 3rd edit., des *Griechischen Staats und Rechtsaltertümer*), 2 vol., Munich, 1920-26 VII

CALDERINI (Aristide), *La manomissionee la condizione dei liberti in Grecia*, Milan, 1908 VIII

— *Cambridge Ancient History*, vol. i-vi, Cambridge, 1923-27 IX

CAVAIGNAC (Eugène), *Histoire de l'antiquité*, 3 vol., Paris, 1913-19.. X

— *Population et capital dans le monde méditerranéen antique* (Publications de la Faculté des Lettres de l'Université de Strasbourg, fasc. xviii), Strasbourg, 1923 XI

CROISET (Alfred), *Les Démocraties antiques*, Paris, 1909 .. XII

CROISET (Maurice), *La Civilisation hellénique. Aperçu historique*, 2 vol., Paris, 1922 XIII

CURTIUS (Ernst), *Griechische Geschichte*, 6th edit., Berlin, 1887-89 (French trans. by BOUCHE-LECLERCQ, with an atlas, 1883) XIV

DEFOURNY (M.), *Aristote, Théorie économique et politique sociale* (Annales de l'Institut supérieur de Philosophie de Louvain, 1914) XV

— *Aristote et l'Éducation* (*ibid.*, vol. iv), Louvain, 1919 .. XVI

— *Aristote. L'Évolution sociale* (*ibid.*, vol. v), Louvain, 1919 XVII

EBELING, *Lexicon Homericum*, 2 vol., Berlin, 1871 XVIII

EHRNEBERG (V.), *Die Rechtsidee im fruhen Griechentum*, Leipzig, 1921................................... XIX

— *Neugrunder des Staates*, Munich, 1925.............. XX

FELDMANN (W.), *Analecta epigraphica ad historiam synœcismorum et sympolitiarum* (Dissertationes philologicæ Argentoratenses, fasc. ix), Strasbourg, 1885 XXI

FOUGÈRES (Gustave), *Mantinée et l'Arcadie orientale*, Paris, 1898 XXII

BIBLIOGRAPHY 397

FRANCOTTE (H.), *La Polis grecque. Recherches sur la formation et l'organisation des cités, des ligues et des confédérations dans la Grèce ancienne* (Studien zur Geschichte und Kultur des Altertums, vol. i, fasc. 3 and 4), Paderborn, 1907 .... **XXIII**

— *L'industrie dans la Grèce ancienne* (Bibliothèque de la Faculté de philosophie et lettres de l'Université de Liège, fasc. vii et viii), 2 vol., Bruxelles, 1900-1901 .... **XXIV**

— *Les finances des cités grecques*, Liège-Paris, 1909 ...... **XXV**

— *Mélanges de droit public grec*, Liège-Paris, 1910 .... **XXVI**

FREEMAN (Edward A.), *History of Federal Government in Greece and Italy*, 2nd edit., by BURY, London, 1873 .... **XXVII**

FUSTEL DE COULANGES, *La Cité antique*, 14th edit., Paris, 1893 .... **XXVIII**

— *Étude sur la propriété à Sparte* (*Nouvelles Recherches sur quelques problèmes d'histoire*, p. 52 ss.) .... **XXIX**

GARDINER (E. Norman), *Olympia: Its History and Remains*, Oxford, 1925 .... **XXX**

GARDNER (Percy), *A History of Ancient Coinage, 700-300 B.C.*, Oxford, 1918 .... **XXXI**

GILBERT (Gustav), *Handbuch der griechischen Staatsaltertümer*, 2 vol., Leipzig, 1881-85, vol. i, 2nd edition, 1893 **XXXII**

GLOTZ (Gustave), *La Solidarité de la famille dans le droit criminel en Grèce*, Paris, 1904 .... **XXXIII**

— *Études sociales et juridiques sur l'antiquité grecque*, Paris, 1906................................... **XXXIV**

— *Ancient Greece at Work*, trans. Dobie, London, 1926 .... **XXXV**

— *Histoire grecque*, vol. i., Paris, 1925 .... **XXXVI**

GROTE, *A History of Greece*, 1st edit., London, 1846 ...... **XXXVII**

GRUNDY (G. B.), *Thucydides and the History of his Age*, London, 1911................................. **XXXVIII**

GUIRAUD (Paul), *La Propriété foncière en Grèce jusqu'à la conquête romaine*, Paris, 1893 .... **XXXIX**

— *La Main-d'œuvre industrielle dans l'ancienne Grèce* (Bibliothèque de la Faculté des Lettres de l'Université de Paris, vol. xii), Paris, 1900 .... **XL**

HEAD (Barclay), *Historia numorum*, 2nd edit., Oxford, 1911 **XLI**

Hellénisation du monde antique, by V. CHAPOT, G. COLIN, Alfred CROISET, etc., Paris, 1914 .... **XLII**

HITZIG (H. F.), *Altgriechische Staatsverträge über Rechtshilfe*, Zurich, no date .... **XLIII**

JANNET (Claudio), *Les Institutions sociales et le droit civil à Sparte*, 2nd edit., Paris, 1880 .... **XLIV**

JARDÉ (Auguste), *The Formation of the Greek People*, trans. Dobie, London, 1926 .... **XLV**

KAERST (Julius), *Geschichte des hellenistischen Zeitalter*, 3 vol., Leipzig, 2nd edit., published 1926 (vol. 2) ...... **XLVI**

KAHRSTEDT (Ulrich), *Griechisches Staatsrecht*, vol. i, Göttingen, 1922............................... **XLVII**

KEIL (Bruno), *Griechische Staatsaltertümer* (Einleitung in der Altertumswissenschaft de GERCKE-NORDEN, vol. iii, 2nd edit., p. 309 ss.), Leipzig-Berlin, 1914 .... **XLVIII**

398 BIBLIOGRAPHY

KESSLER (Josef), *Isokrates und die panhellenische Idee* (Studien zur Geschichte und Kultur des Altertums, vol. iv., fasc. 3), Paderborn, 1910 .... **XLIX**

KIP (Gerhard), *Thessalische Studien, Beiträge zur politischen Geographie, Geschichte und Verfassung der thessalischen Landschaften*, diss., Neuenhaus, 1910 .... **L**

KLOTZSCH (Carl), *Epirotische Geschichte bis zum Jahre* 280 *v. Chr.*, Berlin, 1911 .... **LI**

KUENZI (Adolphe), Ἐπίδοσις, diss., Berne, 1923 .... **LII**

LARFELD (Wilhelm), *Handbuch der griechischen Epigraphik*, Leipzig, vol. i, 1908; vol. ii in 2 parts, 1898-1902 ...... **LIII**

— *Griechische Epigraphik* (Handbuch der klassischen Altertumswissenschaft hgg. von Iwan VON MULLER, vol. i, 5), Munich, 1914 .... **LIV**

LEHMANN-HAUPT (C. F.), *Griechische Geschichte bis zur Schlacht bei Chaironcia* (Einleitung in der Altertumswissenschaft de GERCKE-NORDEN, vol. iii, 2nd edit., p. 3 ss.), Leipzig-Berlin, 1914 .... **LV**

MATHIEU (Georges), *Les Idées politiques d'Isocrate*, Paris, 1925 .... **LVI**

MEYER (Eduard), *Geschichte des Altertums*, 3rd edit., 5 vol., Stuttgart-Berlin, 1910 ss.; 4th edit. of vol. i and ii, 1921 .... **LVII**

— *Forschungen zur alten Geschichte*, 2 vol., Halle, 1899 .. **LVIII**

— *Theopomps Hellenica*, Halle, 1909 .... **LIX**

MONCEAUX (Paul), *La Proxénie grecque*, Paris, 1886...... **LX**

PHILLIPSON (Coleman), *The International Law and Custom of Ancient Greece and Rome*, 2 vol., London, 1911 ...... **LXI**

POEHLMANN (Robert von), *Grundriss der griechischen Geschichte nebst Quellenkunde* (Handbuch der klassischen Altertumswissenschalt hgg. von Iwan VON MULLER, vol. iii, iv), 5th edit., Munich, 1914 .... **LXII**

— *Geschichte der sozialen Frage und des Sozialismus in der antiken Welt*, 3rd edit., 2 vol., Munich, 1925 .... **LXIII**

— *Isokrates und das Problem der Demokratie* (Sb. MA, 1913).. **LXIV**

POHLENZ (Max), *Staatsgedanke und Staatslehre der Griechen* (Wissenschaft und Bildung, vol. clxxxiii), 1923 .... **LXV**

RAEDER (A.), *L'Arbitrage international chez les Hellènes* (Publications of the Norwegian Nobel Institute, vol. i), Christiania, 1912 .... **LXVI**

SCALA (R. von), *Die Staatsverträge der Altertums*, vol. i, Leipzig, 1898 .... **LXVII**

SCHMIDT (Leopold), *Die Ethik der alten Griechen*, 2 vol., Berlin, 1882 .... **LXVIII**

SCHOEMANN (G. F.), *Griechische Altertümer*, 5th edit., revised by LIPSIUS, Berlin, 1897-1902 (French translation by GALUSKI, 1884) .... **LXIX**

SCHOENFELDER (W.), *Die städtischen und Bundesbeamten des griechischen Festlandes vom 4. Jahrhundert v. Chr. Geb. bis in die romische Kaiserzeit*, diss., Leipzig, 1917 .. **LXX**

BIBLIOGRAPHY

399

SWOBODA (Heinrich), *Griechische Staatsaltertümer* (Lehrbuch der griechischen Antiquitaten de K. F. HERMANN, vol. i, iii, 6th edit.), Tübingen, 1913 .... **LXXI**

— *Die griechische Bünde und der moderne Bundesstaat*, Prague, 1915 .... **LXXII**

SZANTO (Emil), *Das griechische Bürgerrecht*, Freiburg, 1892
THALHEIM, *Griechische Rechtsaltertümer* (Lehrbuch der griechischen Antiquitaten de K. F. HERMANN, vol. II, i, 4th edit.), Freiburg-Leipzig, 1895 .... **LXXIII** **LXXIV**

TOD (Marcus Niebuhr), *International Arbitration among the Greeks*, Oxford, 1913 .... **LXXV**

URE (P. N.), *The Origin of Tyranny*, Cambridge, 1922.... **LXXVI**

VINOGRADOFF (Paul), *Outlines of Historical Jurisprudence*. Vol. II: *The Jurisprudence of the Greek City*, Oxford, 1922 **LXXVII**

WALKER (E. M.), *The Hellenica Oxyrhynchia: Its Authorship and Authority*, Oxford, 1913 .... **LXXVIII**

WALLON (H.), *Histoire de l'esclavage dans l'antiquité*, 2nd edit., 3 vol., Paris, 1879 .... **LXXIX**

WILAMOWITZ-MOELLENDORFF (Ulrich von), *Staat und Gesellschaft der Griechen* (Die Kultur der Gegenwart, II, iv, 1), 2nd edit., Leipzig, 1923 .... **LXXX**

WILHELM (Adolf), *Beiträge zur griechischen Inschriftenkunde* (Sonderschriften des österreichischen archäologischen Institutes in Wien, vol. vii), Vienna, 1909 .... **LXXXI**

ZIEBARTH (Erich), *Aus dem griechischen Schulwesen*, Leipzig-Berlin, 2nd edit., 1914 .... **LXXXII**

IV.—WORKS ON ATHENS

ARDAILLON (Édouard), *Les Mines du Laurion dans l'antiquité*, Paris, 1897 .... **LXXXIII**

BEAUCHET (Ludovic), *Histoire du droit privé de la république athénienne*, 4 vol., Paris, 1877.............. **LXXXIV**

BELOCH (Julius), *Die attische Politik seit Perikles*, Leipzig, 1884 .... **LXXXV**

BOECKH (August), *Staatshaushaltung der Athener*, 3rd edit., revised by M. FRAENKEL, 2 vol., Berlin, 1886 .... **LXXXVI**

BRILLANT (Maurice), *Les sécretaires athéniens* (Bibliothèque de l'École des Hautes Études, fasc. cxci), Paris, 1911 .. **LXXXVII**

CALHOUN (George Miller), *Athenian Clubs in Politics and Litigation* (Bulletin of the University of Texas, no. 262), Austin, 1913 .... **LXXXVIII**

CARCOPINO (Jérome), *Histoire de l'ostracisme athénien* (Bibliothèque de la Faculté des Lettres de l'Université de Paris, vol. xxv, p. 85 ss.), Paris, 1909 .... **LXXXIX**

CAVAIGNAC (Eugène), *Études sur l'histoire financière d'Athènes au Ve siècle. Le trésor d'Athènes de 480 à 404*, Paris, 1908................................. **XC**

CLERC (Maxime), *Les métèques athéniens*, Paris, 1893 ..... **XCI**

CLOCHÉ (Paul), *La Restauration démocratique à Athènes*, Paris, 1906................................. **XCII**

CROISET (Maurice), *Aristophane et les partis à Athènes*, Paris, 1906 XCIII

DRERUP (Englebert), [Πρώδου] *Περὶ Πολιτείας, Ein politisches Pamphlet aus Athen*, 404 vor Chr. (Studien zur Geschichte und Kultur des Altertums, vol. ii, fasc. 1), Paderborn, 1908 XCIV

DURRBACH (Félix), *L'Orateur Lycurgue*, Paris, 890........ XCV

FOUCART (Paul), *Mémoire sur les colonies athéniennes au Ve et au IVe siècle* (MAI, vol. ix, 1878, p. 323 ss.) XCVI

FRAENKEL (Max), *Die attischen Geschworenengerichte*, Berlin, 1877 XCVII

FUSTEL DE COULANGES, *Recherches sur le tirage au sort appliqué à la nomination des archontes athéniens* (Nouvelles recherches sur quelques problèmes d'histoire, p. 145 ss.) XCVIII

GERNET (Louis), *L'Approvisionnement d'Athènes en blé au Ve et au VIe siècle* (Bibliothèque de la Faculté des Lettres de l'Université de Paris, vol. xxv, p. 268 ss.), Paris, 1909.. XCIX

GILLIARD (Charles), *Quelques réformes de Solon*, Lausanne, 1907 C

GIRARD (Paul), *L'Éducation athénienne au Ve et au IVe siècle avant J.-C.*, 2nd edit., Paris, 1891 CI

HAUSSOULLIER (B.), *La Vie municipale en Attique. Essai sur l'organisation des dèmes au IVe siècle*, Paris, 1884 .. CII

KALINKA (E.), *Die pseudoxenophontische 'Αθηναίων πολιτεία Einleitung, Uebersetzung, Erklaerung*, Leipzig, 1913 CIII

KIRCHNER (J.), *Prosopographia attica*, 2 vol., Berlin, 1901-03 CIV

LEDL (Artur), *Studien zur älteren athenischen Verfassungsgeschichte*, Heidelberg, 1914 CV

LIPSIUS (H.), *Dos attische Recht und Rechtsverfahren*, 2 vol., Leipzig, 1905-15........................... CVI

LOFBERG (John Oscar), *Sycophancy in Athens*, diss., Chicago, 1917...................................... CVII

MARSHALL (F. H.), *The Second Athenian Confederacy* (Cambridge Historical Essays, vol. xiii), Cambridge, 1905 CVIII

MARTIN (Albert), *Les Cavaliers athéniens*, Paris, 1886..... CIX

MATHIEU (Georges), *Aristote, Constitution d'Athènes* (Bibliothèque de l'École des Hautes Études, fasc. ccxvi), Paris, 1915...................................... CX

MEIER (M. H. E.)-SCHOEMANN (G. F.), *Der attische Prozess*, 2nd edit., revised by J. H. LIPSIUS, 2 vol., Berlin, 1883-87 CXI

PEDROLI (U.), *I tributi delgi alleati d'Atene* (Studi di stor., ant., fasc. 1, 1891, p. 101 ss.) CXII

PERROT (Georges), *Essai sur le droit public d'Athènes*, Paris, 1869.. CXIII

REINACH Adolphe), *Atthis, Les Origines de l'État athénien*, Paris, 1912.. CXIV

BIBLIOGRAPHY

REUSCH (S.), *De diebus contionum ordin. apud Athenienses* (Dissertationes philologicæ Argentoratenses, fasc. iii), Strasbourg, 1879 .... **CXV**

ROMSTEDT (M.), *Die wirtschaftliche Organisation des attischen Reiches*, diss., Lepizig, 1914 .... **CXVI**

SANCTIS (Gaetano de), *'Aτθίs. Storia della repubblica Ateniese dalle origini alle riforme di Clistene*, Rome, 1898, 2nd edit., *dalle origini età di Pericle*, Turin, 1912 .. **CXVII**

SCHAEFFER (Arnold), *Demosthenes und seine Zeit.*, 2nd edit., 3 vols., Leipzig, 1885-87 .... **CXVIII**

SELTMAN (C. T.), *Athens, its History and Coinage before the Persian Invasion*, Cambridge, 1924 .... **CXIX**

SMITH (F. D.), *Athenian Political Commissions*, diss., Chicago, 1920 .... **CXX**

SUNDWALL, *Epigraphische Beiträge zur sozialpolitischen Geschichte Athens in Zeitalter des Demosthenes* (Klio., Beiheft IV), Leipzig, 1906 .... **CXXI**

TOEPFFER (Johannes), *Attische Genealogie*, Berlin, 1889 .. **CXXII**

WEBER (Hans), *Attisches Prozessrecht in den attischen Seebundstaaten* (Studien zur Geschichte und Kultur des Altertums, vol. i, fasc. 5), Paderborn, 1908 .... **CXXIII**

WILAMOWITZ-MOELLENDORFF (Ulrich von), *Aristoteles und Athen*, 2 vol., Berlin, 1893 .... **CXXIV**

WILHELM (Adolf), *Urkunden dramatischer Aufführungen in Athen* (Sonderschriften des österreichischen archäologischen Institutes in Wien, vol. vi), Vienna, 1906.... **CXXV**

ZIMMERN (Alfred), *The Greek Commonwealth. Politics and Economics in Fifth Century Athens*, 4th edit., Oxford, 1924 .... **CXXVI**

INDEX